KOYOHARU GOTOUGE

They're publishing a graphic novel by me! Thank you! And heartfelt thanks to all the readers, my editors over the years, my assistants, everyone in the *Jump* editorial department, everyone at the printer, the people who designed the book, and the many other people who have offered their help!

DEMON SLAYER: KIMETSU NO YAIBA VOLUME 1

Shonen Jump Edition

Story and Art by
KOYOHARU GOTOUGE

KIMETSU NO YAIBA
© 2016 by Koyoharu Gotouge
All rights reserved. First published in Japan
in 2016 by SHUEISHA Inc., Tokyo. English
translation rights arranged by SHUEISHA Inc.

TRANSLATION John Werry
ENGLISH ADAPTATION Stan!
TOUCH-UP ART & LETTERING John Hunt
DESIGN Adam Grano
EDITOR Mike Montesa

The stories, characters and incidents mentioned
in this publication are entirely fictional.

Printed in Italy

Published by VIZ Media, LLC
P.O. Box 77010
San Francisco, CA 94107

33
First printing, July 2018
Thirty-third printing, July 2024

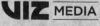

VIZ MEDIA   SHONEN JUMP

viz.com

1

CRUELTY

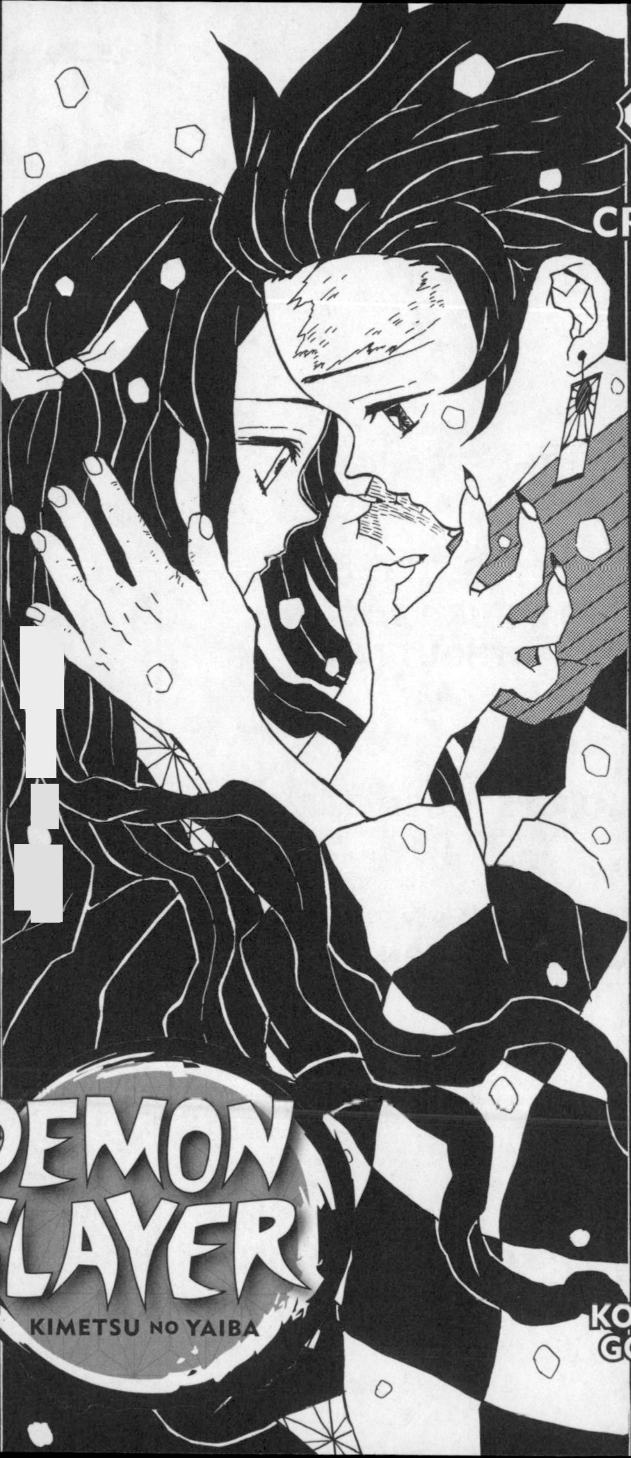

DEMON SLAYER

KIMETSU NO YAIBA

KOYOHARU GOTOUGE

CONTENTS

DEMON SLAYER
KIMETSU NO YAIBA

1

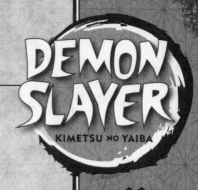

CRUELTY

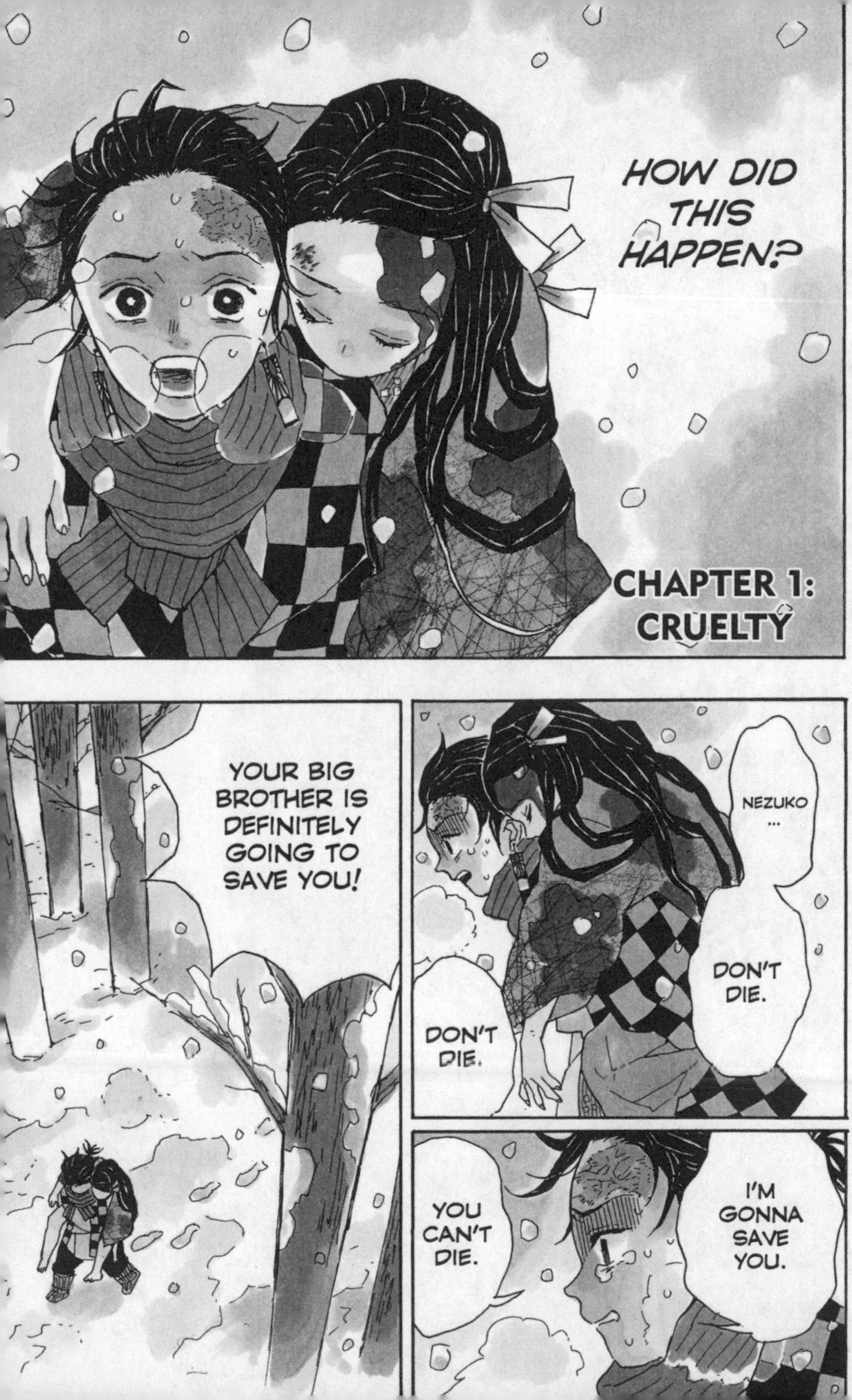
HOW DID THIS HAPPEN?
CHAPTER 1: CRUELTY
NEZUKO ...
DON'T DIE.
DON'T DIE.
I'M GONNA SAVE YOU.
YOU CAN'T DIE.
YOUR BIG BROTHER IS DEFINITELY GOING TO SAVE YOU!

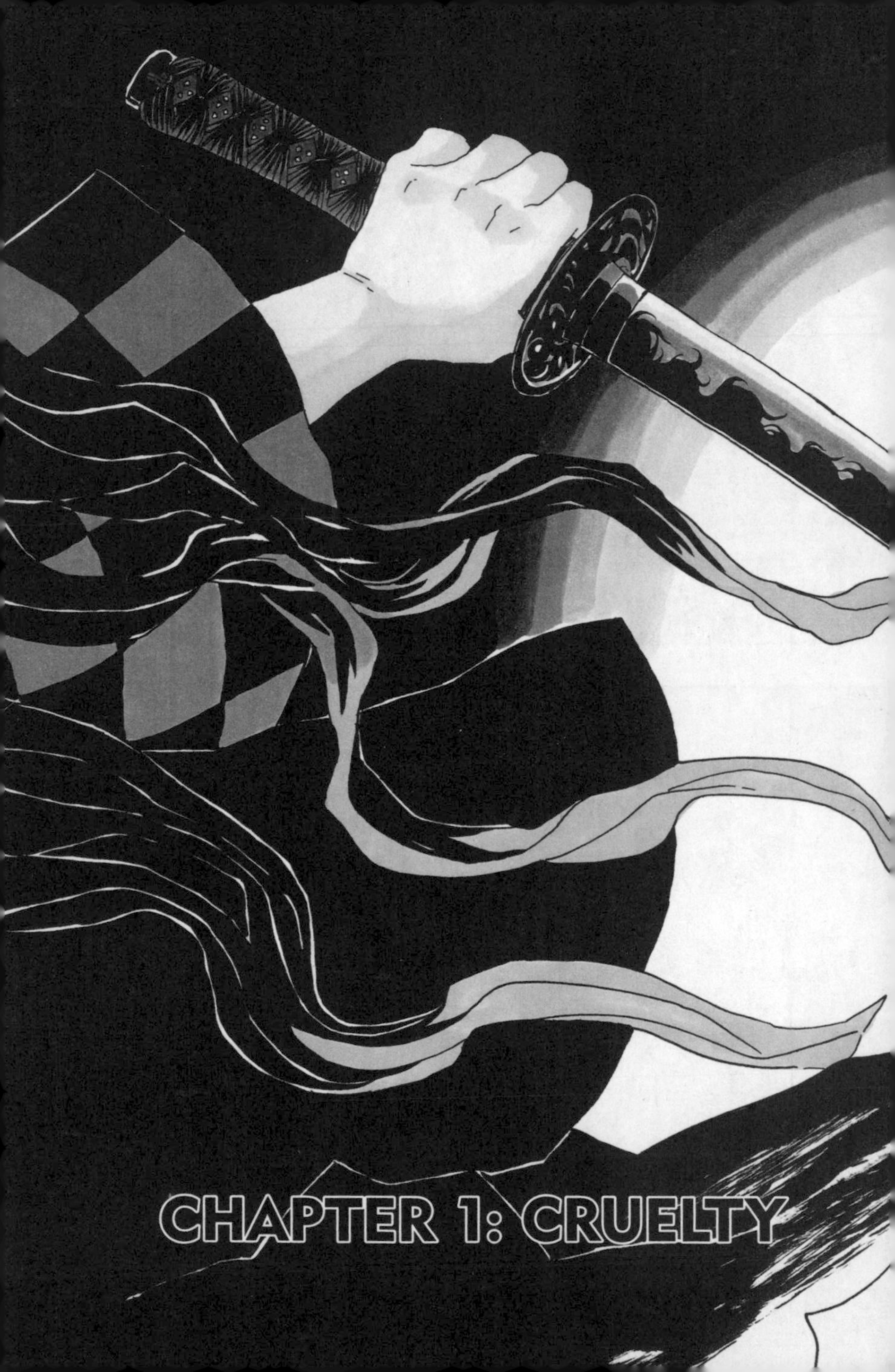
CHAPTER 1: CRUELTY

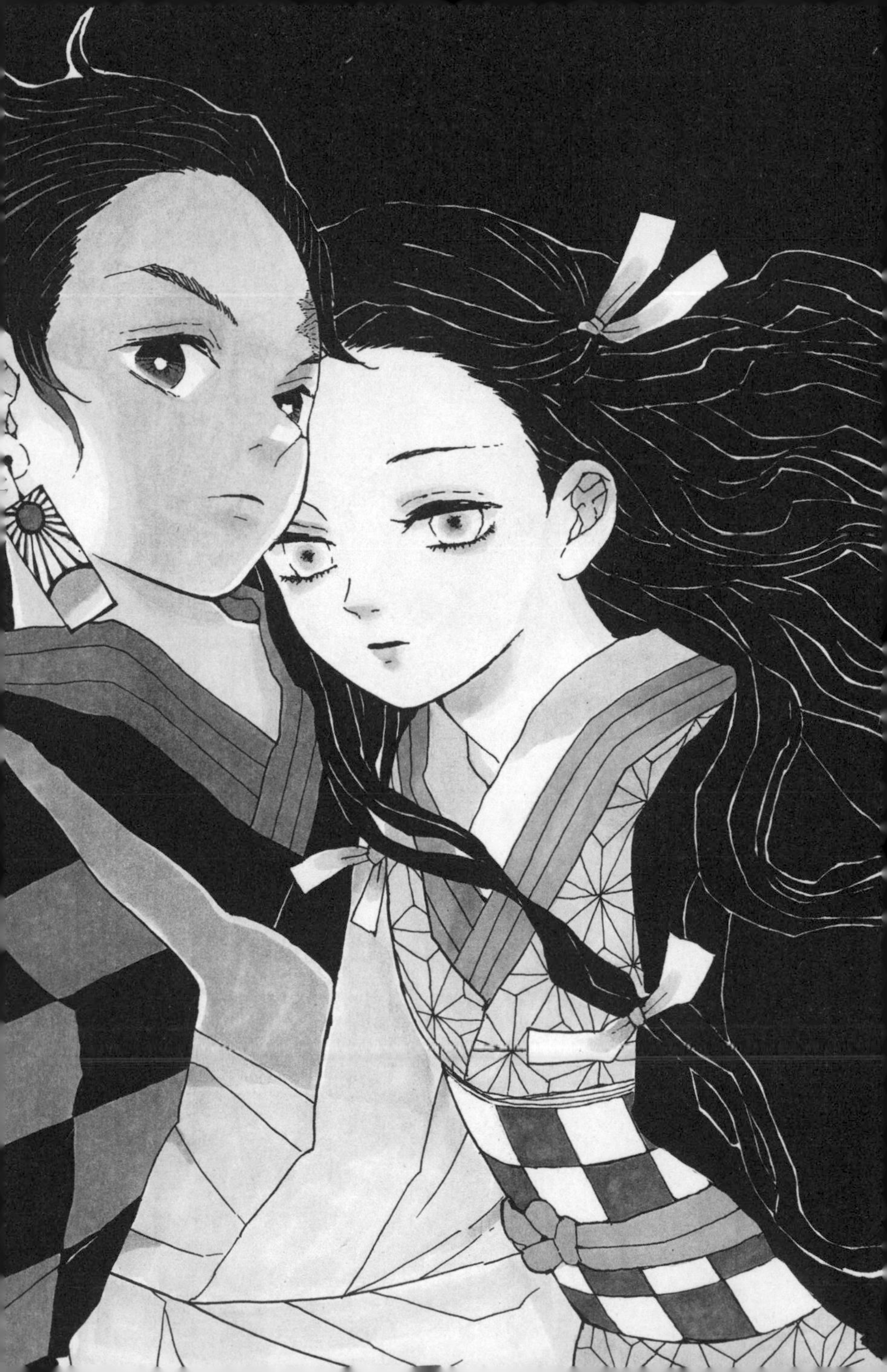

DEMON SLAYER

KIMETSU NO YAIBA

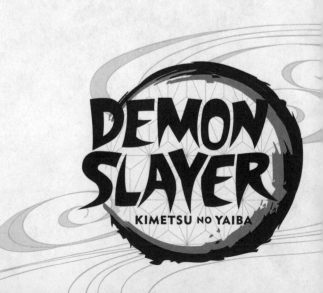

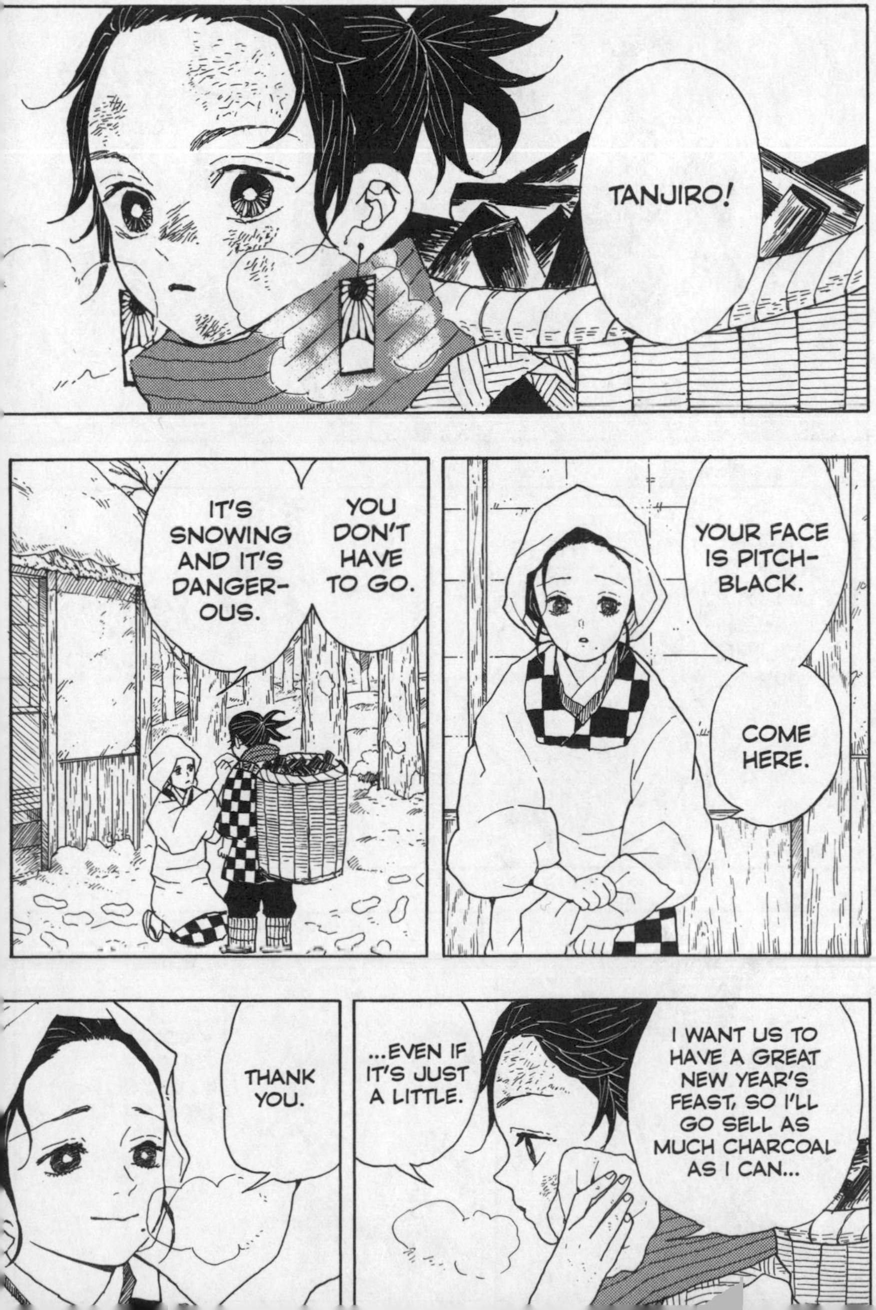
TANJIRO!
YOUR FACE IS PITCH-BLACK.
COME HERE.
YOU DON'T HAVE TO GO.
IT'S SNOWING AND IT'S DANGER-OUS.
I WANT US TO HAVE A GREAT NEW YEAR'S FEAST, SO I'LL GO SELL AS MUCH CHARCOAL AS I CAN...
...EVEN IF IT'S JUST A LITTLE.
THANK YOU.

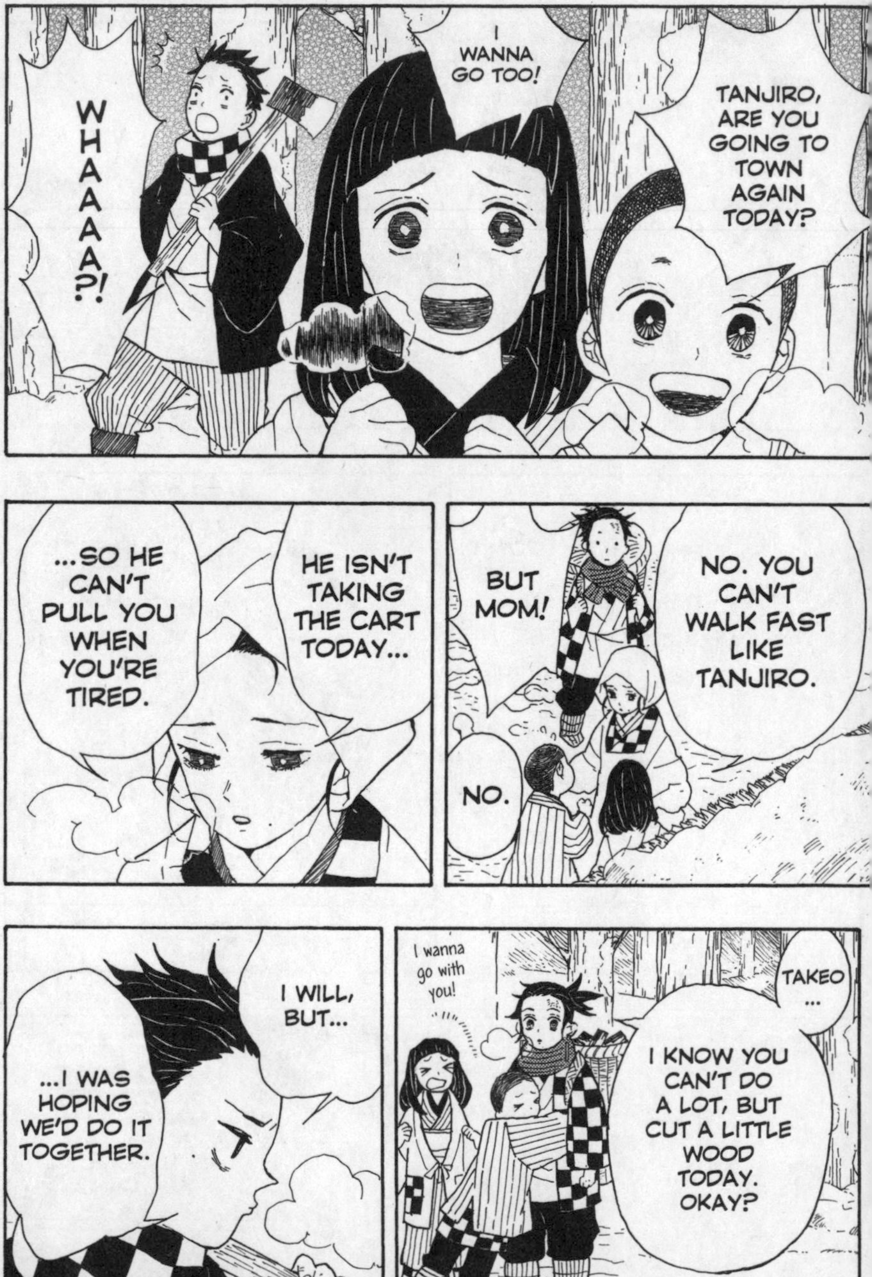
TANJIRO, ARE YOU GOING TO TOWN AGAIN TODAY?
I WANNA GO TOO!
WHAAAAA?!
NO. YOU CAN'T WALK FAST LIKE TANJIRO.
BUT MOM!
NO.
HE ISN'T TAKING THE CART TODAY...
...SO HE CAN'T PULL YOU WHEN YOU'RE TIRED.
TAKEO ...
I KNOW YOU CAN'T DO A LOT, BUT CUT A LITTLE WOOD TODAY. OKAY?
I wanna go with you!
I WILL, BUT...
...I WAS HOPING WE'D DO IT TOGETHER.

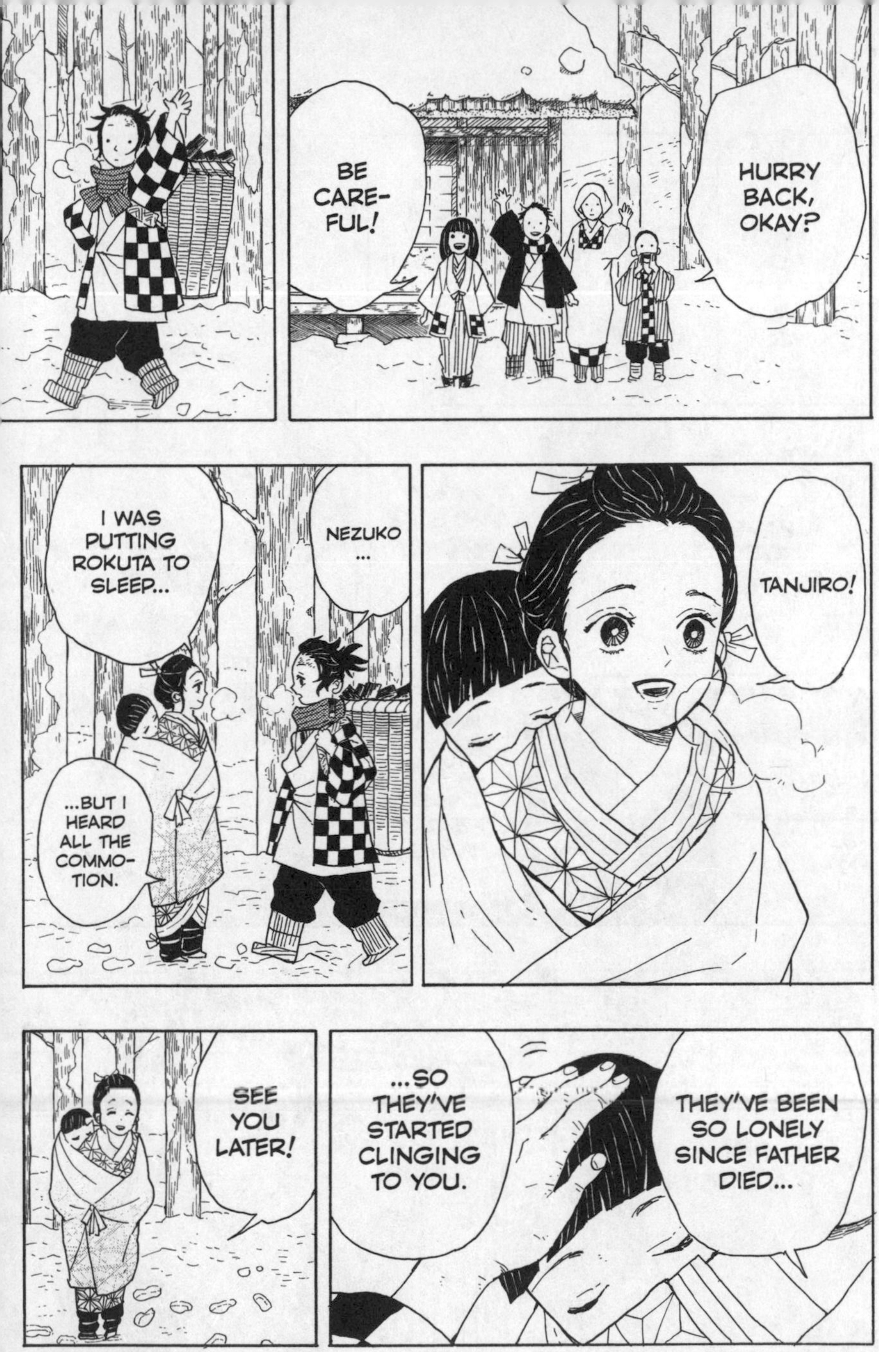
HURRY BACK, OKAY?
BE CARE-FUL!
TANJIRO!
NEZUKO ...
I WAS PUTTING ROKUTA TO SLEEP...
...BUT I HEARD ALL THE COMMO-TION.
THEY'VE BEEN SO LONELY SINCE FATHER DIED...
...SO THEY'VE STARTED CLINGING TO YOU.
SEE YOU LATER!

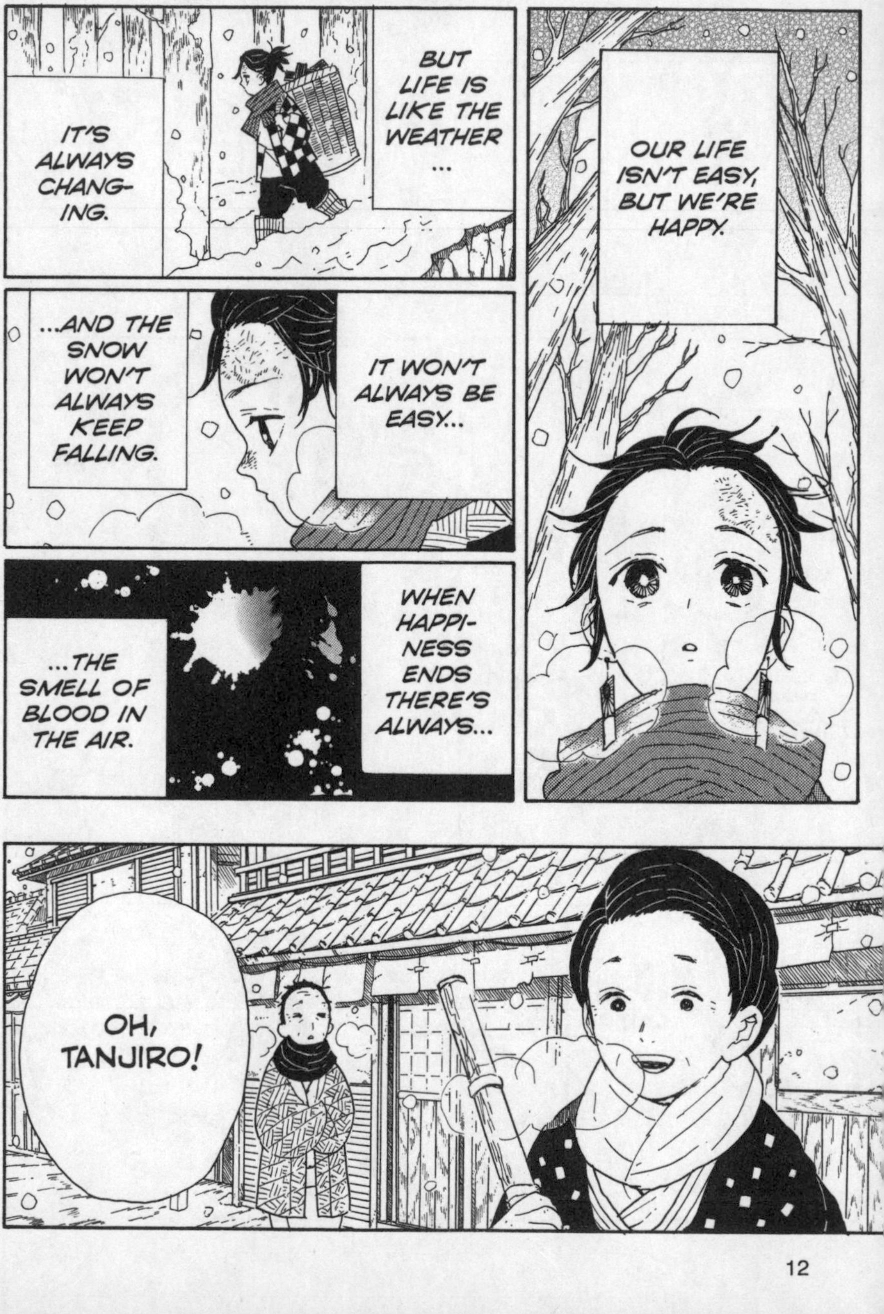
OUR LIFE ISN'T EASY, BUT WE'RE HAPPY.
BUT LIFE IS LIKE THE WEATHER ...
IT'S ALWAYS CHANGING.
IT WON'T ALWAYS BE EASY...
...AND THE SNOW WON'T ALWAYS KEEP FALLING.
WHEN HAPPINESS ENDS THERE'S ALWAYS...
...THE SMELL OF BLOOD IN THE AIR.
OH, TANJIRO!

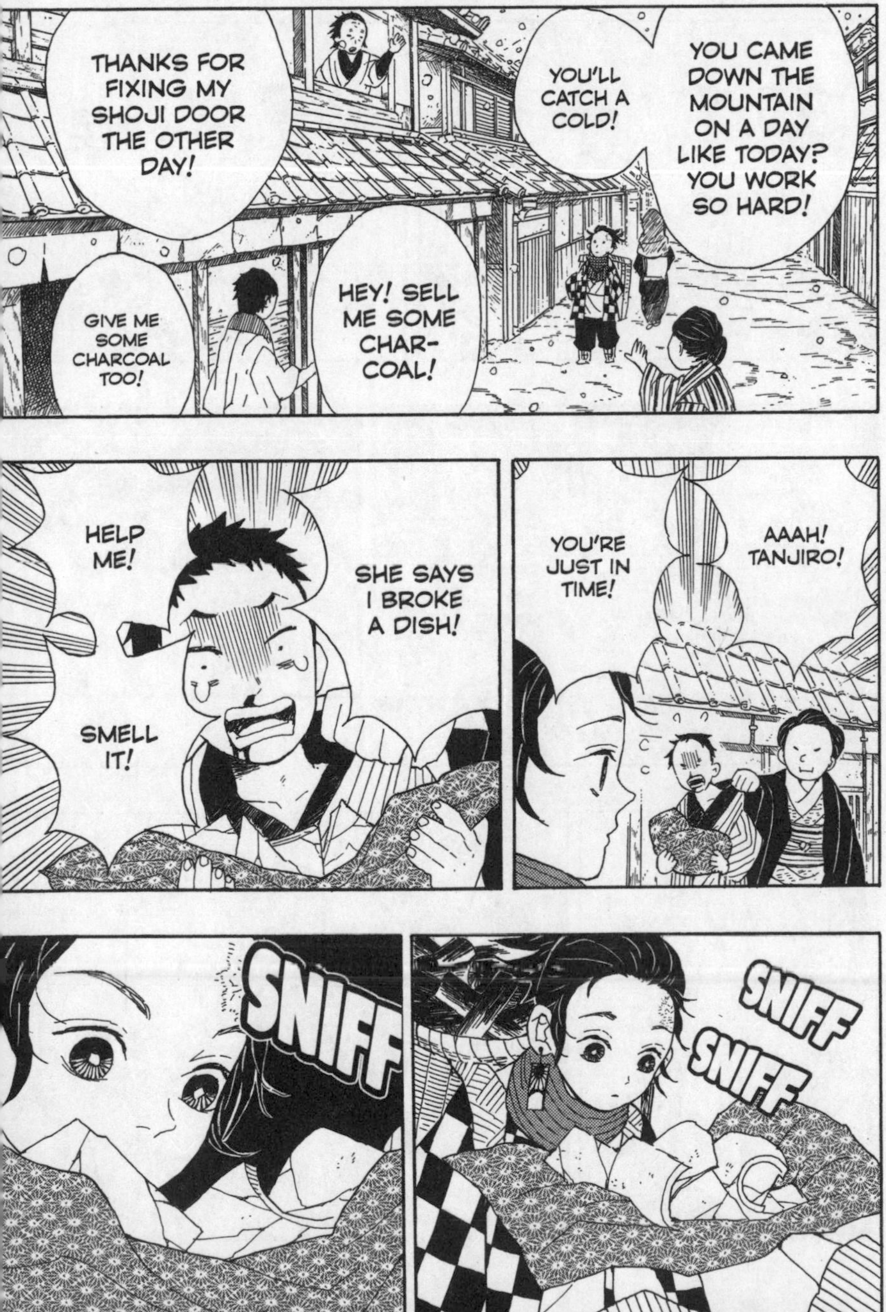
YOU CAME DOWN THE MOUNTAIN ON A DAY LIKE TODAY? YOU WORK SO HARD!
YOU'LL CATCH A COLD!
THANKS FOR FIXING MY SHOJI DOOR THE OTHER DAY!
HEY! SELL ME SOME CHAR-COAL!
GIVE ME SOME CHARCOAL TOO!
AAAH! TANJIRO!
YOU'RE JUST IN TIME!
SHE SAYS I BROKE A DISH!
HELP ME!
SMELL IT!
SNIFF
SNIFF
SNIFF

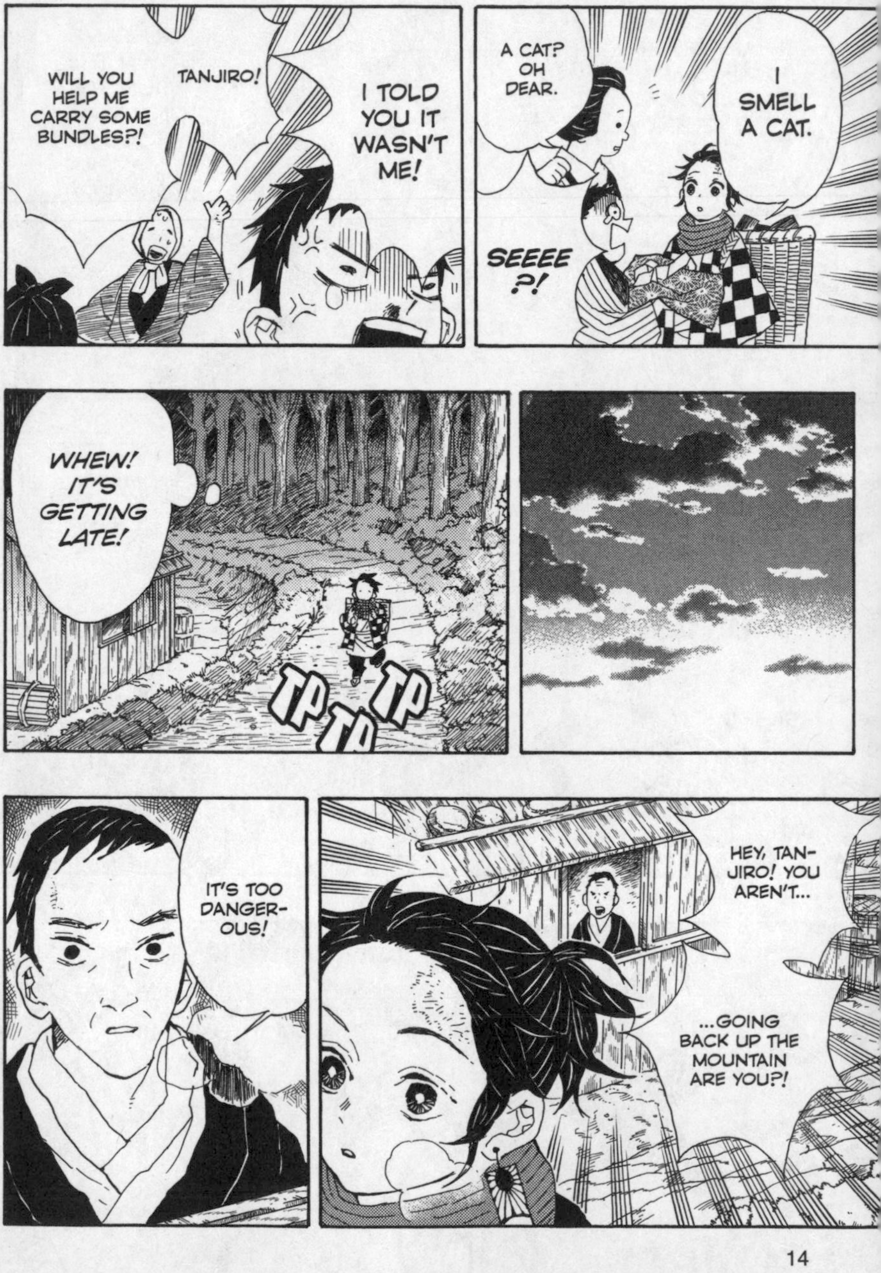
I SMELL A CAT.
A CAT? OH DEAR.
SEEEE ?!
I TOLD YOU IT WASN'T ME!
TANJIRO!
WILL YOU HELP ME CARRY SOME BUNDLES?!
WHEW! IT'S GETTING LATE!
TP TP TP
HEY, TAN-JIRO! YOU AREN'T...
...GOING BACK UP THE MOUNTAIN ARE YOU?!
IT'S TOO DANGER-OUS!

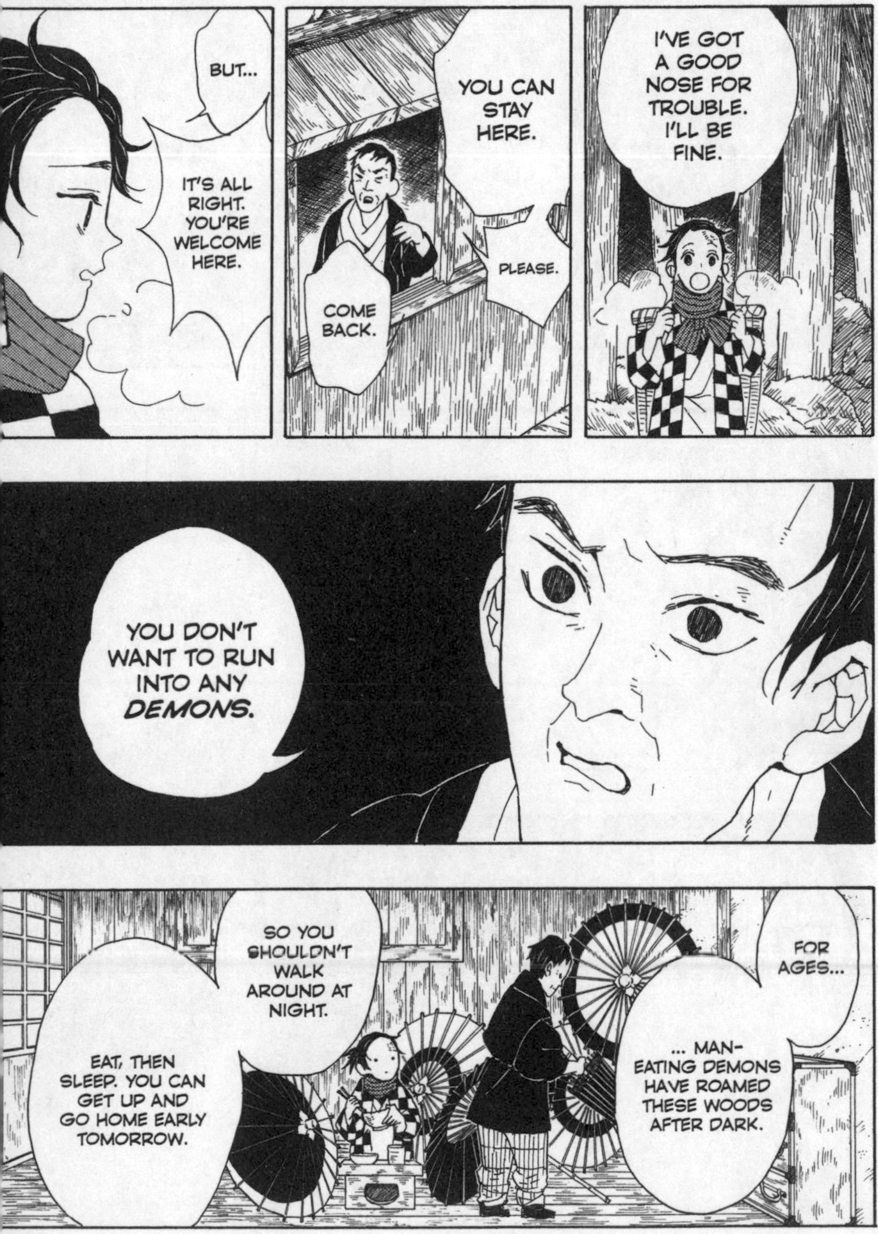
I'VE GOT A GOOD NOSE FOR TROUBLE. I'LL BE FINE.
YOU CAN STAY HERE.
PLEASE.
COME BACK.
BUT...
IT'S ALL RIGHT. YOU'RE WELCOME HERE.
YOU DON'T WANT TO RUN INTO ANY *DEMONS*.
FOR AGES...
... MAN-EATING DEMONS HAVE ROAMED THESE WOODS AFTER DARK.
SO YOU SHOULDN'T WALK AROUND AT NIGHT.
EAT, THEN SLEEP. YOU CAN GET UP AND GO HOME EARLY TOMORROW.

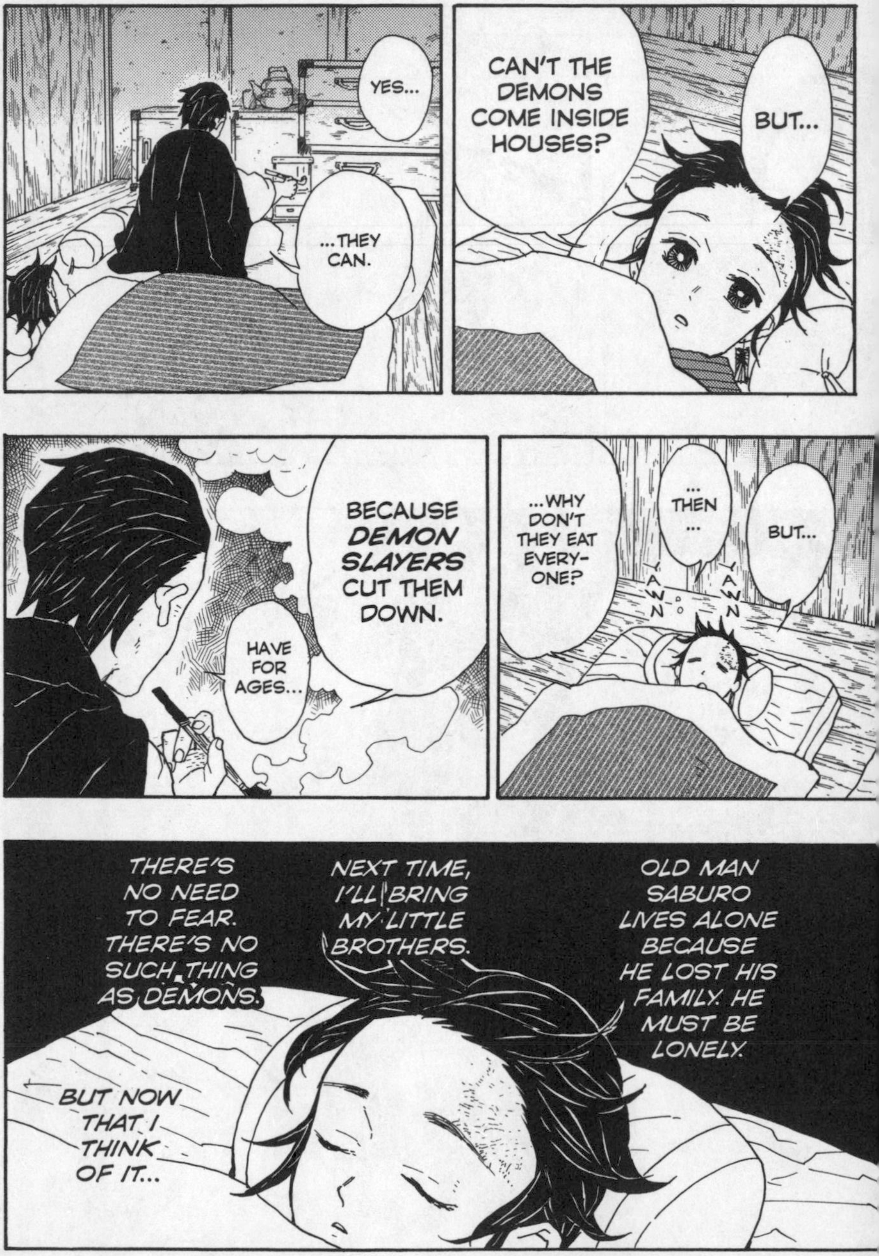
BUT...
CAN'T THE DEMONS COME INSIDE HOUSES?
YES...
...THEY CAN.
BUT...
...THEN...
...WHY DON'T THEY EAT EVERY-ONE?
YAWN
YAWN
BECAUSE DEMON SLAYERS CUT THEM DOWN.
HAVE FOR AGES...
OLD MAN SABURO LIVES ALONE BECAUSE HE LOST HIS FAMILY. HE MUST BE LONELY.
NEXT TIME, I'LL BRING MY LITTLE BROTHERS.
THERE'S NO NEED TO FEAR. THERE'S NO SUCH THING AS DEMONS.
BUT NOW THAT I THINK OF IT...

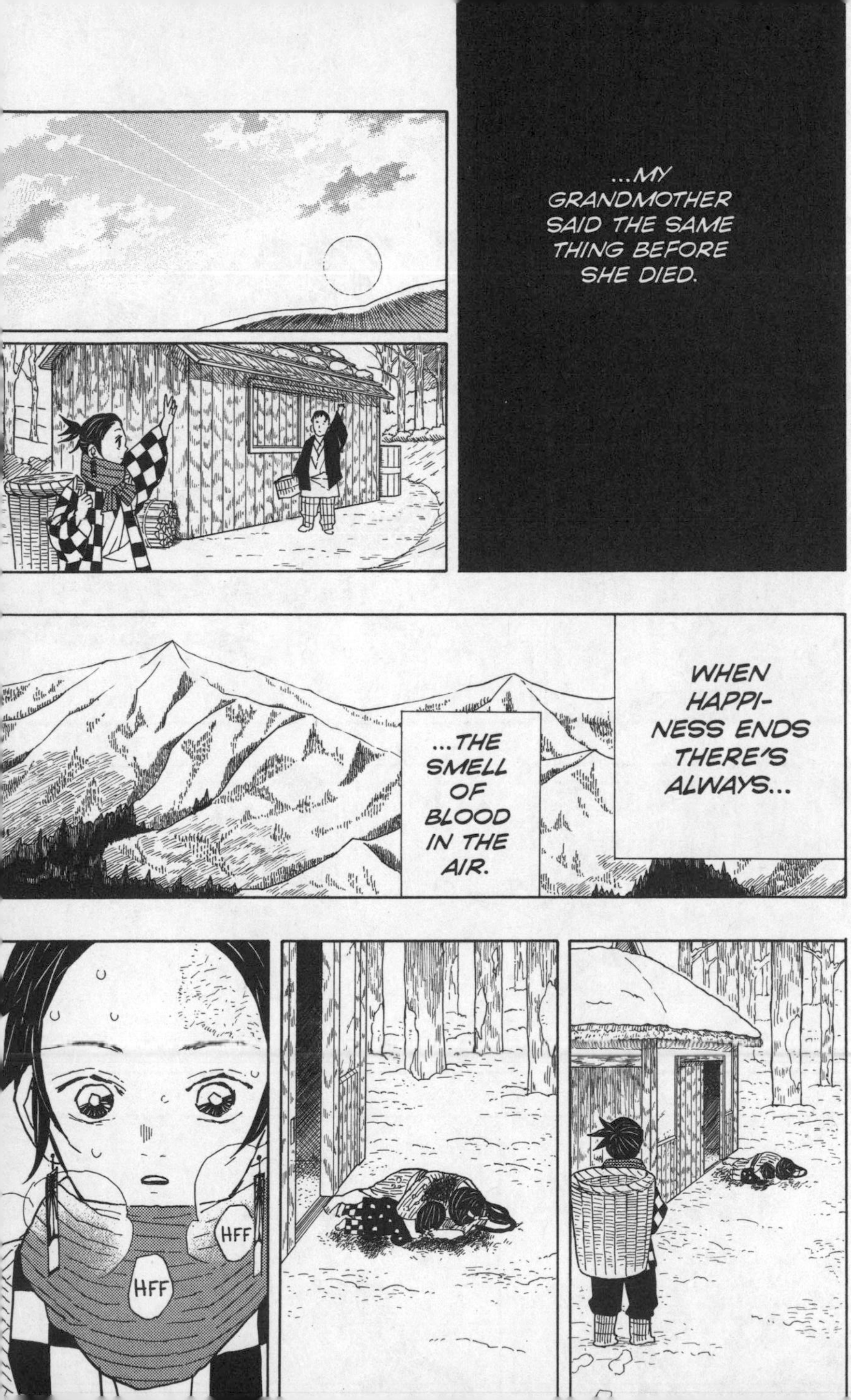
...MY GRANDMOTHER SAID THE SAME THING BEFORE SHE DIED.
WHEN HAPPINESS ENDS THERE'S ALWAYS...
...THE SMELL OF BLOOD IN THE AIR.
HFF
HFF

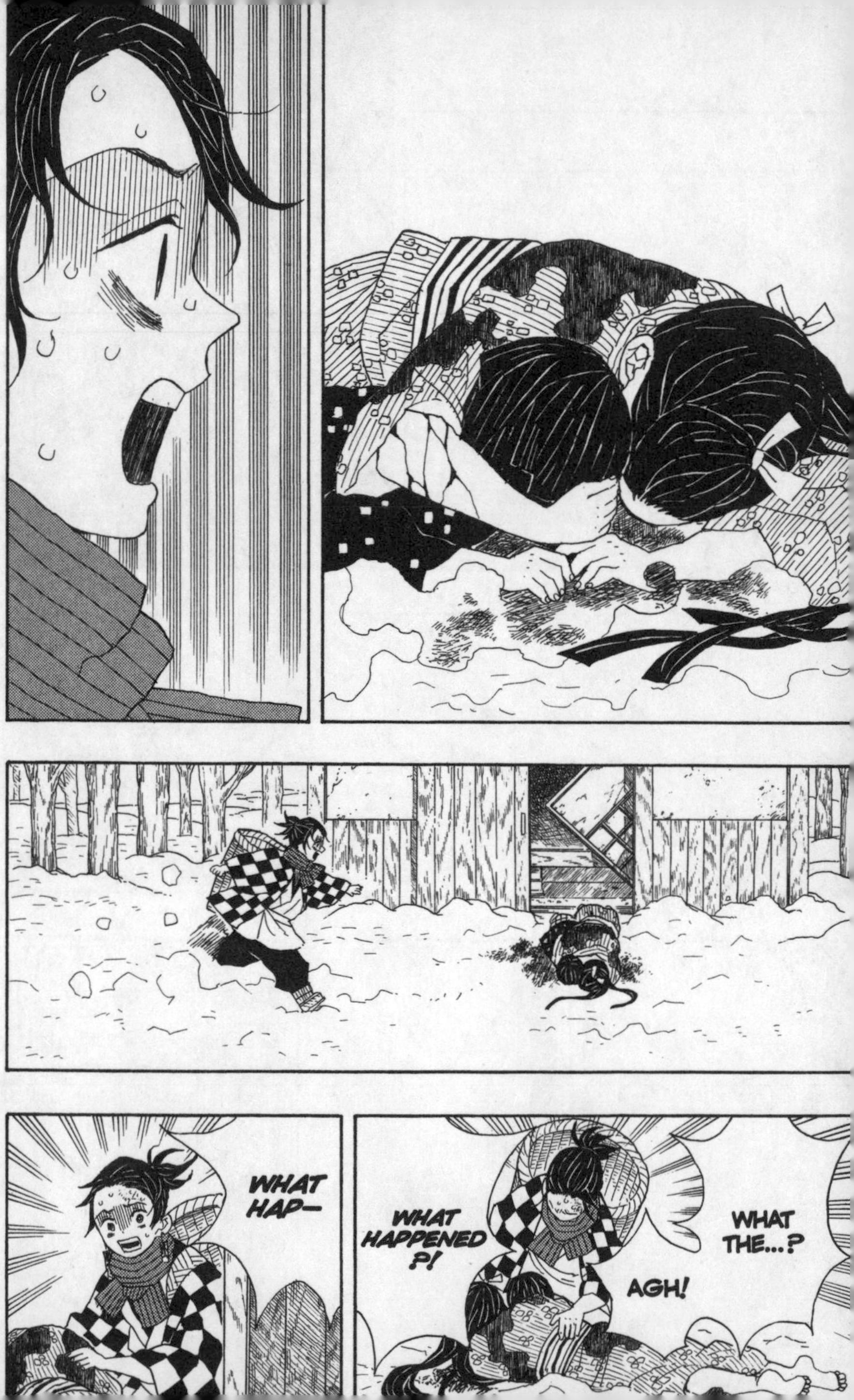
WHAT THE...?
WHAT HAPPENED ?!
AGH!
WHAT HAP—

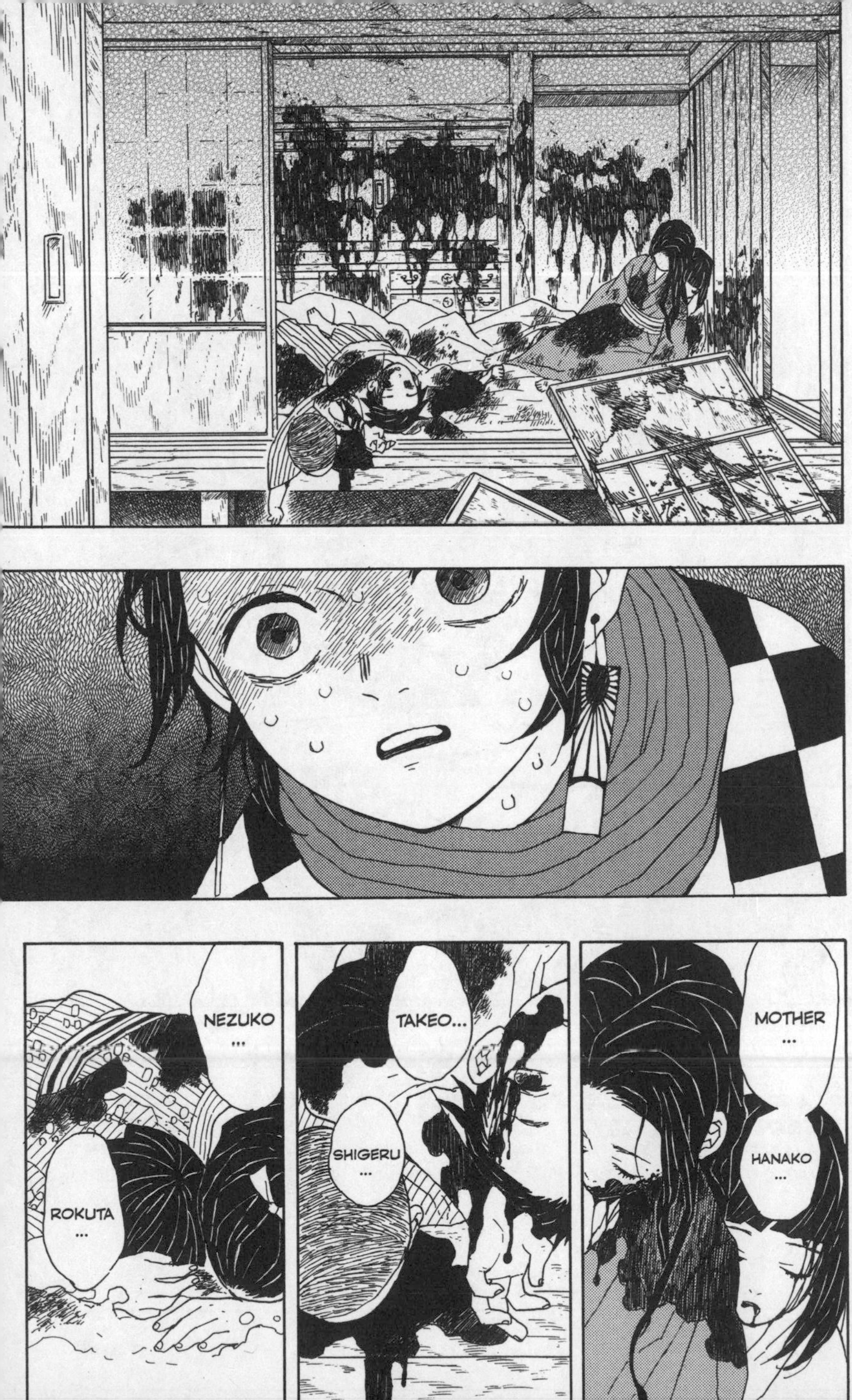
MOTHER ...
HANAKO ...
TAKEO...
SHIGERU ...
NEZUKO ...
ROKUTA ...

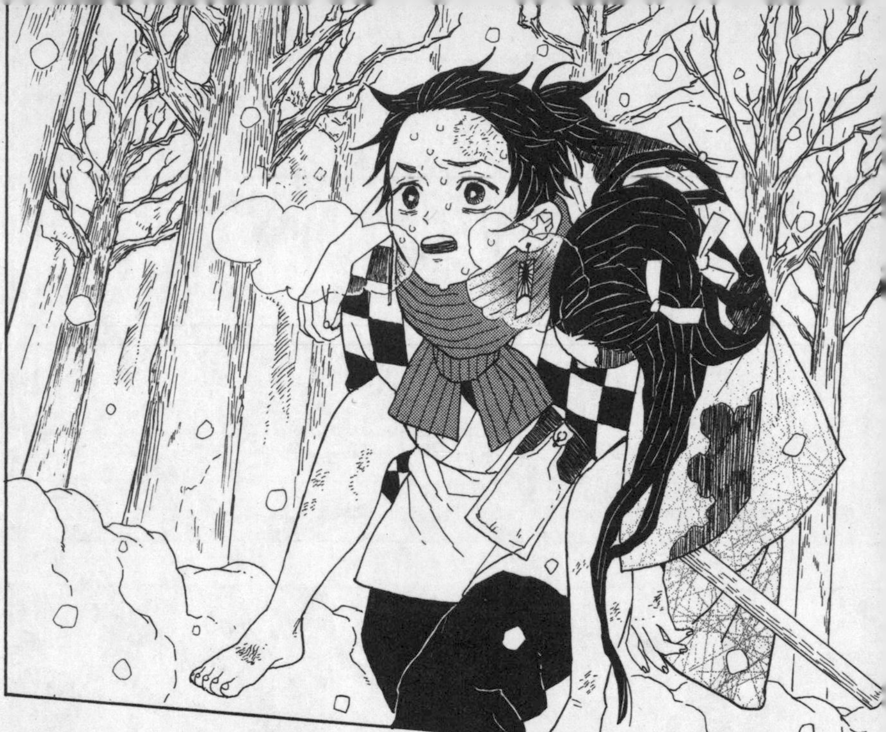

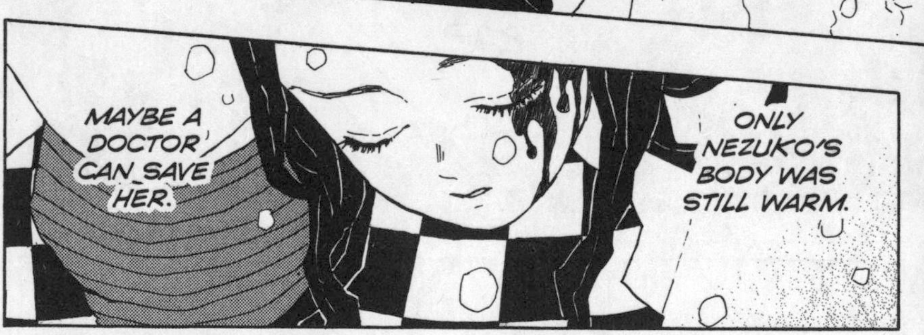
ONLY NEZUKO'S BODY WAS STILL WARM.
MAYBE A DOCTOR CAN SAVE HER.

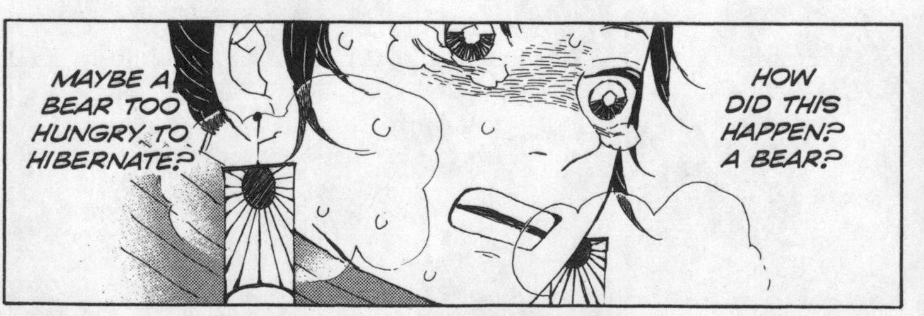
HOW DID THIS HAPPEN? A BEAR?
MAYBE A BEAR TOO HUNGRY TO HIBERNATE?

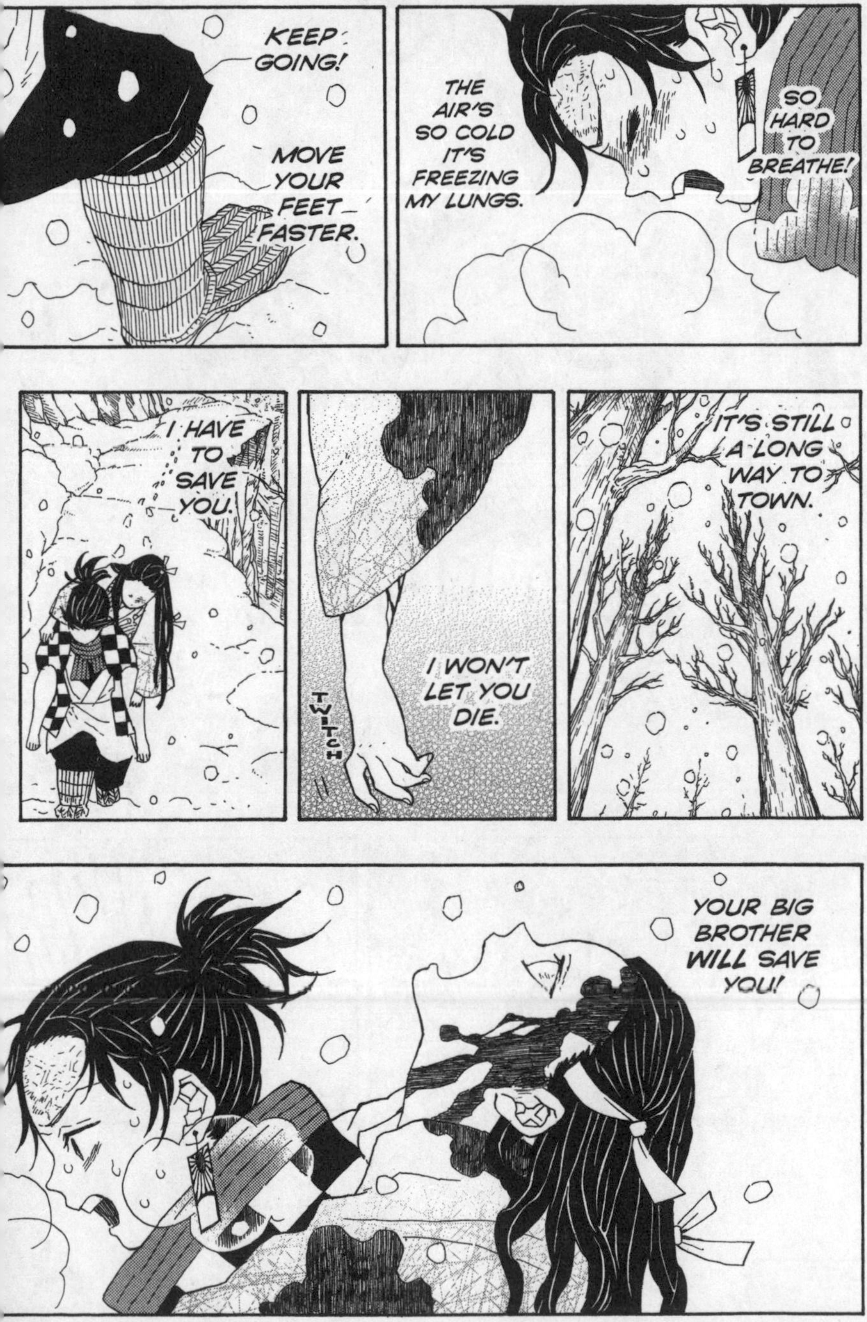
THE AIR'S SO COLD IT'S FREEZING MY LUNGS.
SO HARD TO BREATHE!
KEEP GOING!
MOVE YOUR FEET FASTER.
IT'S STILL A LONG WAY TO TOWN.
I WON'T LET YOU DIE.
TWITCH
I HAVE TO SAVE YOU.
YOUR BIG BROTHER WILL SAVE YOU!

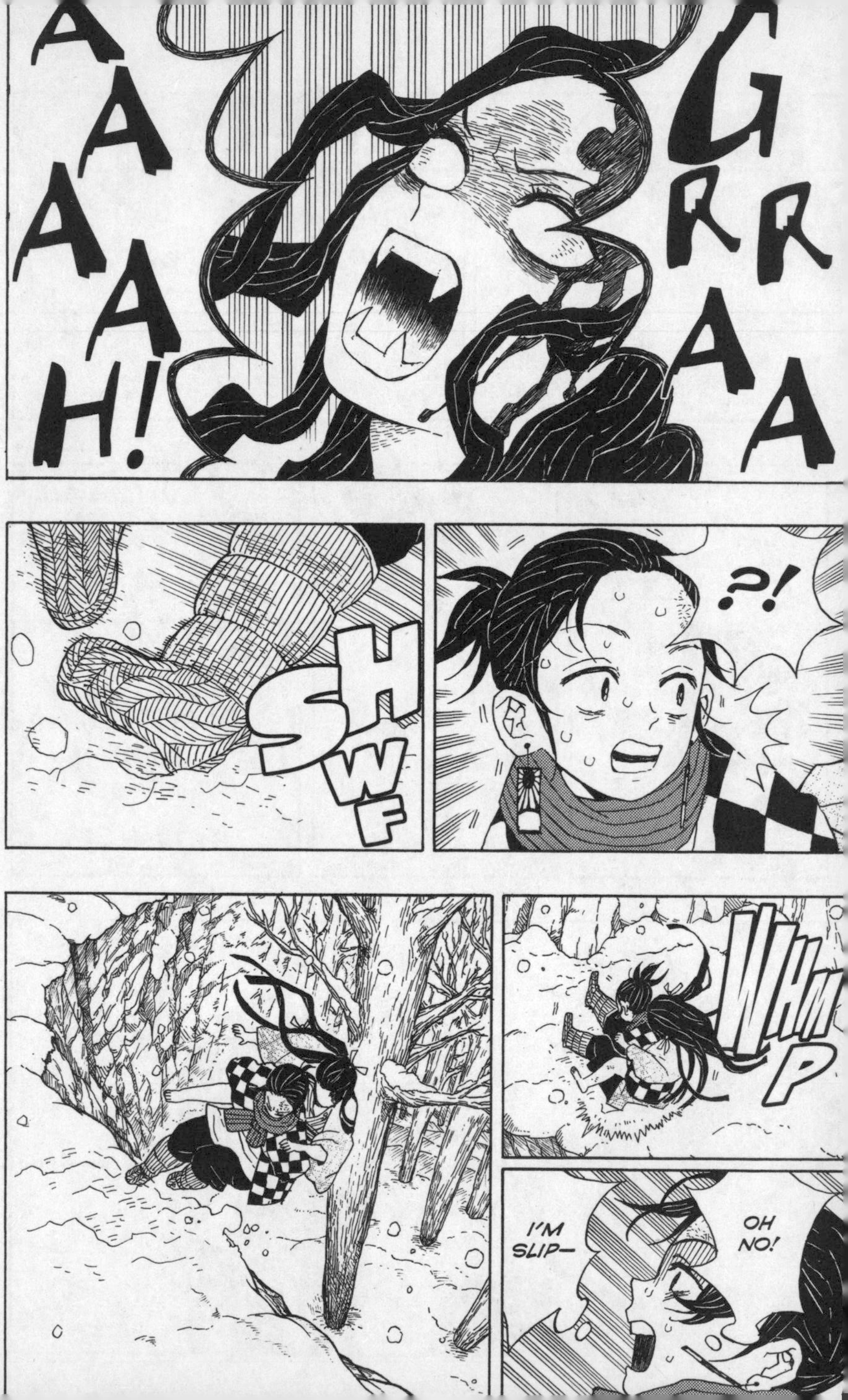
GRRAA
AAAAH!
?!
SHWF
WHMP
OH NO!
I'M SLIP—

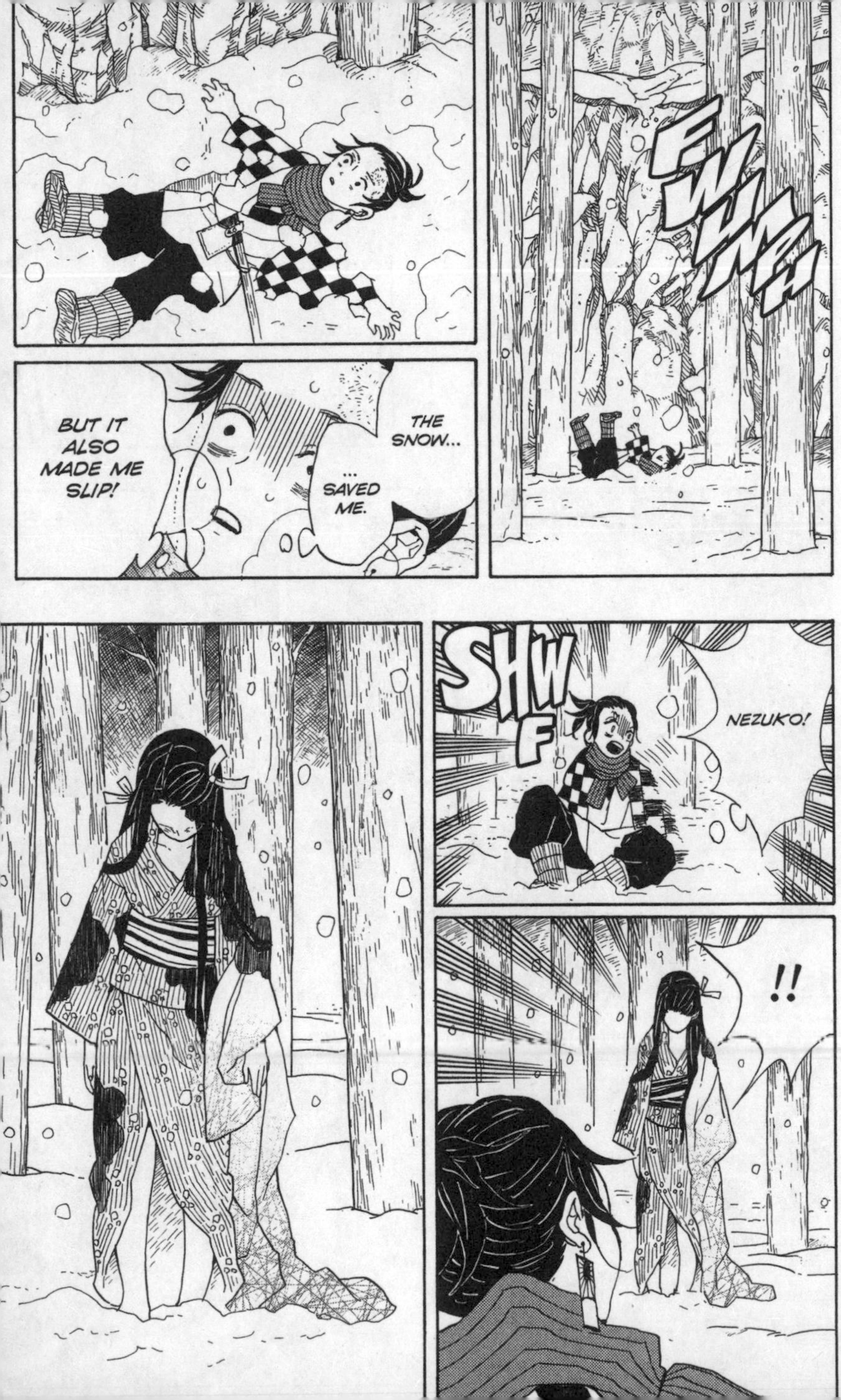
FWUMPH
THE SNOW...
...SAVED ME.
BUT IT ALSO MADE ME SLIP!
SHWF
NEZUKO!
!!

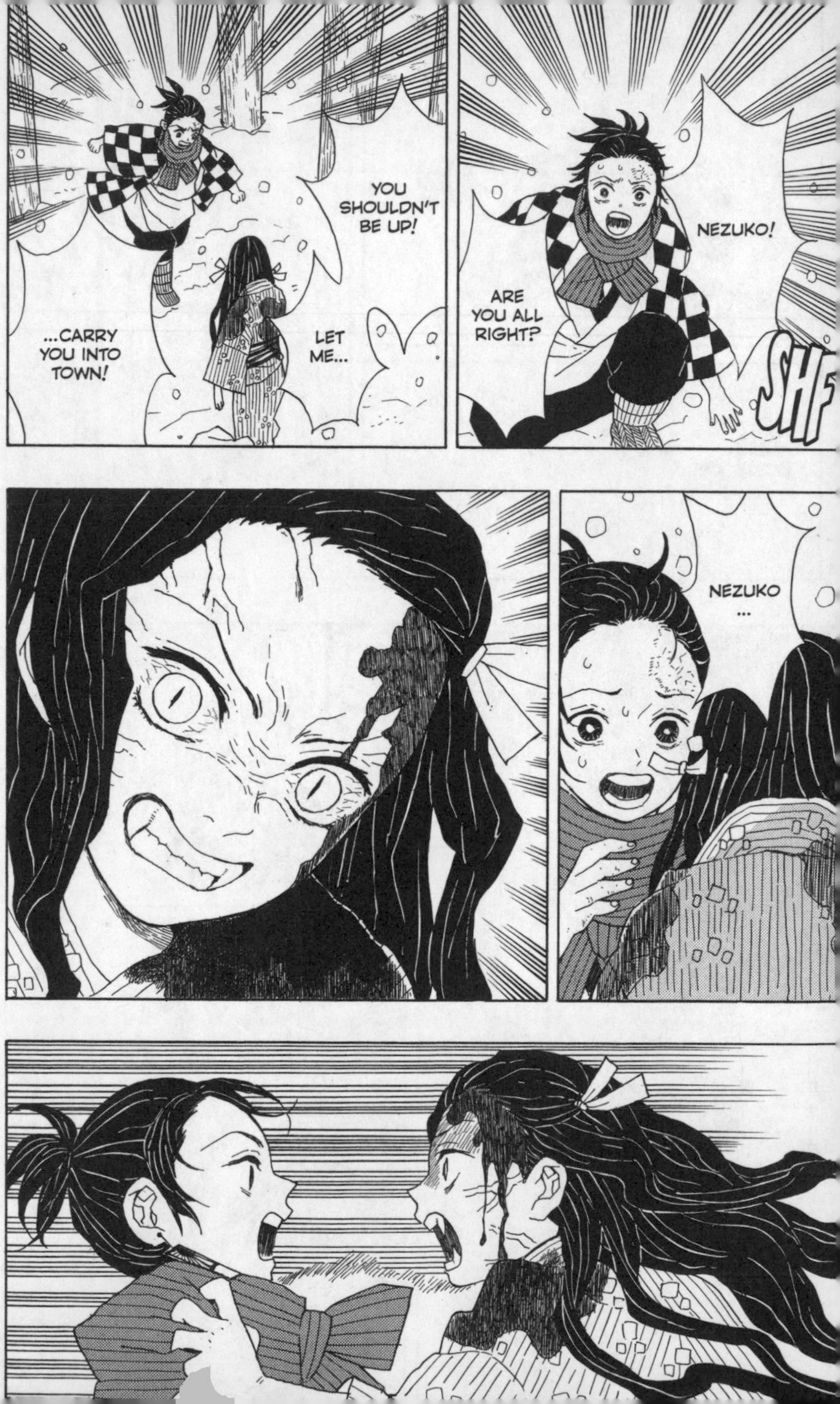
NEZUKO!
ARE YOU ALL RIGHT?
SHF
YOU SHOULDN'T BE UP!
LET ME...
...CARRY YOU INTO TOWN!
NEZUKO ...

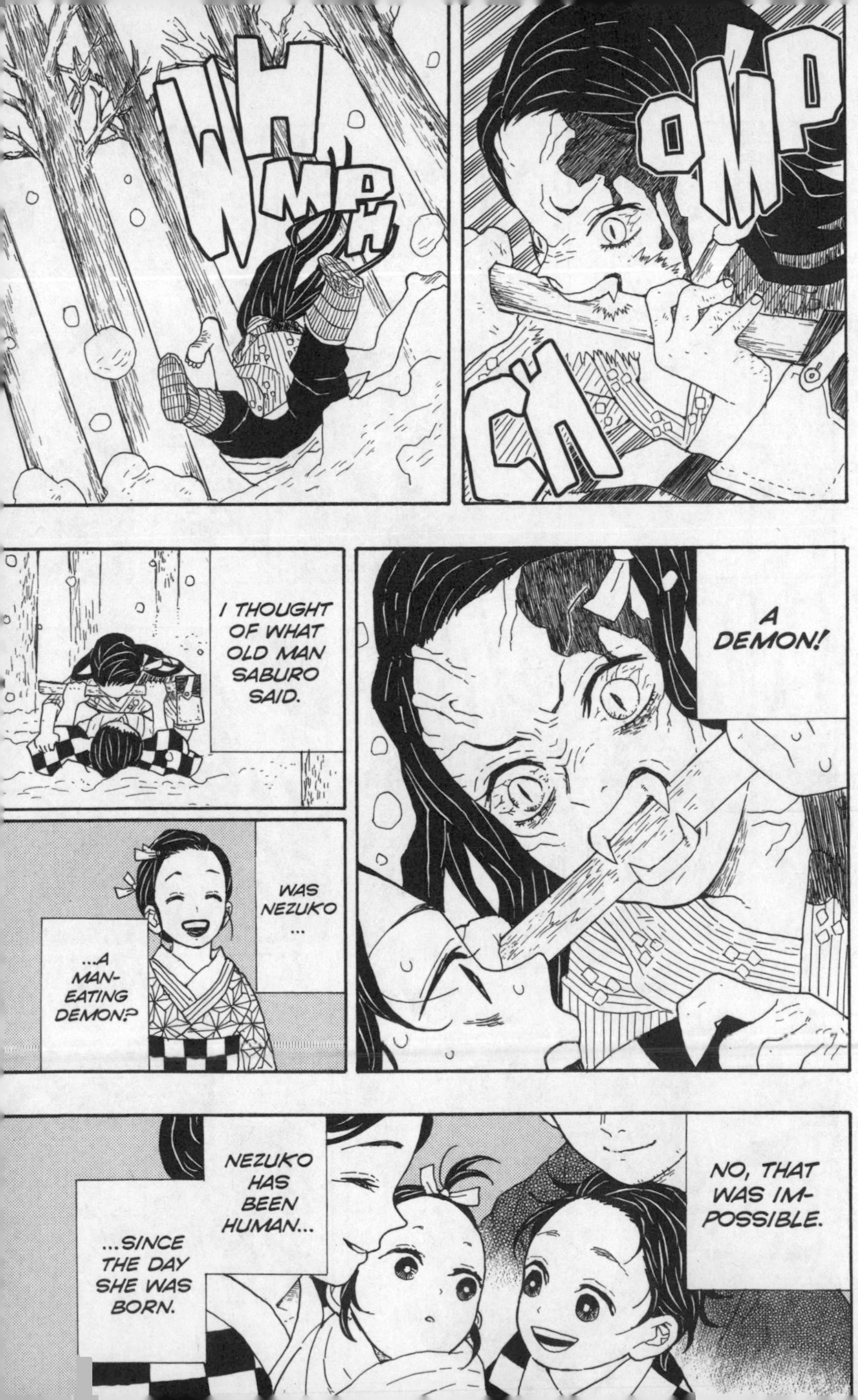
OMP
CH
A DEMON!
I THOUGHT OF WHAT OLD MAN SABURO SAID.
WAS NEZUKO ...
...A MAN-EATING DEMON?
NO, THAT WAS IMPOSSIBLE.
NEZUKO HAS BEEN HUMAN...
...SINCE THE DAY SHE WAS BORN.

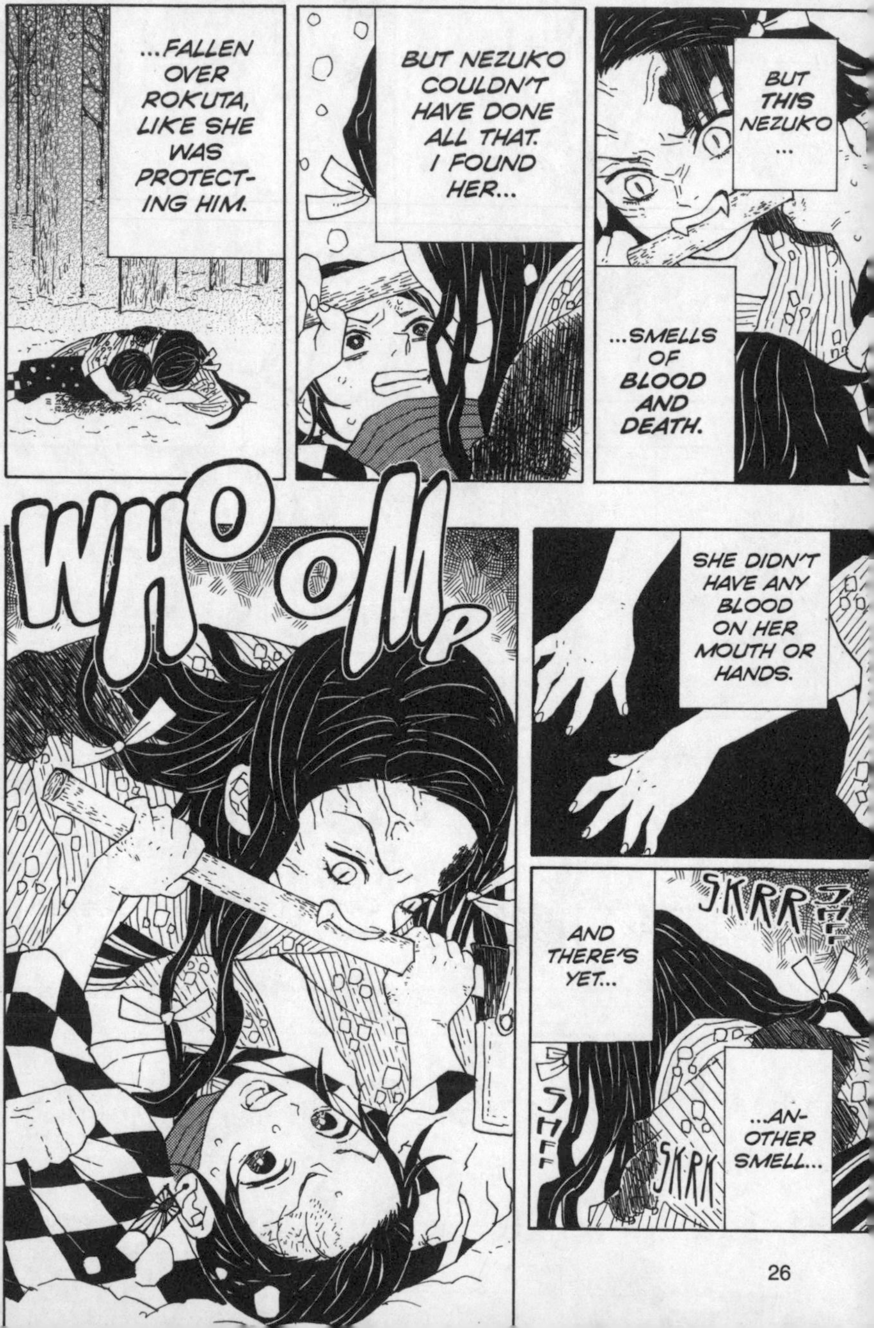
BUT THIS NEZUKO ...
...SMELLS OF BLOOD AND DEATH.
BUT NEZUKO COULDN'T HAVE DONE ALL THAT. I FOUND HER...
...FALLEN OVER ROKUTA, LIKE SHE WAS PROTECT-ING HIM.
SHE DIDN'T HAVE ANY BLOOD ON HER MOUTH OR HANDS.
SKRR
AND THERE'S YET...
SHFF
SKRK
...AN-OTHER SMELL...
WHOOMP

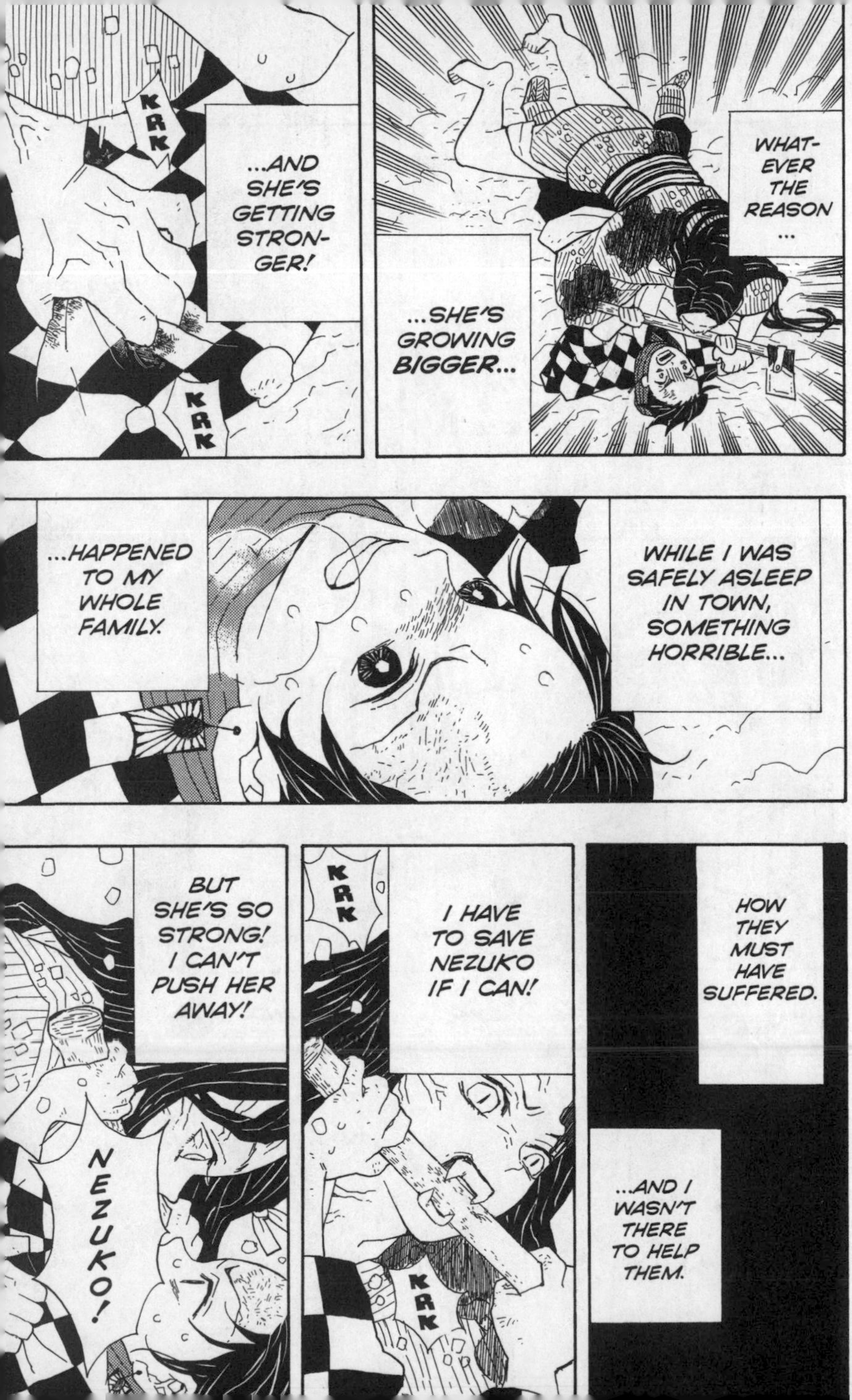
WHATEVER THE REASON...
...SHE'S GROWING BIGGER...
KRK
...AND SHE'S GETTING STRONGER!
KRK
WHILE I WAS SAFELY ASLEEP IN TOWN, SOMETHING HORRIBLE...
...HAPPENED TO MY WHOLE FAMILY.
HOW THEY MUST HAVE SUFFERED.
...AND I WASN'T THERE TO HELP THEM.
KRK
I HAVE TO SAVE NEZUKO IF I CAN!
KRK
BUT SHE'S SO STRONG! I CAN'T PUSH HER AWAY!
NEZUKO!

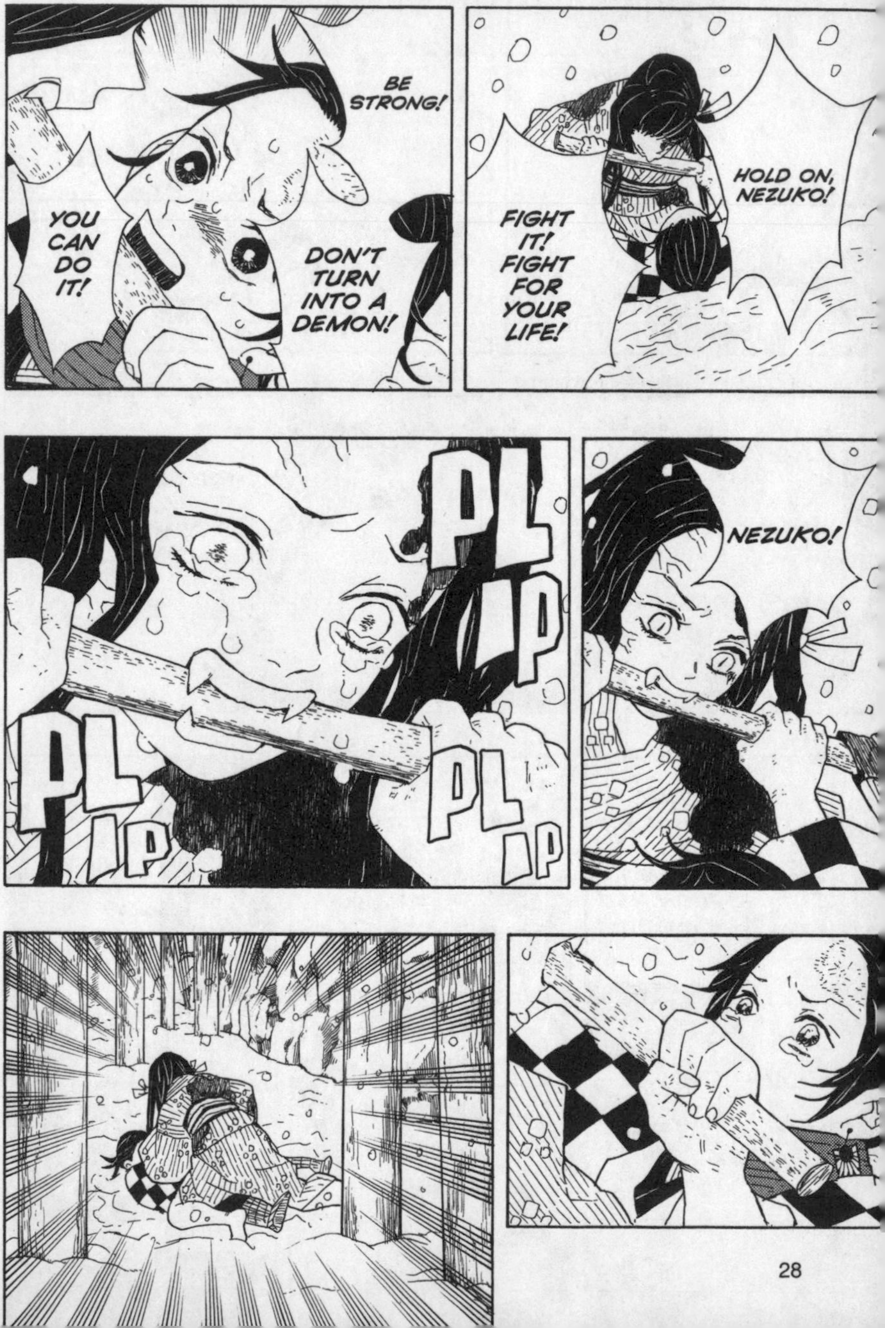
HOLD ON, NEZUKO!
FIGHT IT! FIGHT FOR YOUR LIFE!
BE STRONG!
DON'T TURN INTO A DEMON!
YOU CAN DO IT!
NEZUKO!
PLIP
PLIP
PLIP

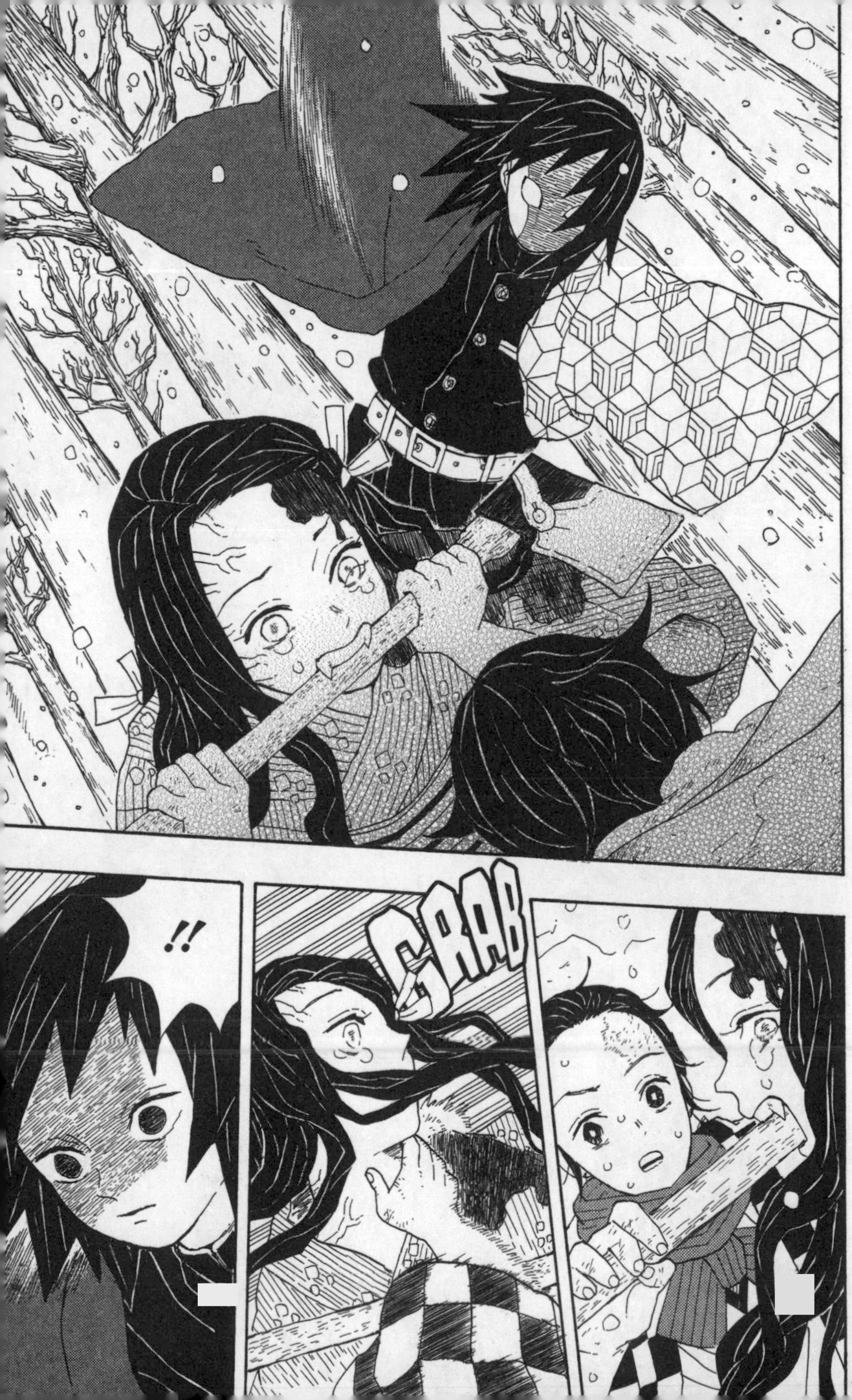
GRAB
!!

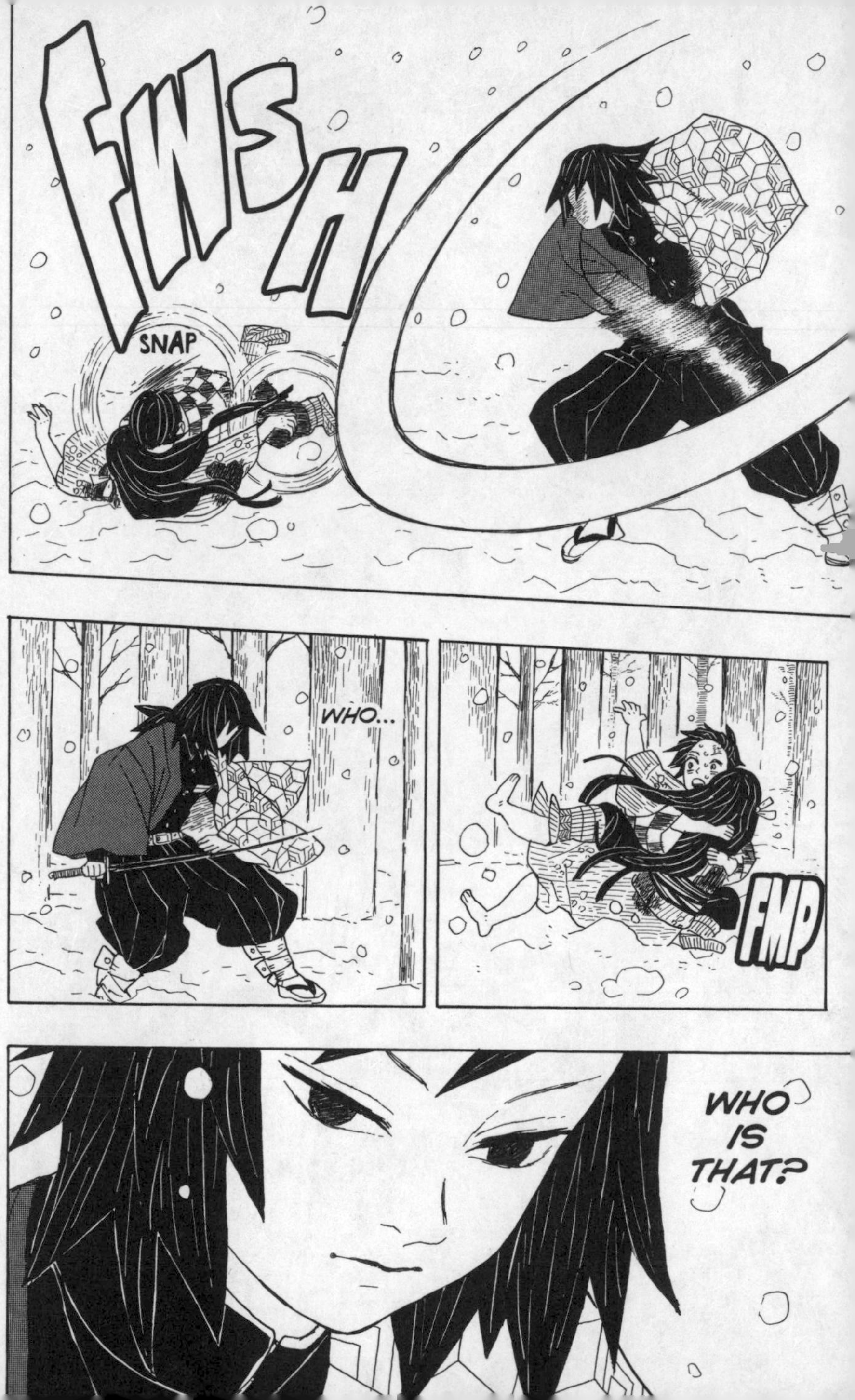
FWSH
SNAP
FMP
WHO...
WHO IS THAT?

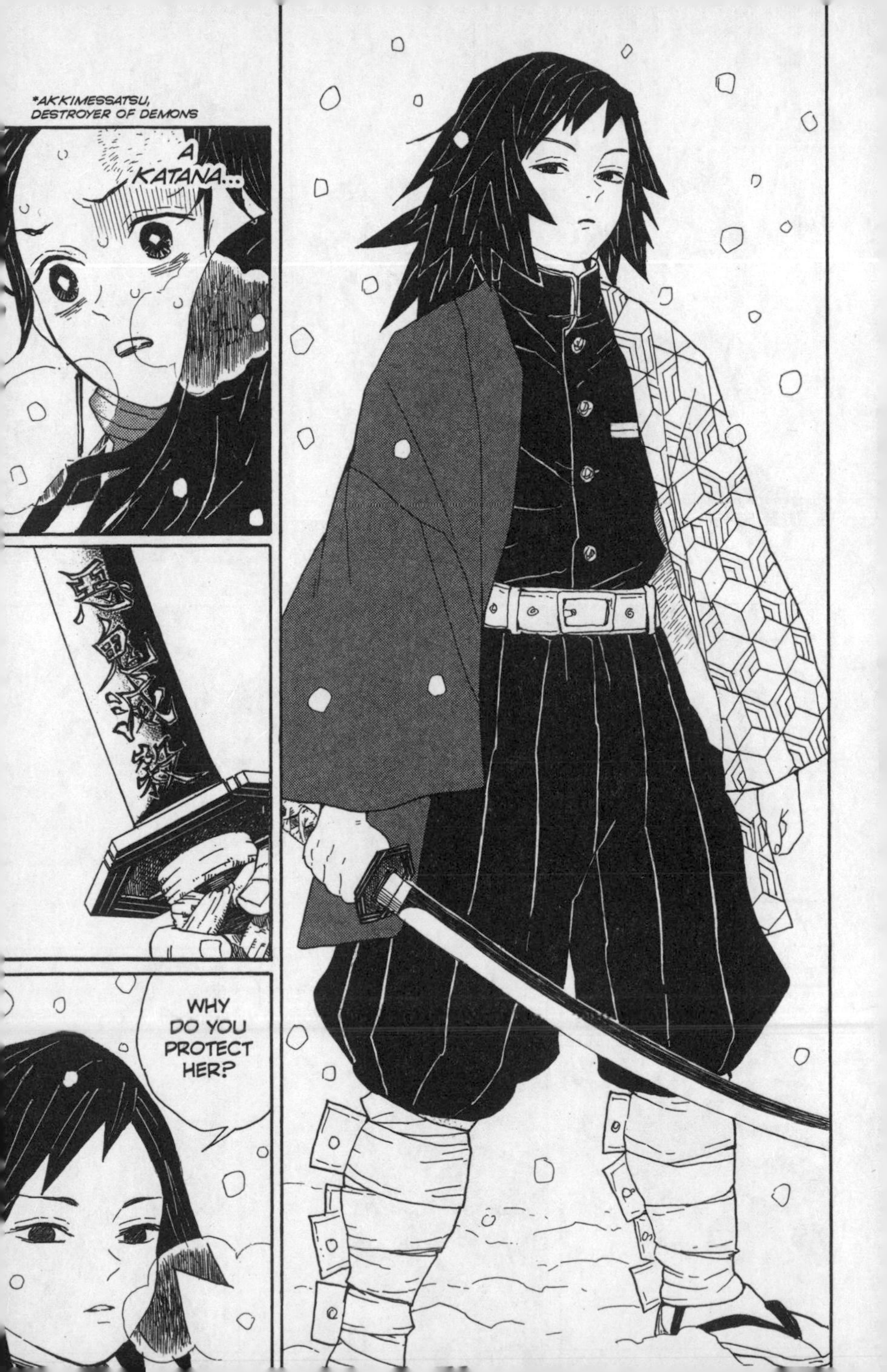
*AKKIMESSATSU, DESTROYER OF DEMONS
A KATANA...
WHY DO YOU PROTECT HER?

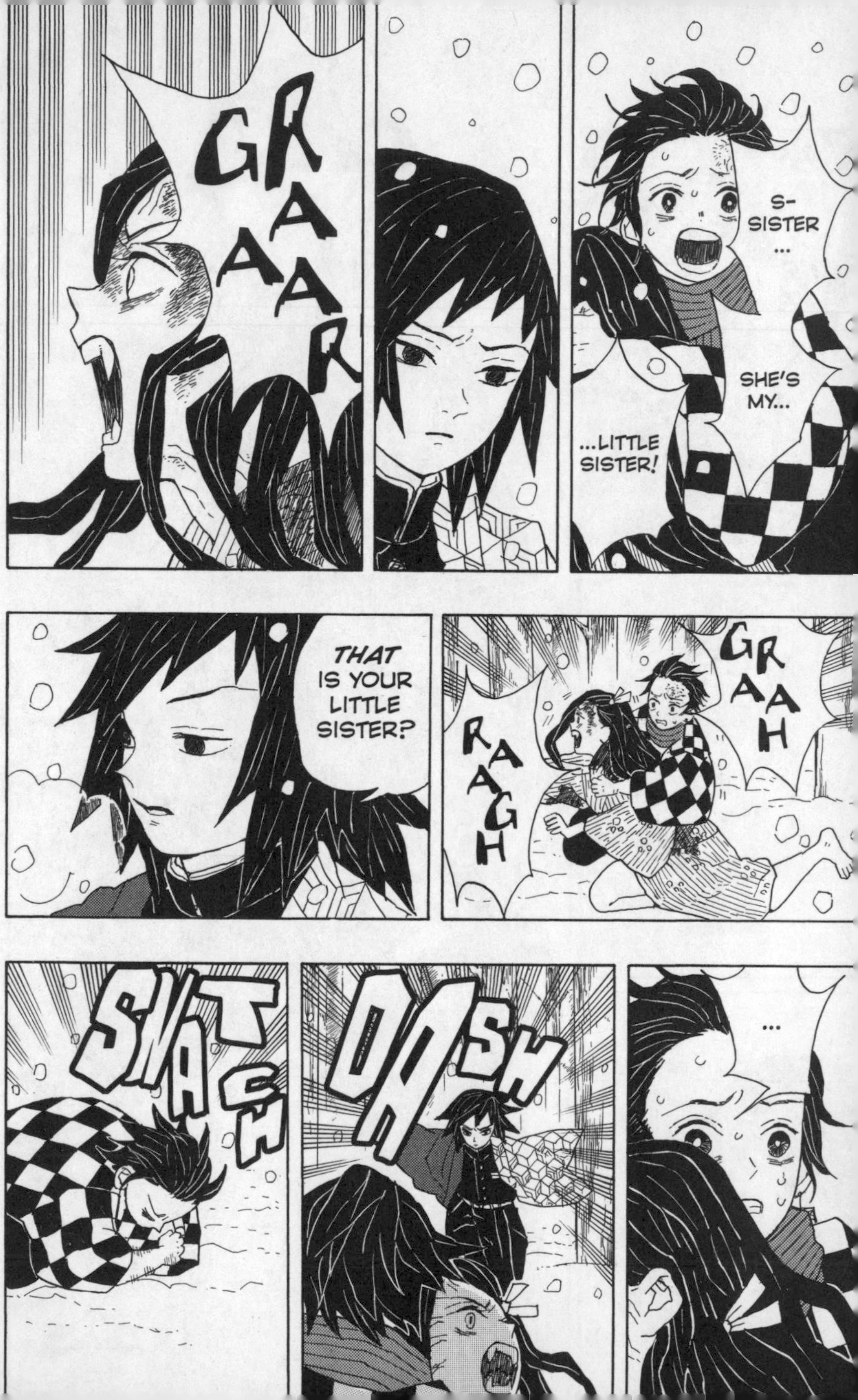

S-SISTER...
SHE'S MY...
...LITTLE SISTER!
GRAAAR
GRAAH
RAAGH
THAT IS YOUR LITTLE SISTER?
...
DASH
SNATCH

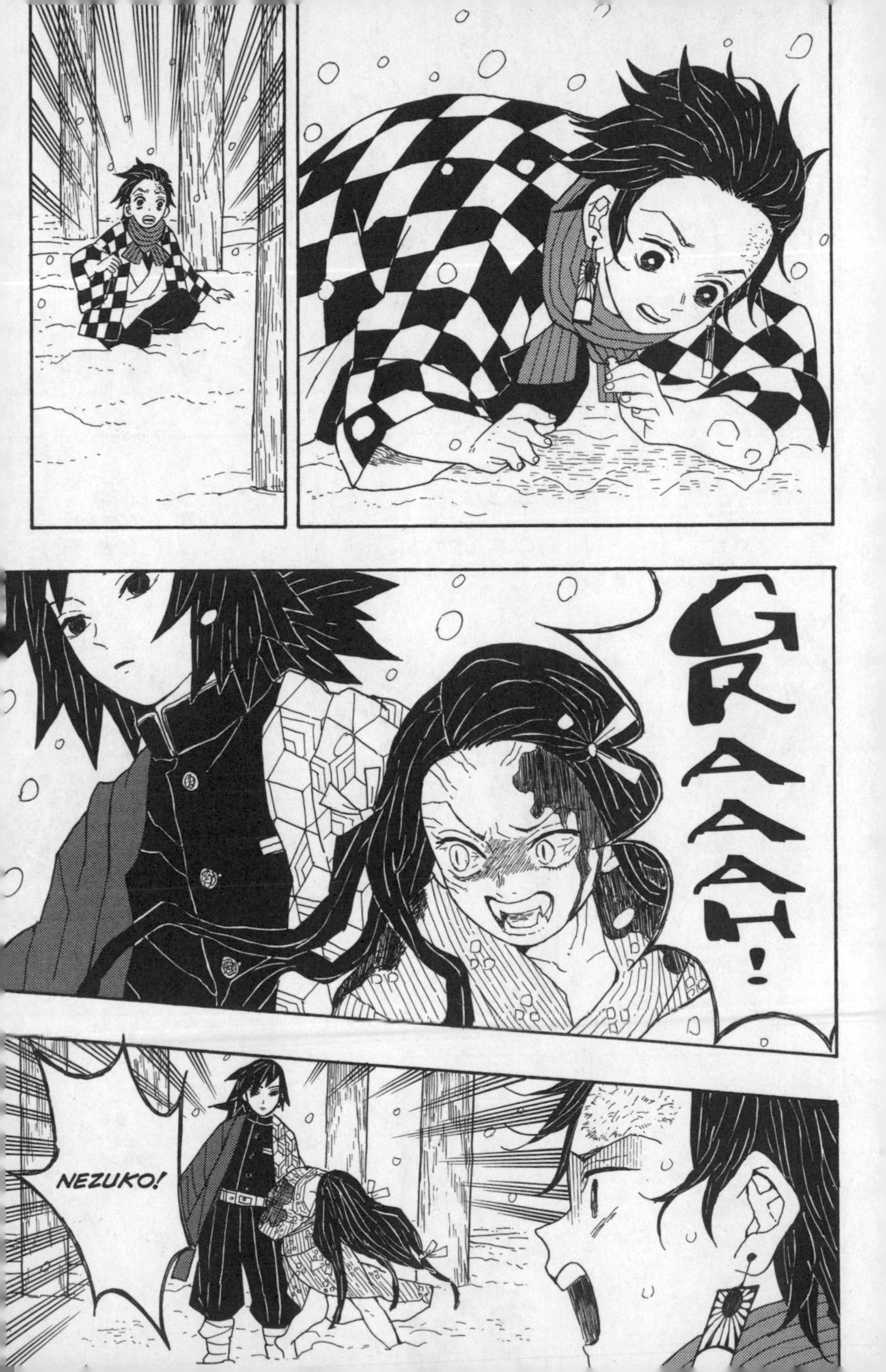
GRAAAH!
NEZUKO!

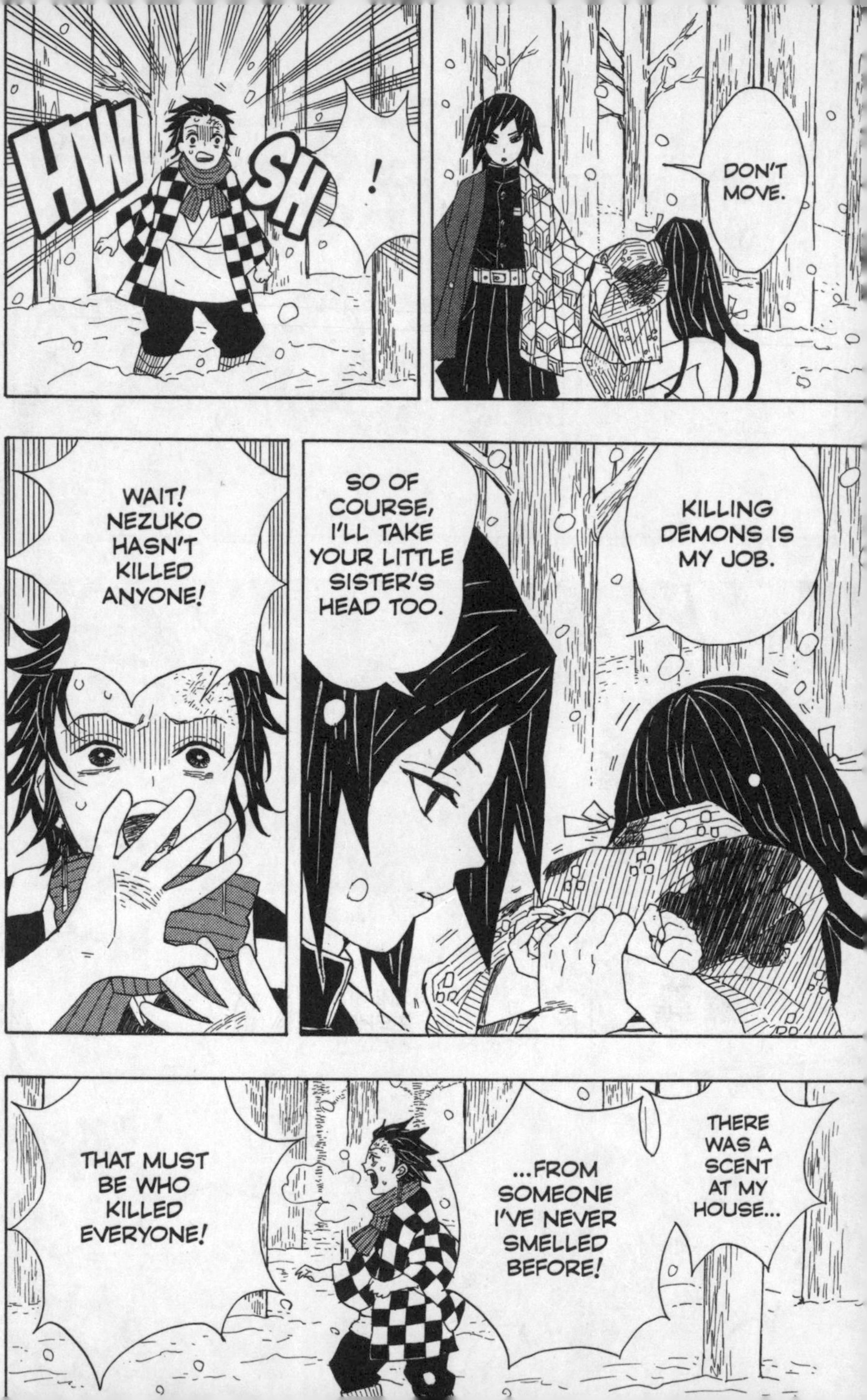
DON'T MOVE.
HWSH
!
KILLING DEMONS IS MY JOB.
SO OF COURSE, I'LL TAKE YOUR LITTLE SISTER'S HEAD TOO.
WAIT! NEZUKO HASN'T KILLED ANYONE!
THERE WAS A SCENT AT MY HOUSE...
...FROM SOMEONE I'VE NEVER SMELLED BEFORE!
THAT MUST BE WHO KILLED EVERYONE!

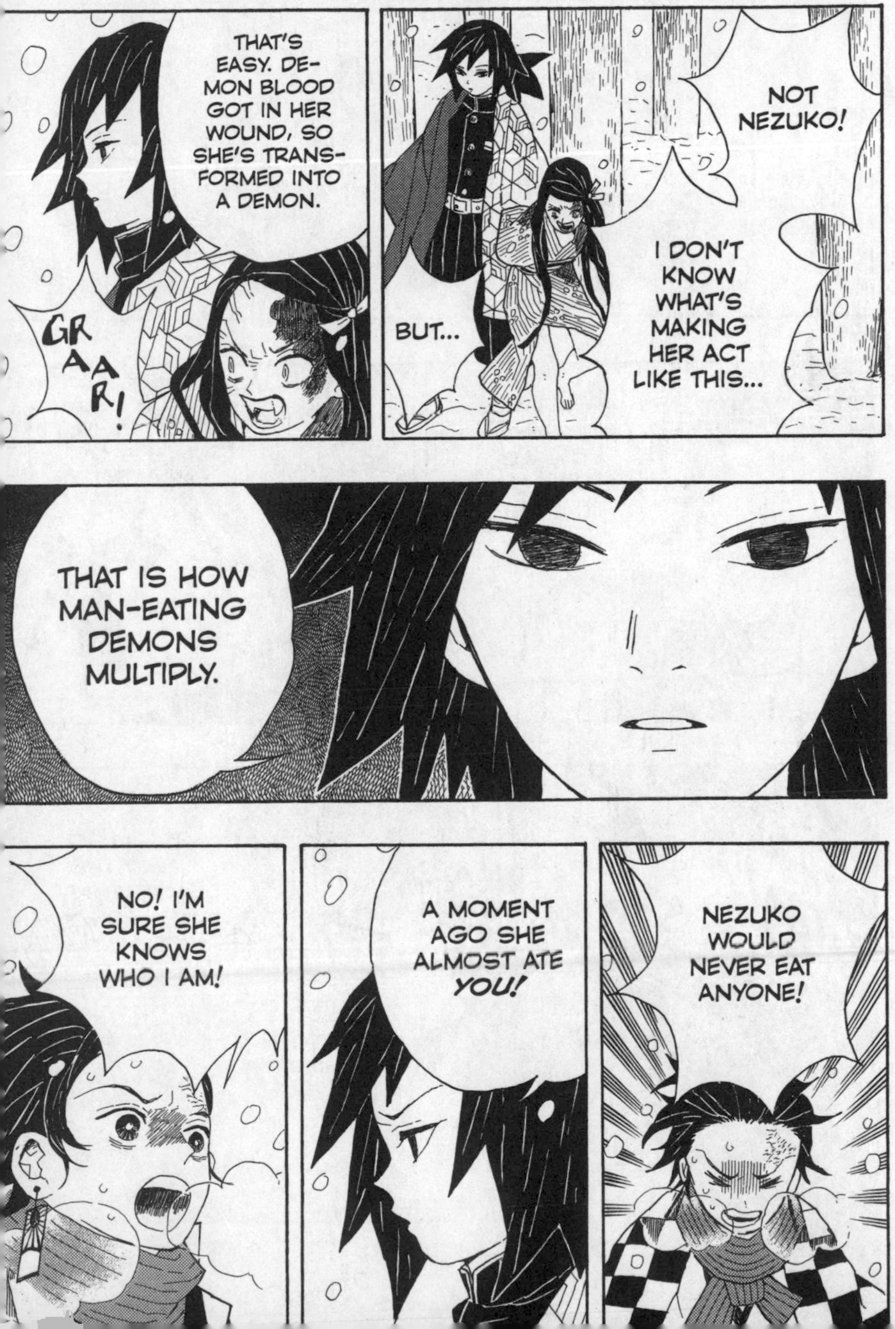
NOT NEZUKO!
I DON'T KNOW WHAT'S MAKING HER ACT LIKE THIS...
BUT...
THAT'S EASY. DEMON BLOOD GOT IN HER WOUND, SO SHE'S TRANSFORMED INTO A DEMON.
GRAAAR!
THAT IS HOW MAN-EATING DEMONS MULTIPLY.
NEZUKO WOULD NEVER EAT ANYONE!
A MOMENT AGO SHE ALMOST ATE *YOU!*
NO! I'M SURE SHE KNOWS WHO I AM!

I'LL FIND A WAY TO *CURE* HER!

I'LL MAKE HER *HUMAN* AGAIN!

I *WON'T* LET HER HURT ANYONE!

I'LL FIND A WAY! I SWEAR! PLEASE DON'T KILL HER!

A HUMAN WHO BECOMES A DEMON CANNOT GO BACK.

SHE WON'T GET BETTER.

SHN NG

...SO...

I'LL ALSO FIND THE ONE THAT KILLED MY FAMILY!

I'LL DO ALL THAT, SO...

...SO...

I CAN'T LOSE NEZUKO TOO!

STOP!

PLEASE, STOP.

PLEASE...

PLEASE DON'T KILL MY LITTLE SISTER!

PLEASE...

NEVER LEAVE YOURSELF SO *DEFENSELESS* IN FRONT OF AN ENEMY!

STOP BOWING SO PITIFULLY!

IF THAT WORKED, YOUR FAMILY WOULD STILL BE ALIVE!

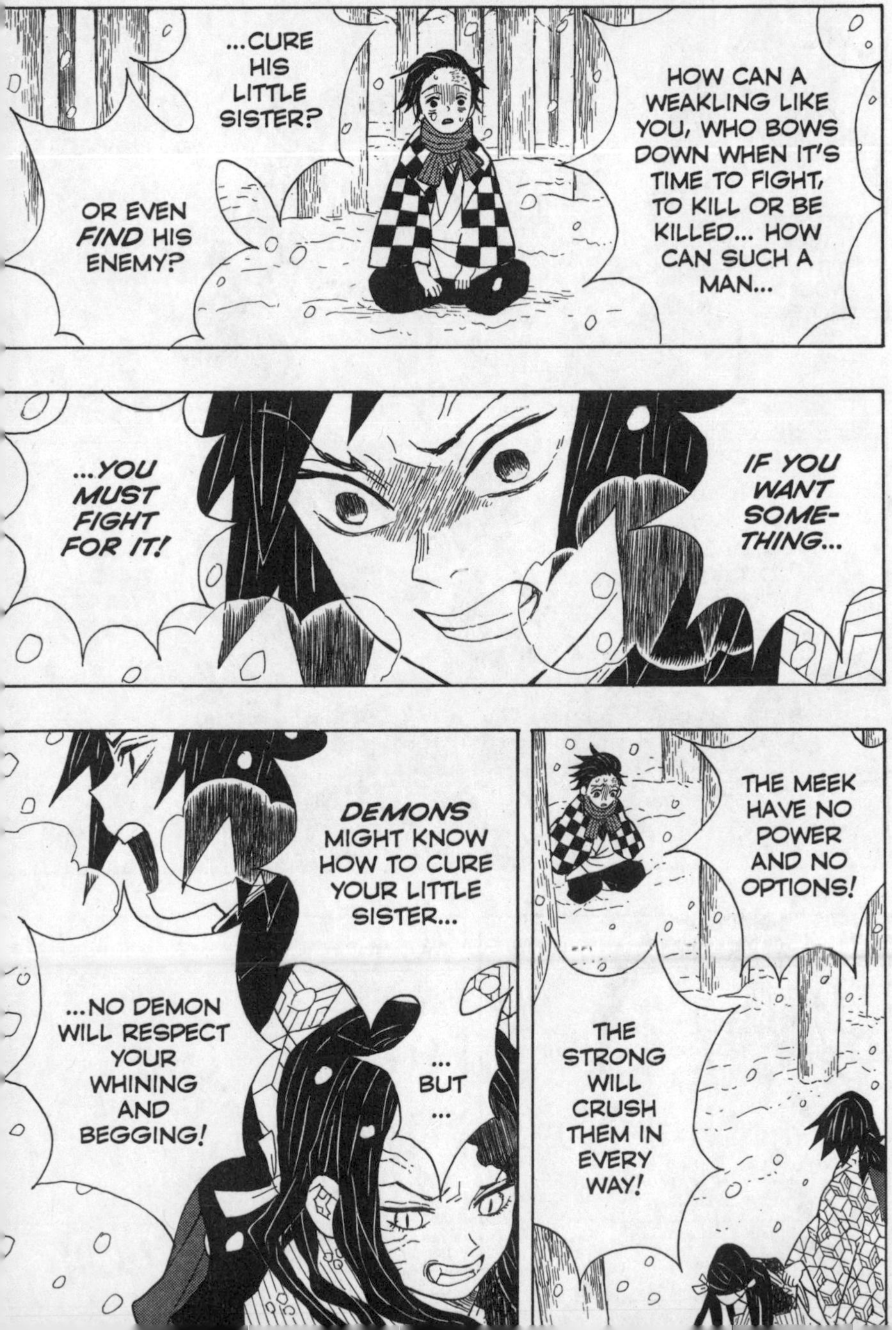
HOW CAN A WEAKLING LIKE YOU, WHO BOWS DOWN WHEN IT'S TIME TO FIGHT, TO KILL OR BE KILLED... HOW CAN SUCH A MAN...
...CURE HIS LITTLE SISTER?
OR EVEN *FIND* HIS ENEMY?
IF YOU WANT SOME-THING...
...YOU MUST FIGHT FOR IT!
THE MEEK HAVE NO POWER AND NO OPTIONS!
THE STRONG WILL CRUSH THEM IN EVERY WAY!
DEMONS MIGHT KNOW HOW TO CURE YOUR LITTLE SISTER...
...BUT...
...NO DEMON WILL RESPECT YOUR WHINING AND BEGGING!

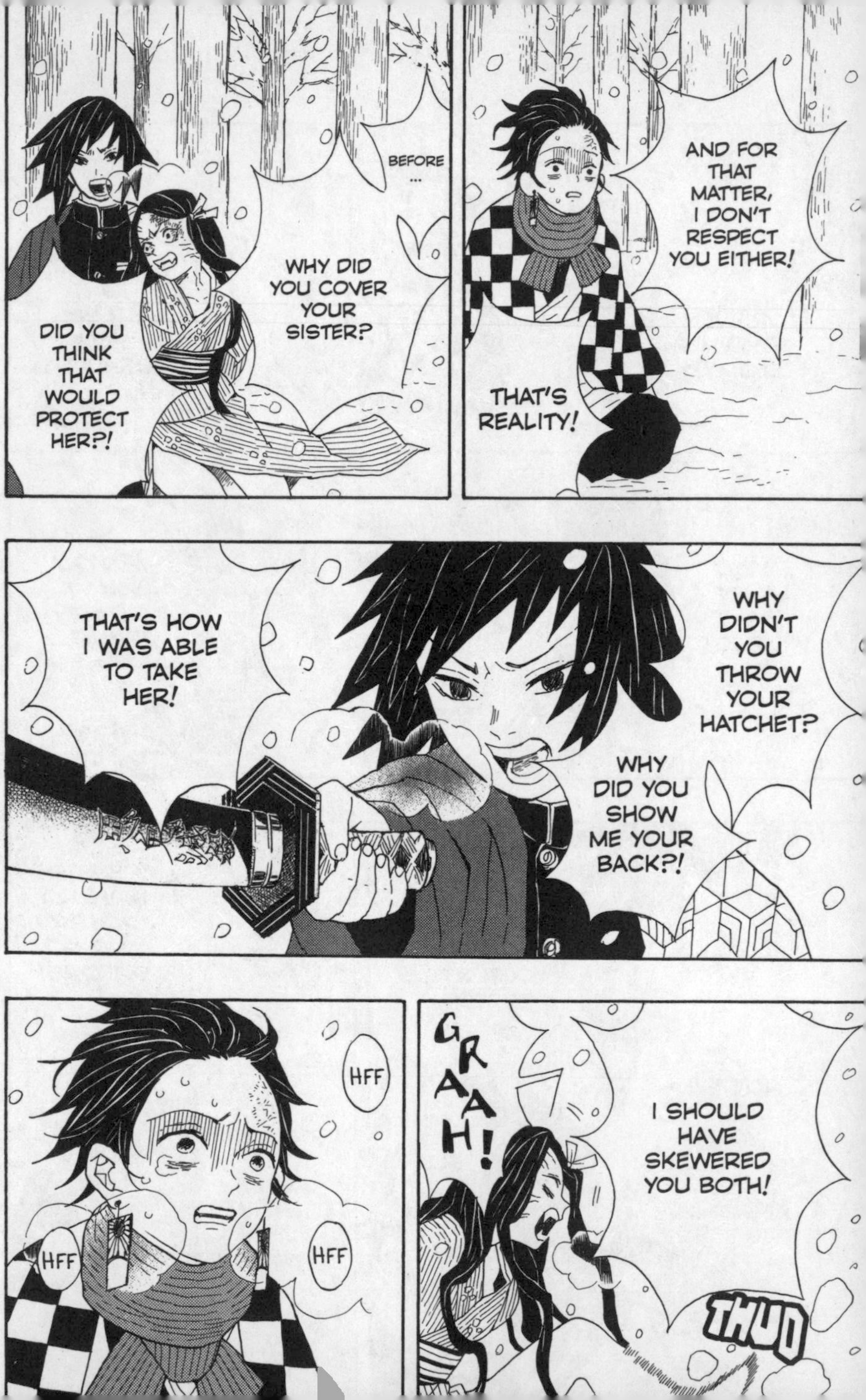
AND FOR THAT MATTER, I DON'T RESPECT YOU EITHER!
THAT'S REALITY!
BEFORE ...
WHY DID YOU COVER YOUR SISTER?
DID YOU THINK THAT WOULD PROTECT HER?!
WHY DIDN'T YOU THROW YOUR HATCHET?
WHY DID YOU SHOW ME YOUR BACK?!
THAT'S HOW I WAS ABLE TO TAKE HER!
GRAAH!
I SHOULD HAVE SKEWERED YOU BOTH!
THUD
HFF
HFF
HFF

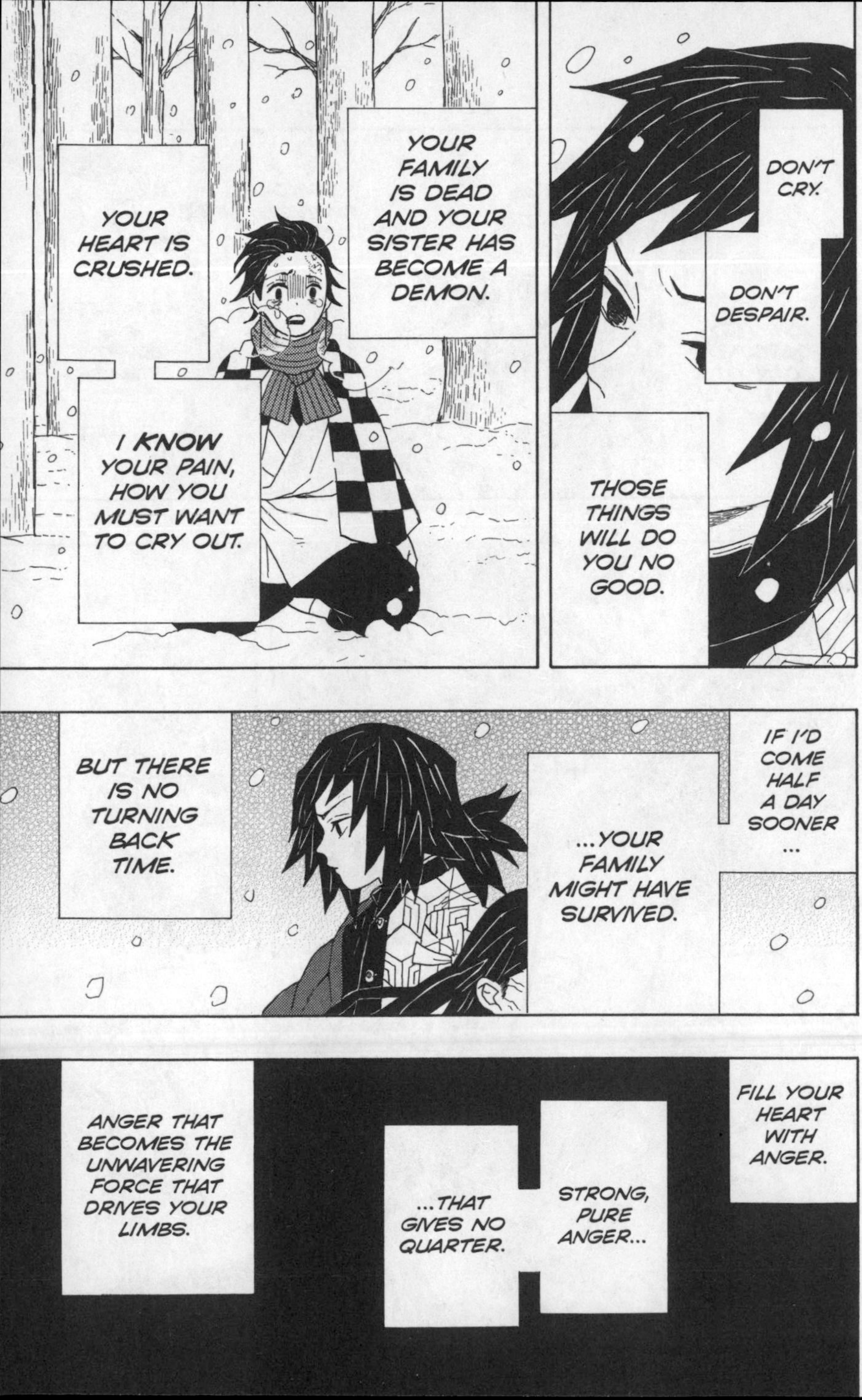
DON'T CRY.
DON'T DESPAIR.
THOSE THINGS WILL DO YOU NO GOOD.
YOUR FAMILY IS DEAD AND YOUR SISTER HAS BECOME A DEMON.
YOUR HEART IS CRUSHED.
I KNOW YOUR PAIN, HOW YOU MUST WANT TO CRY OUT.
IF I'D COME HALF A DAY SOONER ...
...YOUR FAMILY MIGHT HAVE SURVIVED.
BUT THERE IS NO TURNING BACK TIME.
FILL YOUR HEART WITH ANGER.
STRONG, PURE ANGER...
...THAT GIVES NO QUARTER.
ANGER THAT BECOMES THE UNWAVERING FORCE THAT DRIVES YOUR LIMBS.

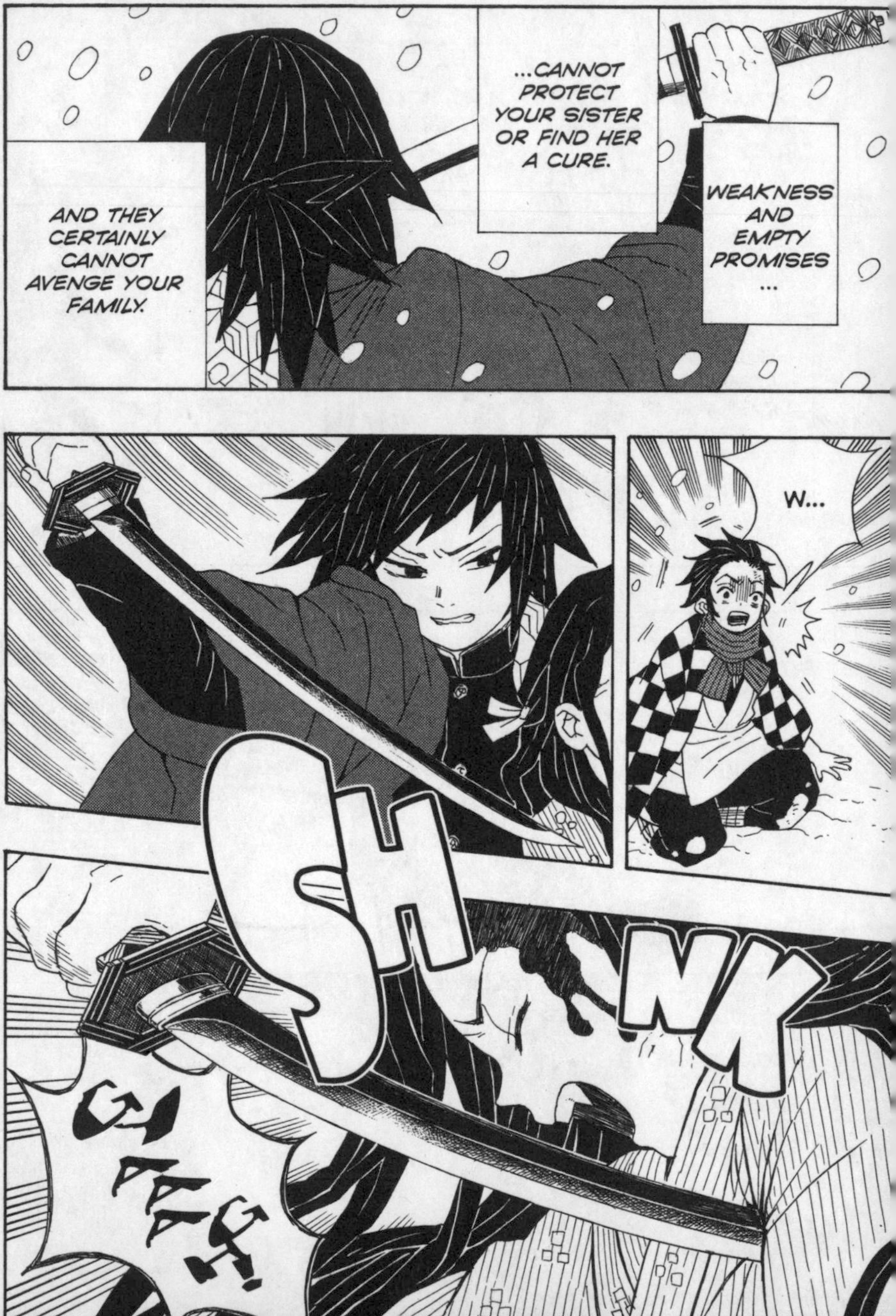
WEAKNESS AND EMPTY PROMISES ...
...CANNOT PROTECT YOUR SISTER OR FIND HER A CURE.
AND THEY CERTAINLY CANNOT AVENGE YOUR FAMILY.
W...
SHNK
GHAAAGH!

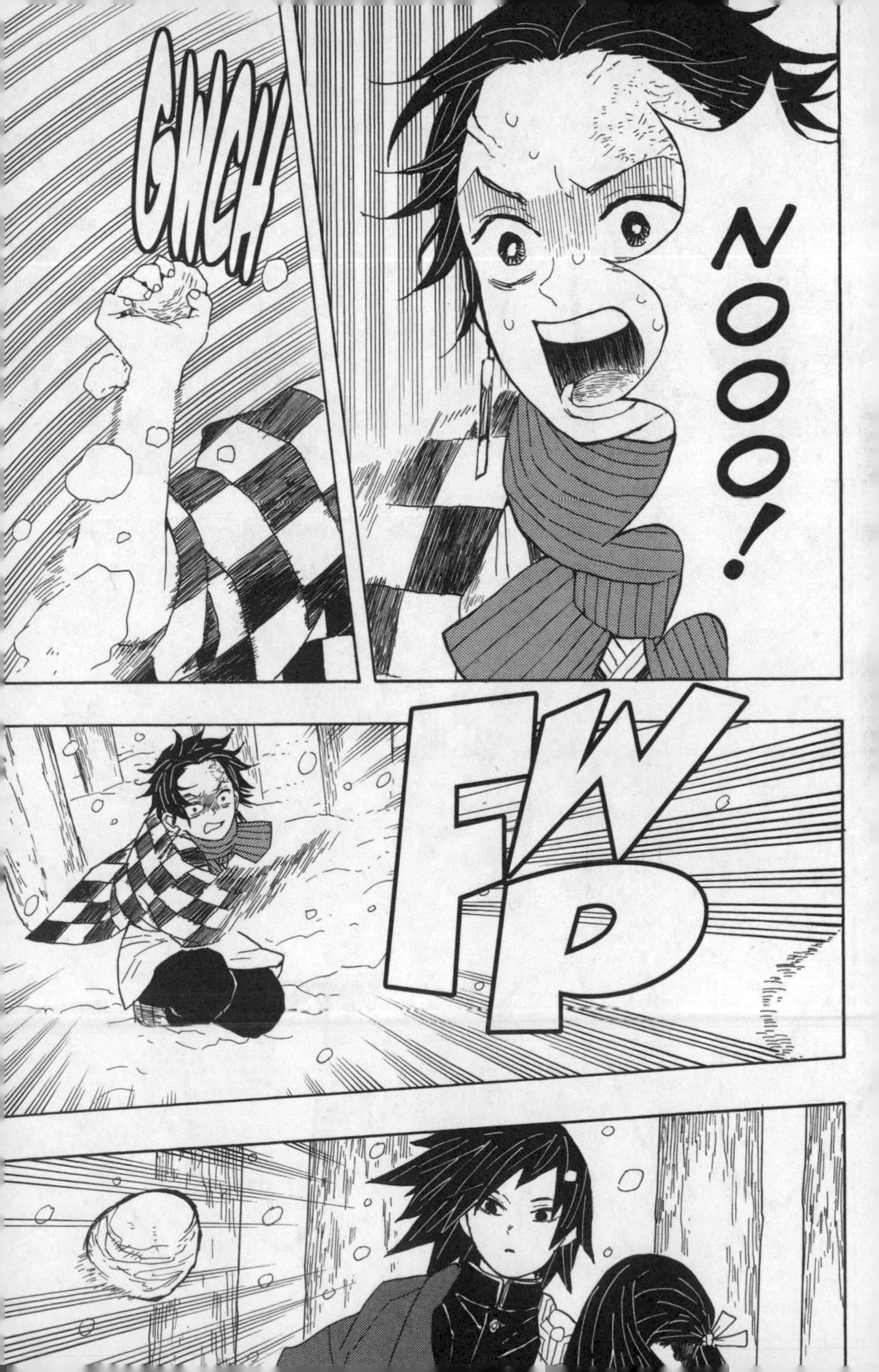
NOOOO!
GNCH!
FWP

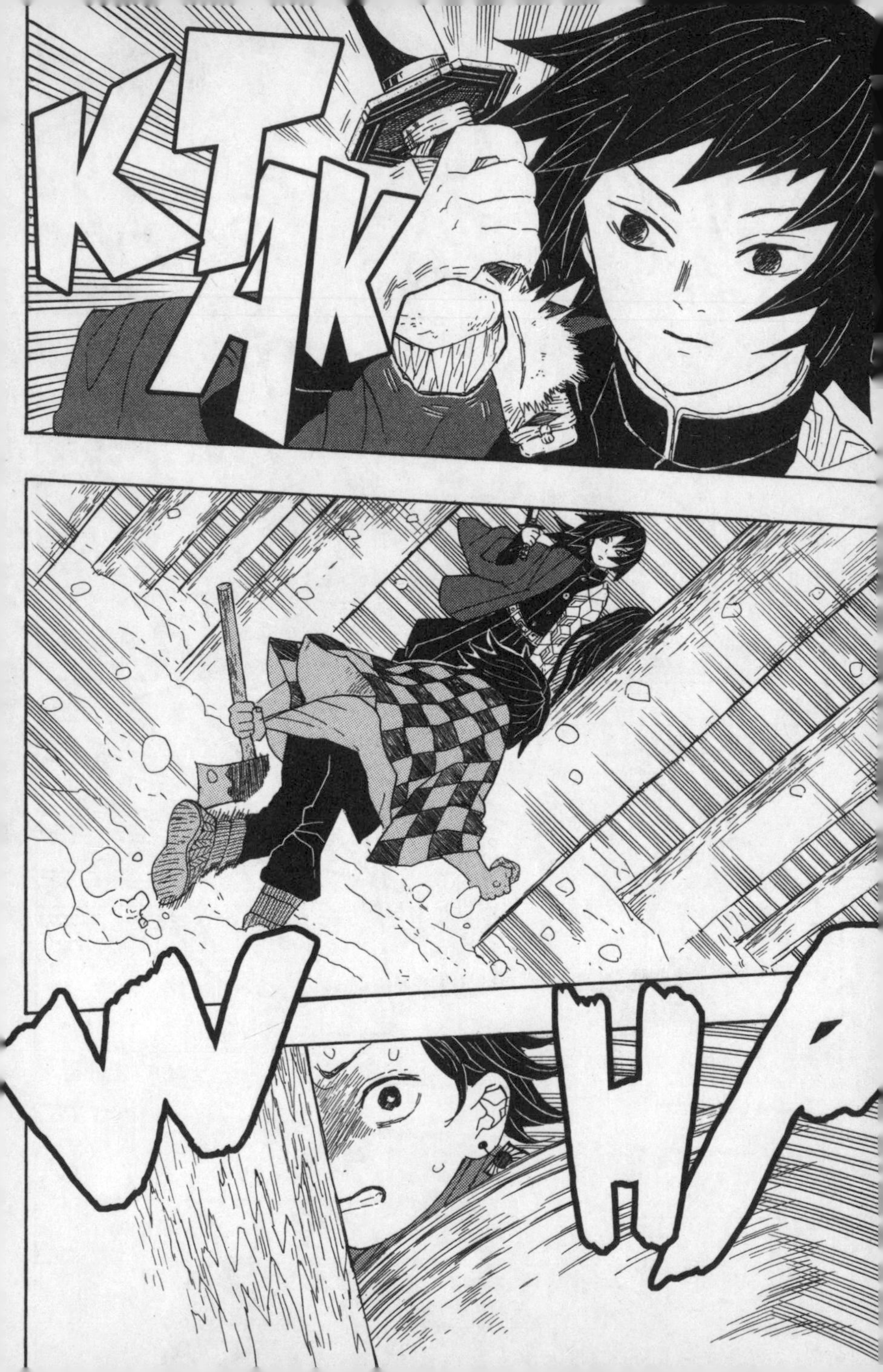
KTAK
WH

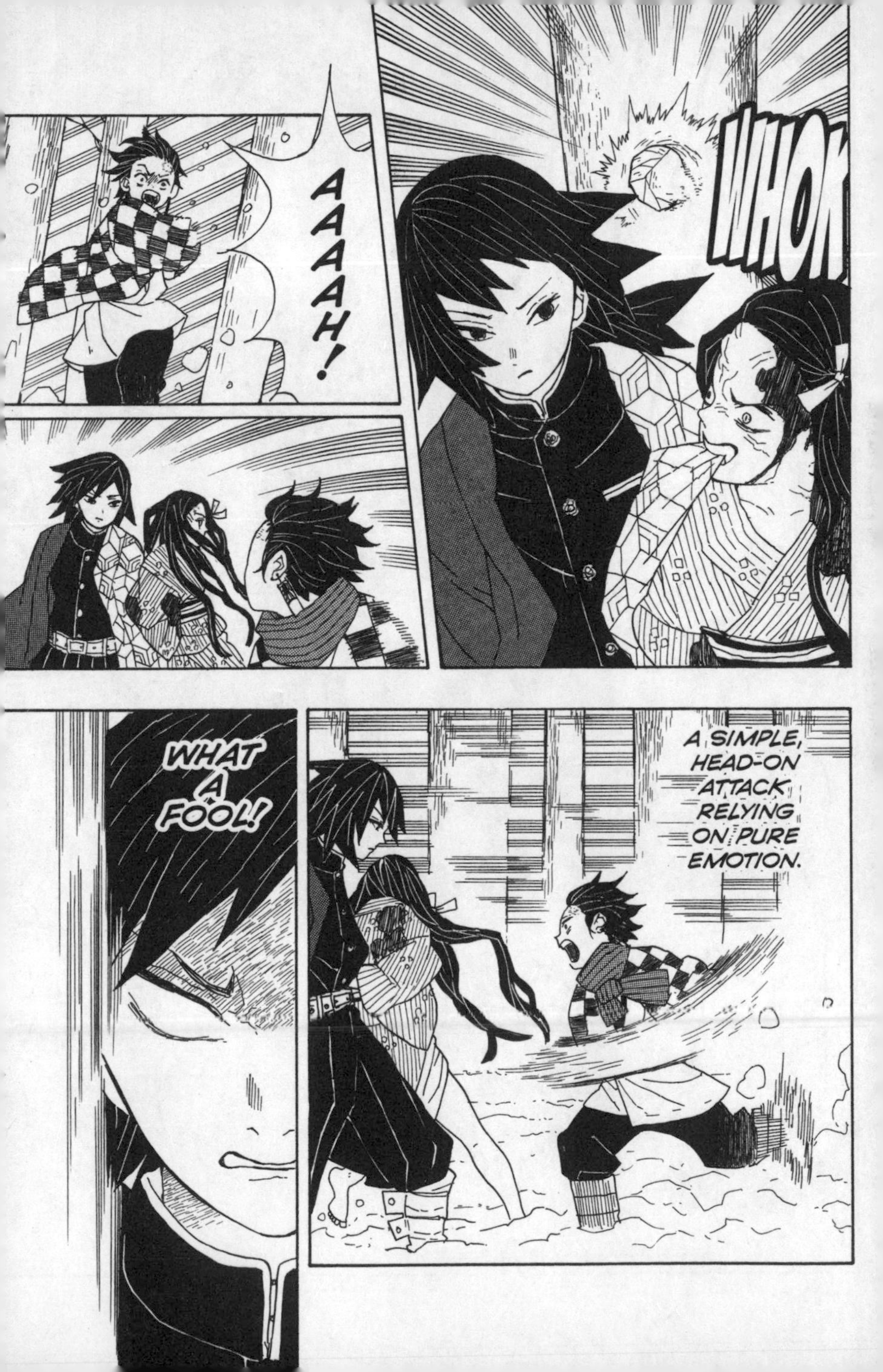
WHOK
AAAAAH!
A SIMPLE, HEAD-ON ATTACK RELYING ON PURE EMOTION.
WHAT A FOOL!

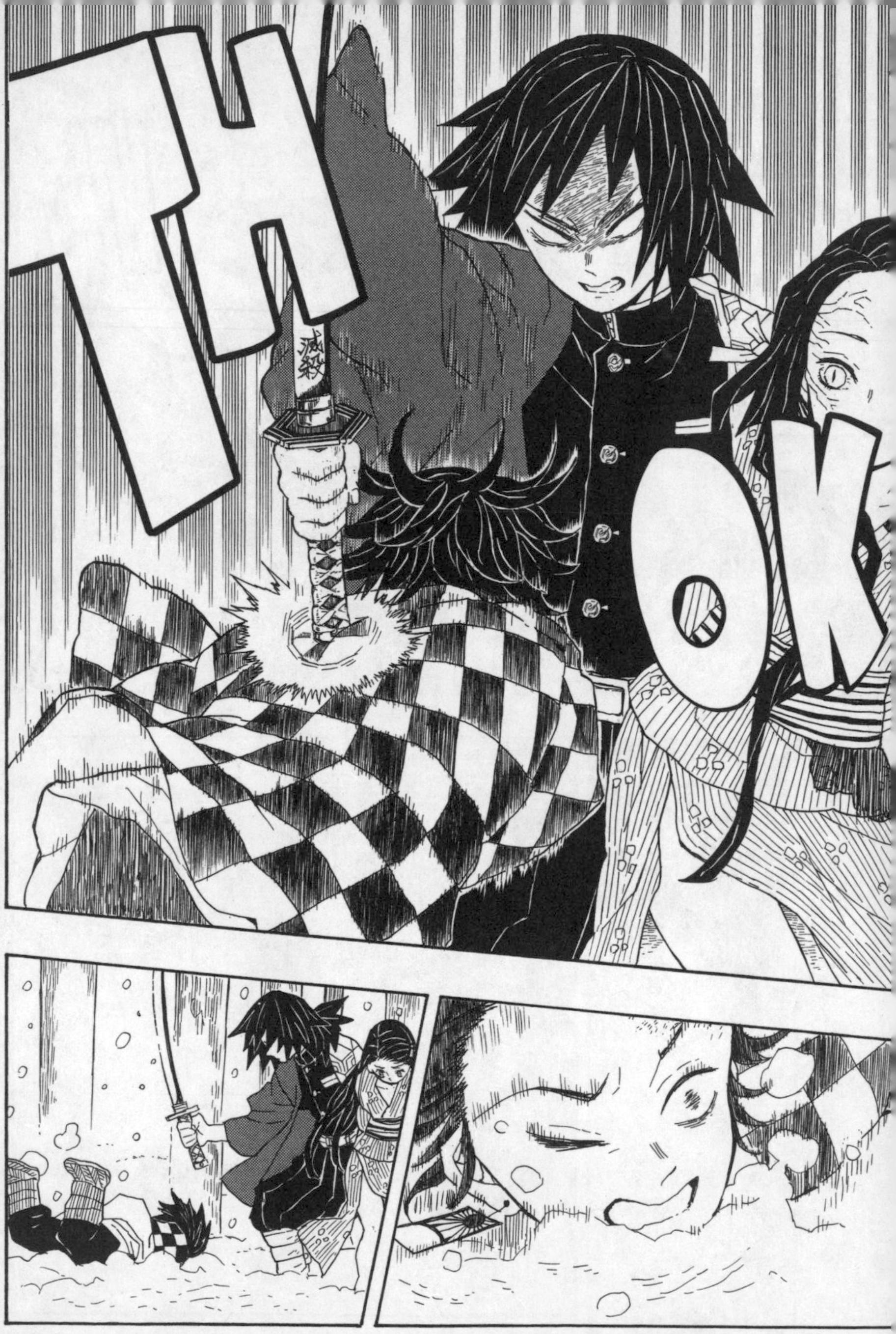
THOK

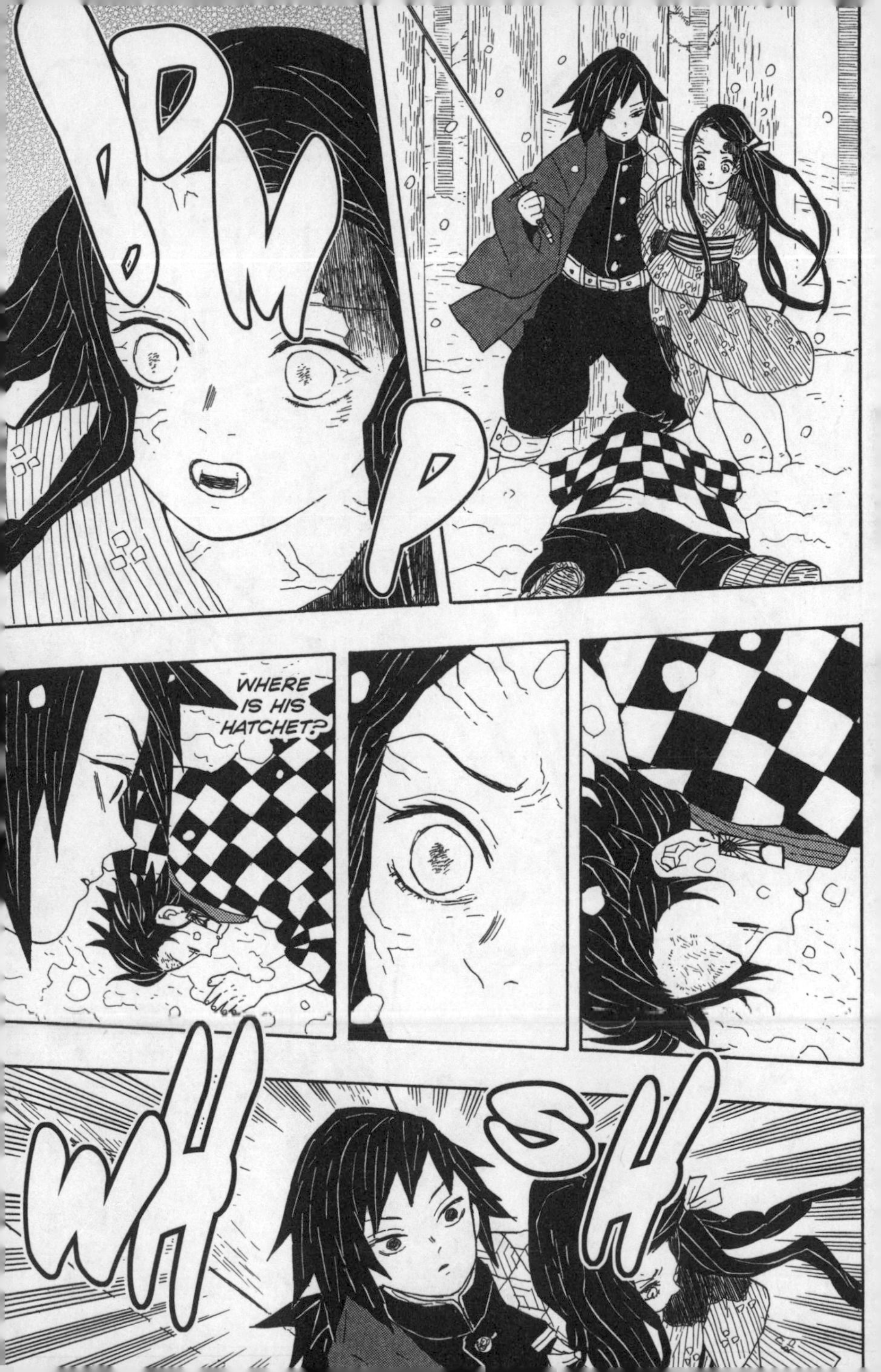
WHERE IS HIS HATCHET?

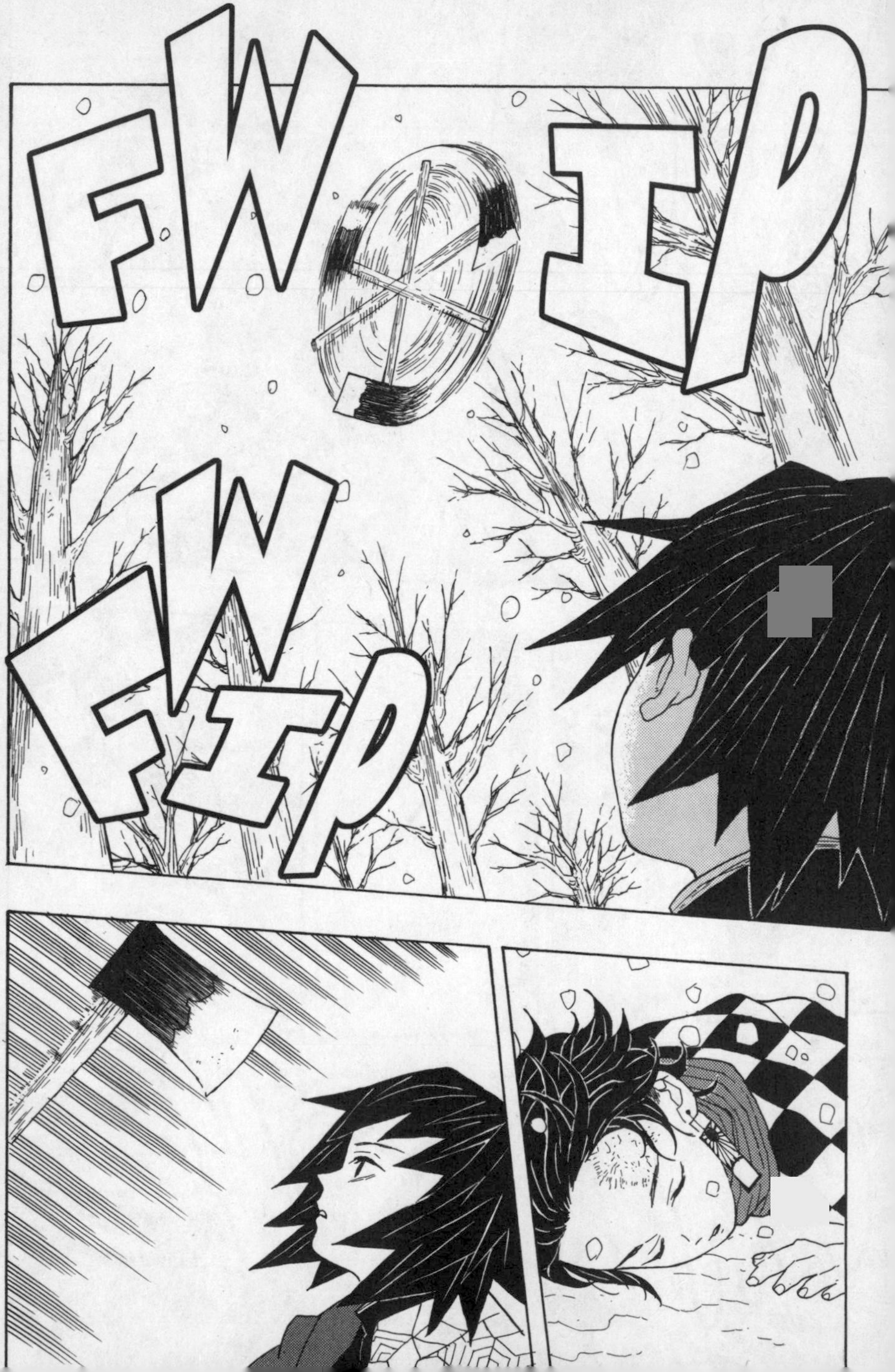
FWIP
FWIP

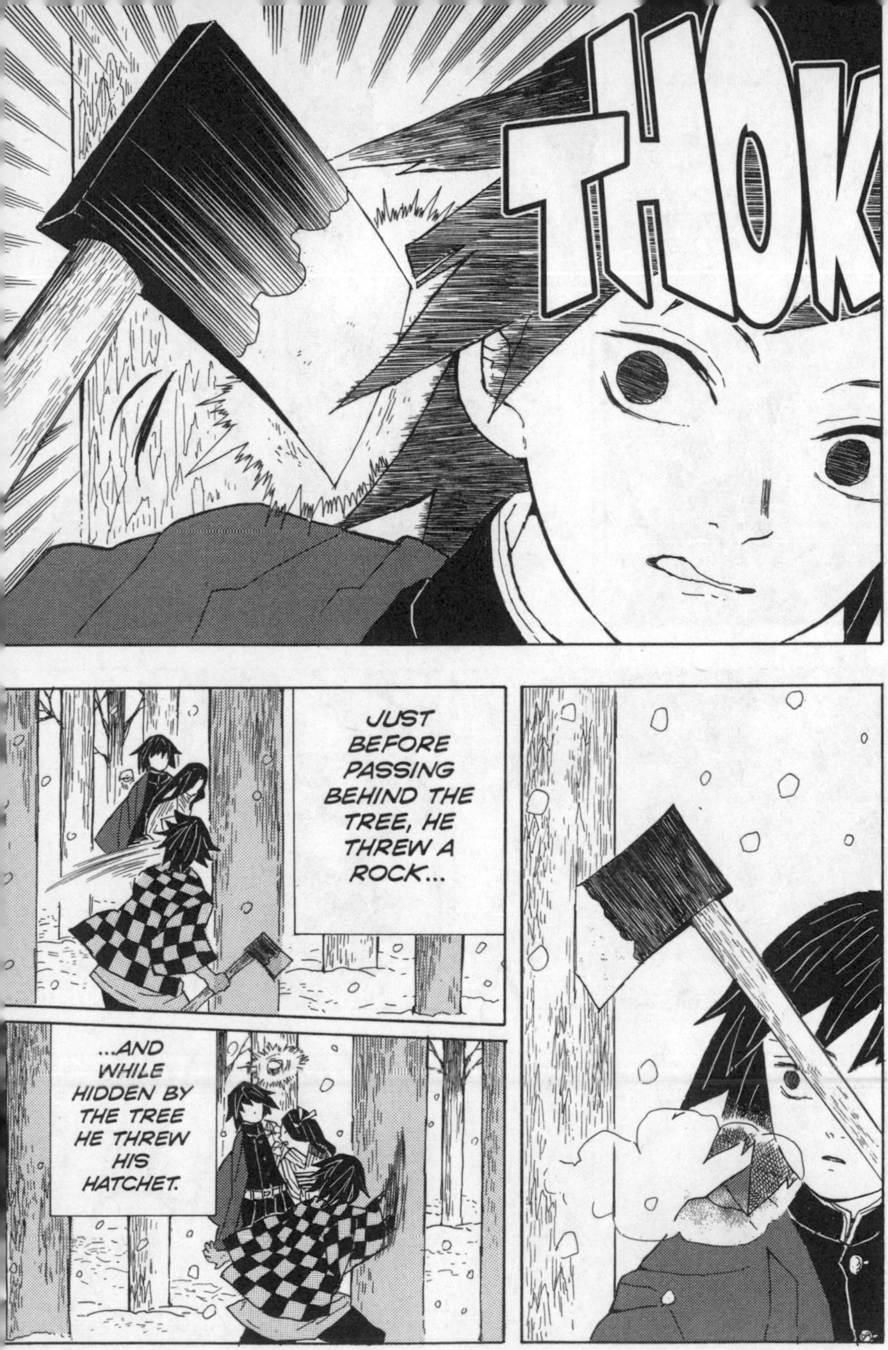
THOK
JUST BEFORE PASSING BEHIND THE TREE, HE THREW A ROCK...
...AND WHILE HIDDEN BY THE TREE HE THREW HIS HATCHET.

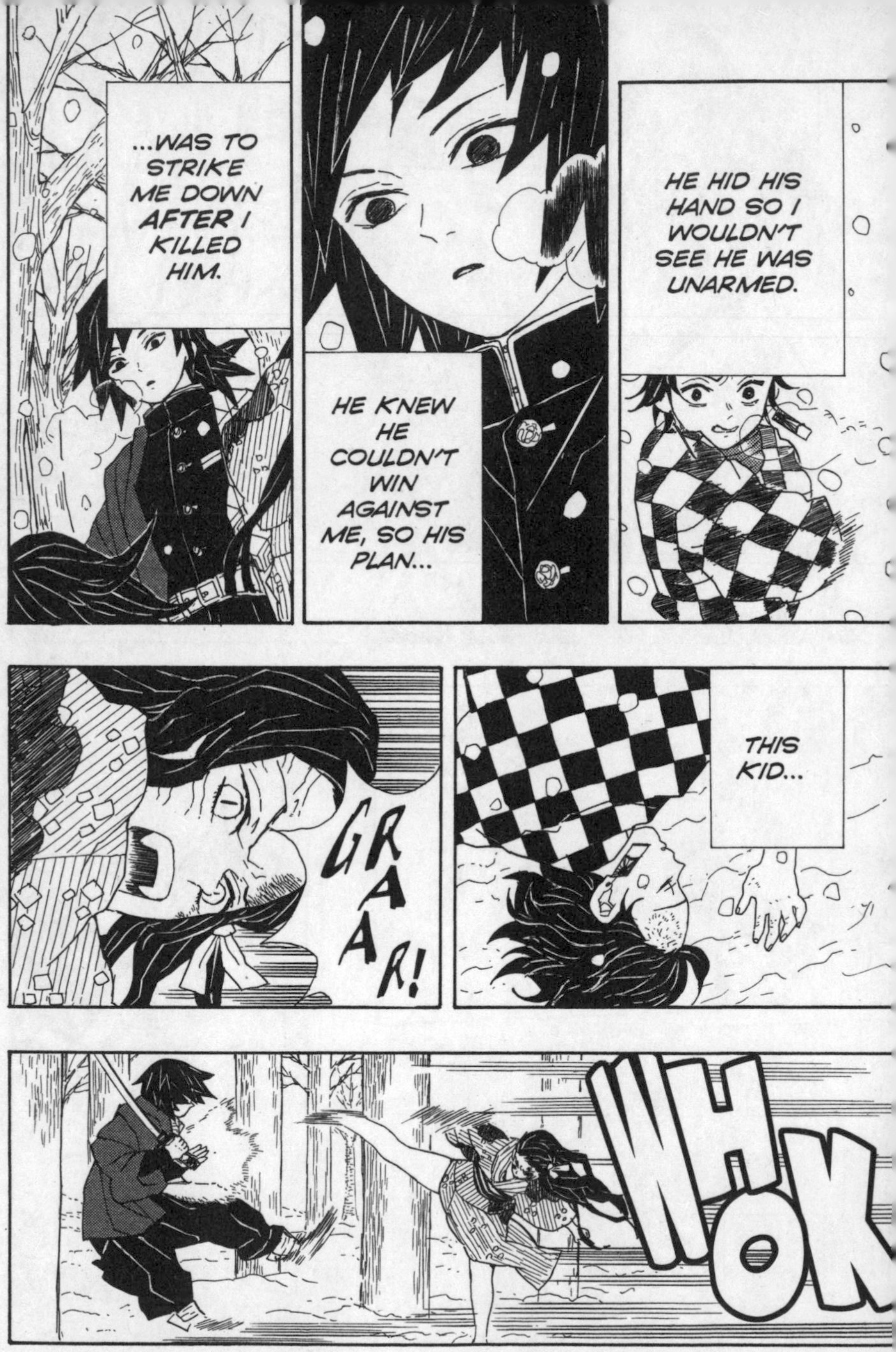
HE HID HIS HAND SO I WOULDN'T SEE HE WAS UNARMED.
HE KNEW HE COULDN'T WIN AGAINST ME, SO HIS PLAN...
...WAS TO STRIKE ME DOWN AFTER I KILLED HIM.
THIS KID...
GRAAR!
WHOK

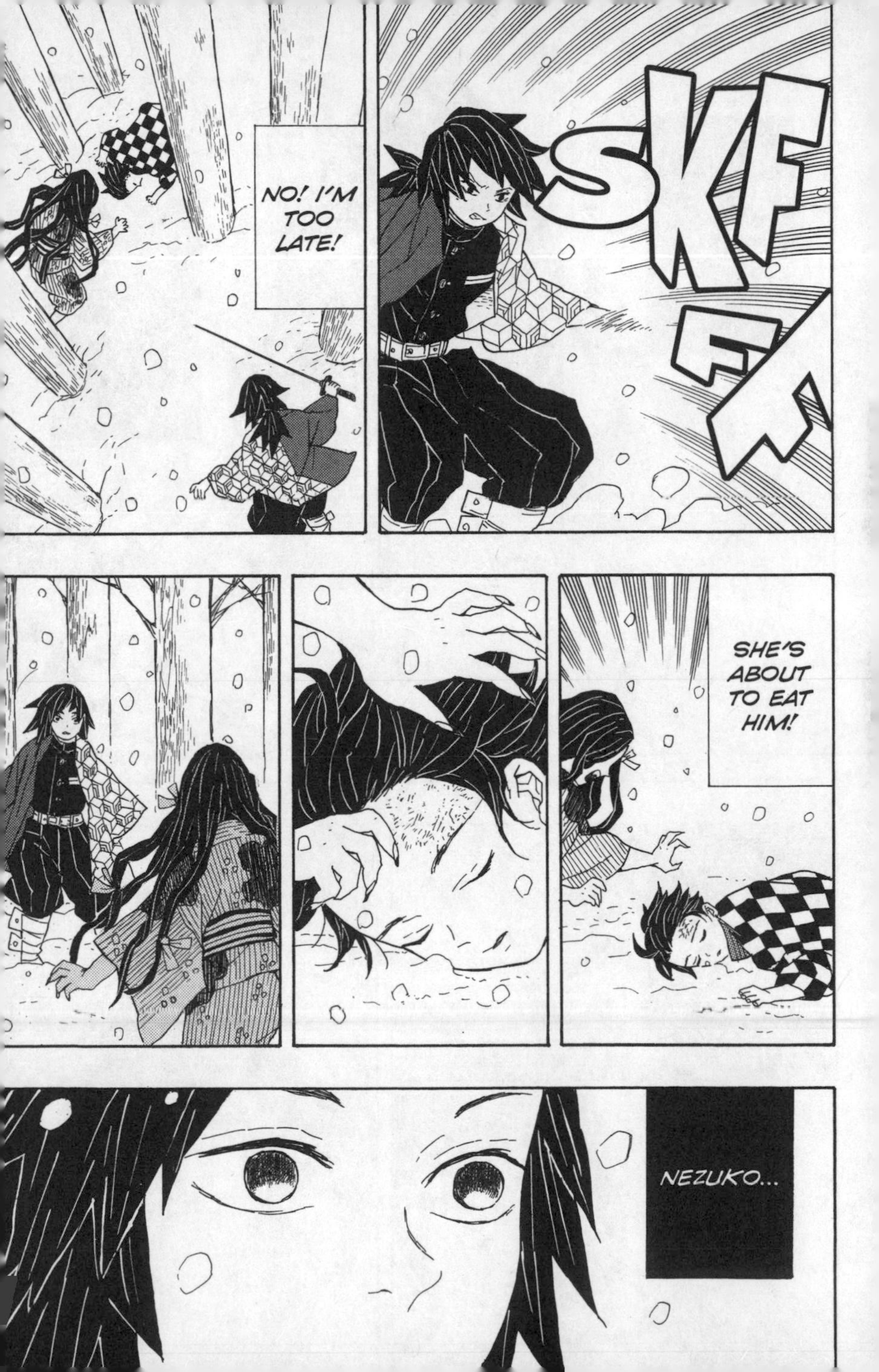
SKFFT
NO! I'M TOO LATE!
SHE'S ABOUT TO EAT HIM!
NEZUKO...

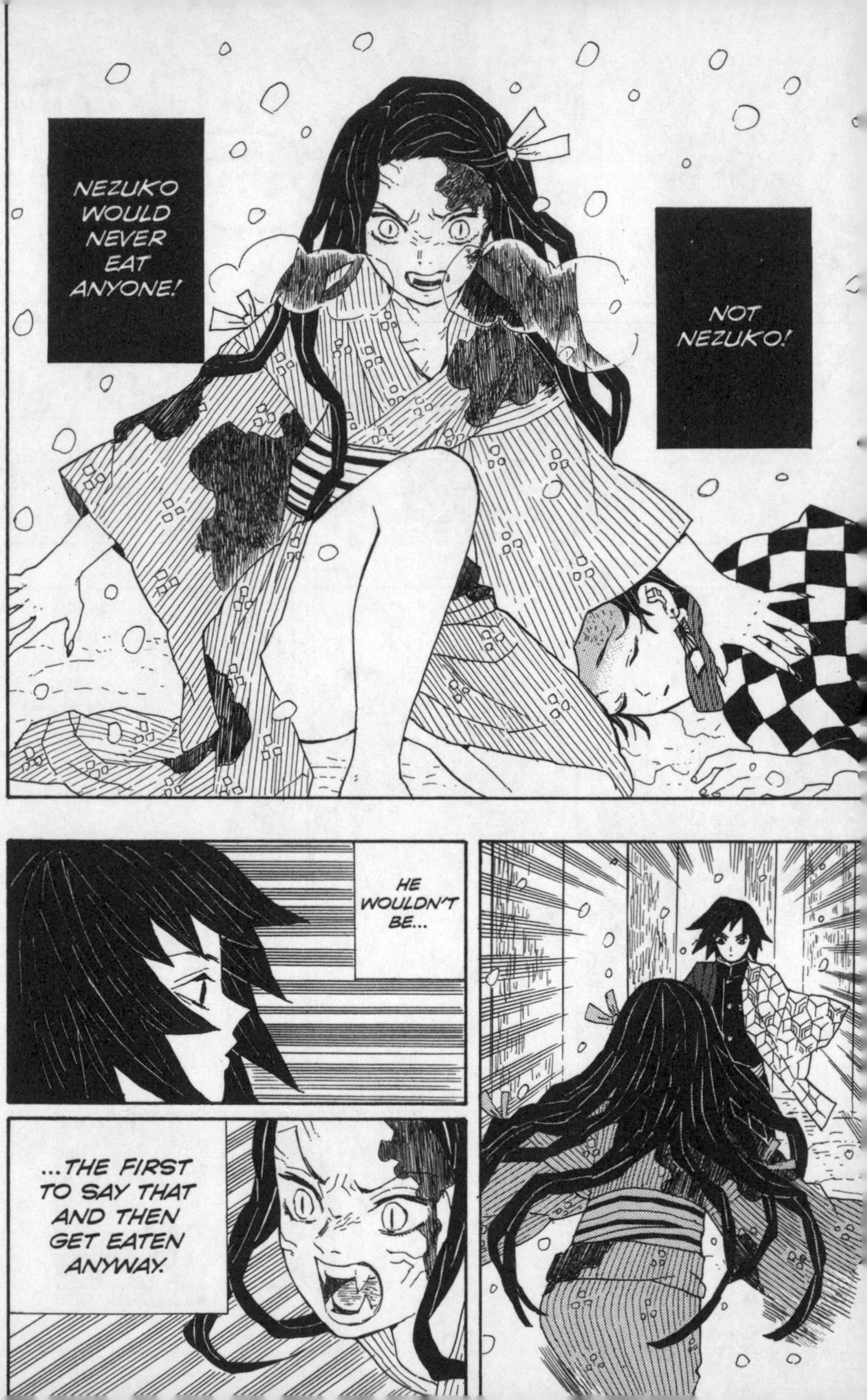
NEZUKO WOULD NEVER EAT ANYONE!
NOT NEZUKO!
HE WOULDN'T BE...
...THE FIRST TO SAY THAT AND THEN GET EATEN ANYWAY.

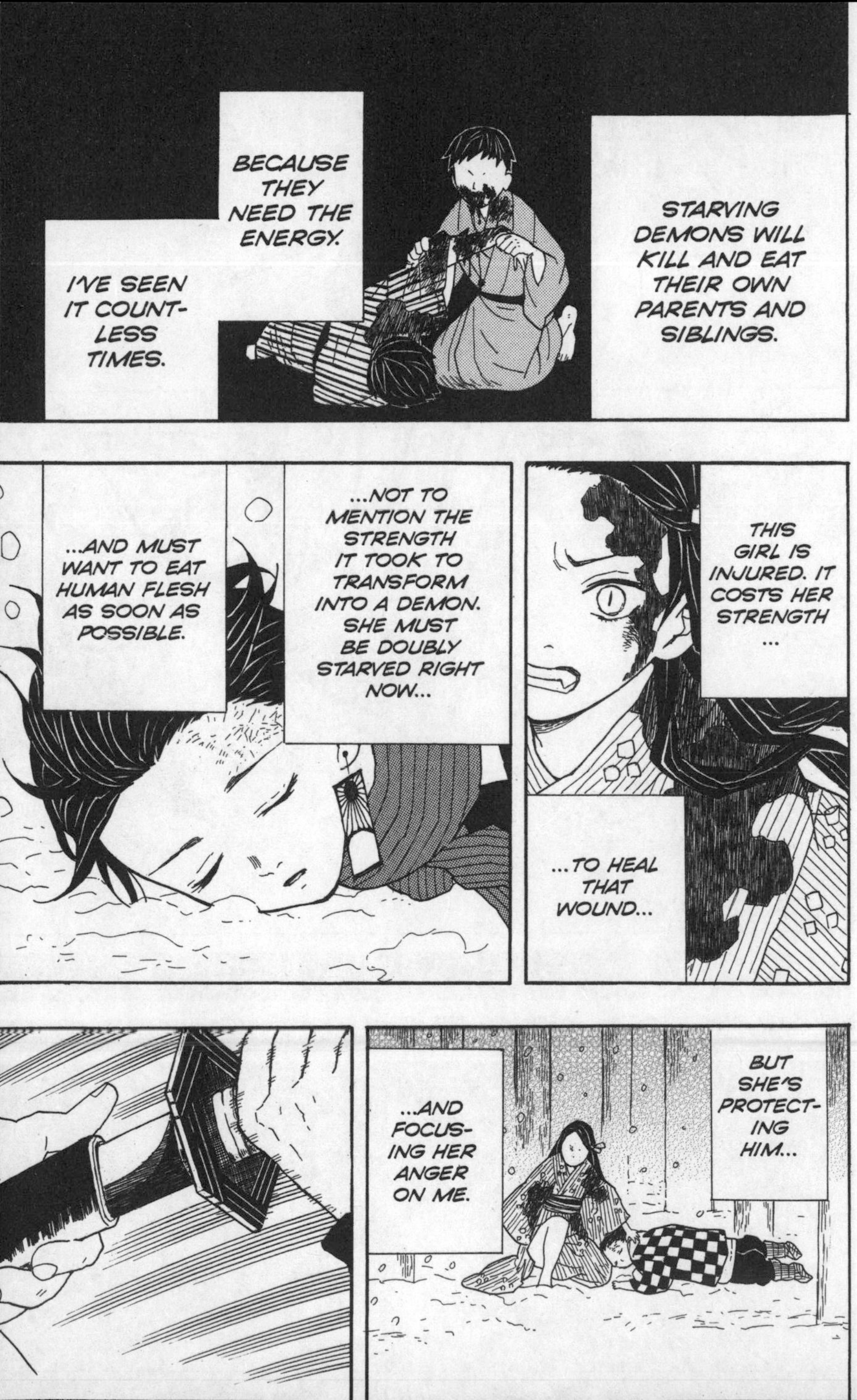
STARVING DEMONS WILL KILL AND EAT THEIR OWN PARENTS AND SIBLINGS.
BECAUSE THEY NEED THE ENERGY.
I'VE SEEN IT COUNTLESS TIMES.
THIS GIRL IS INJURED. IT COSTS HER STRENGTH...
...TO HEAL THAT WOUND...
...NOT TO MENTION THE STRENGTH IT TOOK TO TRANSFORM INTO A DEMON. SHE MUST BE DOUBLY STARVED RIGHT NOW...
...AND MUST WANT TO EAT HUMAN FLESH AS SOON AS POSSIBLE.
BUT SHE'S PROTECTING HIM...
...AND FOCUSING HER ANGER ON ME.

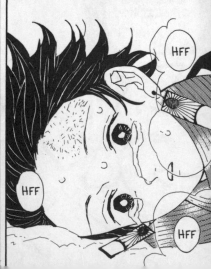

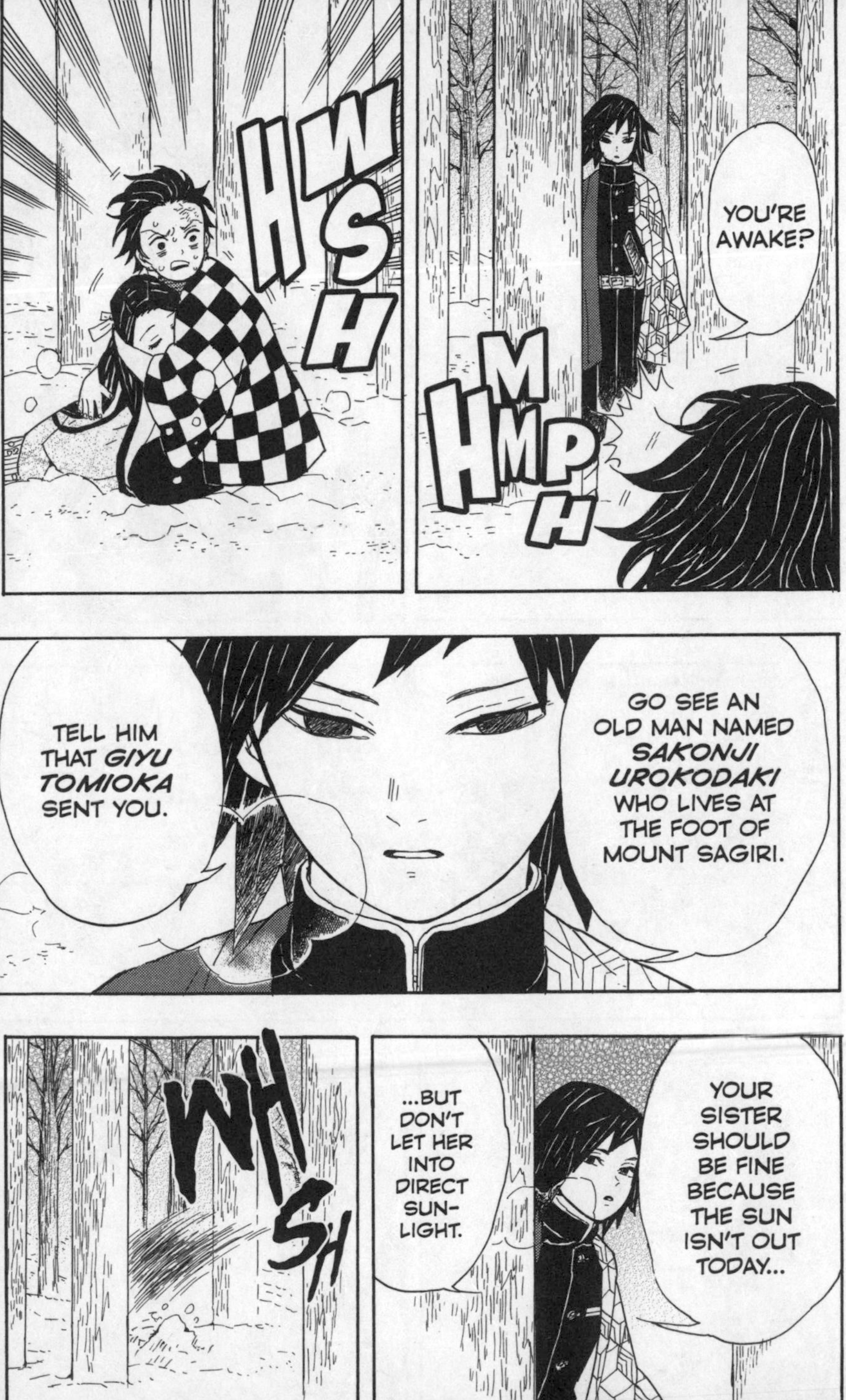
YOU'RE AWAKE?
HMMPH
HWSH
GO SEE AN OLD MAN NAMED *SAKONJI UROKODAKI* WHO LIVES AT THE FOOT OF MOUNT SAGIRI.
TELL HIM THAT *GIYU TOMIOKA* SENT YOU.
YOUR SISTER SHOULD BE FINE BECAUSE THE SUN ISN'T OUT TODAY...
...BUT DON'T LET HER INTO DIRECT SUN-LIGHT.
WHSH

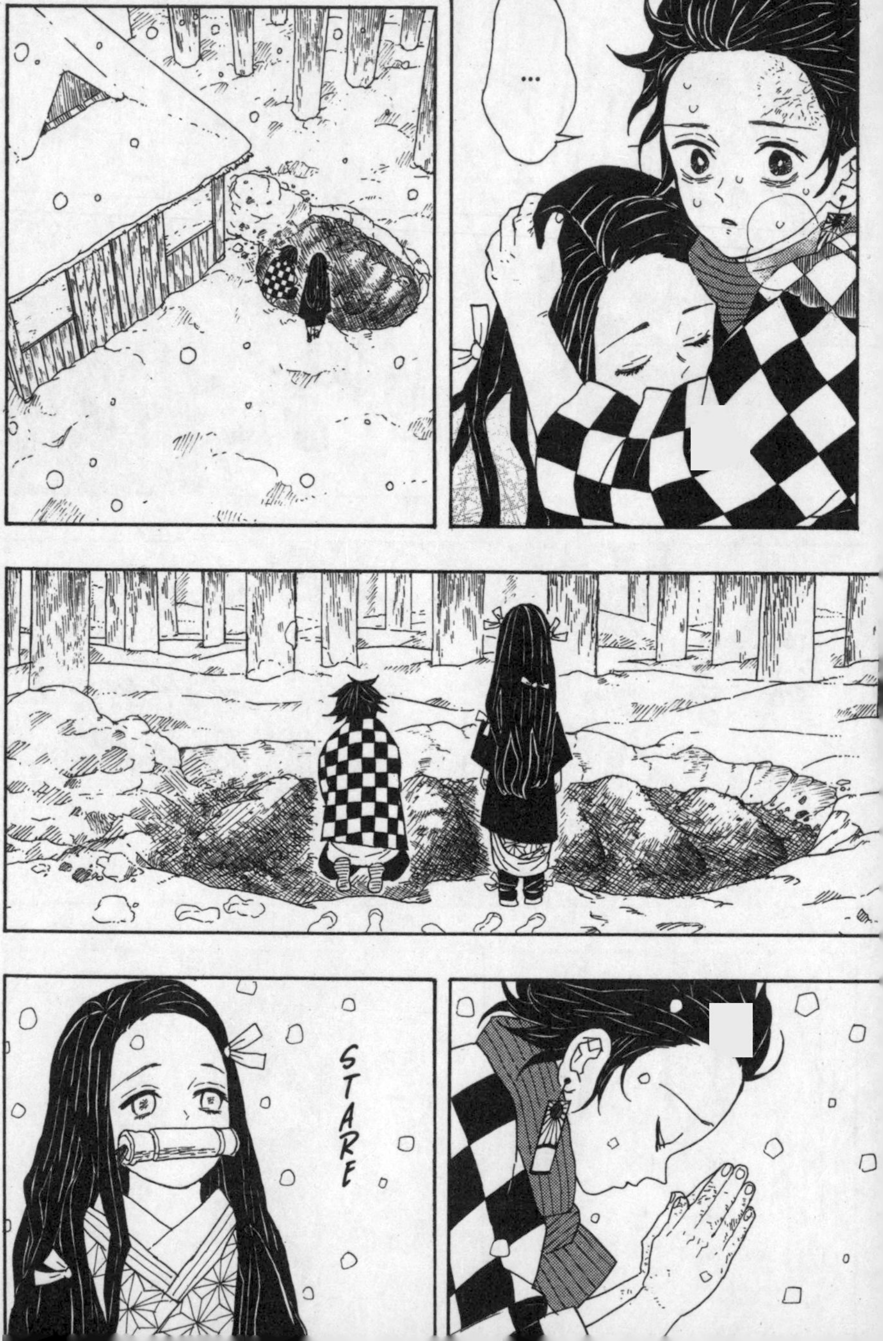
...
STARE

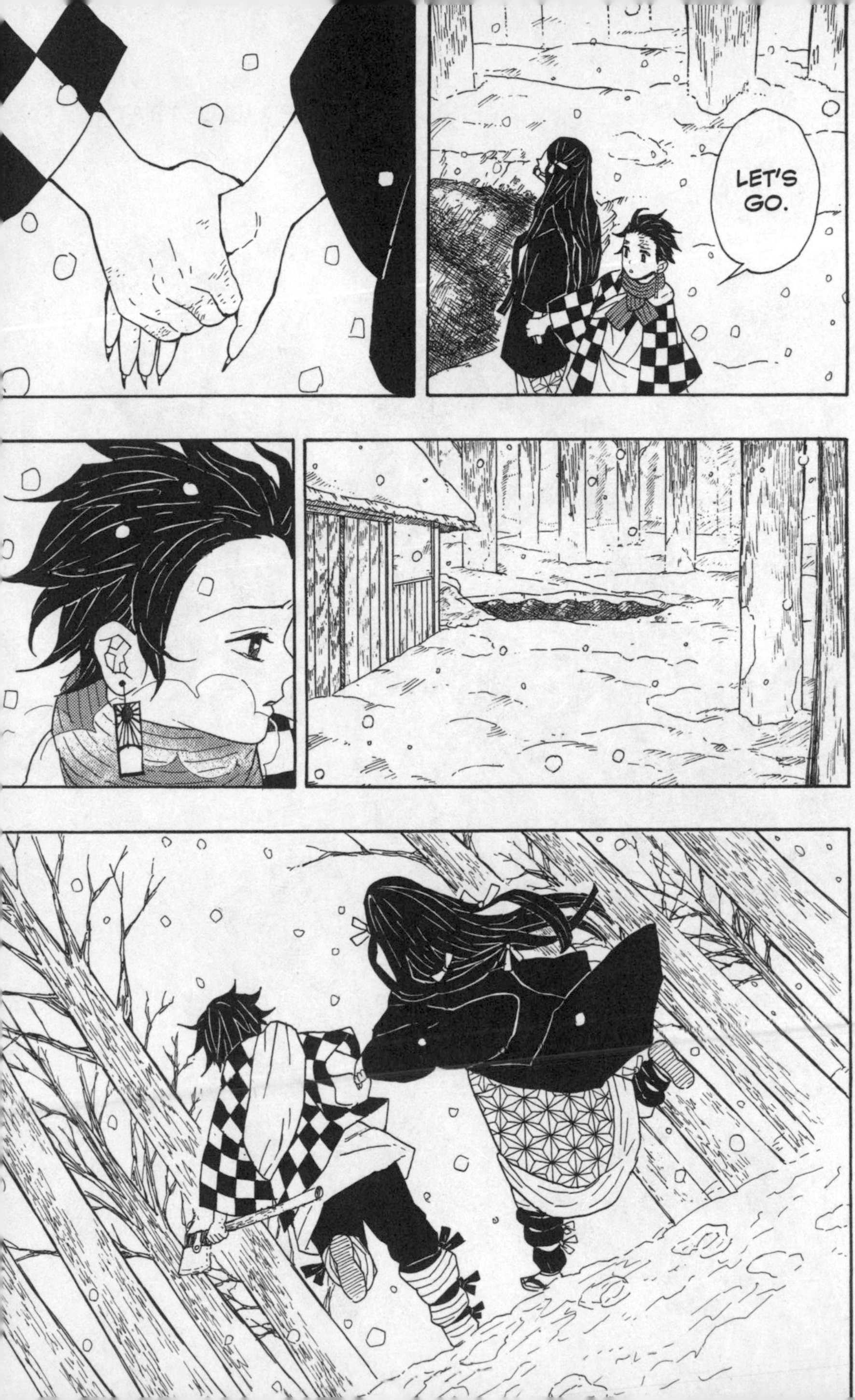
LET'S GO.

PRODUCTION ART, ILLUSTRATION ①

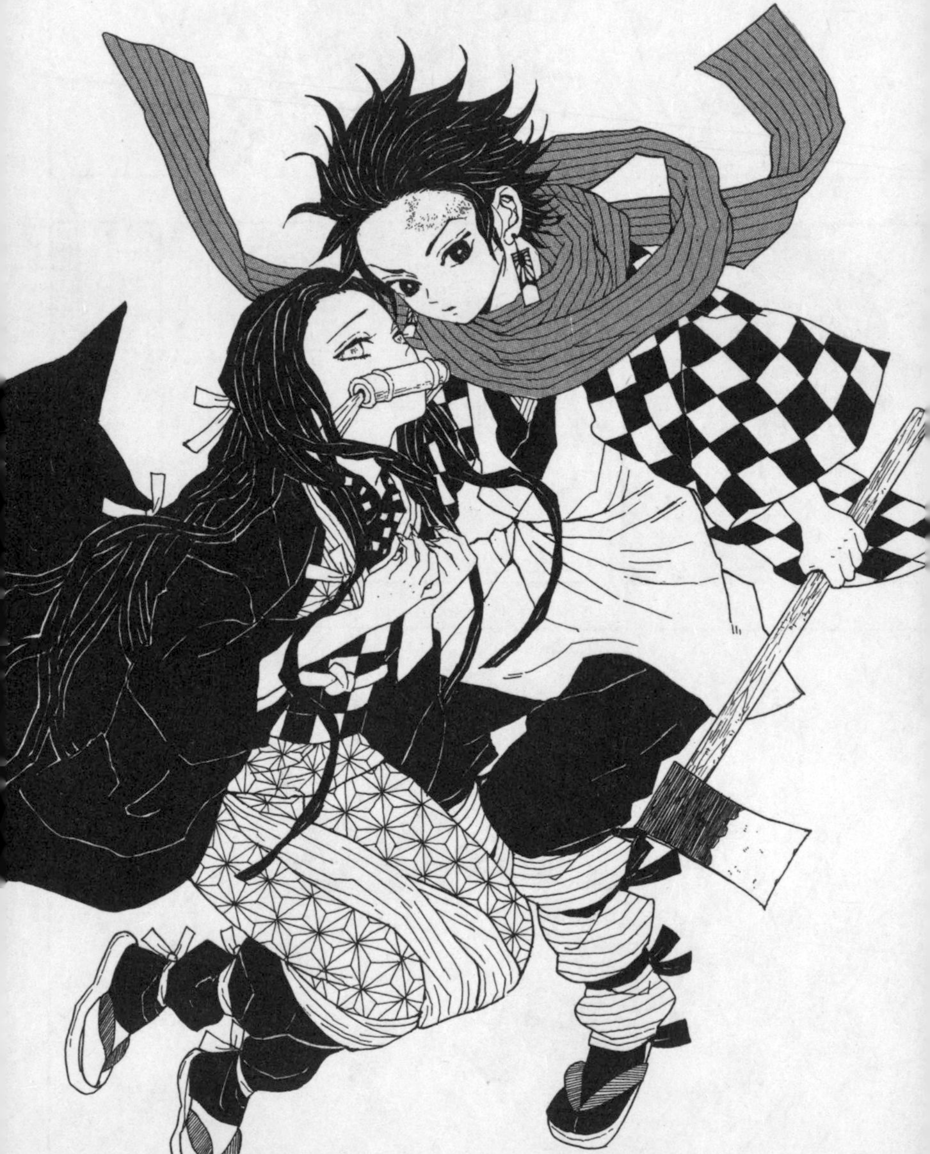

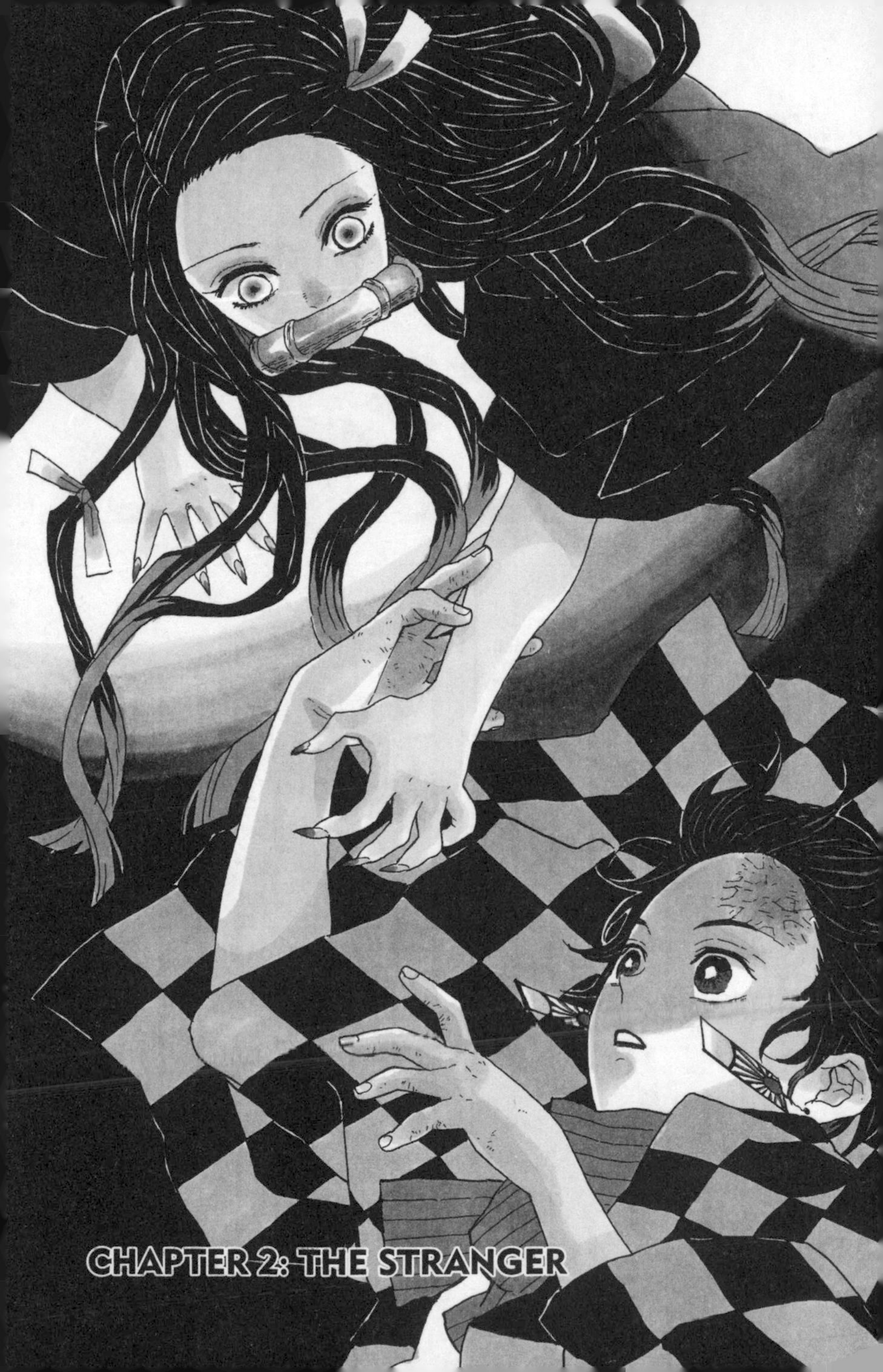
CHAPTER 2: THE STRANGER

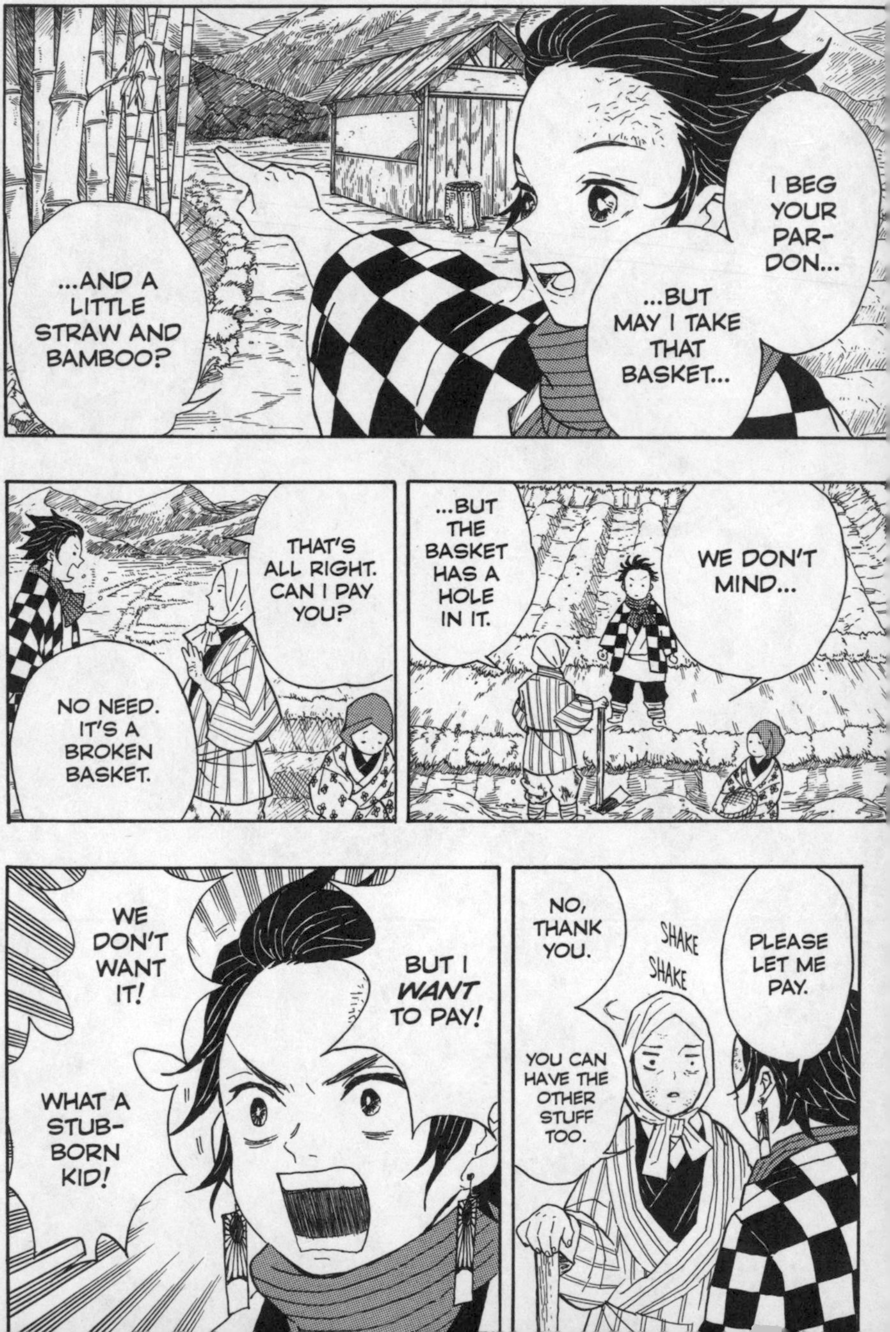
I BEG YOUR PARDON...
...BUT MAY I TAKE THAT BASKET...
...AND A LITTLE STRAW AND BAMBOO?
WE DON'T MIND...
...BUT THE BASKET HAS A HOLE IN IT.
THAT'S ALL RIGHT. CAN I PAY YOU?
NO NEED. IT'S A BROKEN BASKET.
PLEASE LET ME PAY.
SHAKE
SHAKE
NO, THANK YOU.
YOU CAN HAVE THE OTHER STUFF TOO.
BUT I *WANT* TO PAY!
WE DON'T WANT IT!
WHAT A STUBBORN KID!

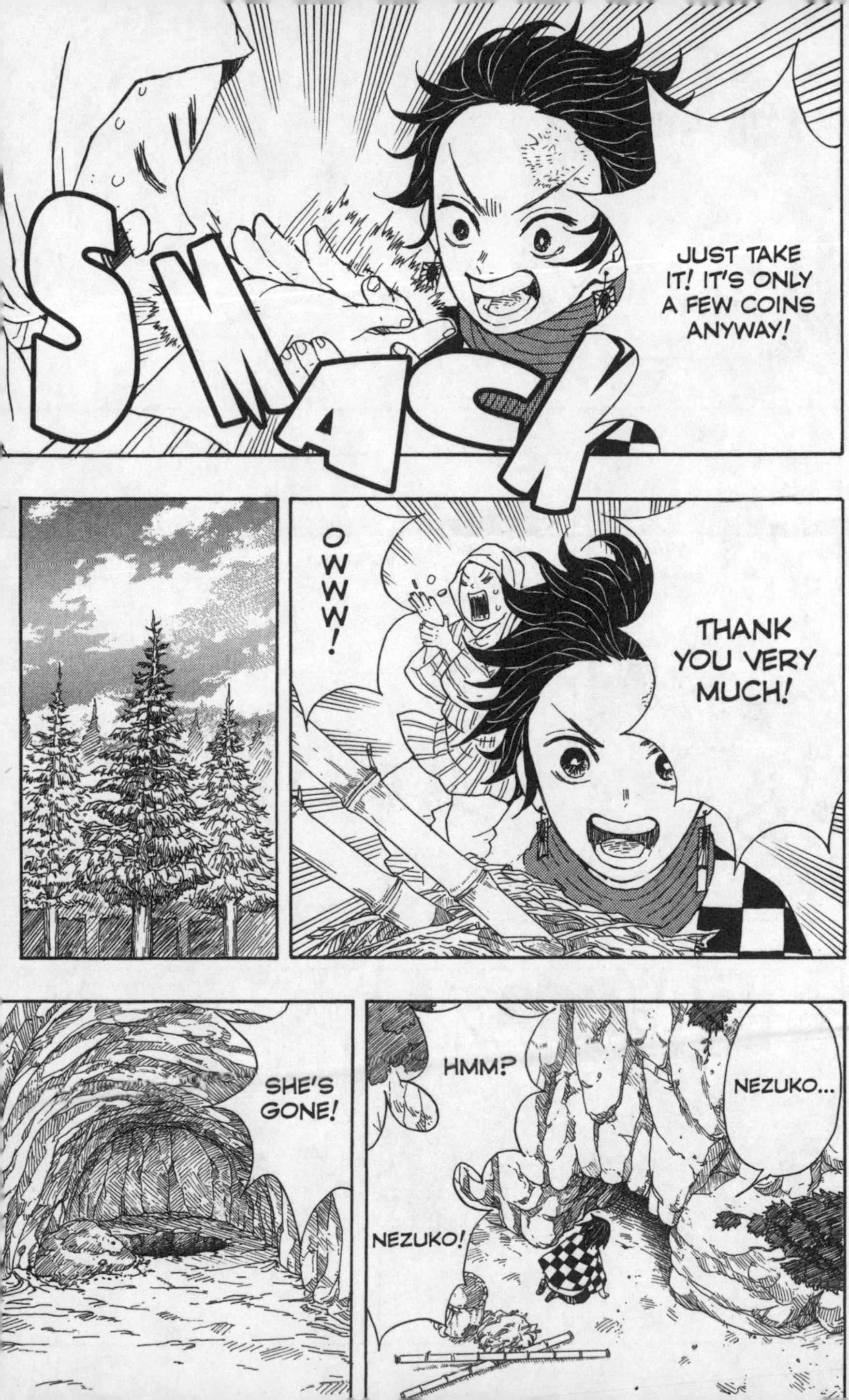
JUST TAKE IT! IT'S ONLY A FEW COINS ANYWAY!
SMACK
THANK YOU VERY MUCH!
OWWW!
NEZUKO...
HMM?
NEZUKO!
SHE'S GONE!

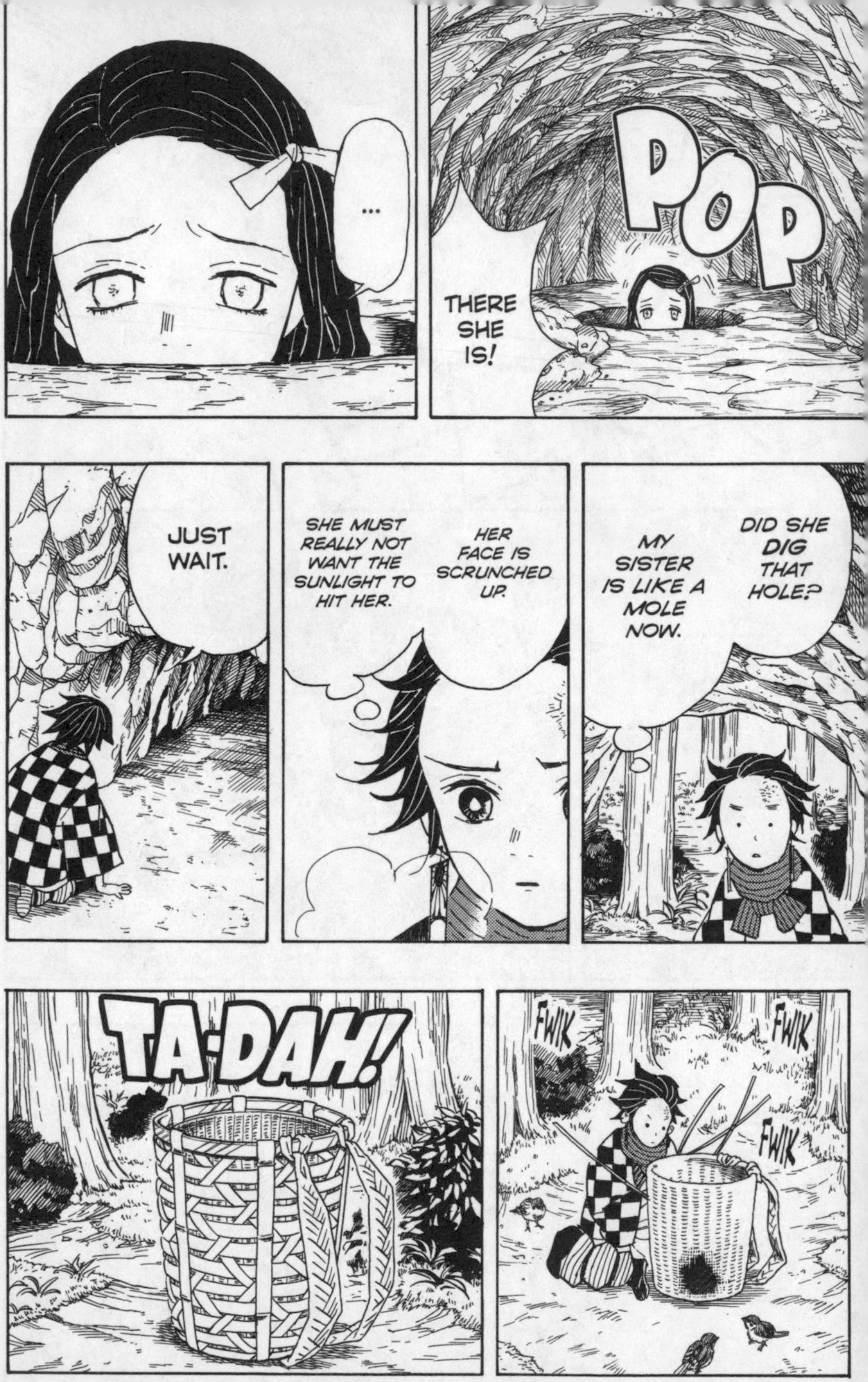
POP
THERE SHE IS!
...
DID SHE DIG THAT HOLE?
MY SISTER IS LIKE A MOLE NOW.
HER FACE IS SCRUNCHED UP.
SHE MUST REALLY NOT WANT THE SUNLIGHT TO HIT HER.
JUST WAIT.
FWIK
FWIK
FWIK
TA-DAH!

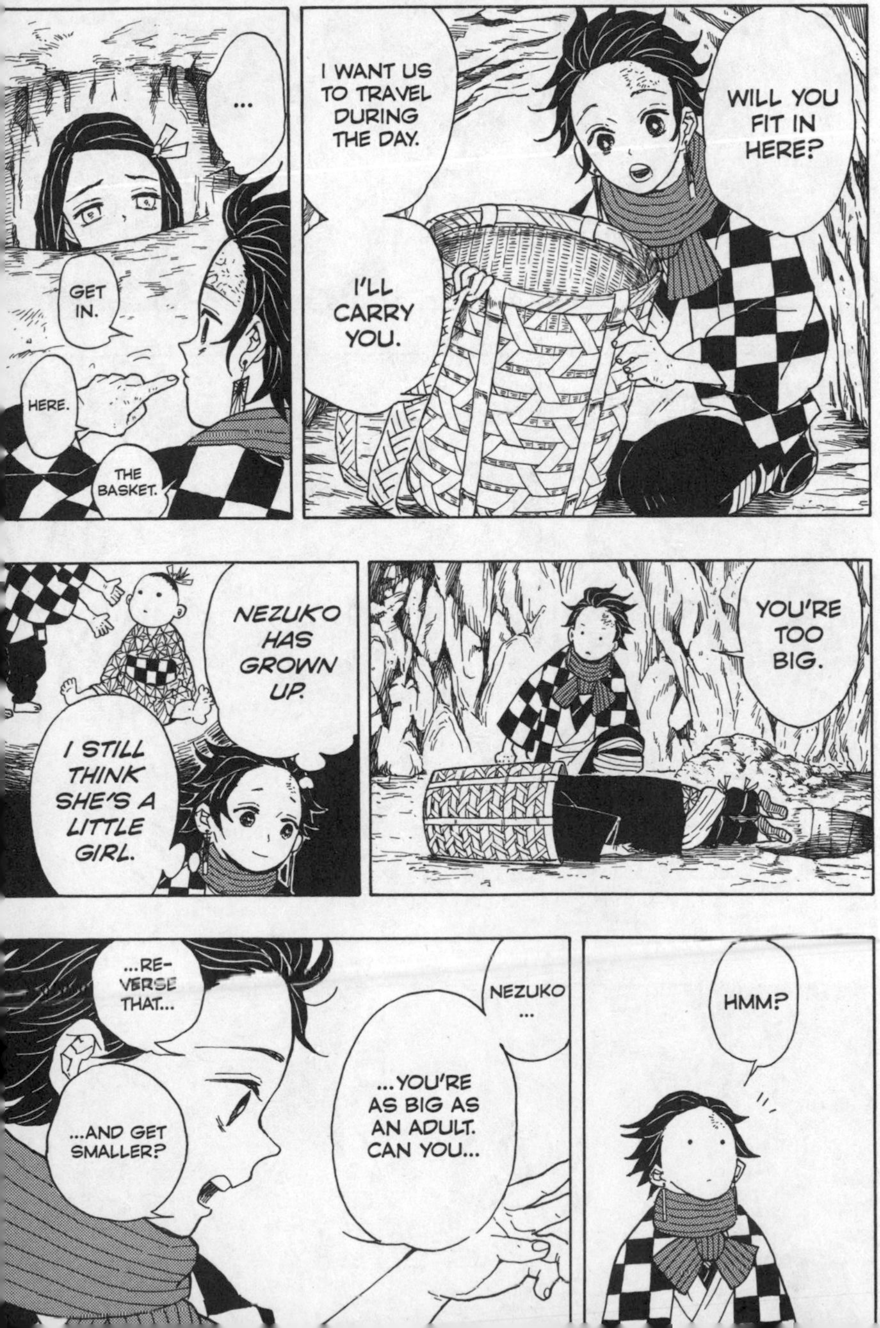
WILL YOU FIT IN HERE?
I WANT US TO TRAVEL DURING THE DAY.
I'LL CARRY YOU.
...
GET IN.
HERE.
THE BASKET.
YOU'RE TOO BIG.
NEZUKO HAS GROWN UP.
I STILL THINK SHE'S A LITTLE GIRL.
HMM?
NEZUKO ...
...YOU'RE AS BIG AS AN ADULT. CAN YOU...
...RE-VERSE THAT...
...AND GET SMALLER?

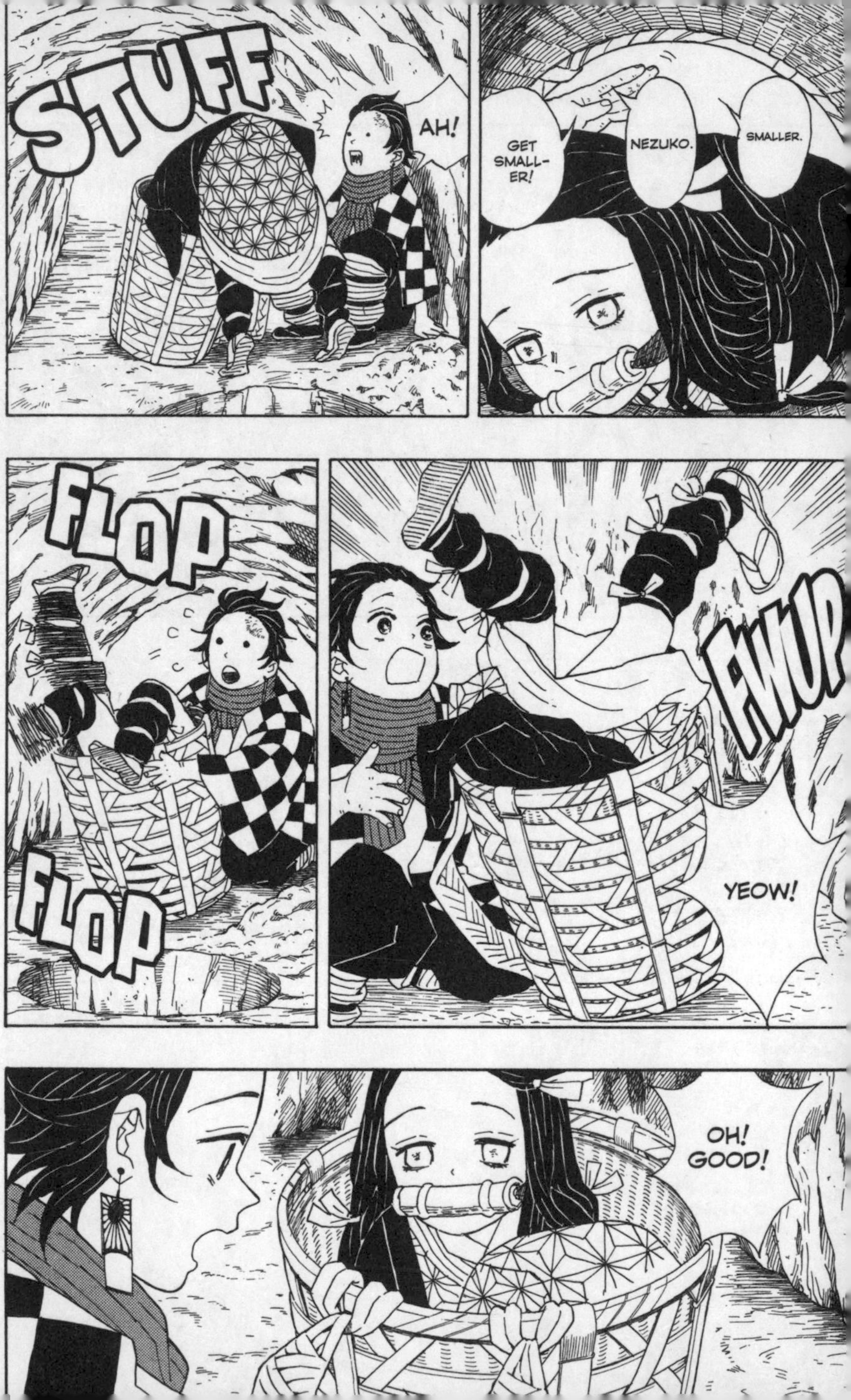
SMALLER.
NEZUKO.
GET SMALL-ER!
STUFF
AH!
FWUP
YEOW!
FLOP
FLOP
OH! GOOD!

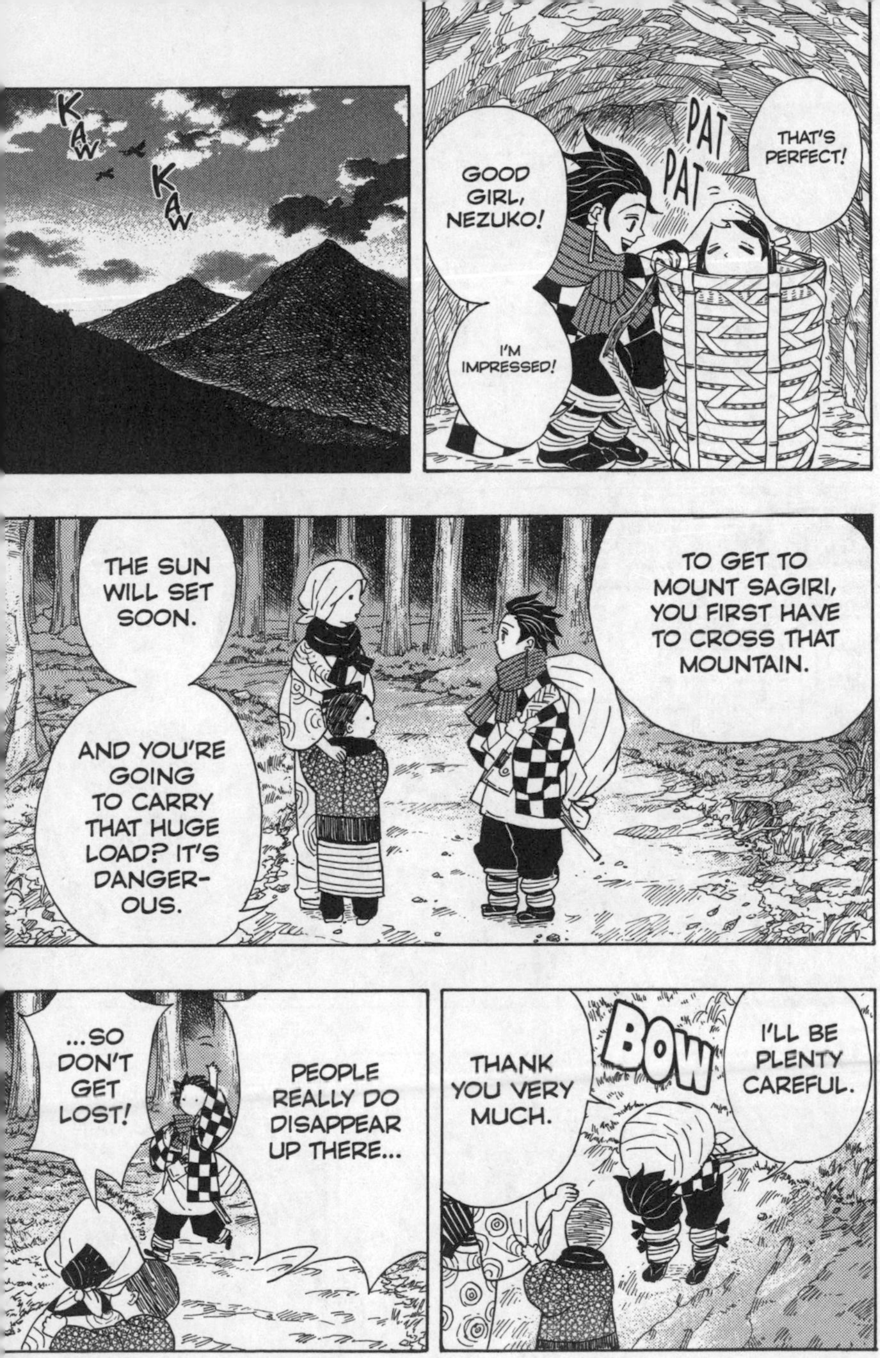
THAT'S PERFECT!
PAT PAT
GOOD GIRL, NEZUKO!
I'M IMPRESSED!
KAW KAW
TO GET TO MOUNT SAGIRI, YOU FIRST HAVE TO CROSS THAT MOUNTAIN.
THE SUN WILL SET SOON.
AND YOU'RE GOING TO CARRY THAT HUGE LOAD? IT'S DANGER-OUS.
I'LL BE PLENTY CAREFUL.
BOW
THANK YOU VERY MUCH.
PEOPLE REALLY DO DISAPPEAR UP THERE...
...SO DON'T GET LOST!

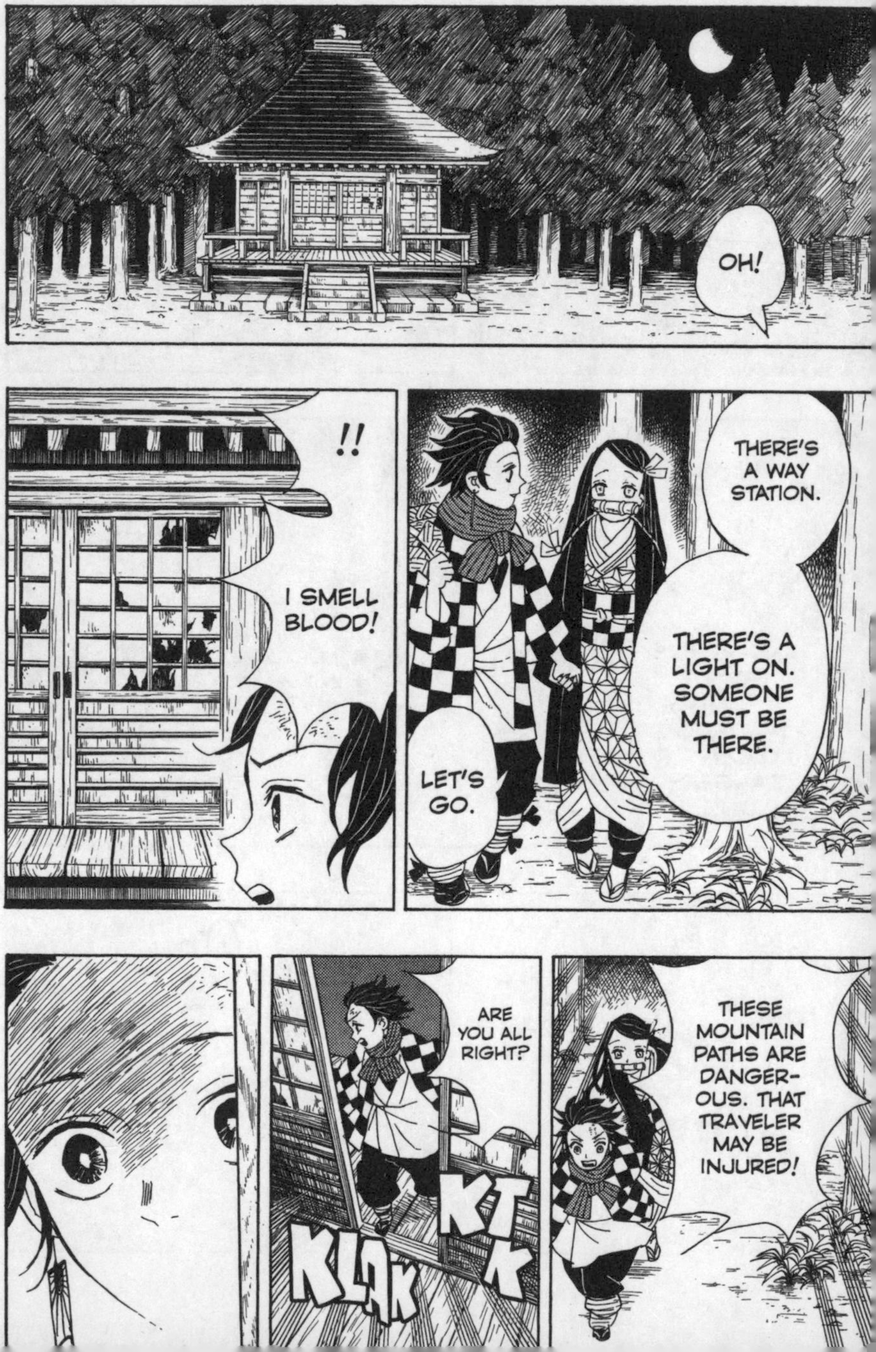
OH!
THERE'S A WAY STATION.
THERE'S A LIGHT ON. SOMEONE MUST BE THERE.
LET'S GO.
!!
I SMELL BLOOD!
THESE MOUNTAIN PATHS ARE DANGER-OUS. THAT TRAVELER MAY BE INJURED!
ARE YOU ALL RIGHT?
KTK
KLAK

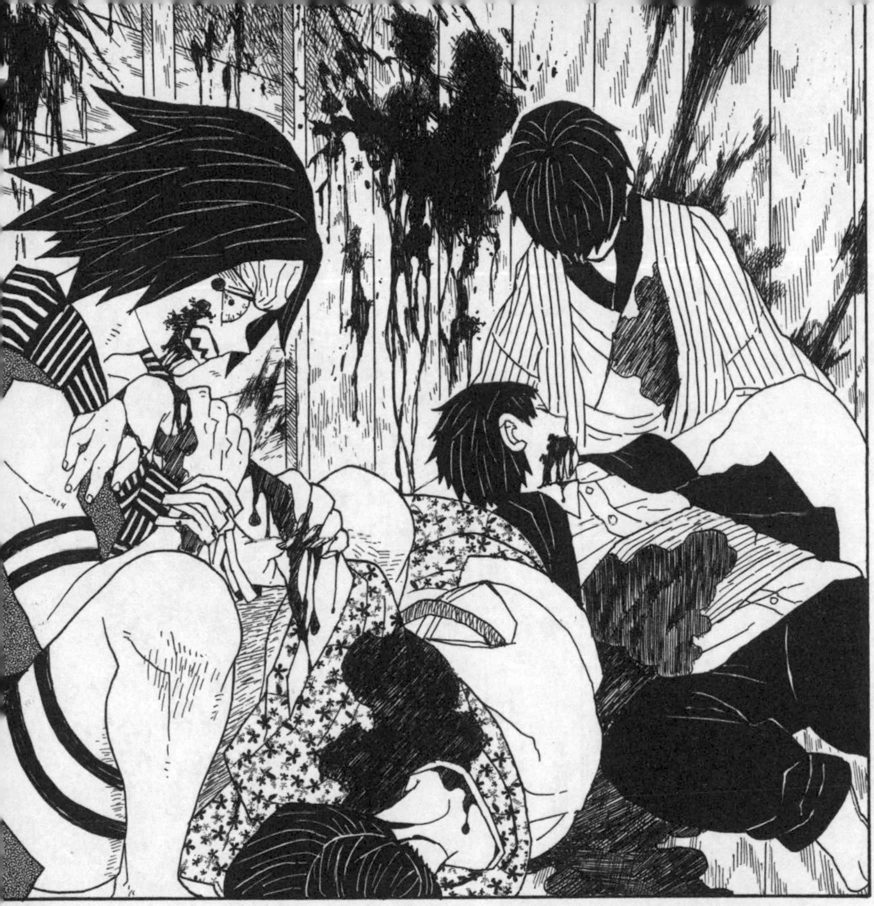

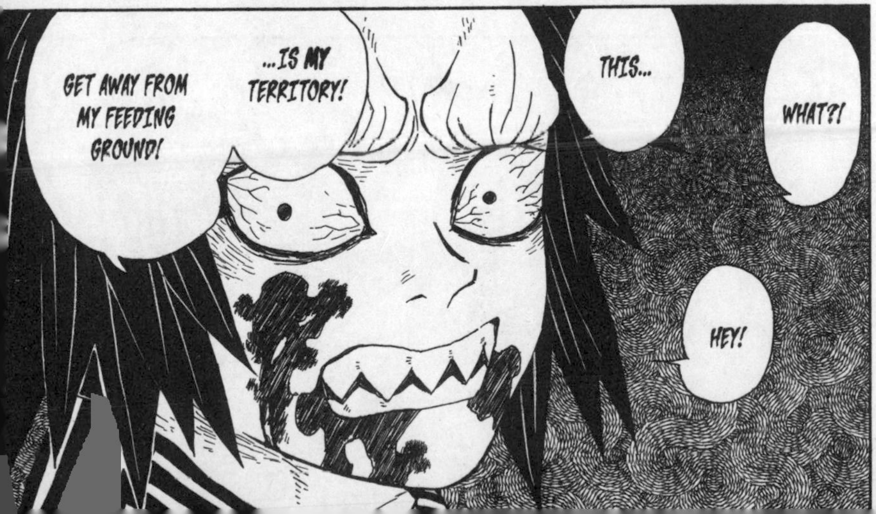
WHAT?!
HEY!
THIS...
...IS MY TERRITORY!
GET AWAY FROM MY FEEDING GROUND!

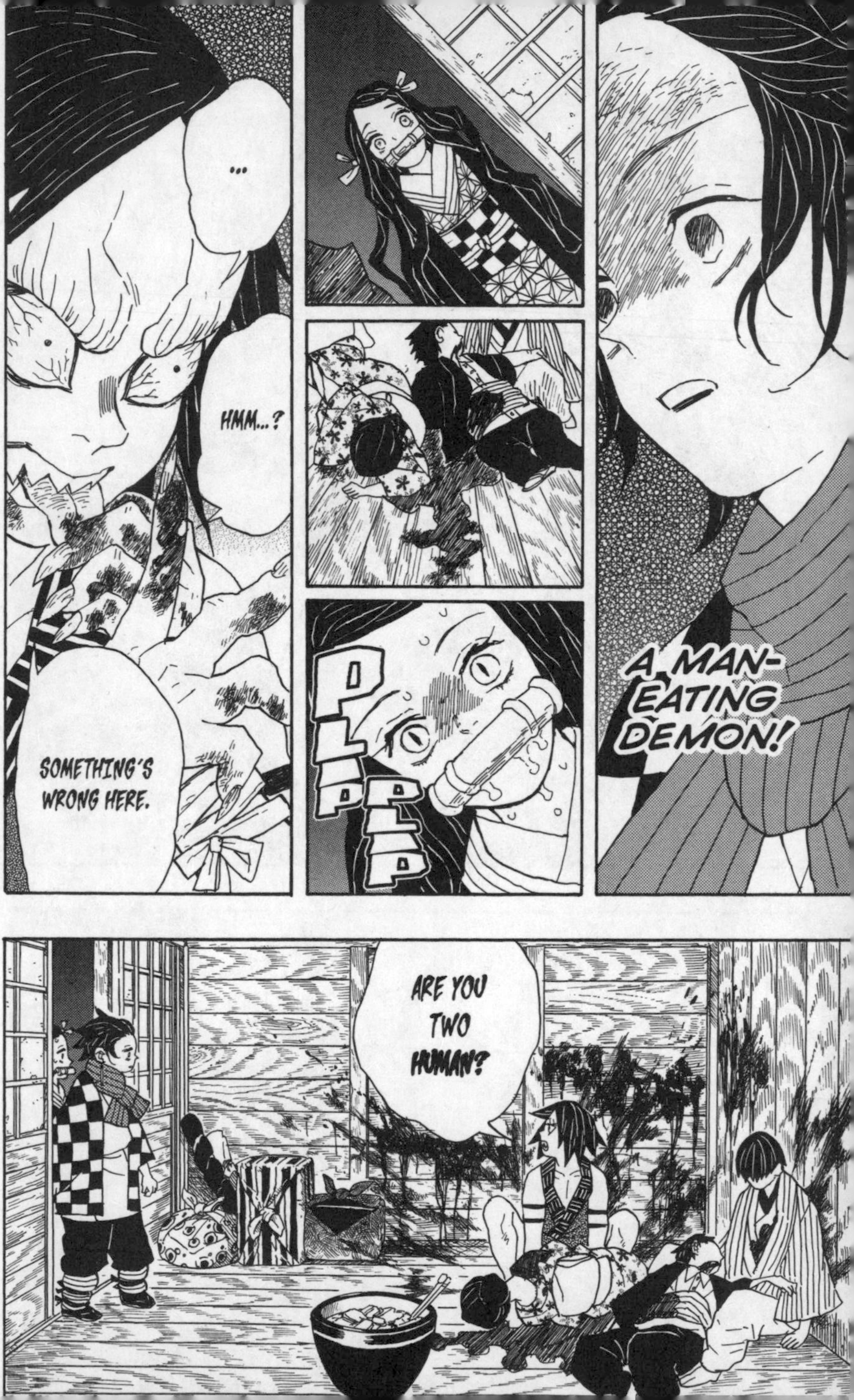
A MAN-EATING DEMON!
PLIP PLIP
...
HMM...?
SOMETHING'S WRONG HERE.
ARE YOU TWO HUMAN?

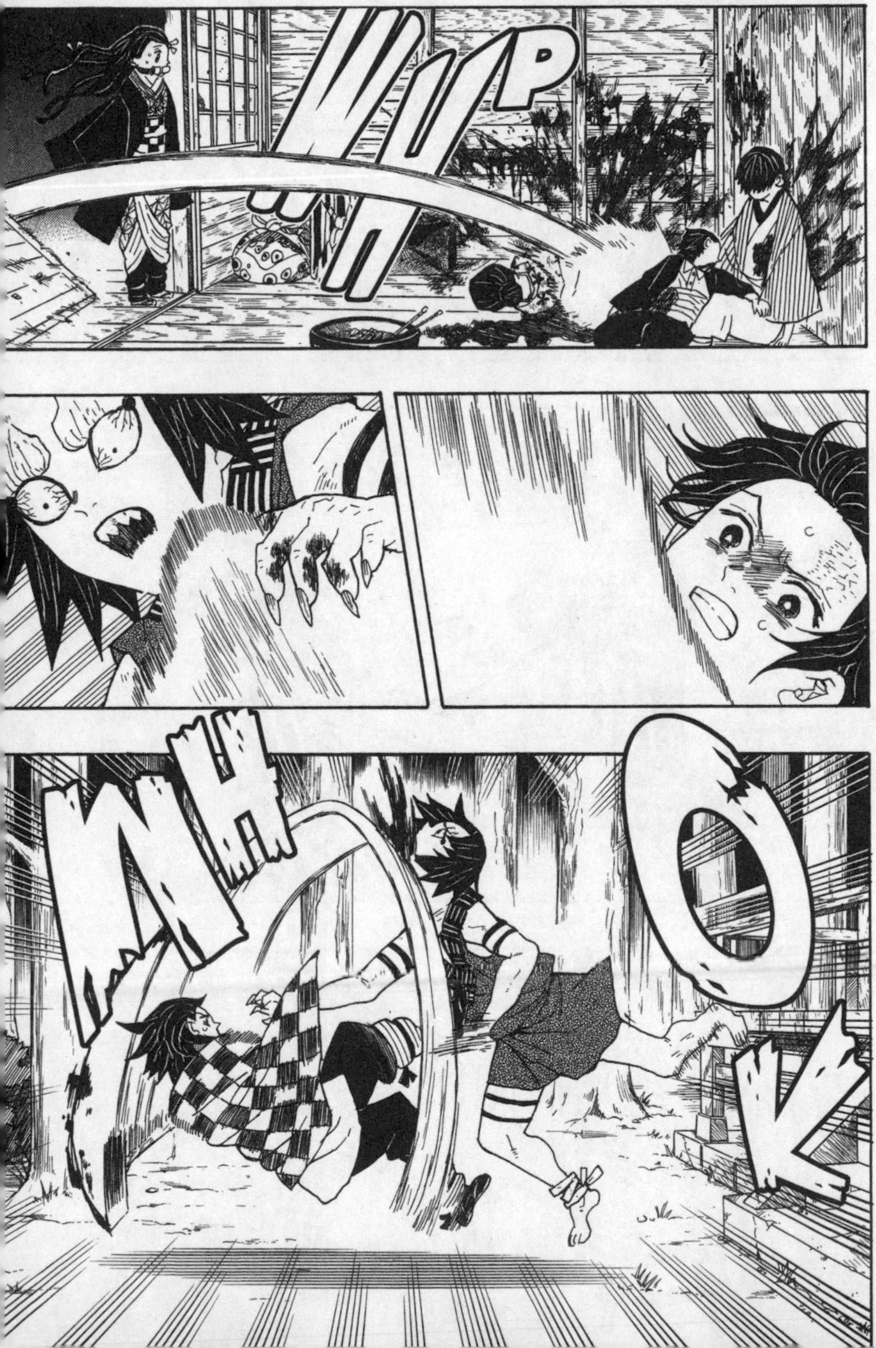
WHIP
WHOK

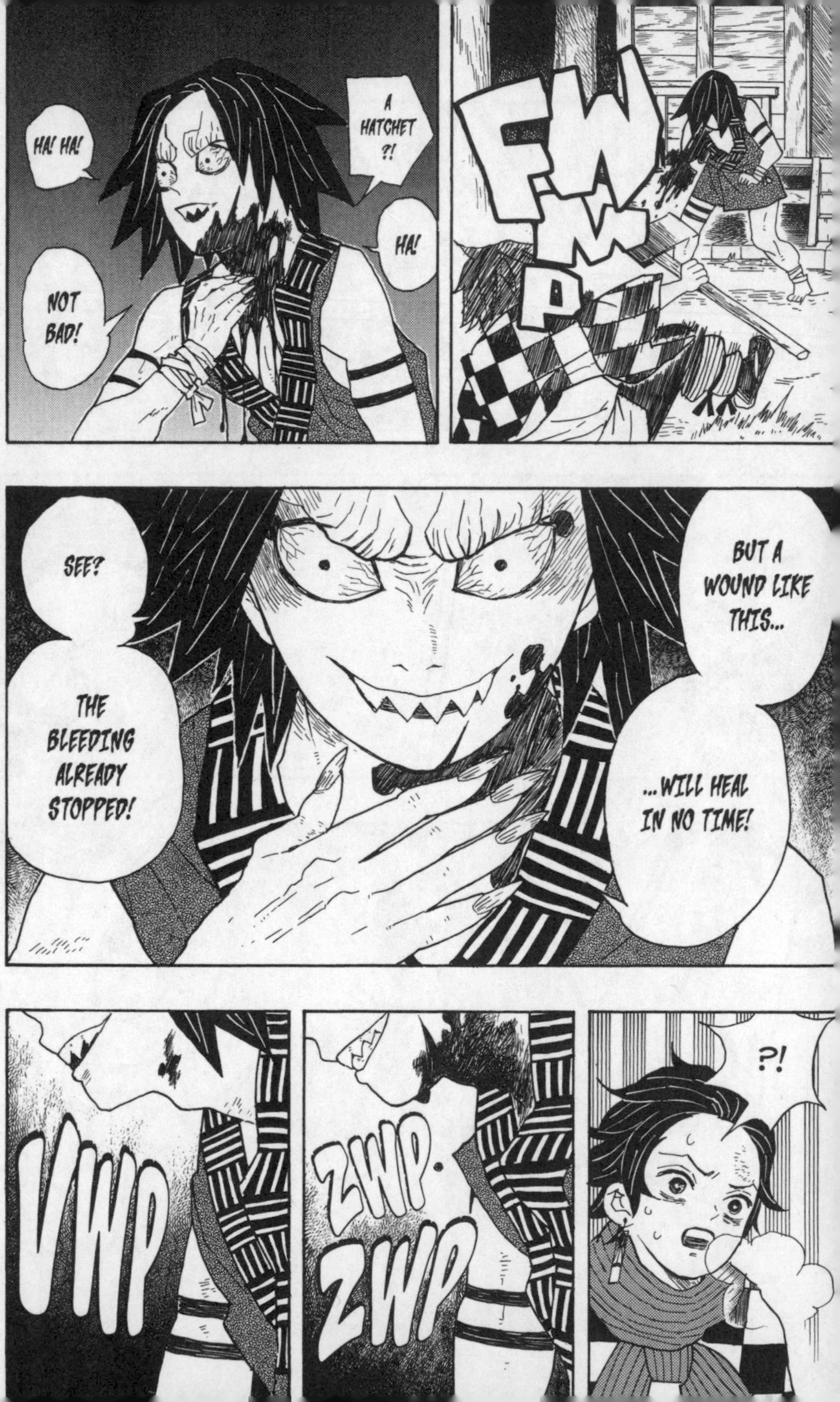
FWMP
A HATCHET ?!
HA! HA!
HA!
NOT BAD!
BUT A WOUND LIKE THIS...
...WILL HEAL IN NO TIME!
SEE?
THE BLEEDING ALREADY STOPPED!
?!
ZWP
ZWP
ZWP
VWP

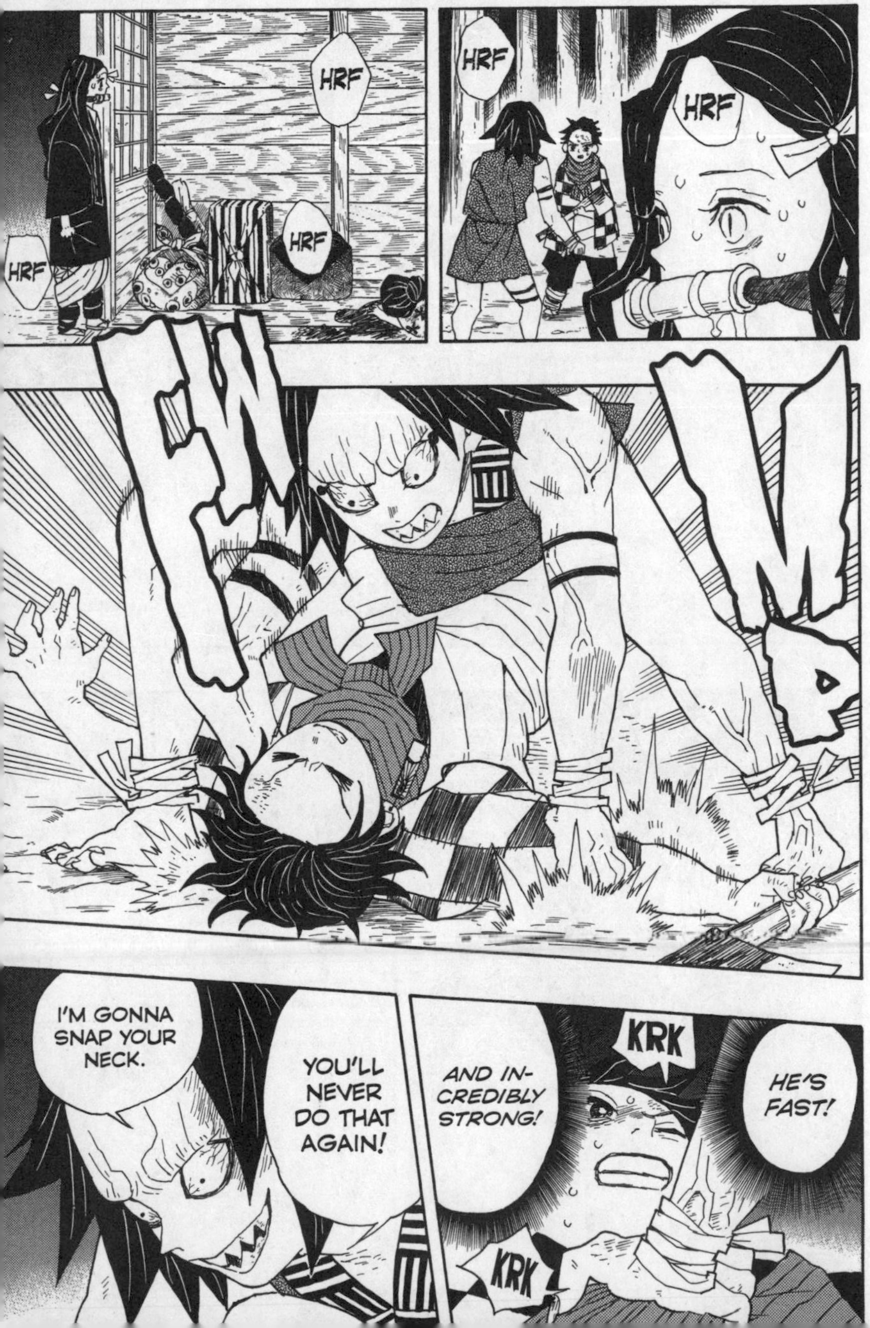
HRF
HRF
HRF
HRF
HRF
KRK
HE'S FAST!
AND IN-CREDIBLY STRONG!
KRK
YOU'LL NEVER DO THAT AGAIN!
I'M GONNA SNAP YOUR NECK.

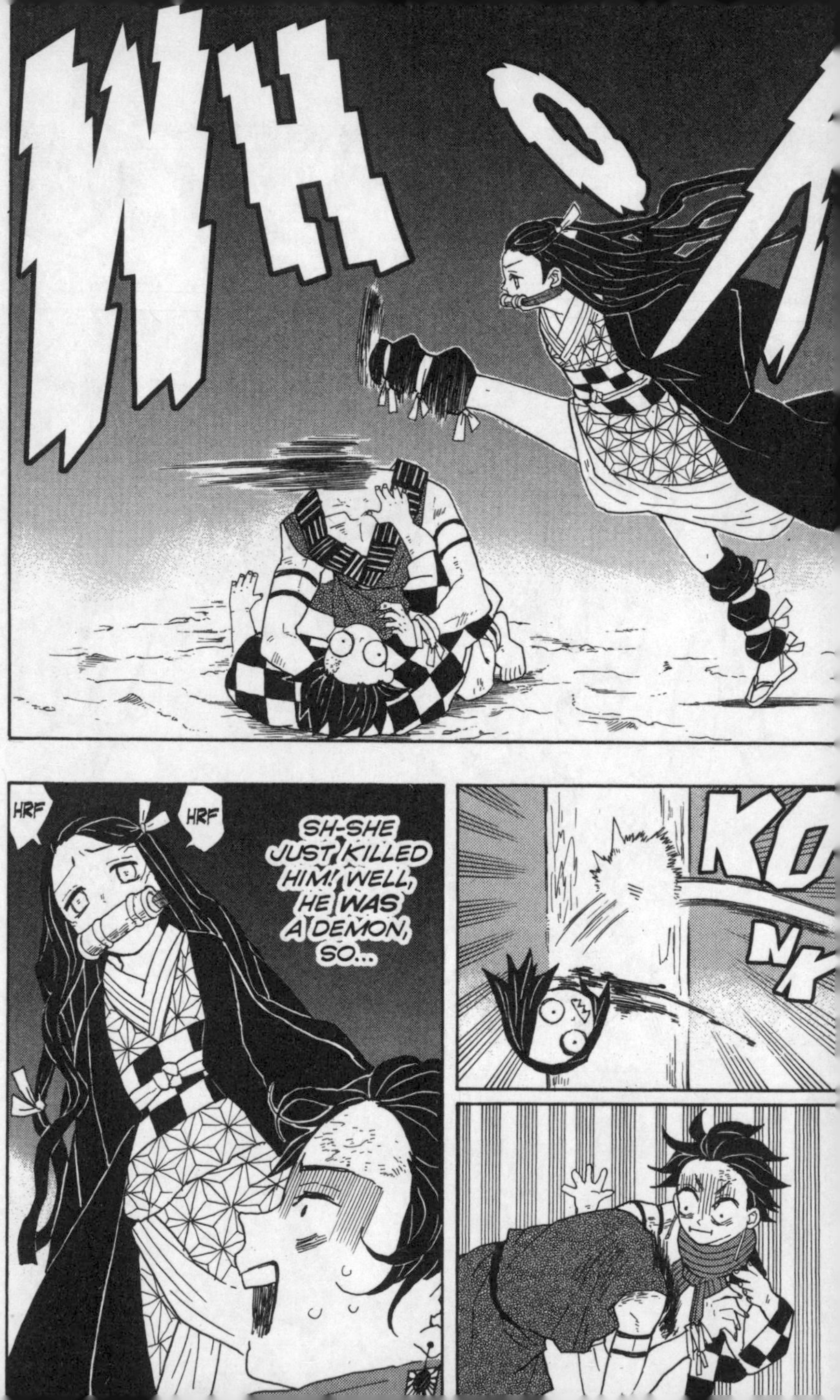
KO
NK
HRF
HRF
SH-SHE JUST KILLED HIM! WELL, HE WAS A DEMON, SO...

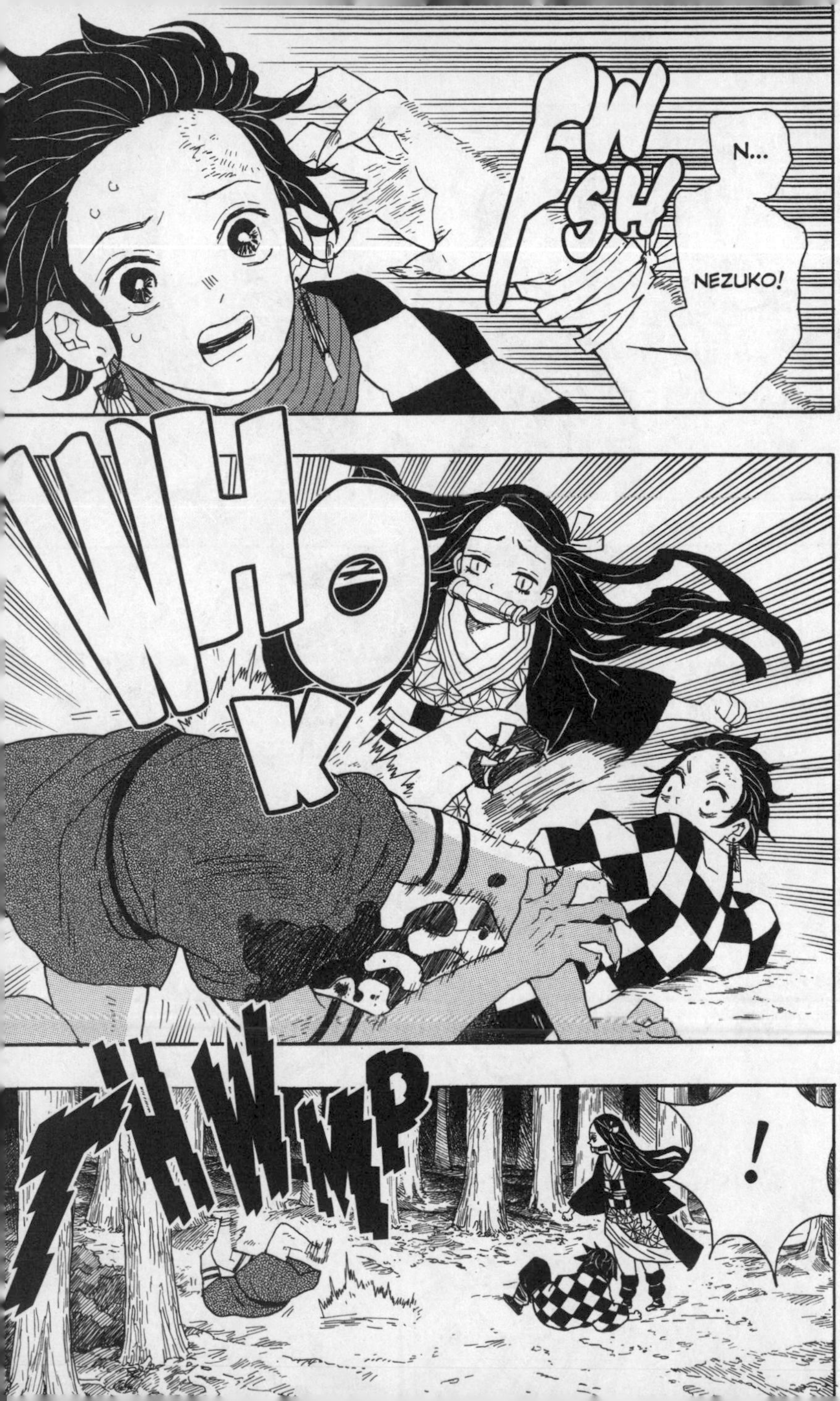
N...
NEZUKO!
FWSH
WHOK
THWMP
!

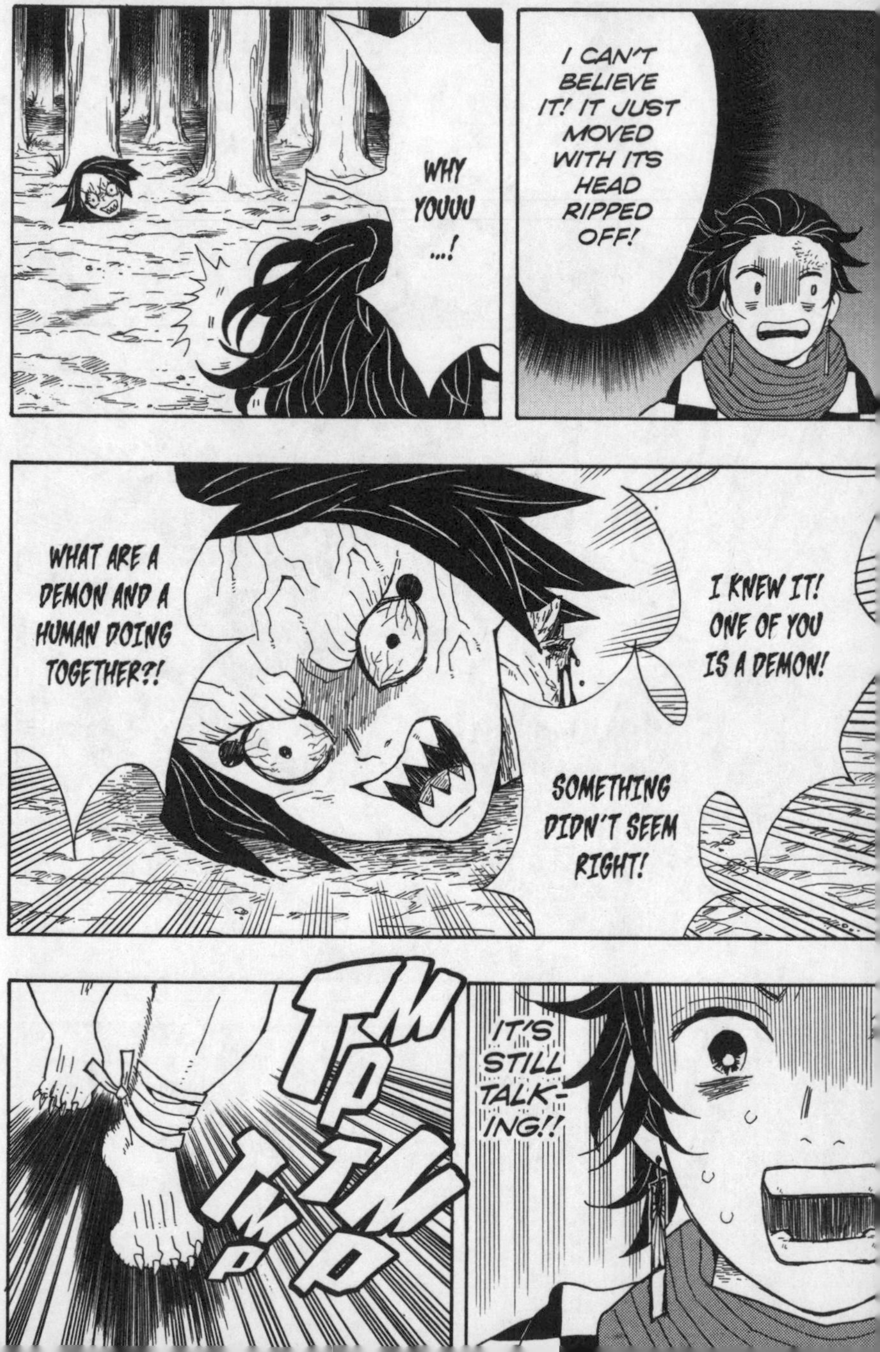
I CAN'T BELIEVE IT! IT JUST MOVED WITH ITS HEAD RIPPED OFF!
WHY YOUUU ...!
I KNEW IT! ONE OF YOU IS A DEMON!
SOMETHING DIDN'T SEEM RIGHT!
WHAT ARE A DEMON AND A HUMAN DOING TOGETHER?!
IT'S STILL TALK-ING!!
TMP TMP TMP

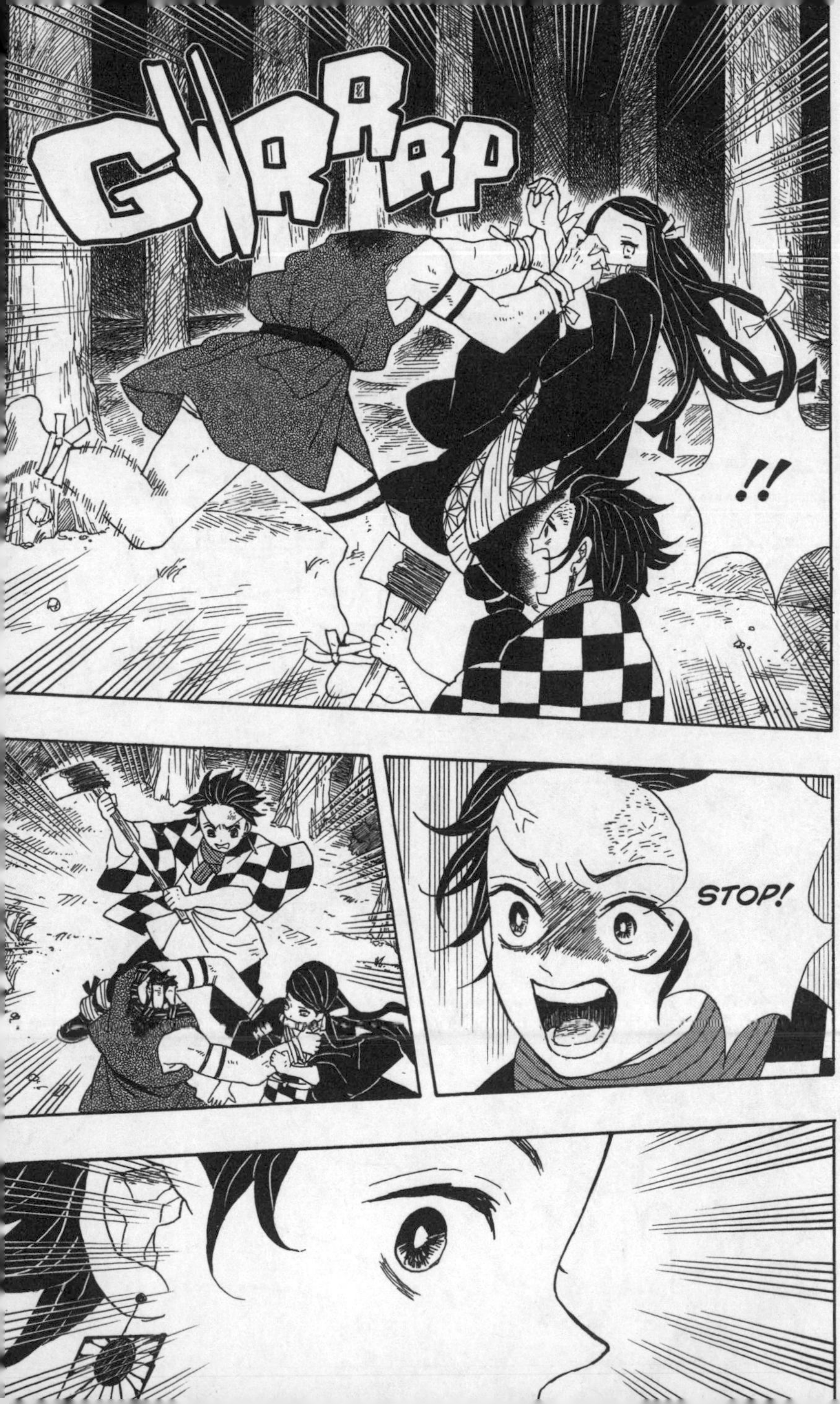
GWRRAP
!!
STOP!

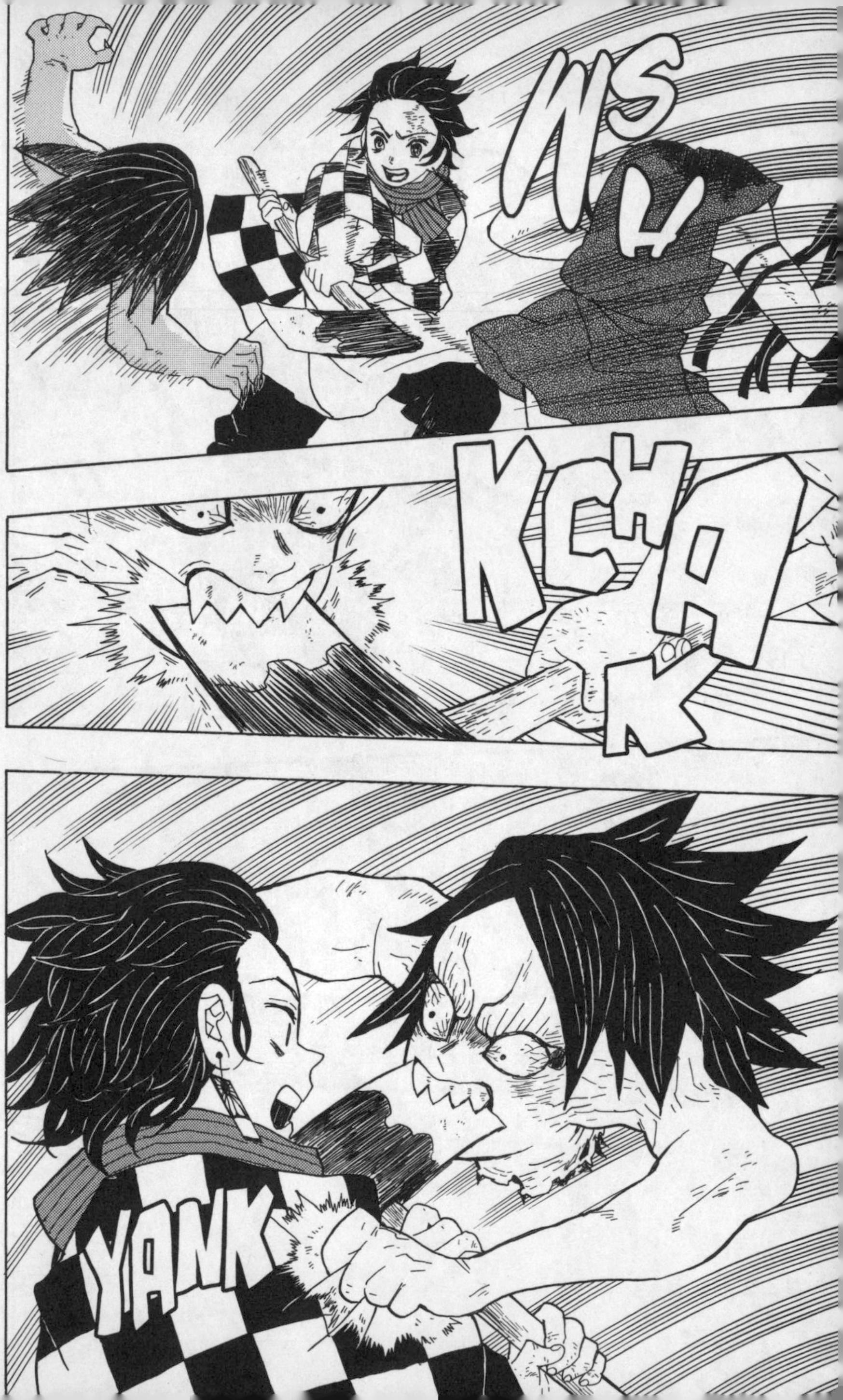
WSH
KCHAK
YANK

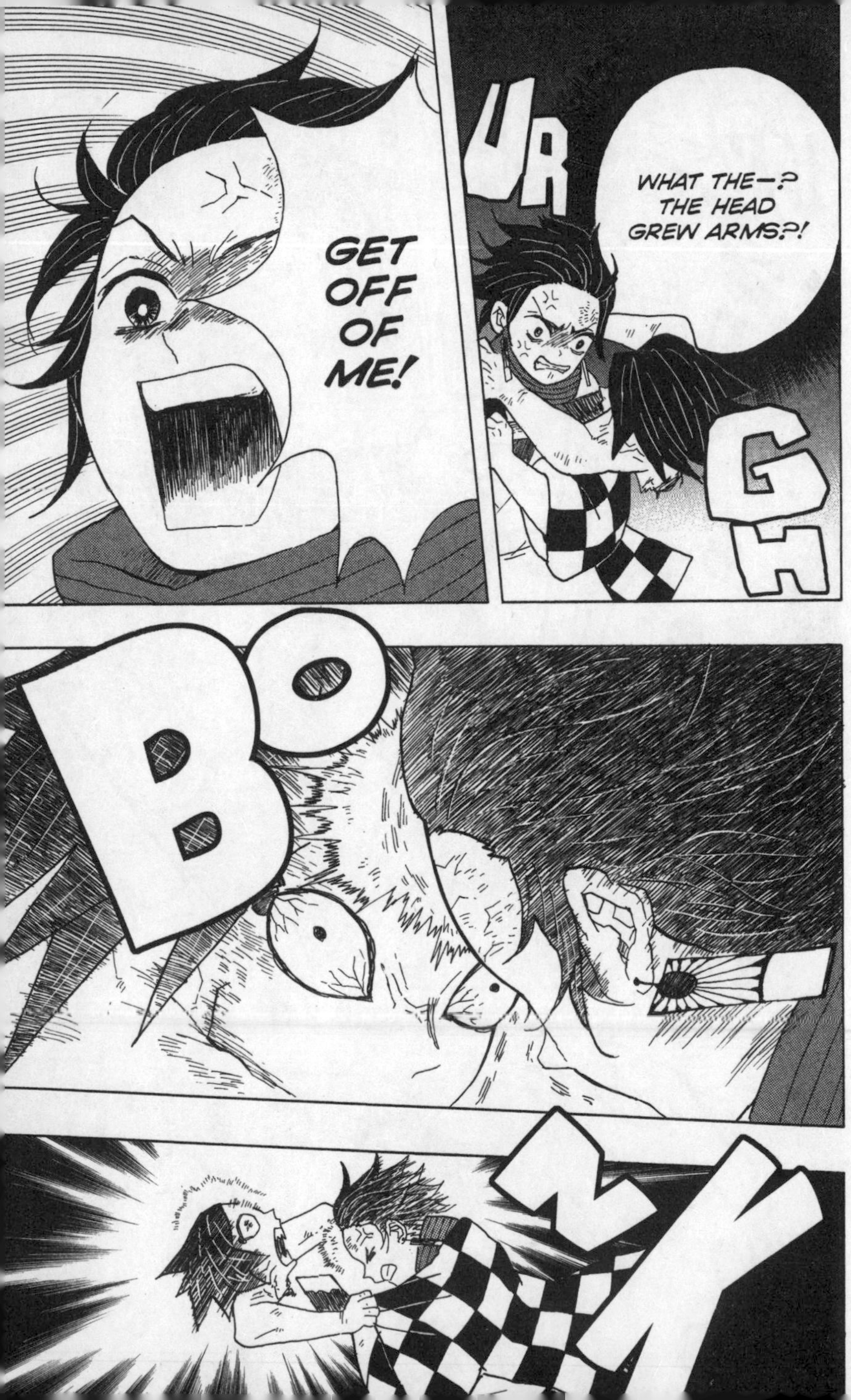
UR
WHAT THE—? THE HEAD GREW ARMS?!
GH
GET OFF OF ME!

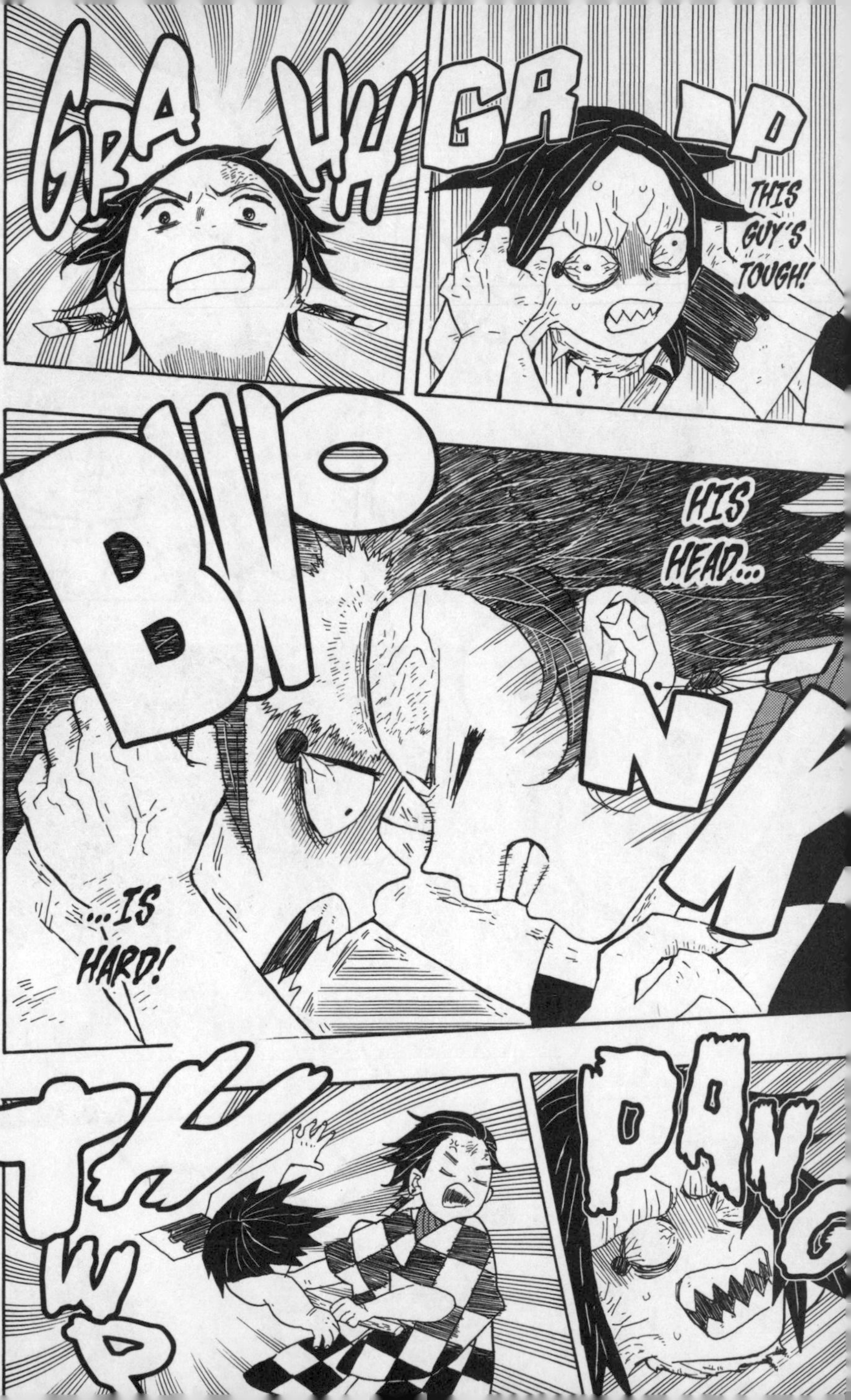
GRIP
THIS GUY'S TOUGH!
GRA UH
BWOONK
HIS HEAD...
...IS HARD!
PANG
THWP

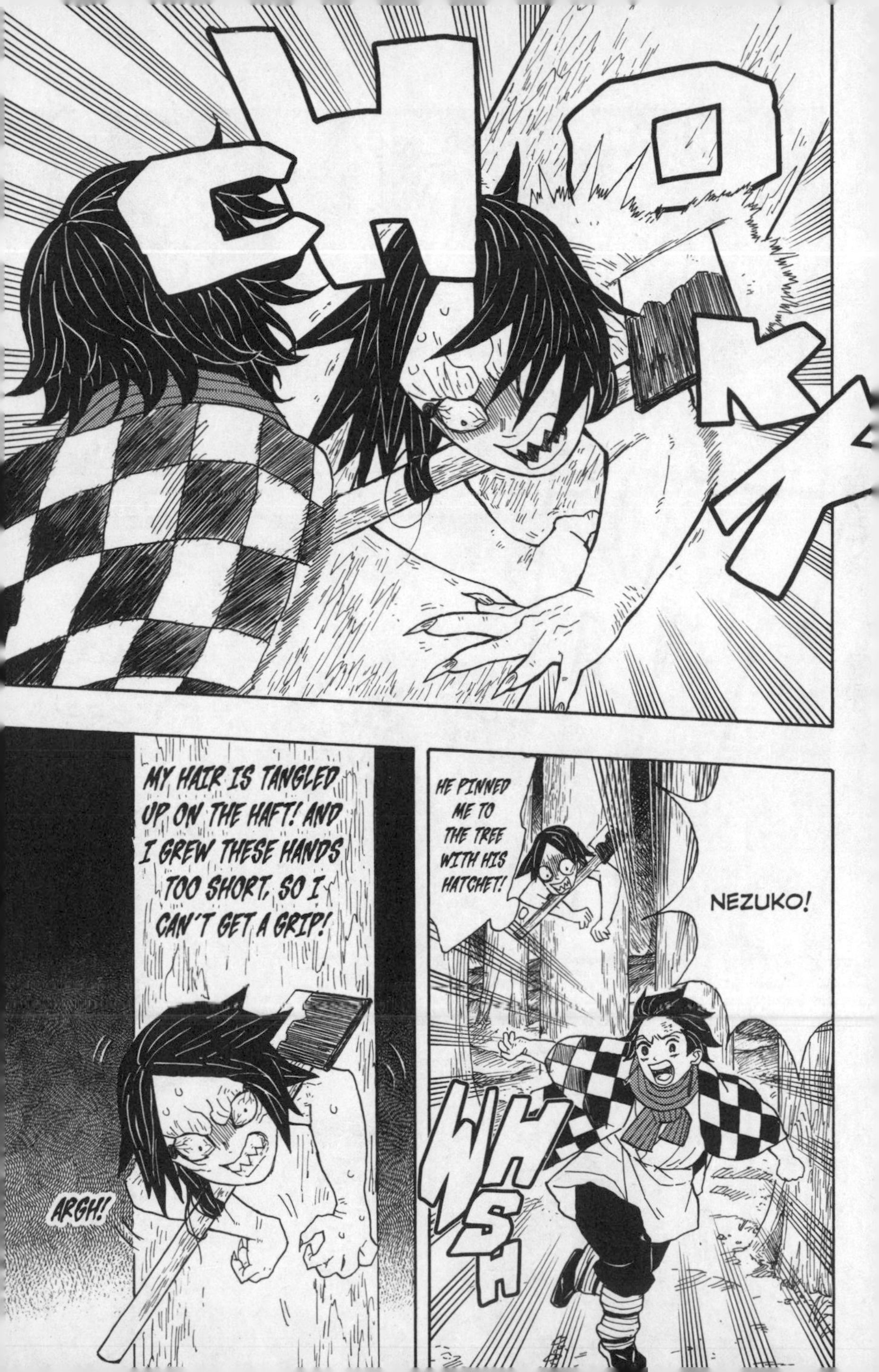
NEZUKO!
HE PINNED ME TO THE TREE WITH HIS HATCHET!
WHSH
MY HAIR IS TANGLED UP ON THE HAFT! AND I GREW THESE HANDS TOO SHORT, SO I CAN'T GET A GRIP!
ARGH!

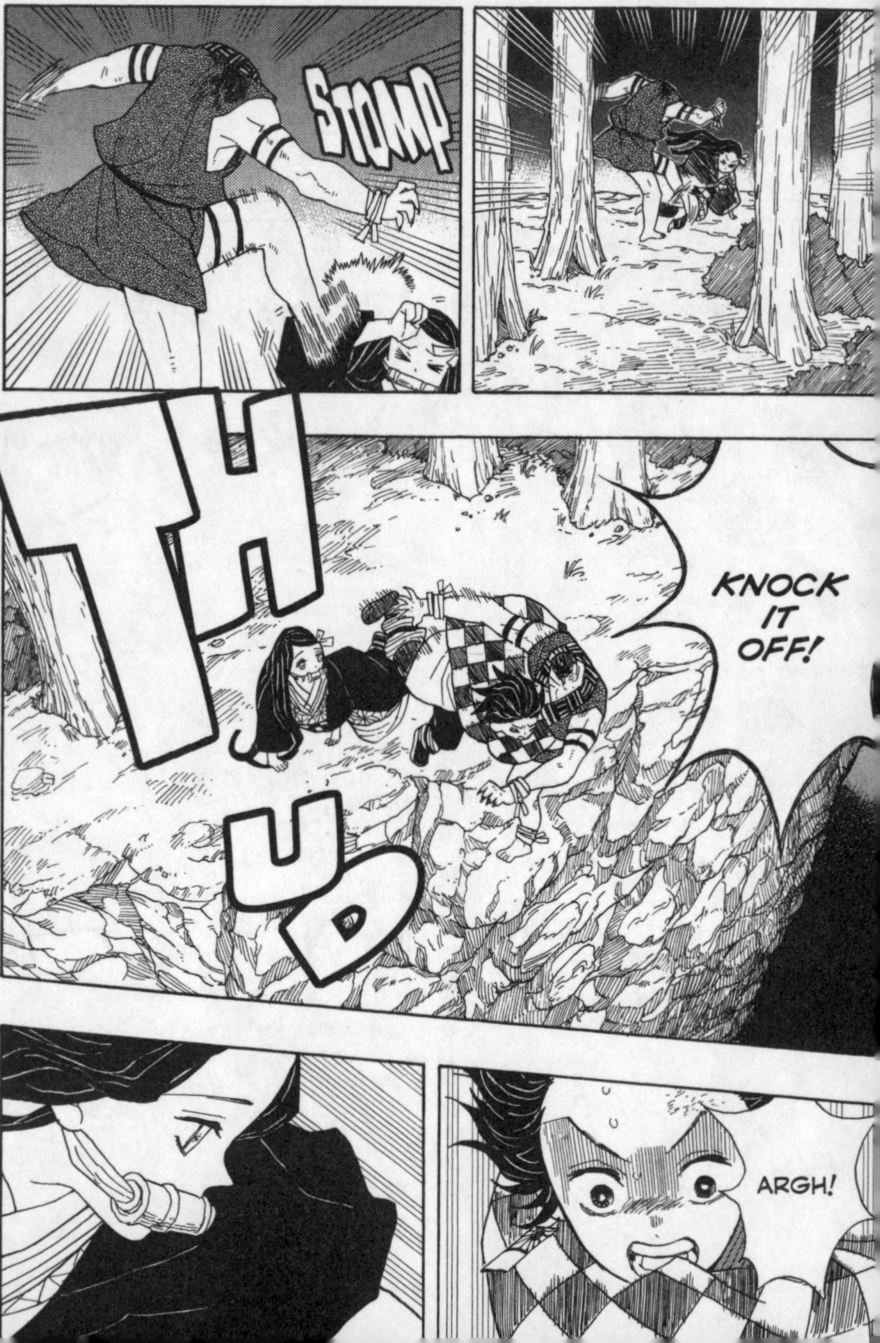
STOMP
KNOCK IT OFF!
THUD
ARGH!

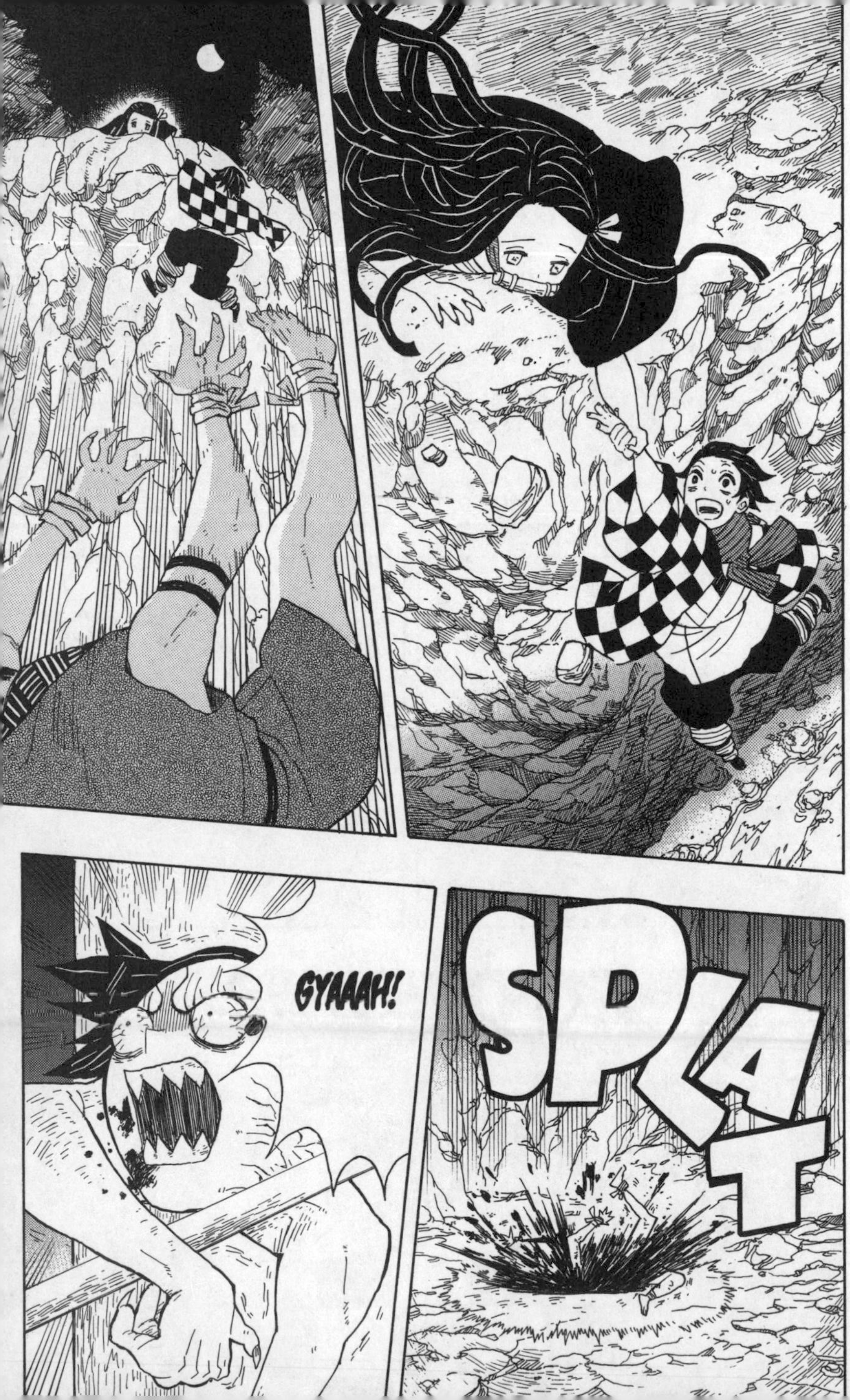
SPLAT
GYAAAH!

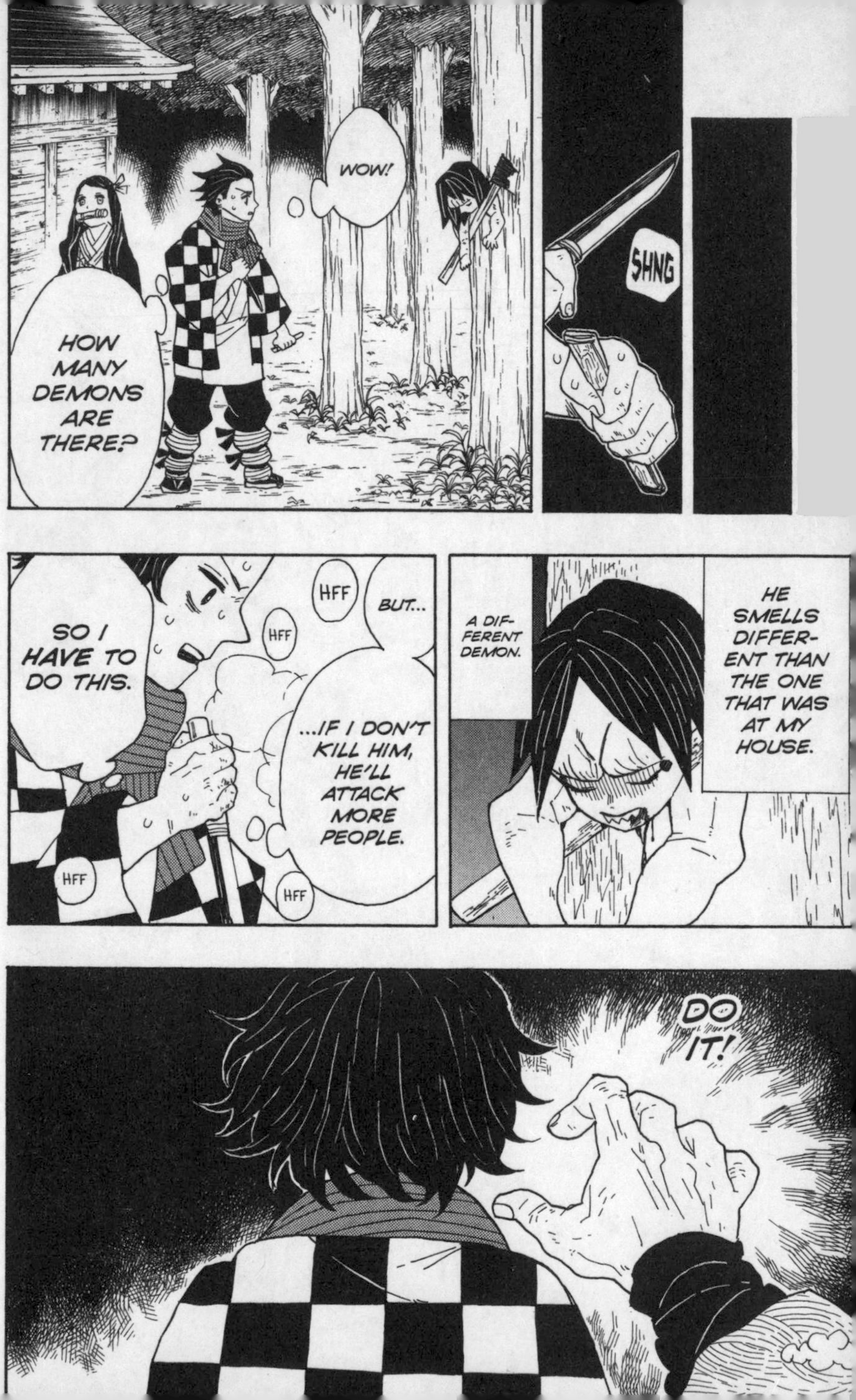
SHNG
WOW!
HOW MANY DEMONS ARE THERE?
HE SMELLS DIFFERENT THAN THE ONE THAT WAS AT MY HOUSE.
A DIFFERENT DEMON.
BUT...
HFF
HFF
SO I HAVE TO DO THIS.
...IF I DON'T KILL HIM, HE'LL ATTACK MORE PEOPLE.
HFF
HFF
DO IT!

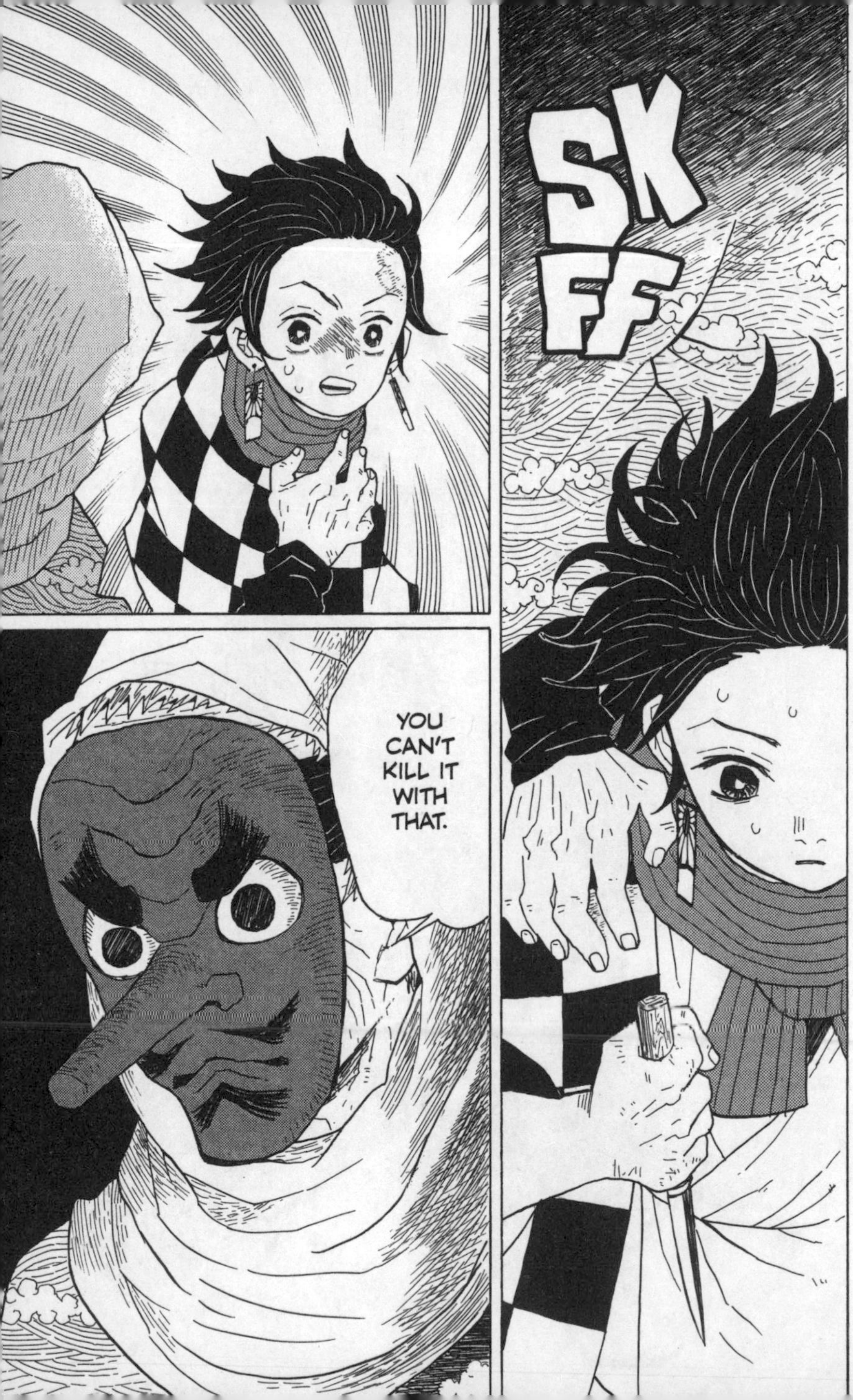
SKFF
YOU CAN'T KILL IT WITH THAT.

PRODUCTION ART, ILLUSTRATION ②

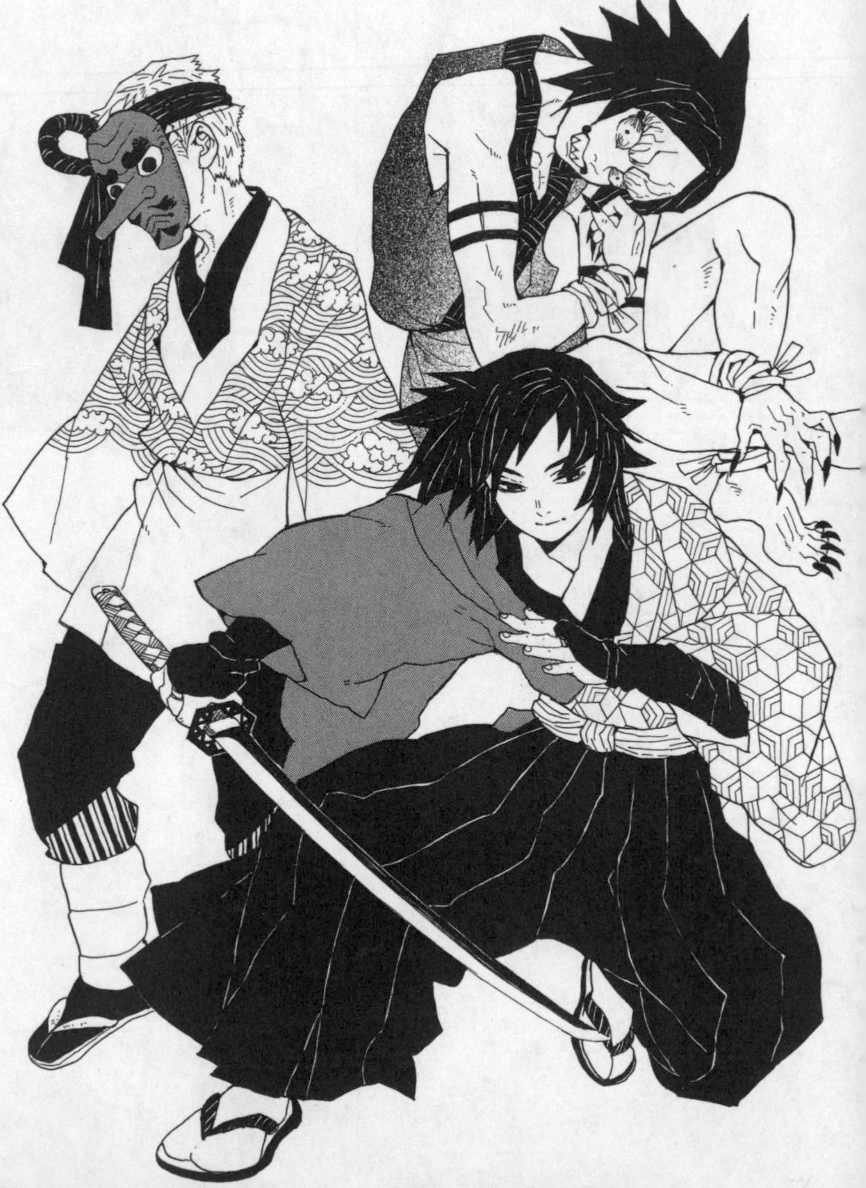

CHAPTER 3: RETURN BY DAWN

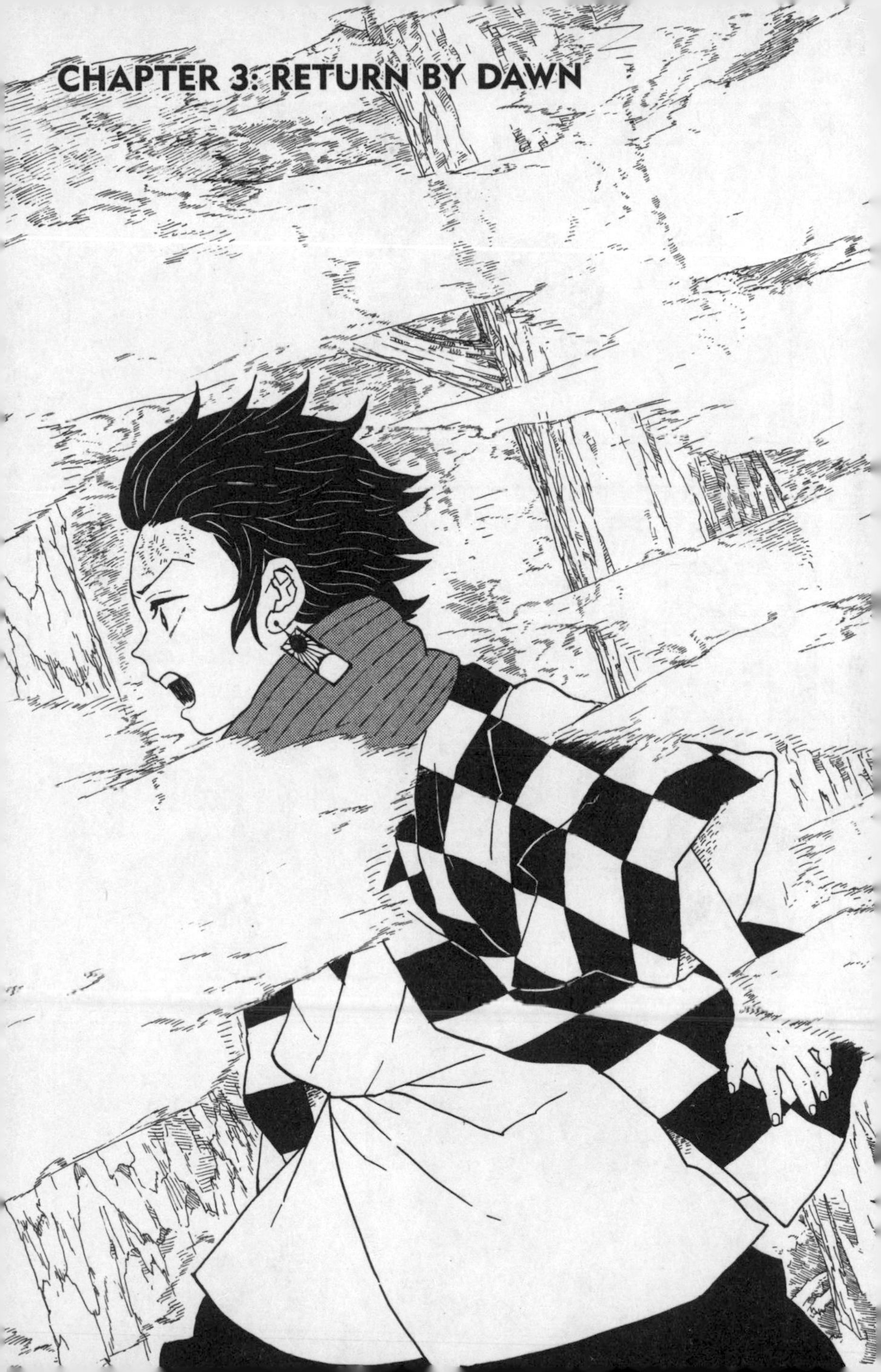

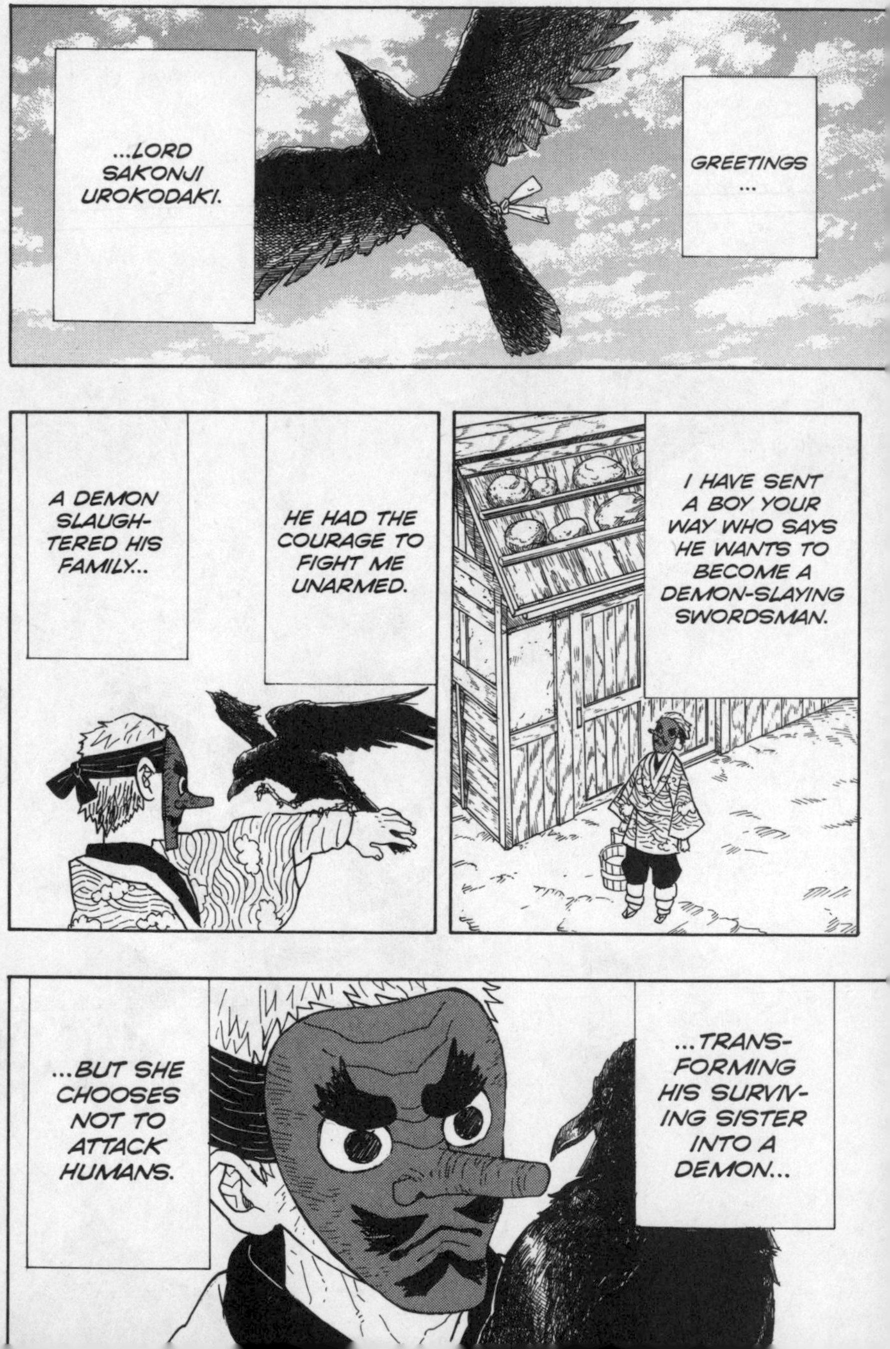
GREETINGS ...
...LORD SAKONJI UROKODAKI.
I HAVE SENT A BOY YOUR WAY WHO SAYS HE WANTS TO BECOME A DEMON-SLAYING SWORDSMAN.
HE HAD THE COURAGE TO FIGHT ME UNARMED.
A DEMON SLAUGH-TERED HIS FAMILY...
...TRANS-FORMING HIS SURVIV-ING SISTER INTO A DEMON...
...BUT SHE CHOOSES NOT TO ATTACK HUMANS.

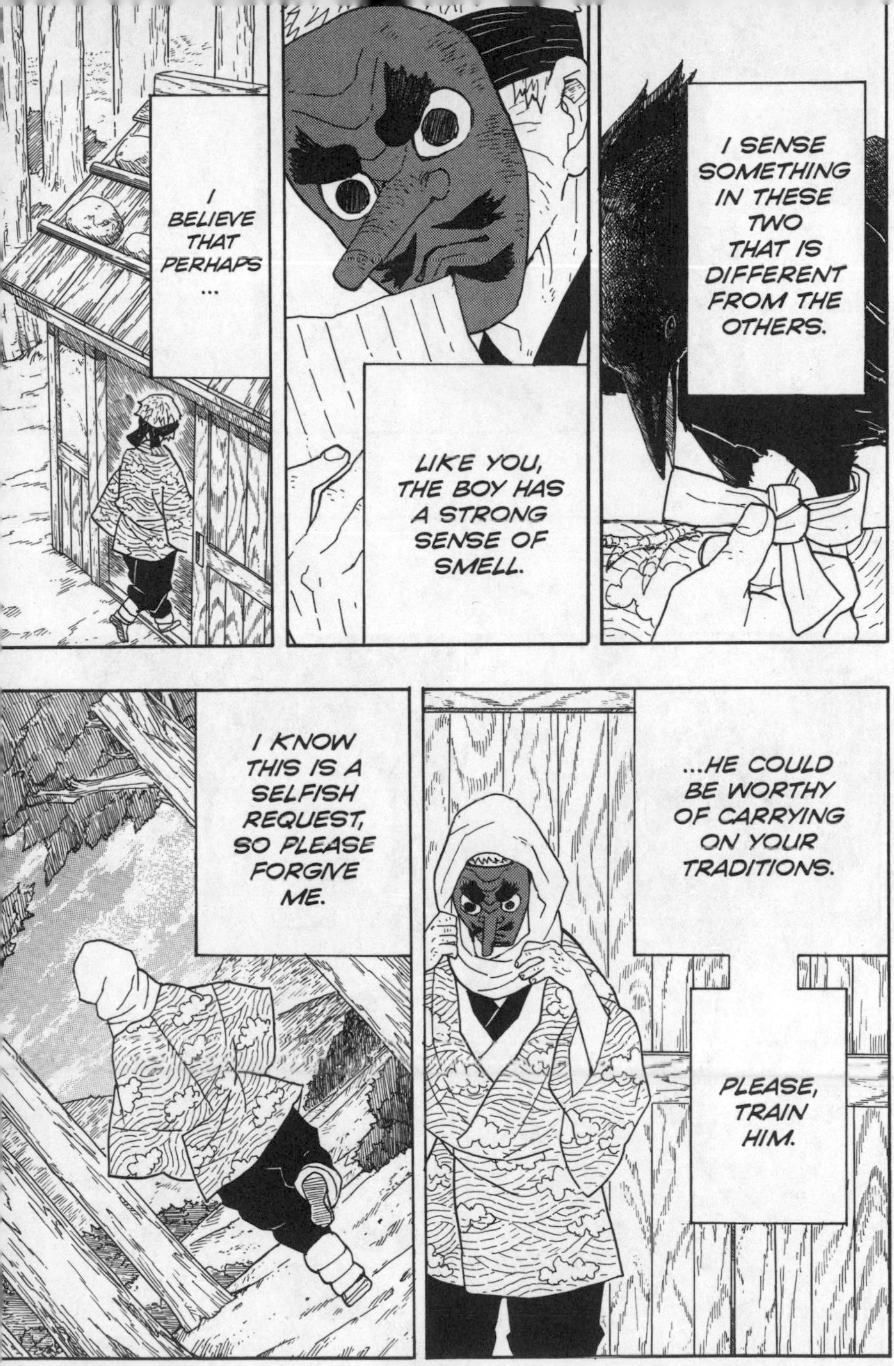
I SENSE SOMETHING IN THESE TWO THAT IS DIFFERENT FROM THE OTHERS.
LIKE YOU, THE BOY HAS A STRONG SENSE OF SMELL.
I BELIEVE THAT PERHAPS ...
...HE COULD BE WORTHY OF CARRYING ON YOUR TRADITIONS.
PLEASE, TRAIN HIM.
I KNOW THIS IS A SELFISH REQUEST, SO PLEASE FORGIVE ME.

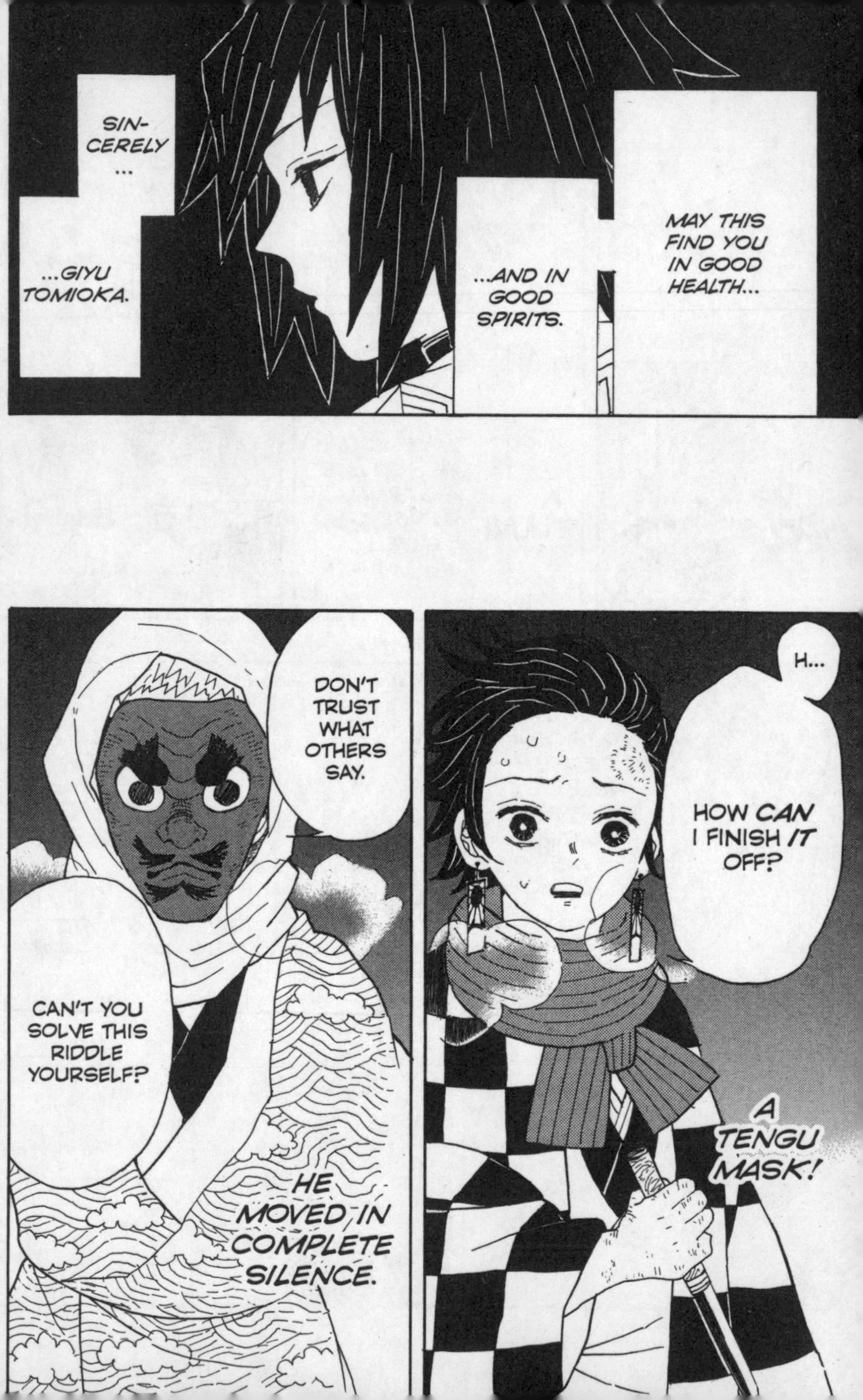
MAY THIS FIND YOU IN GOOD HEALTH...
...AND IN GOOD SPIRITS.
SIN-CERELY ...
...GIYU TOMIOKA.
H...
HOW CAN I FINISH *IT* OFF?
A TENGU MASK!
DON'T TRUST WHAT OTHERS SAY.
CAN'T YOU SOLVE THIS RIDDLE YOURSELF?
HE MOVED IN COMPLETE SILENCE.

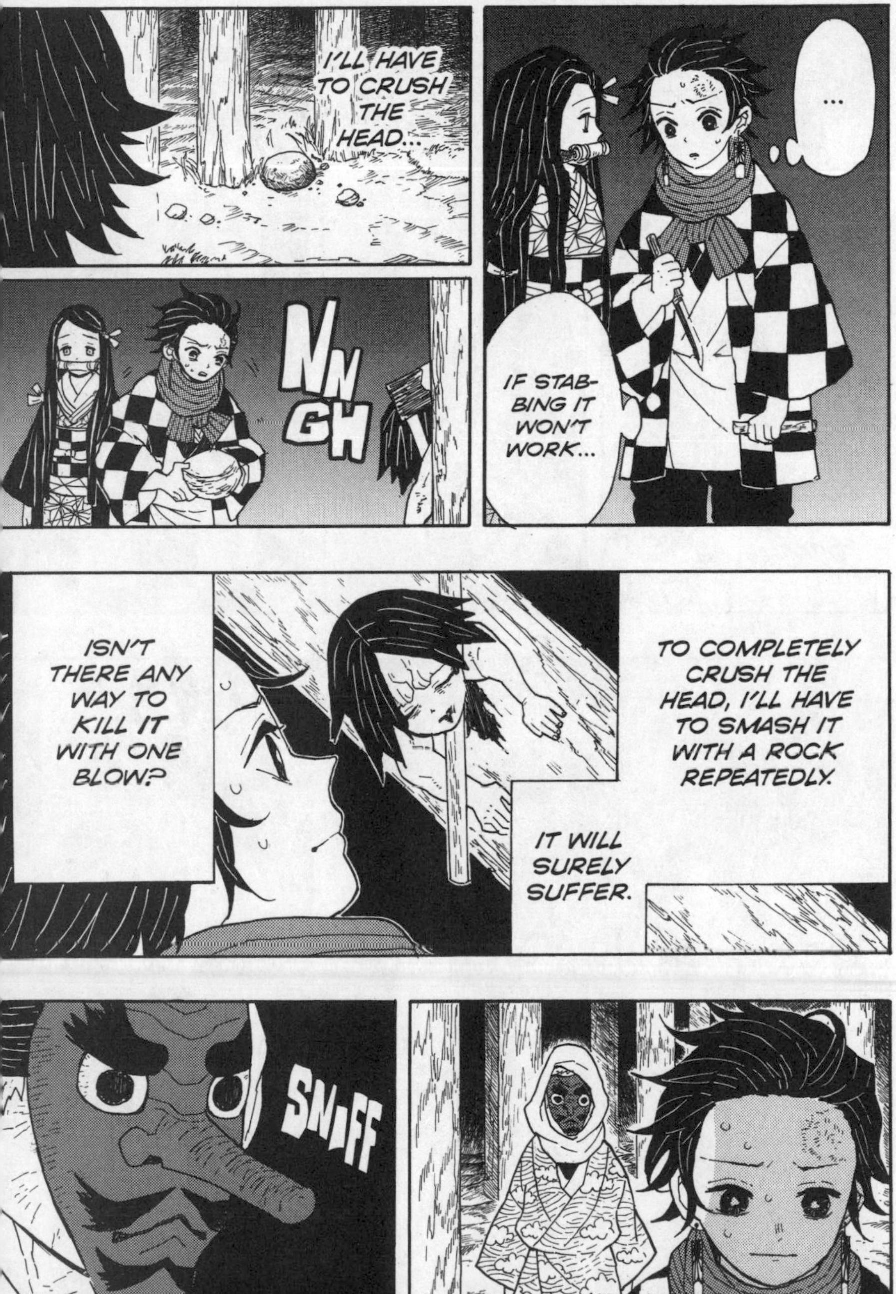
...
IF STAB-BING IT WON'T WORK...
I'LL HAVE TO CRUSH THE HEAD...
NNGH
TO COMPLETELY CRUSH THE HEAD, I'LL HAVE TO SMASH IT WITH A ROCK REPEATEDLY.
IT WILL SURELY SUFFER.
ISN'T THERE ANY WAY TO KILL IT WITH ONE BLOW?
SNIFF

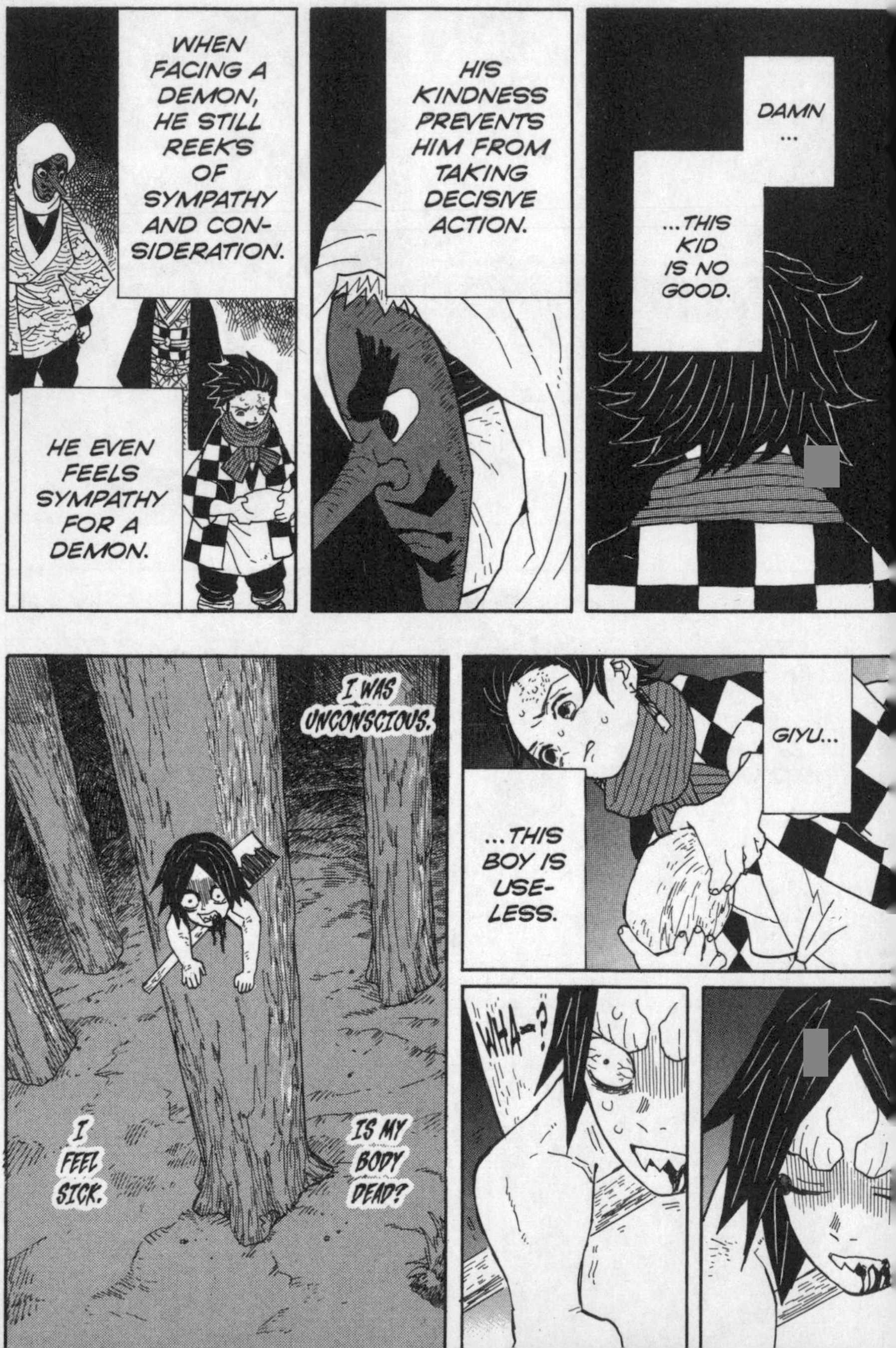
DAMN ...
...THIS KID IS NO GOOD.
HIS KINDNESS PREVENTS HIM FROM TAKING DECISIVE ACTION.
WHEN FACING A DEMON, HE STILL REEKS OF SYMPATHY AND CON-SIDERATION.
HE EVEN FEELS SYMPATHY FOR A DEMON.
GIYU...
...THIS BOY IS USE-LESS.
WHA--?
I WAS UNCONSCIOUS.
IS MY BODY DEAD?
I FEEL SICK.

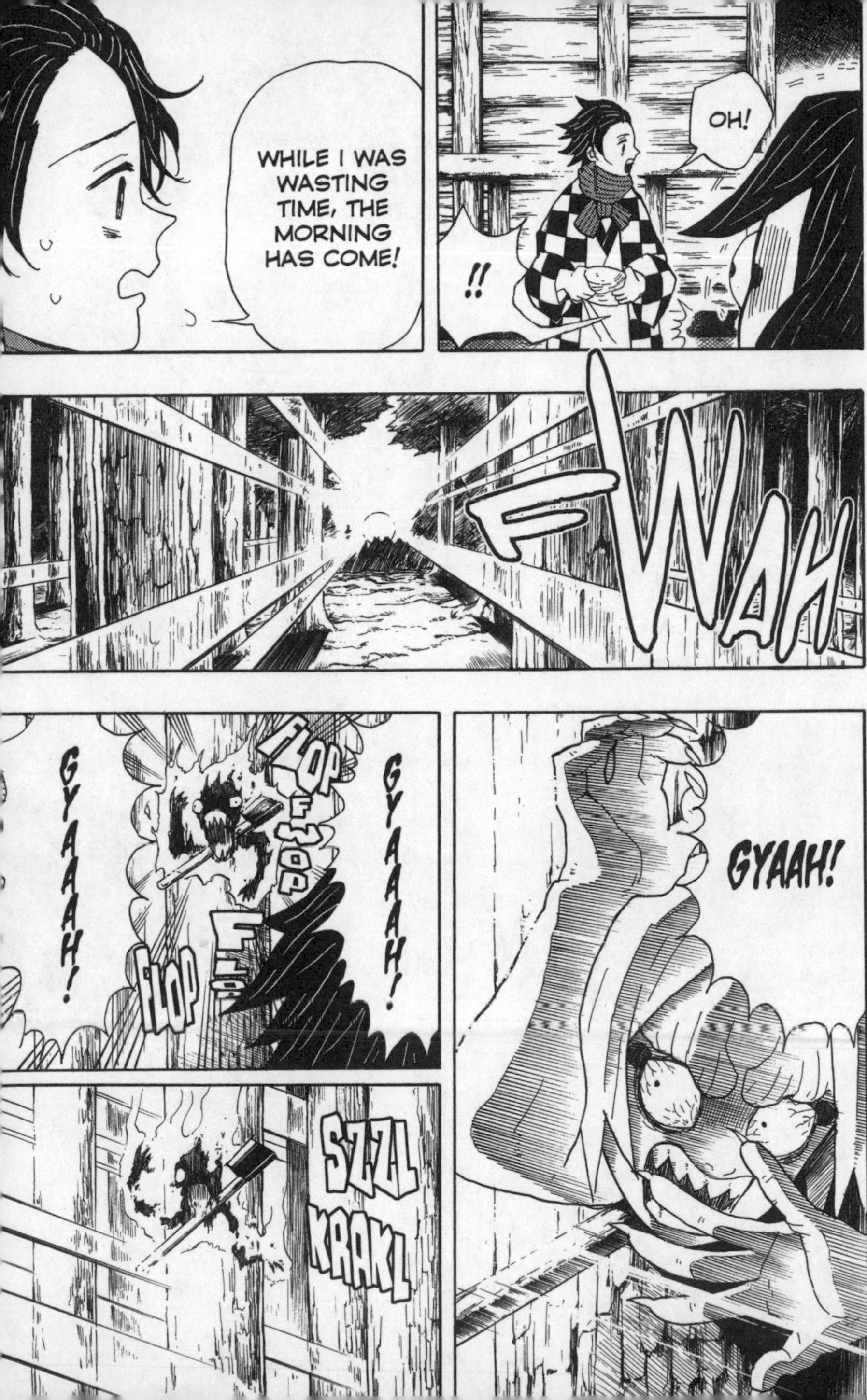
OH!
!!
WHILE I WAS WASTING TIME, THE MORNING HAS COME!
FWAH
GYAAH!
GYAAAAH!
FLOP
FWOP
FLOP
FLOP
GYAAAAH!
SZZL
KRAKL

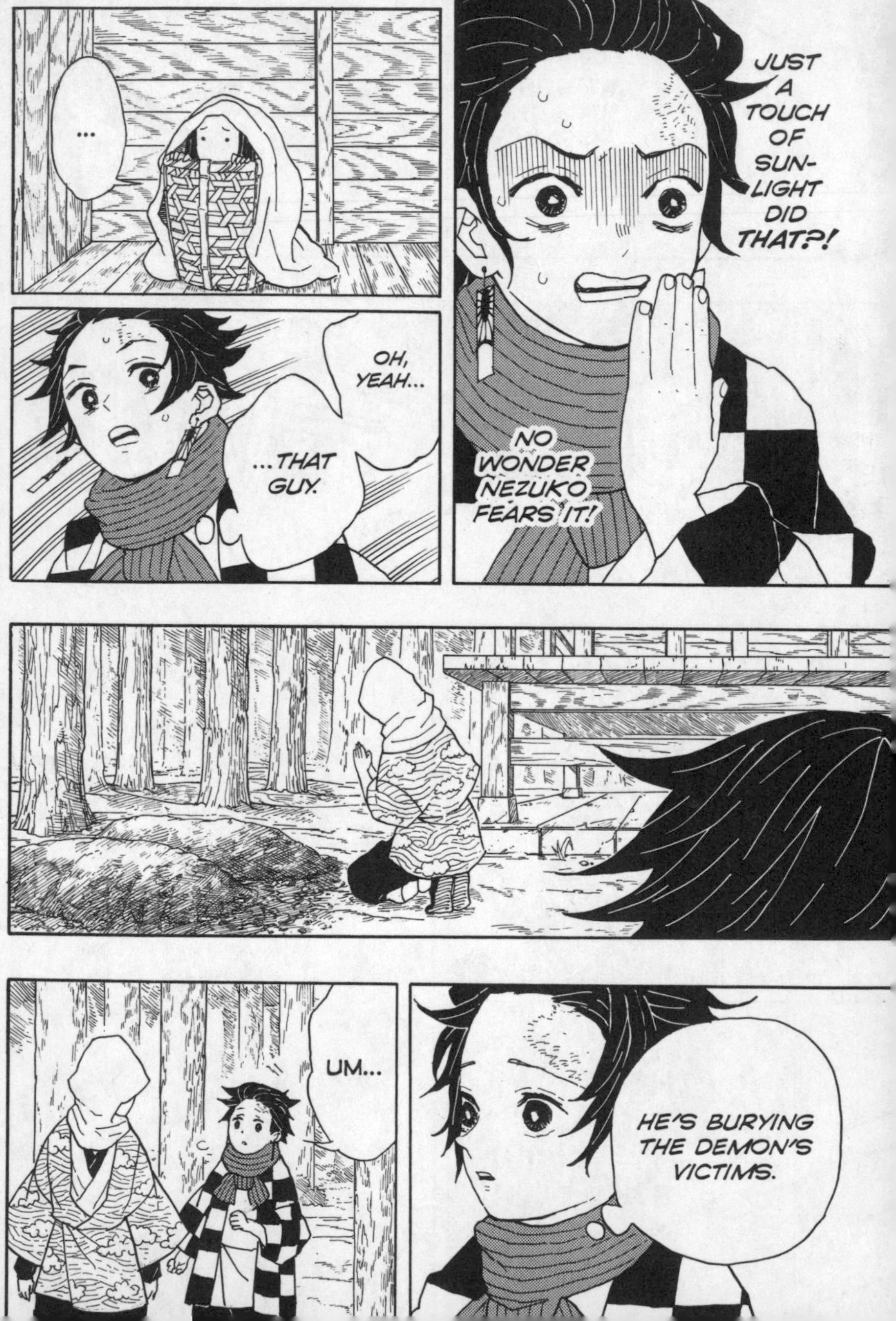
JUST A TOUCH OF SUN-LIGHT DID THAT?!
NO WONDER NEZUKO FEARS IT!
...
OH, YEAH...
...THAT GUY.
HE'S BURYING THE DEMON'S VICTIMS.
UM...

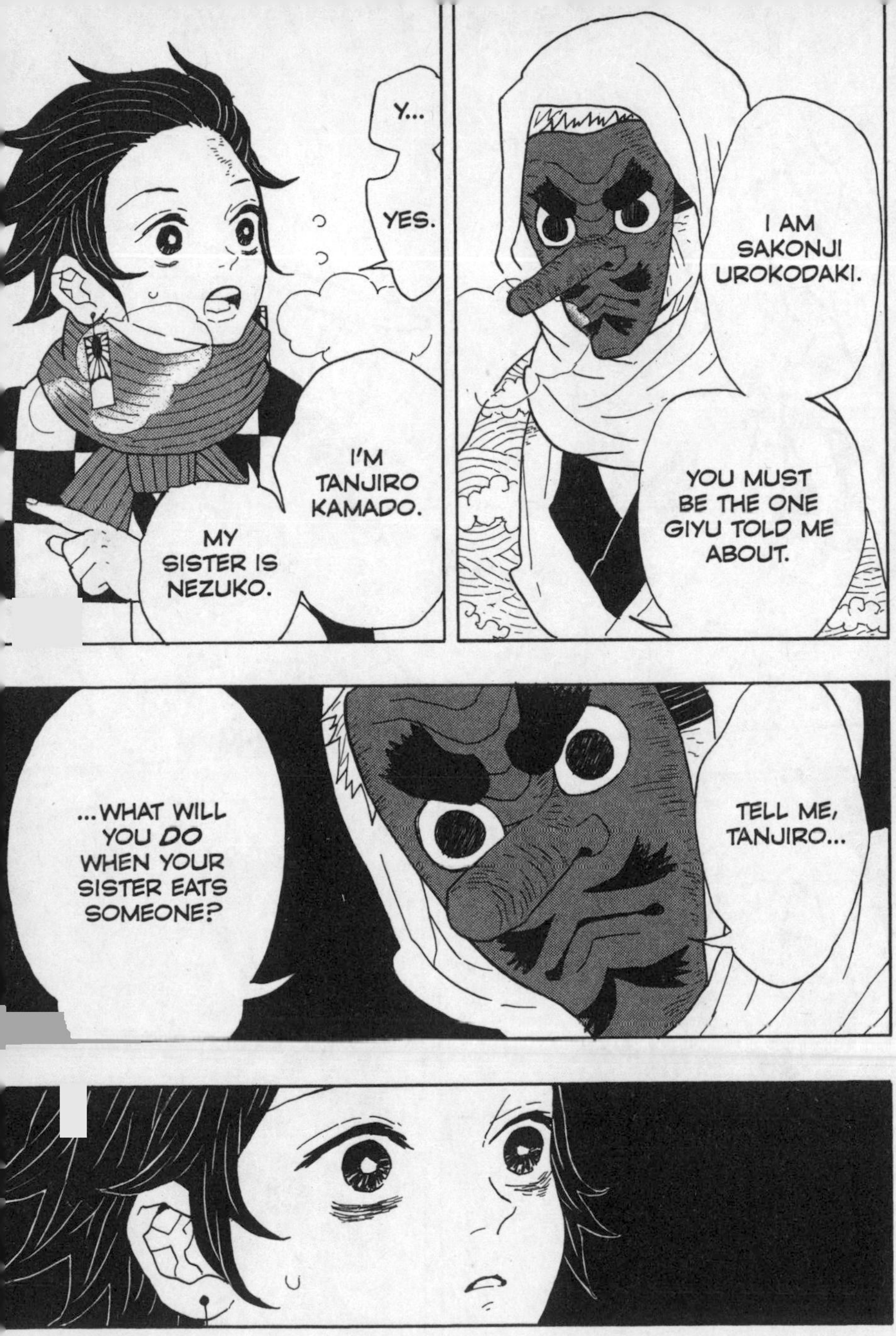
I AM SAKONJI UROKODAKI.
YOU MUST BE THE ONE GIYU TOLD ME ABOUT.
Y...
YES.
I'M TANJIRO KAMADO.
MY SISTER IS NEZUKO.
TELL ME, TANJIRO...
...WHAT WILL YOU *DO* WHEN YOUR SISTER EATS SOMEONE?

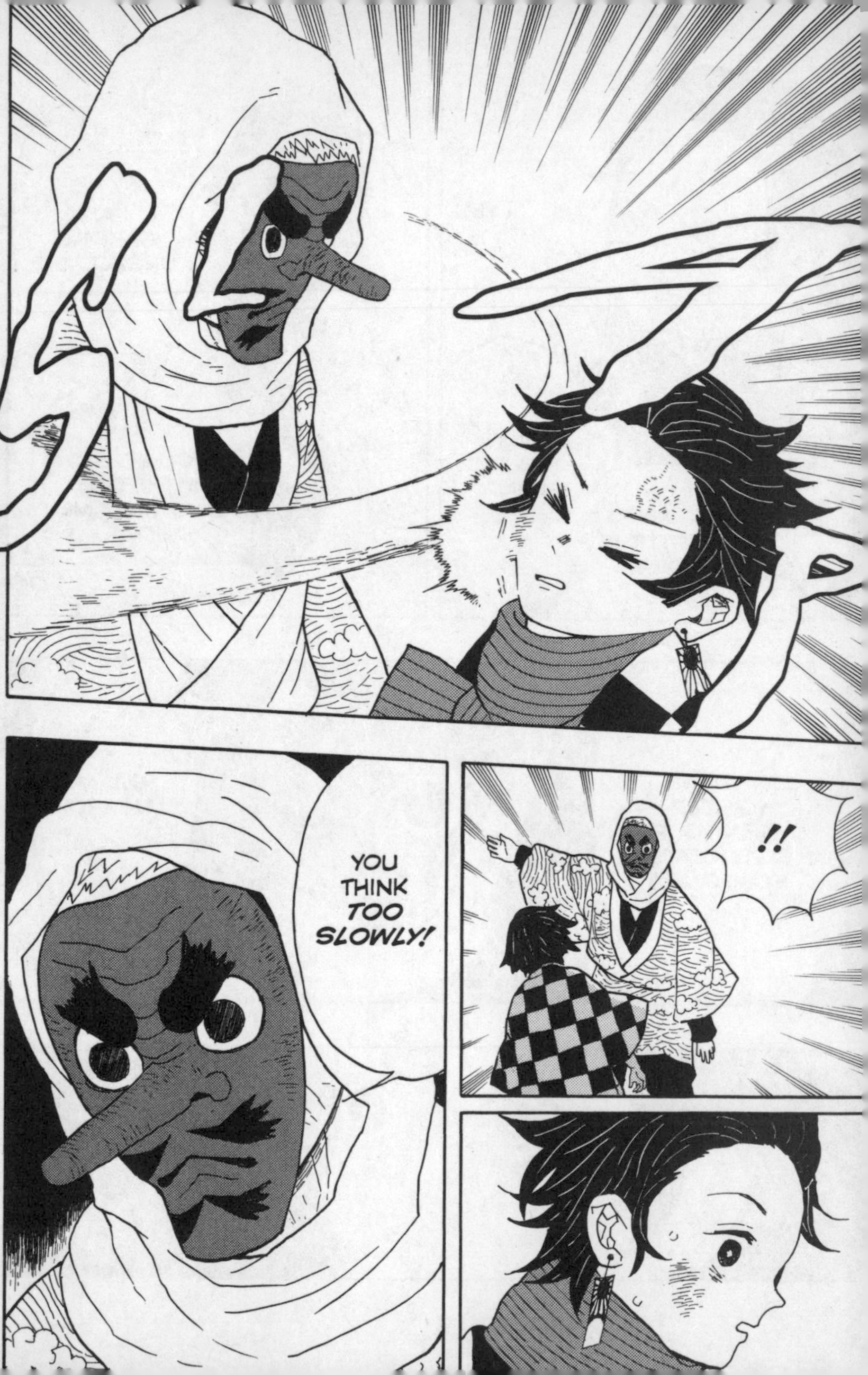
!!
YOU THINK TOO SLOWLY!

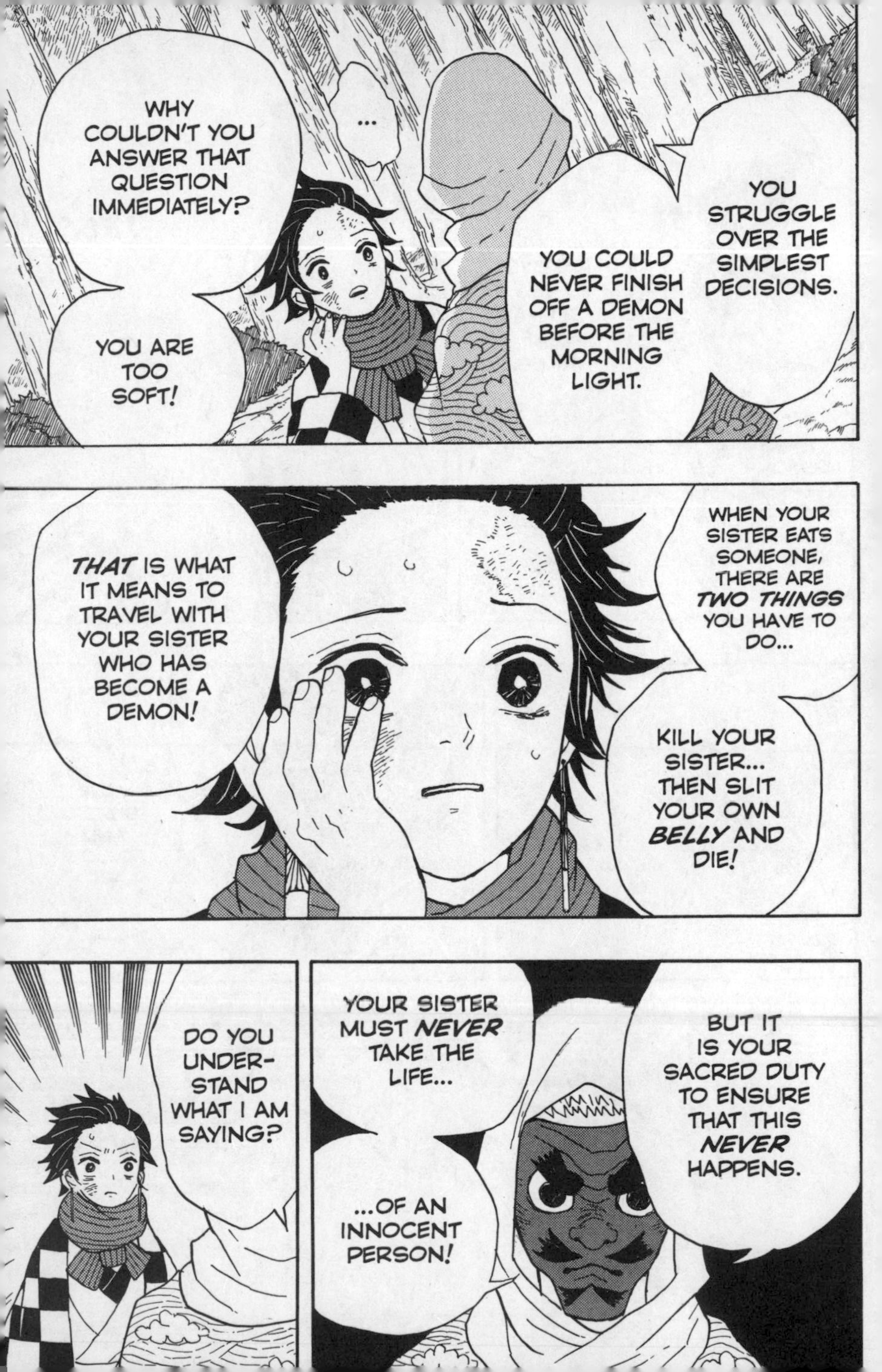
YOU STRUGGLE OVER THE SIMPLEST DECISIONS.
YOU COULD NEVER FINISH OFF A DEMON BEFORE THE MORNING LIGHT.
...
WHY COULDN'T YOU ANSWER THAT QUESTION IMMEDIATELY?
YOU ARE TOO SOFT!
WHEN YOUR SISTER EATS SOMEONE, THERE ARE *TWO THINGS* YOU HAVE TO DO...
KILL YOUR SISTER... THEN SLIT YOUR OWN *BELLY* AND DIE!
THAT IS WHAT IT MEANS TO TRAVEL WITH YOUR SISTER WHO HAS BECOME A DEMON!
YOUR SISTER MUST *NEVER* TAKE THE LIFE...
...OF AN INNOCENT PERSON!
BUT IT IS YOUR SACRED DUTY TO ENSURE THAT THIS *NEVER* HAPPENS.
DO YOU UNDER-STAND WHAT I AM SAYING?

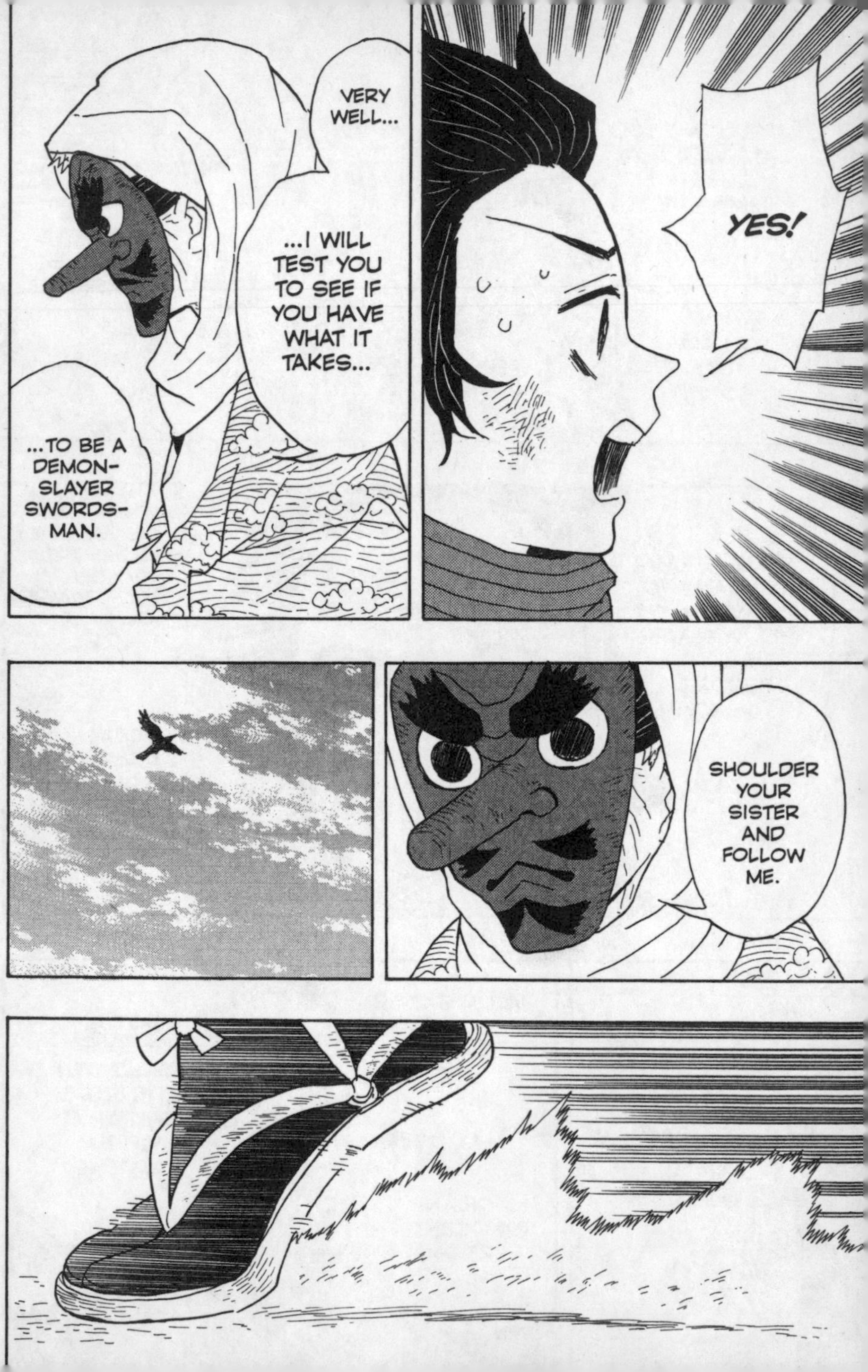
YES!
VERY WELL...
...I WILL TEST YOU TO SEE IF YOU HAVE WHAT IT TAKES...
...TO BE A DEMON-SLAYER SWORDS-MAN.
SHOULDER YOUR SISTER AND FOLLOW ME.

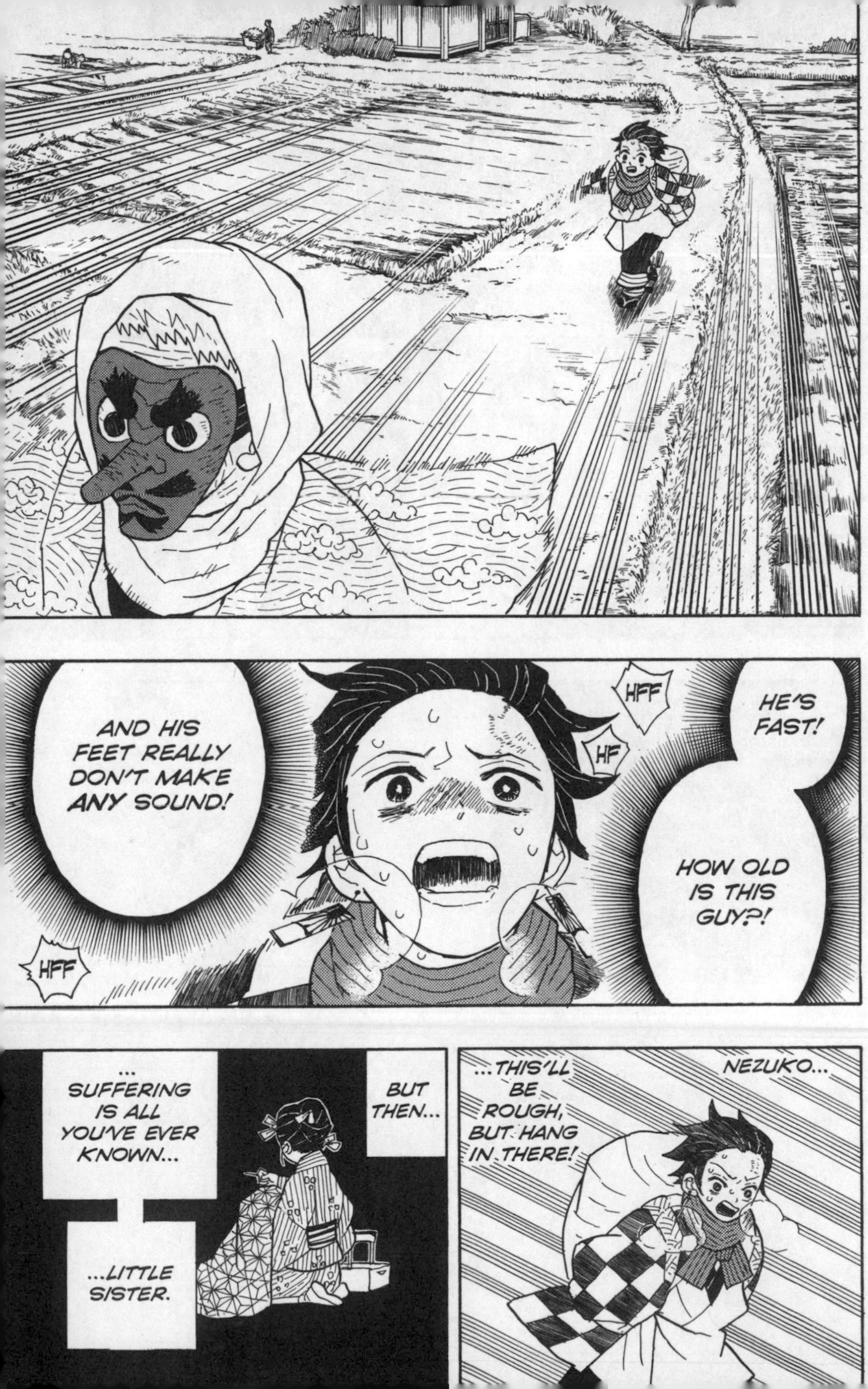
HE'S FAST!
HOW OLD IS THIS GUY?!
HFF
HF
AND HIS FEET REALLY DON'T MAKE ANY SOUND!
HFF
NEZUKO...
...THIS'LL BE ROUGH, BUT HANG IN THERE!
BUT THEN...
...SUFFERING IS ALL YOU'VE EVER KNOWN...
...LITTLE SISTER.

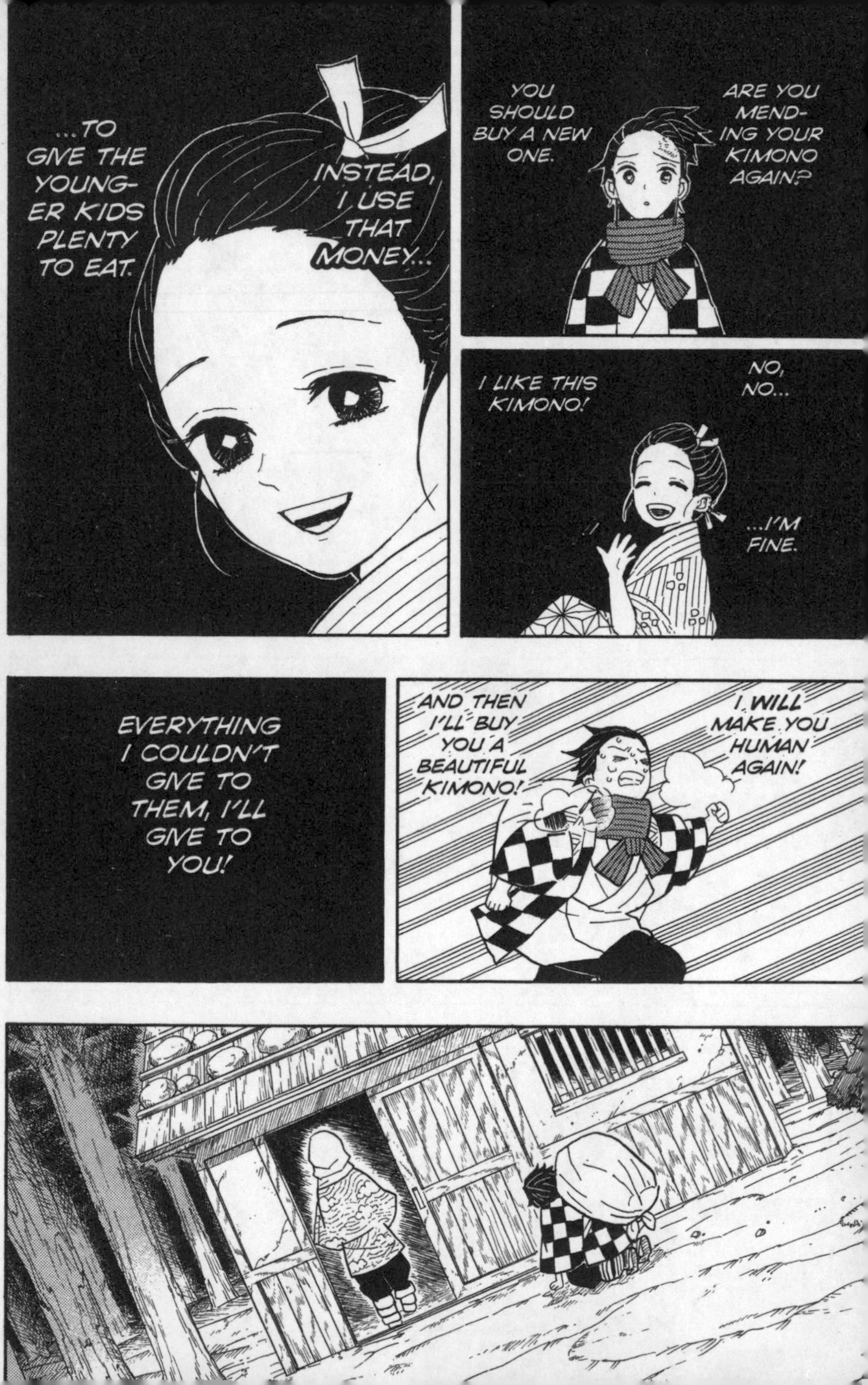
ARE YOU MEND-ING YOUR KIMONO AGAIN?
YOU SHOULD BUY A NEW ONE.
NO, NO...
I LIKE THIS KIMONO!
...I'M FINE.
INSTEAD, I USE THAT MONEY...
...TO GIVE THE YOUNG-ER KIDS PLENTY TO EAT.
I WILL MAKE YOU HUMAN AGAIN!
AND THEN I'LL BUY YOU A BEAUTIFUL KIMONO!
EVERYTHING I COULDN'T GIVE TO THEM, I'LL GIVE TO YOU!

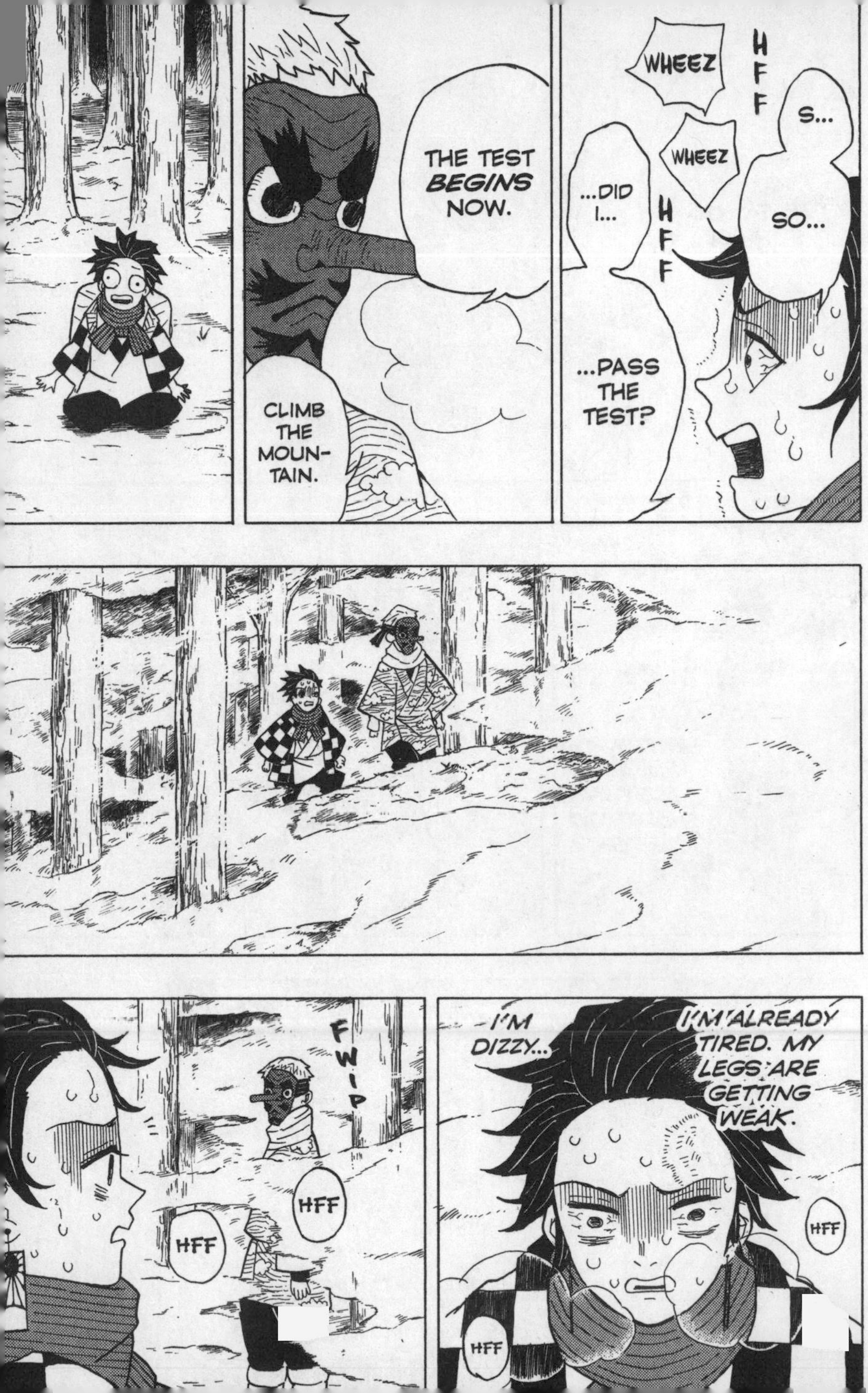
S...
WHEEZ
HFF
WHEEZ
SO...
...DID I...
HFF
...PASS THE TEST?
THE TEST BEGINS NOW.
CLIMB THE MOUNTAIN.
I'M ALREADY TIRED. MY LEGS ARE GETTING WEAK.
I'M DIZZY...
HFF
HFF
FWIP
HFF
HFF

THIS TIME, I WILL NOT WAIT UNTIL SUNRISE.

NOW YOU MUST DESCEND TO THE HOUSE AT THE FOOT OF THE MOUNTAIN.

HFF

HFF

OH, I GET IT.

HE THINKS I'LL GET LOST IN THIS THICK FOG.

IS THAT ALL?

HFF

HFF

HASH

HUH?

I'VE ALREADY MEMORIZED UROKODAKI'S SCENT.

THAT'S EASY! I HAVE A SHARP NOSE!

I JUST HAVE TO GET BACK BEFORE SUNRISE.

HFF

HFF

HFF

I GET IT!

A COVERED PIT!

WSH

UH-OH! HERE WE GO AGAIN!

THESE ARE ALL TRAPS.

THAT'S THE CHALLENGE!

MMPH

THWOK

I'M IN BIG TROUBLE.

HFF

HFF

WHUD

AND I JUST NOTICED... UP ON THIS MOUNTAIN...

IF I KEEP SETTING OFF EVERY TRAP, I WON'T GET DOWN THE MOUNTAIN BY MORNING.

HFF HFF HFF

IT'S MUCH WORSE THAN THE MOUNTAIN WE LIVED ON!

...THE AIR'S SO THIN I CAN BARELY BREATHE!

HFF

HFF

CONTROL YOUR BREATHING. SNIFF OUT THE TRAPS.

I FEEL LIKE I MIGHT PASS OUT!

NO! I'VE GOTTA GET BACK!

THAT'S WHY I FEEL SO TIRED AND DIZZY.

YES! I CAN SMELL THEM!

TRAPS HAVE TO BE SET BY SOMEONE, AND THOSE SCENTS MUST LINGER.

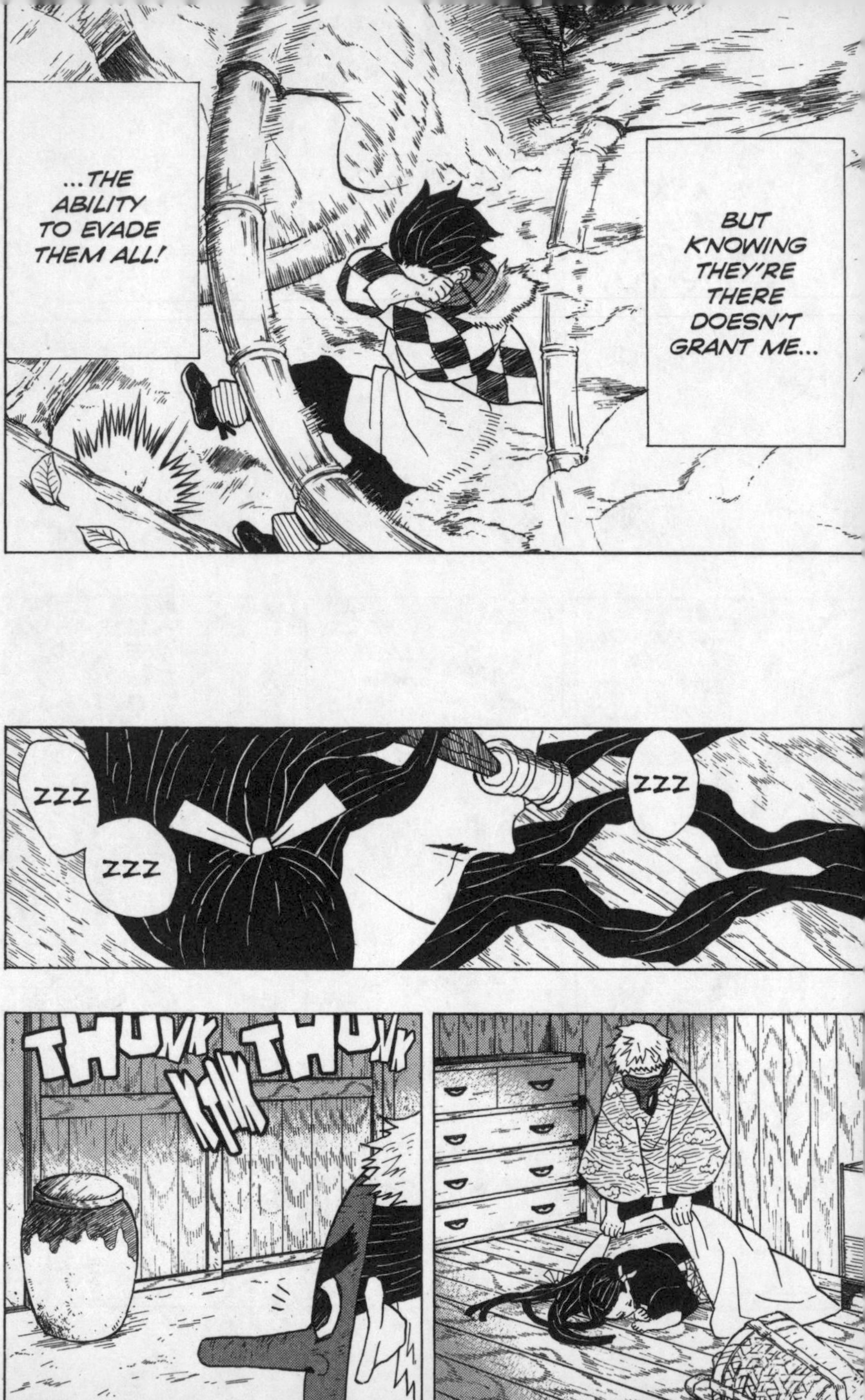
BUT KNOWING THEY'RE THERE DOESN'T GRANT ME...
...THE ABILITY TO EVADE THEM ALL!
ZZZ
ZZZ
ZZZ
THUNK
THUNK
KTNK

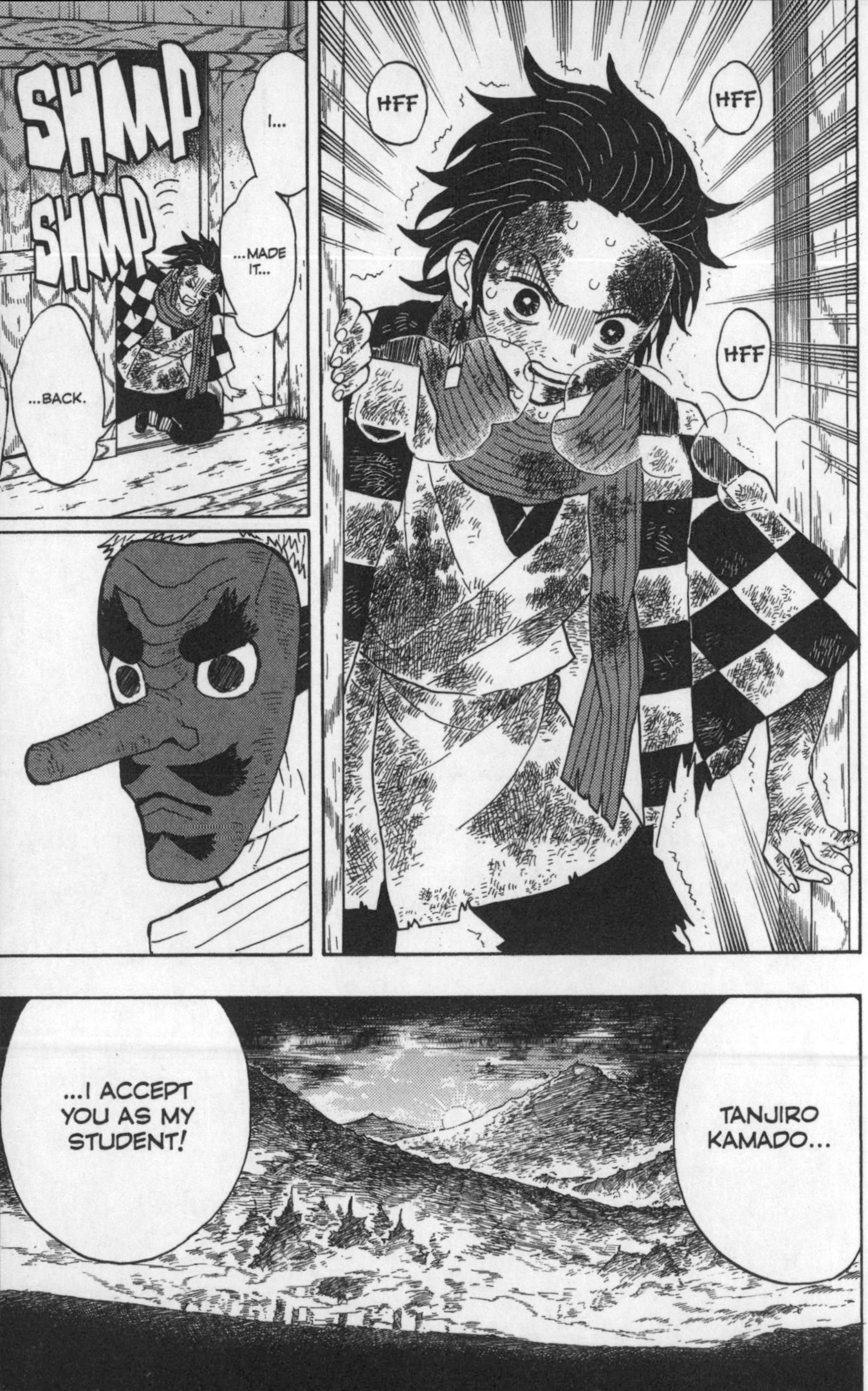
HFF
HFF
HFF
SHMP
SHMP
I...
...MADE IT...
...BACK.
TANJIRO KAMADO...
...I ACCEPT YOU AS MY STUDENT!

Taisho Whispers
& Rumors

○ 鬼滅奇譚 (Mysterious Story of the Demon Slayer)
(Kimetsu Kitan)

○ 鬼鬼滅滅 (Demon Demon Slayer Slayer)
(Kikimetsumetsu)

○ 悪鬼滅々 (Evil Demon Slayer)
(Akkimetsumetsu)

○ 鬼殺の刃 (Sword of the Demon Killer)
(Kisatsu no Yaiba)

○ 滅々鬼譚 (Strange Tale of the Demon Slayer)
(Metsumetsu Kitan)

○ 鬼殺譚 (Tale of the Demon Killer)
(Kisatsutan)

○ 空想鬼滅奇譚 (The Fantastic Strange Tale of the Demon Slayer)
(Kuso Kimetsu Kitan)

○ 鬼狩りカグツチ (Demon Hunting God of Fire)
(Onigari Kagutsuchi)

○ 炭のカグツチ (Charred God of Fire)
(Sumi no Kagutsuchi)

* "Kitan" means an unusual and myste-rious story.

* "Kagutsuchi" is a god of fire.

Hello, I'm Gotoge.

I hear these titles were under consideration.

Which one do you like?

CHAPTER 4: TANJIRO'S JOURNAL, PART 1

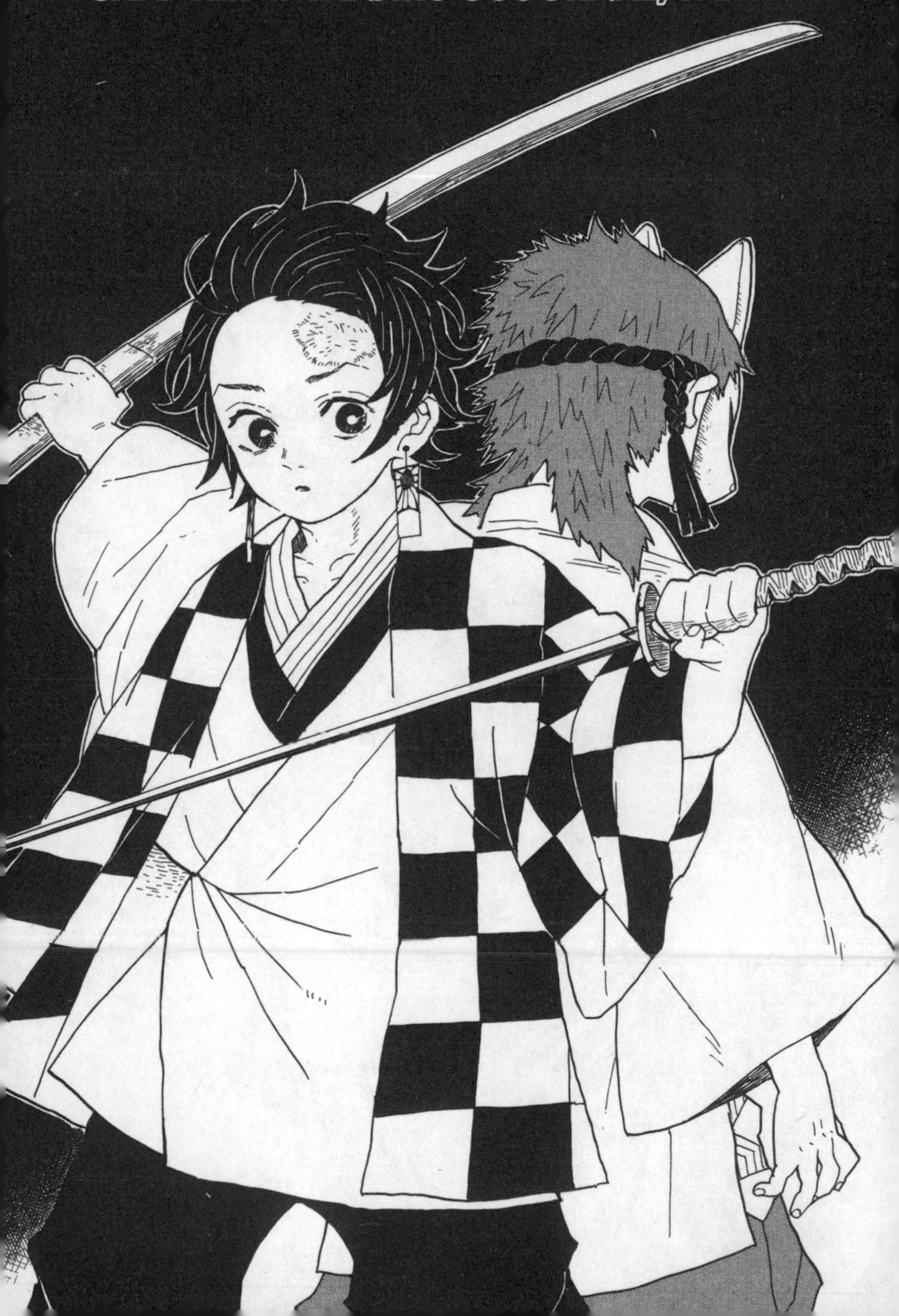

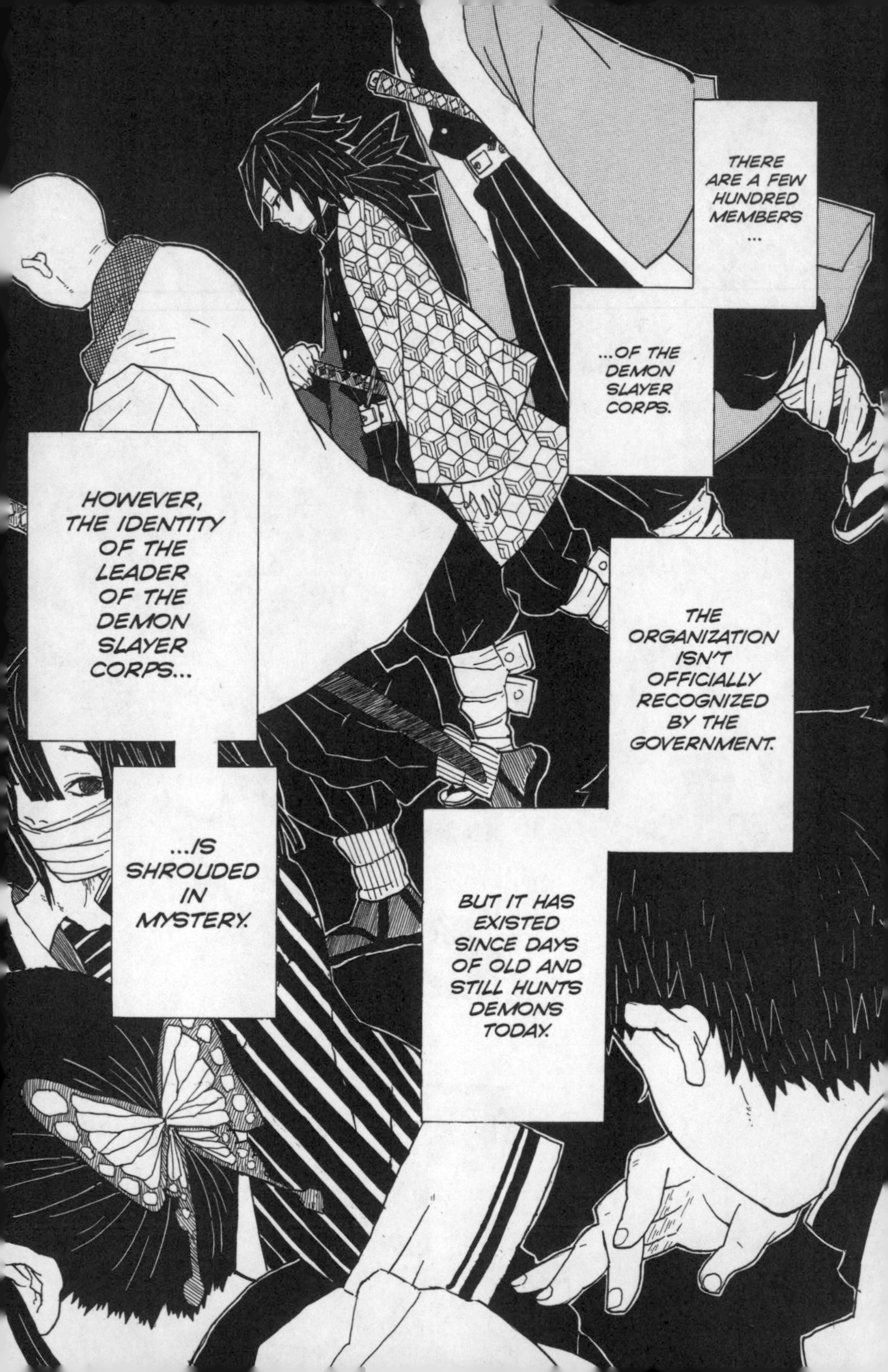
THERE ARE A FEW HUNDRED MEMBERS ...
...OF THE DEMON SLAYER CORPS.
THE ORGANIZATION ISN'T OFFICIALLY RECOGNIZED BY THE GOVERNMENT.
BUT IT HAS EXISTED SINCE DAYS OF OLD AND STILL HUNTS DEMONS TODAY.
HOWEVER, THE IDENTITY OF THE LEADER OF THE DEMON SLAYER CORPS...
...IS SHROUDED IN MYSTERY.

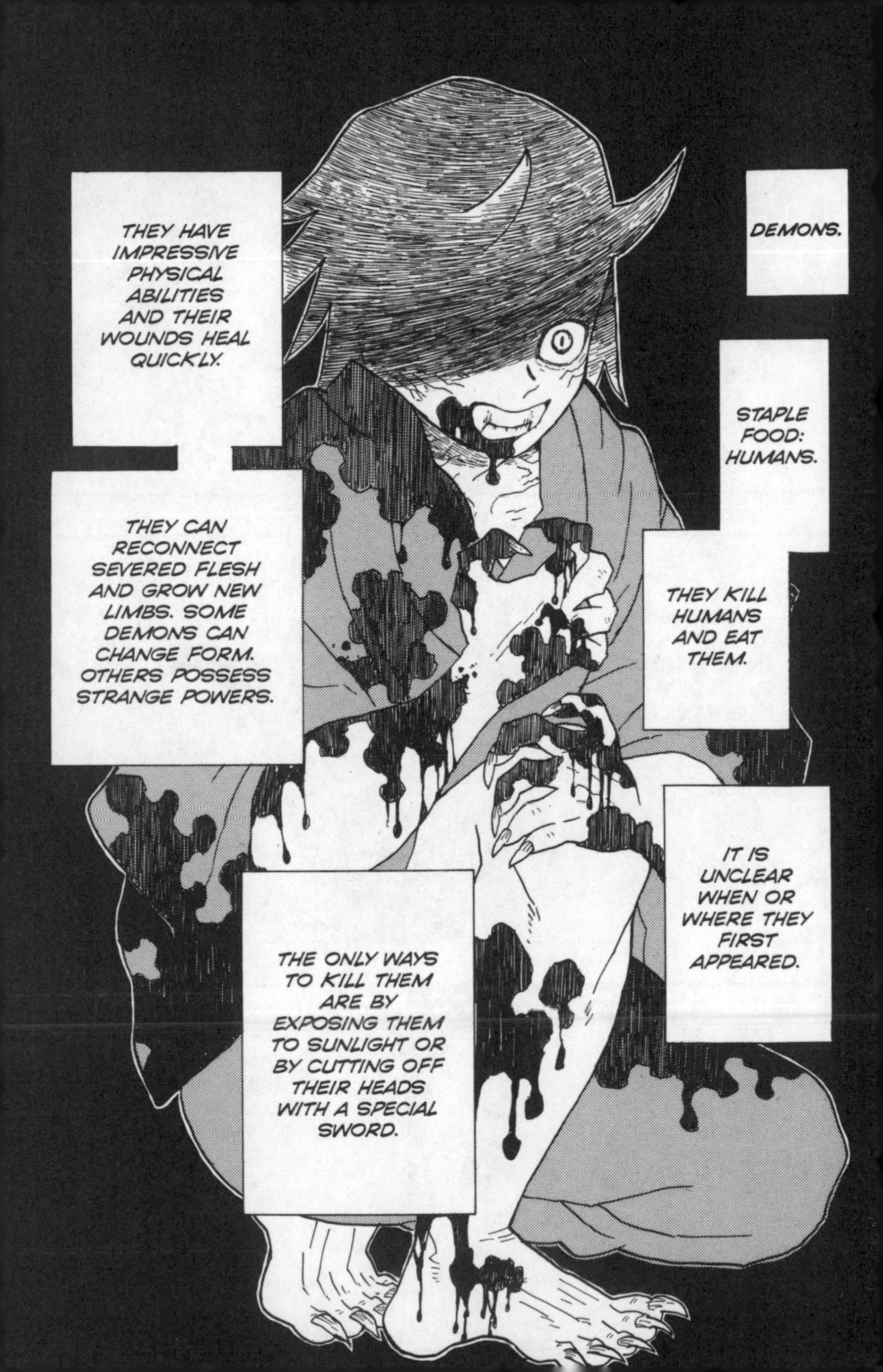
DEMONS.
STAPLE FOOD: HUMANS.
THEY KILL HUMANS AND EAT THEM.
THEY HAVE IMPRESSIVE PHYSICAL ABILITIES AND THEIR WOUNDS HEAL QUICKLY.
THEY CAN RECONNECT SEVERED FLESH AND GROW NEW LIMBS. SOME DEMONS CAN CHANGE FORM. OTHERS POSSESS STRANGE POWERS.
IT IS UNCLEAR WHEN OR WHERE THEY FIRST APPEARED.
THE ONLY WAYS TO KILL THEM ARE BY EXPOSING THEM TO SUNLIGHT OR BY CUTTING OFF THEIR HEADS WITH A SPECIAL SWORD.

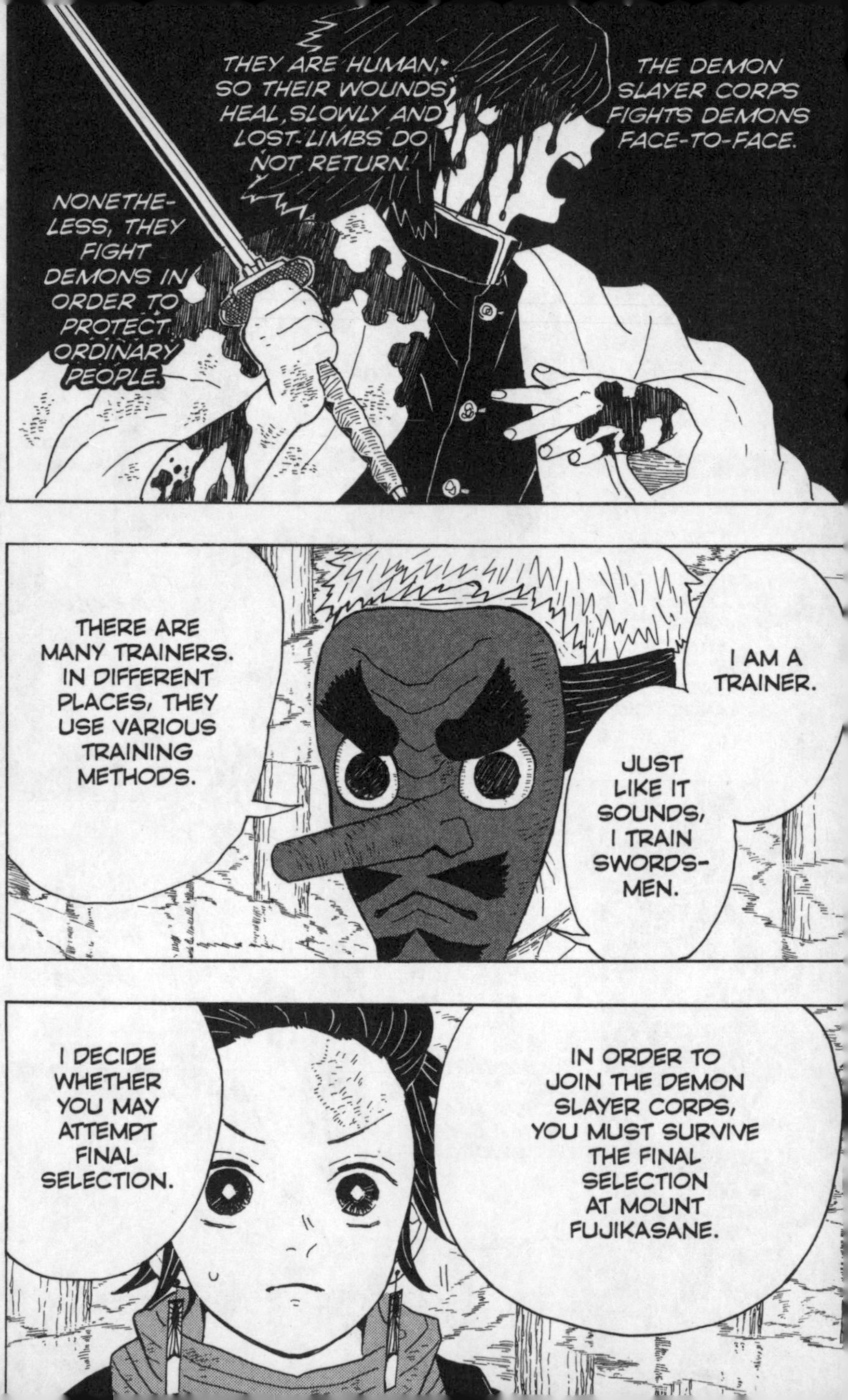
THE DEMON SLAYER CORPS FIGHTS DEMONS FACE-TO-FACE.
THEY ARE HUMAN, SO THEIR WOUNDS HEAL SLOWLY AND LOST LIMBS DO NOT RETURN.
NONETHELESS, THEY FIGHT DEMONS IN ORDER TO PROTECT ORDINARY PEOPLE.
I AM A TRAINER.
JUST LIKE IT SOUNDS, I TRAIN SWORDSMEN.
THERE ARE MANY TRAINERS. IN DIFFERENT PLACES, THEY USE VARIOUS TRAINING METHODS.
IN ORDER TO JOIN THE DEMON SLAYER CORPS, YOU MUST SURVIVE THE FINAL SELECTION AT MOUNT FUJIKASANE.
I DECIDE WHETHER YOU MAY ATTEMPT FINAL SELECTION.

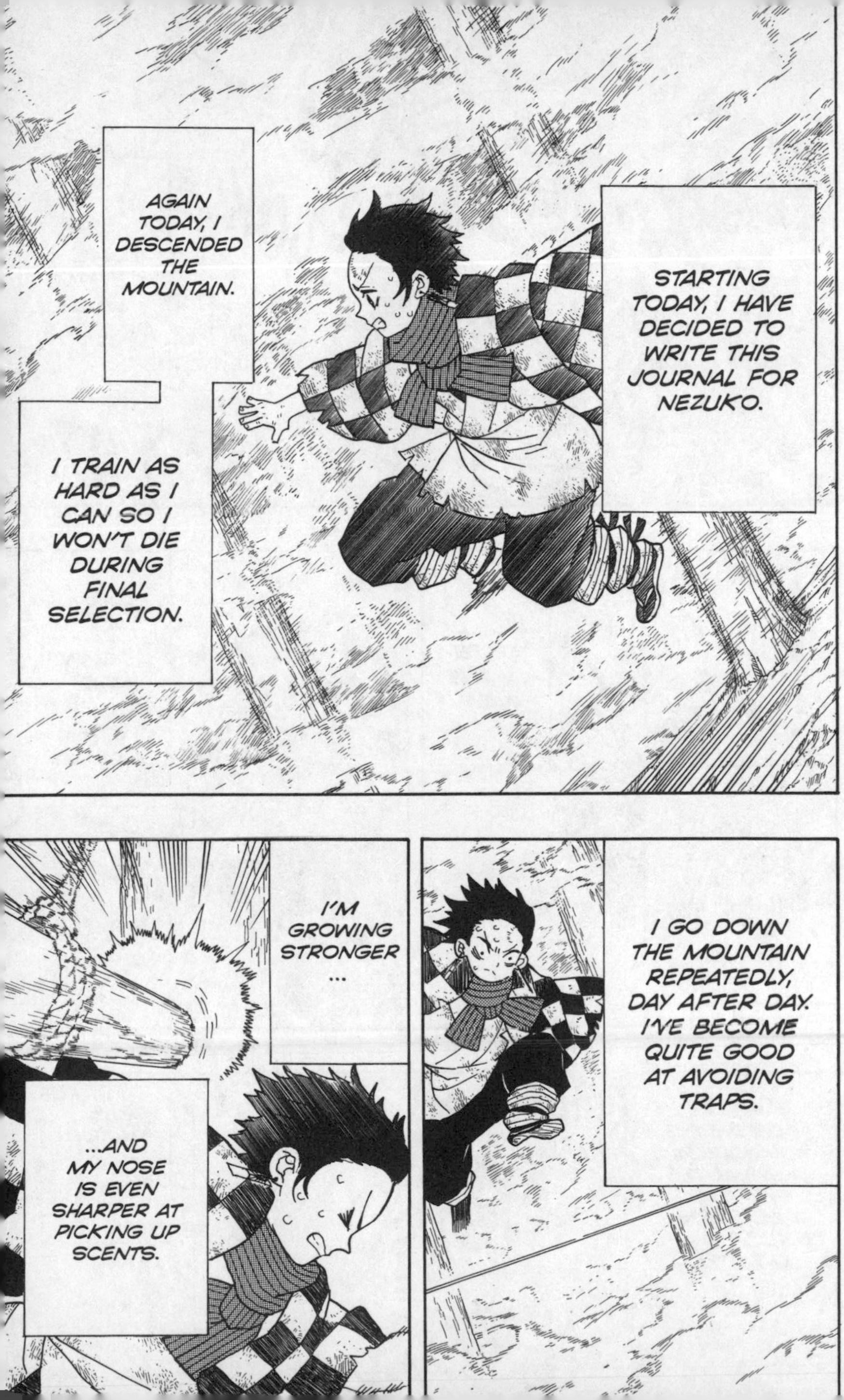
STARTING TODAY, I HAVE DECIDED TO WRITE THIS JOURNAL FOR NEZUKO.
AGAIN TODAY, I DESCENDED THE MOUNTAIN.
I TRAIN AS HARD AS I CAN SO I WON'T DIE DURING FINAL SELECTION.
I GO DOWN THE MOUNTAIN REPEATEDLY, DAY AFTER DAY. I'VE BECOME QUITE GOOD AT AVOIDING TRAPS.
I'M GROWING STRONGER ...
...AND MY NOSE IS EVEN SHARPER AT PICKING UP SCENTS.

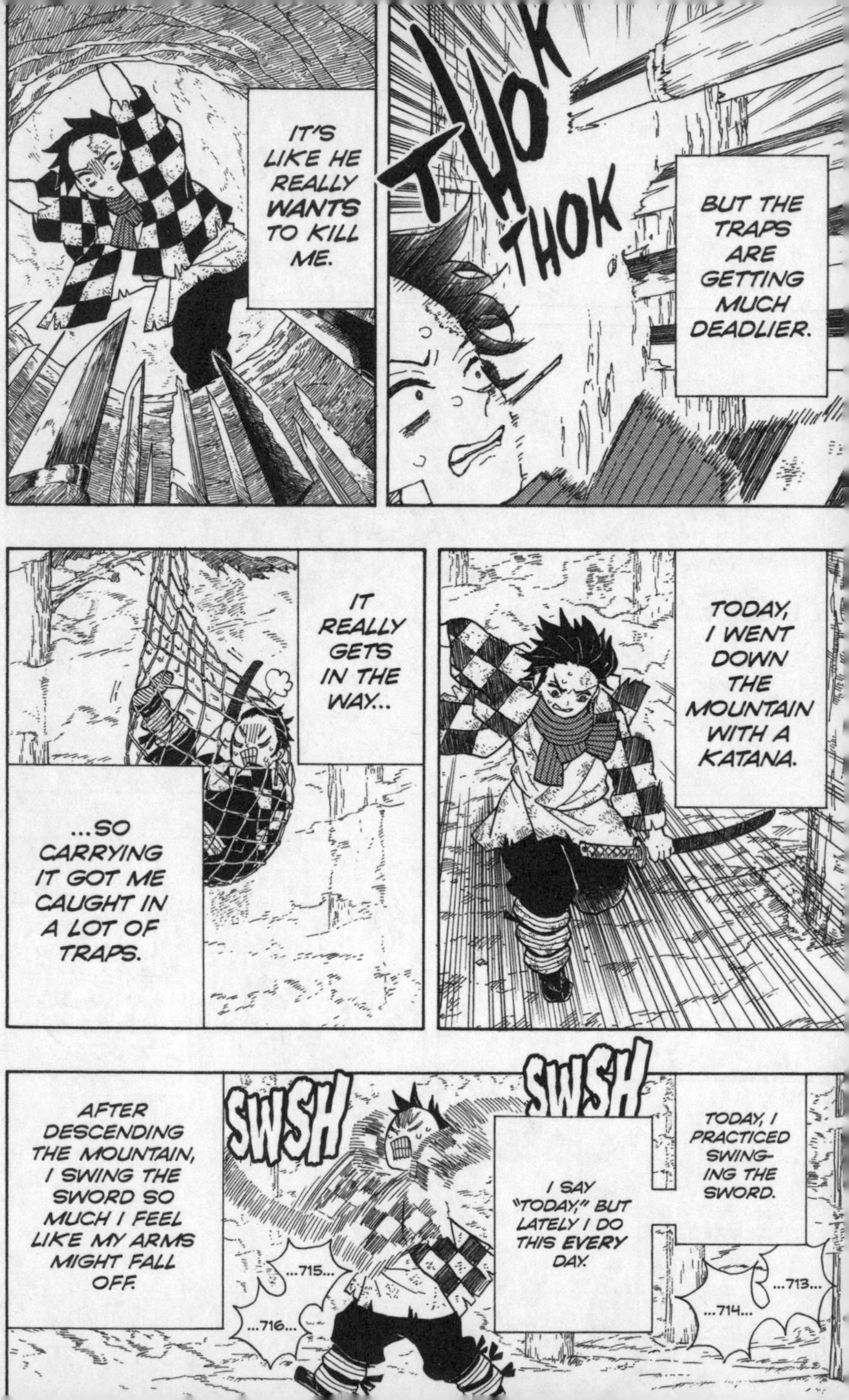
THOK
THOK
BUT THE TRAPS ARE GETTING MUCH DEADLIER.
IT'S LIKE HE REALLY WANTS TO KILL ME.
TODAY, I WENT DOWN THE MOUNTAIN WITH A KATANA.
IT REALLY GETS IN THE WAY...
...SO CARRYING IT GOT ME CAUGHT IN A LOT OF TRAPS.
TODAY, I PRACTICED SWING-ING THE SWORD.
...713...
...714...
SWSH
I SAY "TODAY," BUT LATELY I DO THIS EVERY DAY.
...715...
...716...
SWSH
AFTER DESCENDING THE MOUNTAIN, I SWING THE SWORD SO MUCH I FEEL LIKE MY ARMS MIGHT FALL OFF.

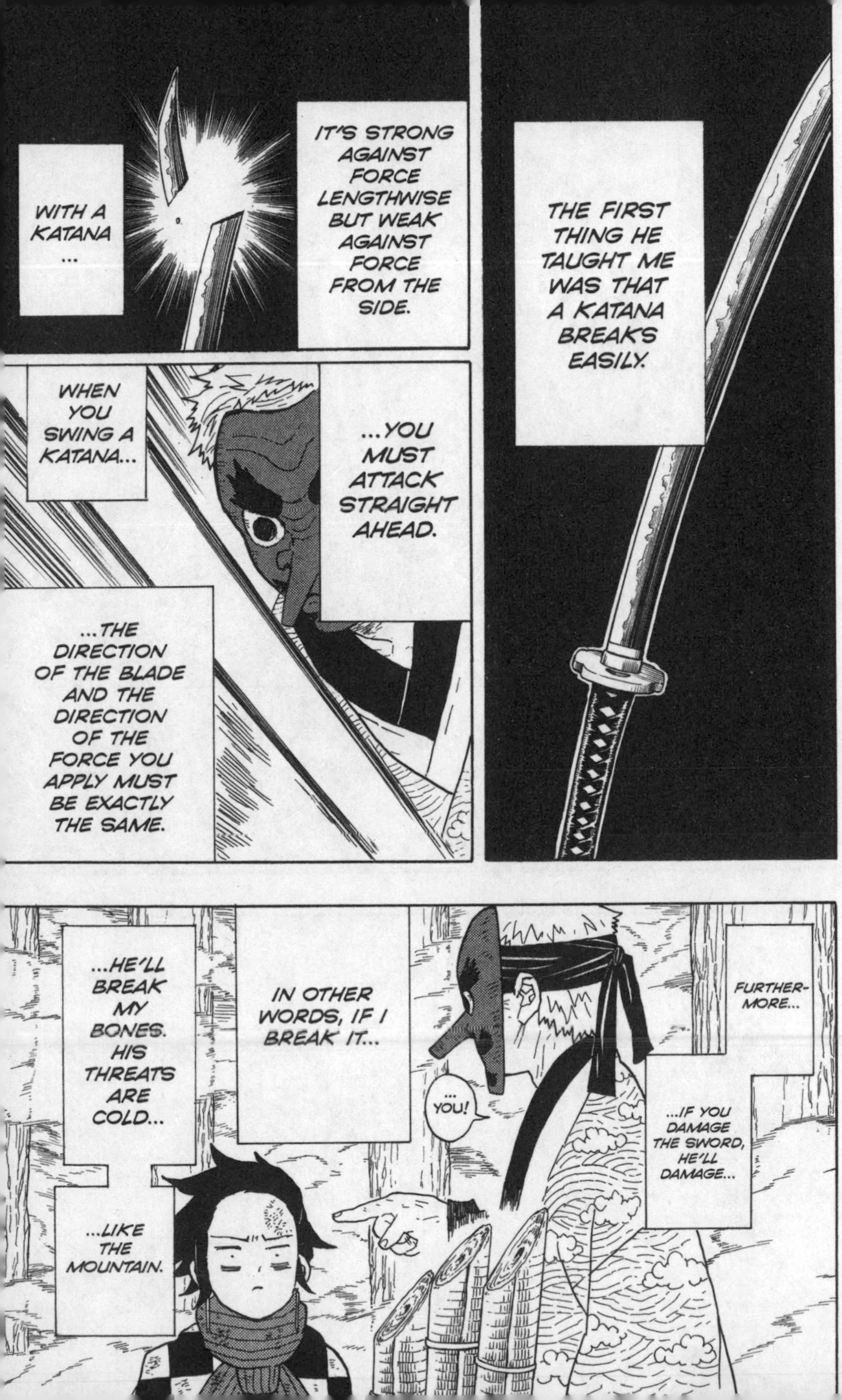
THE FIRST THING HE TAUGHT ME WAS THAT A KATANA BREAKS EASILY.
WITH A KATANA ...
IT'S STRONG AGAINST FORCE LENGTHWISE BUT WEAK AGAINST FORCE FROM THE SIDE.
WHEN YOU SWING A KATANA...
...YOU MUST ATTACK STRAIGHT AHEAD.
...THE DIRECTION OF THE BLADE AND THE DIRECTION OF THE FORCE YOU APPLY MUST BE EXACTLY THE SAME.
FURTHER-MORE...
...IF YOU DAMAGE THE SWORD, HE'LL DAMAGE...
...YOU!
IN OTHER WORDS, IF I BREAK IT...
...HE'LL BREAK MY BONES. HIS THREATS ARE COLD...
...LIKE THE MOUNTAIN.

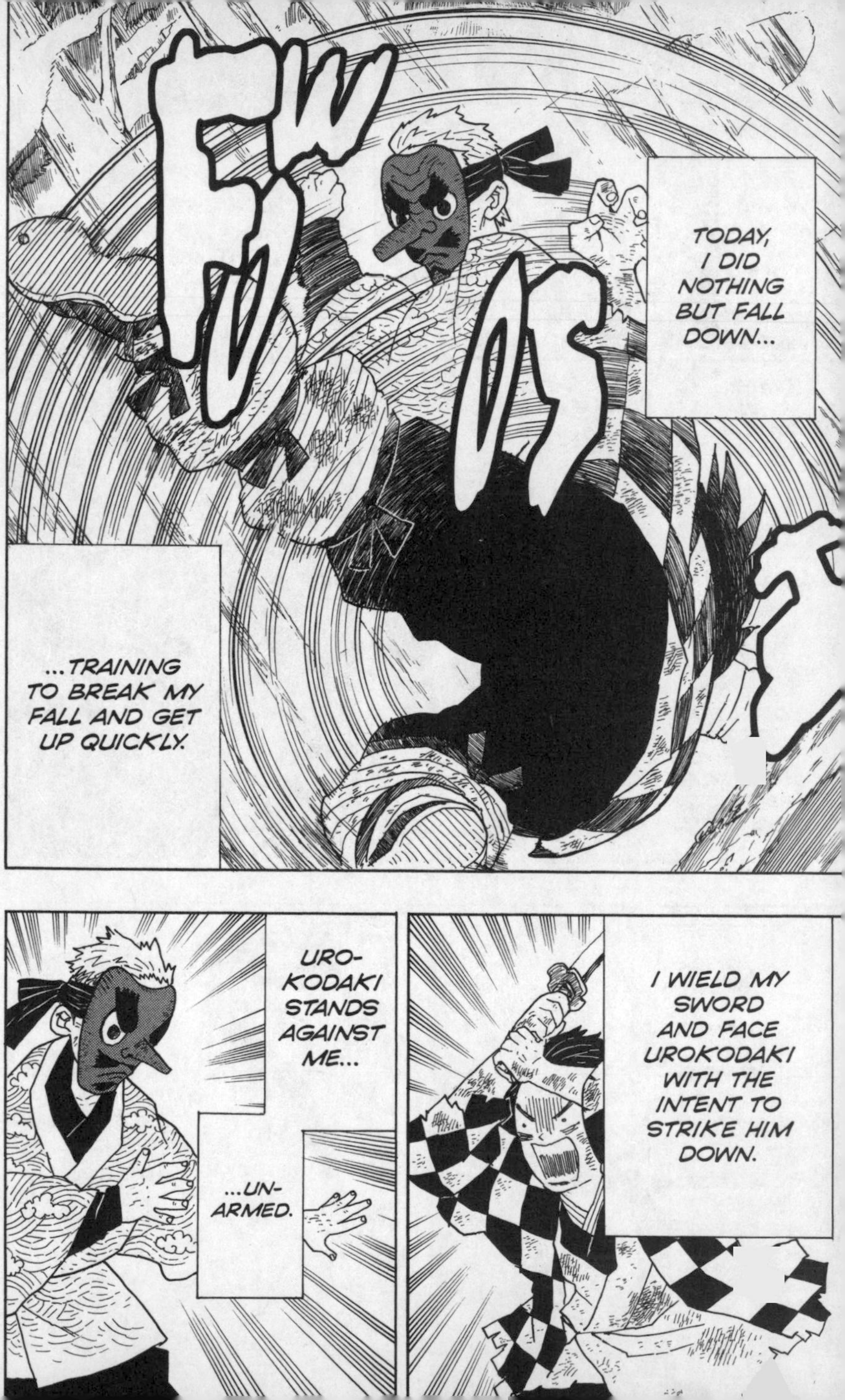
TODAY, I DID NOTHING BUT FALL DOWN...
...TRAINING TO BREAK MY FALL AND GET UP QUICKLY.
I WIELD MY SWORD AND FACE UROKODAKI WITH THE INTENT TO STRIKE HIM DOWN.
URO-KODAKI STANDS AGAINST ME...
...UN-ARMED.

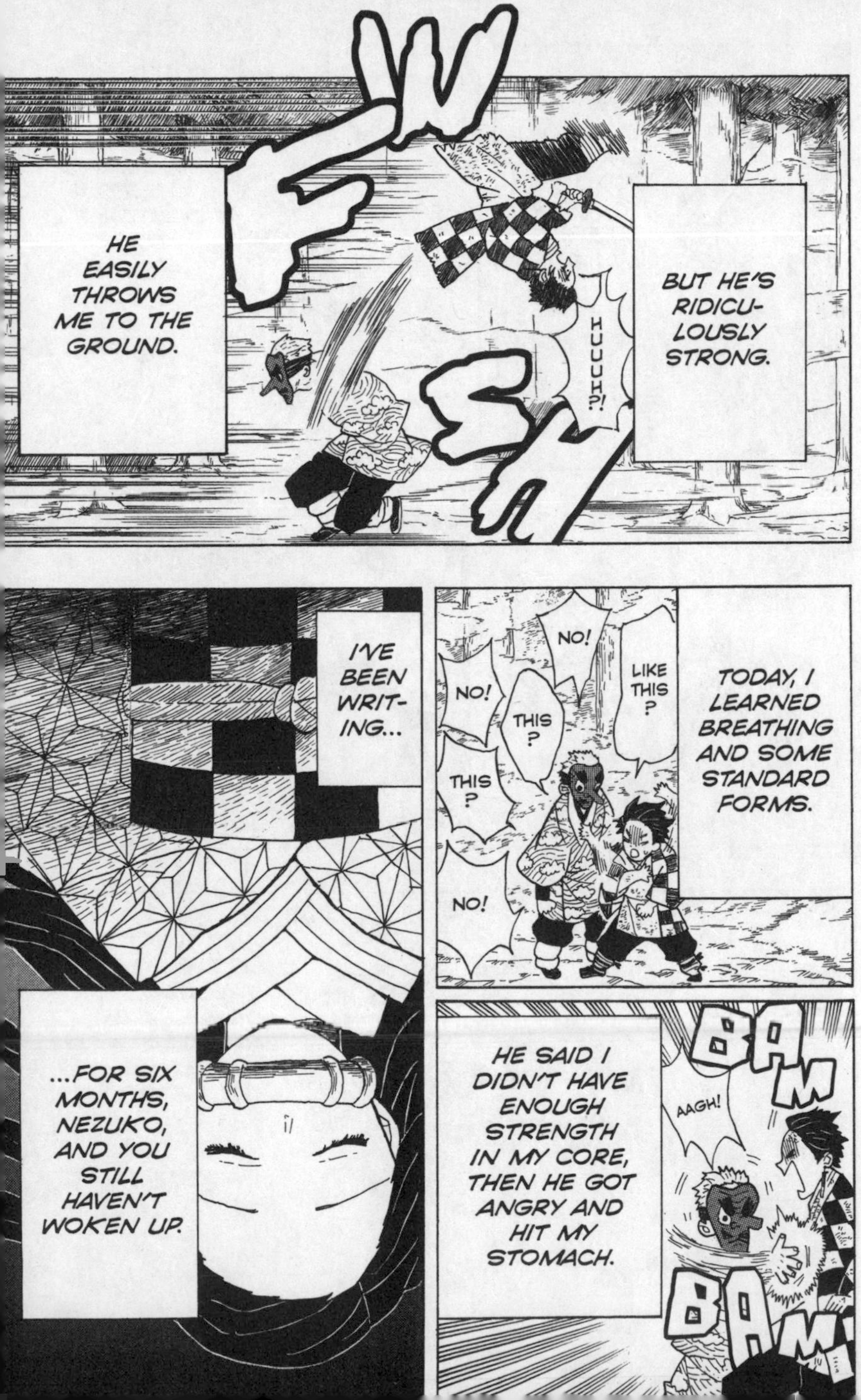

BUT HE'S RIDICU-LOUSLY STRONG.
HUUUH?!
HE EASILY THROWS ME TO THE GROUND.
TODAY, I LEARNED BREATHING AND SOME STANDARD FORMS.
LIKE THIS?
NO!
THIS?
NO!
THIS?
NO!
BAM
HE SAID I DIDN'T HAVE ENOUGH STRENGTH IN MY CORE, THEN HE GOT ANGRY AND HIT MY STOMACH.
AAGH!
BAM!
I'VE BEEN WRIT-ING...
...FOR SIX MONTHS, NEZUKO, AND YOU STILL HAVEN'T WOKEN UP.

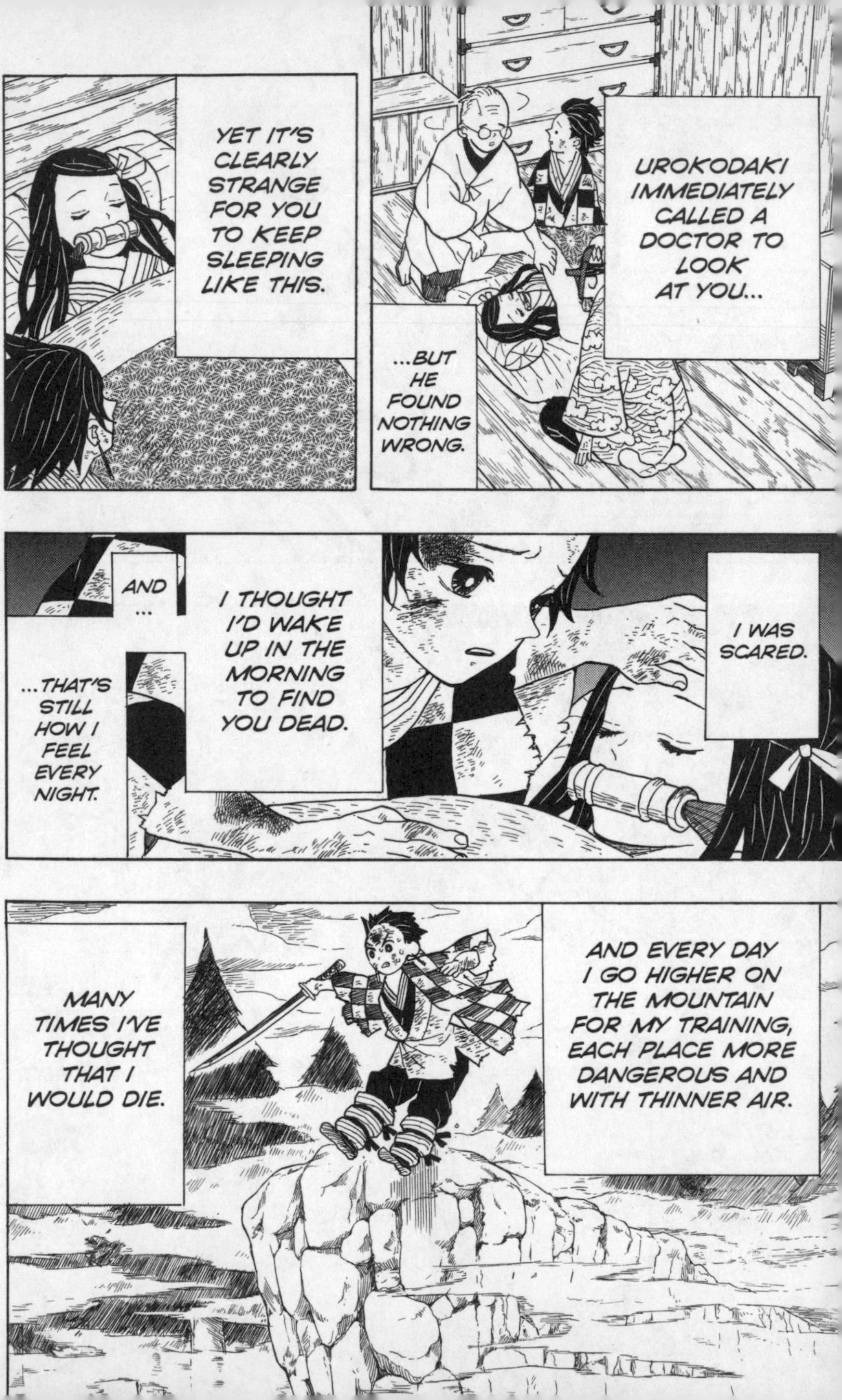
URAKODAKI IMMEDIATELY CALLED A DOCTOR TO LOOK AT YOU...
...BUT HE FOUND NOTHING WRONG.
YET IT'S CLEARLY STRANGE FOR YOU TO KEEP SLEEPING LIKE THIS.
I WAS SCARED.
I THOUGHT I'D WAKE UP IN THE MORNING TO FIND YOU DEAD.
AND ...
...THAT'S STILL HOW I FEEL EVERY NIGHT.
AND EVERY DAY I GO HIGHER ON THE MOUNTAIN FOR MY TRAINING, EACH PLACE MORE DANGEROUS AND WITH THINNER AIR.
MANY TIMES I'VE THOUGHT THAT I WOULD DIE.

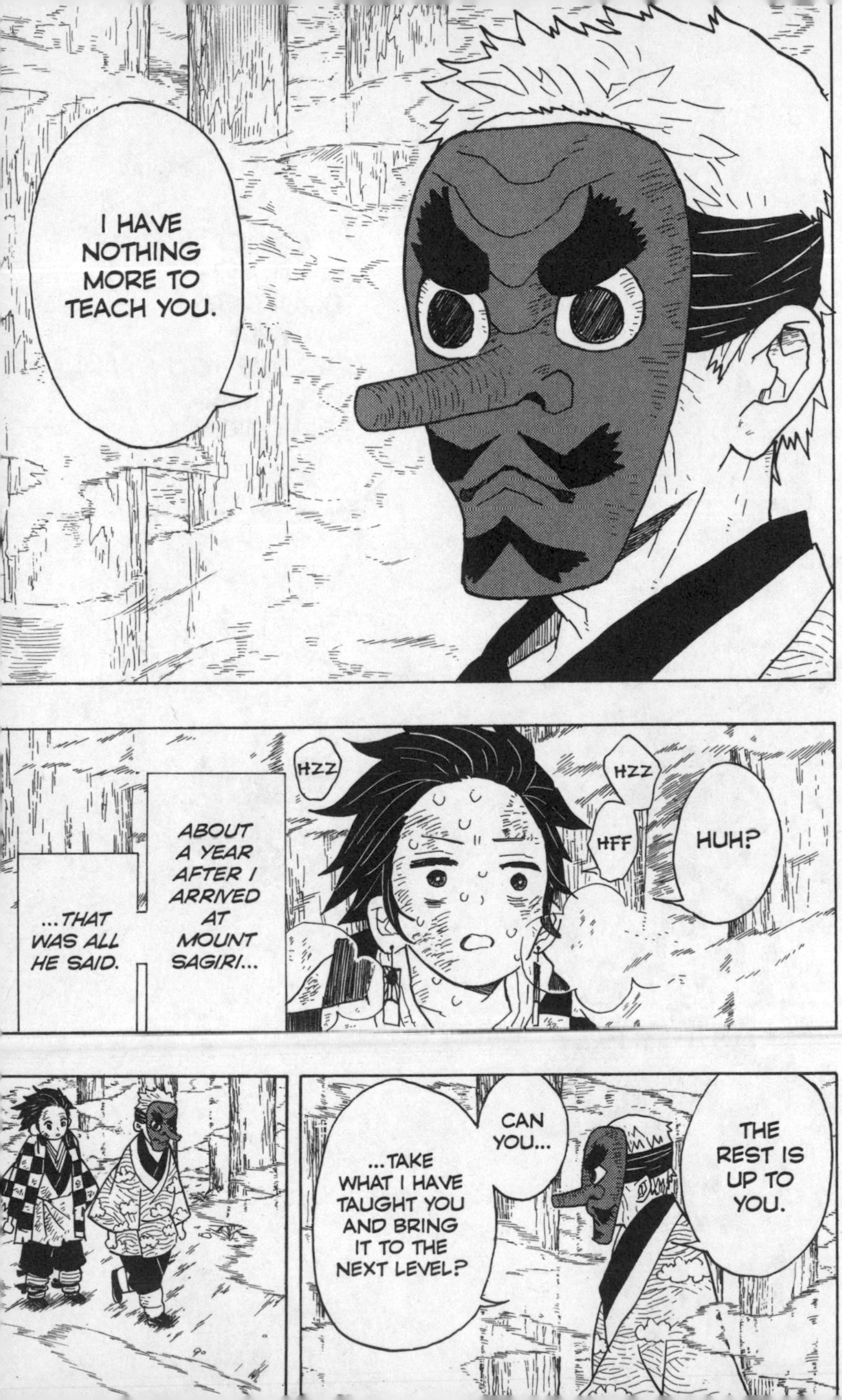
I HAVE NOTHING MORE TO TEACH YOU.
HZZ
HUH?
HFF
HZZ
ABOUT A YEAR AFTER I ARRIVED AT MOUNT SAGIRI...
...THAT WAS ALL HE SAID.
THE REST IS UP TO YOU.
CAN YOU...
...TAKE WHAT I HAVE TAUGHT YOU AND BRING IT TO THE NEXT LEVEL?

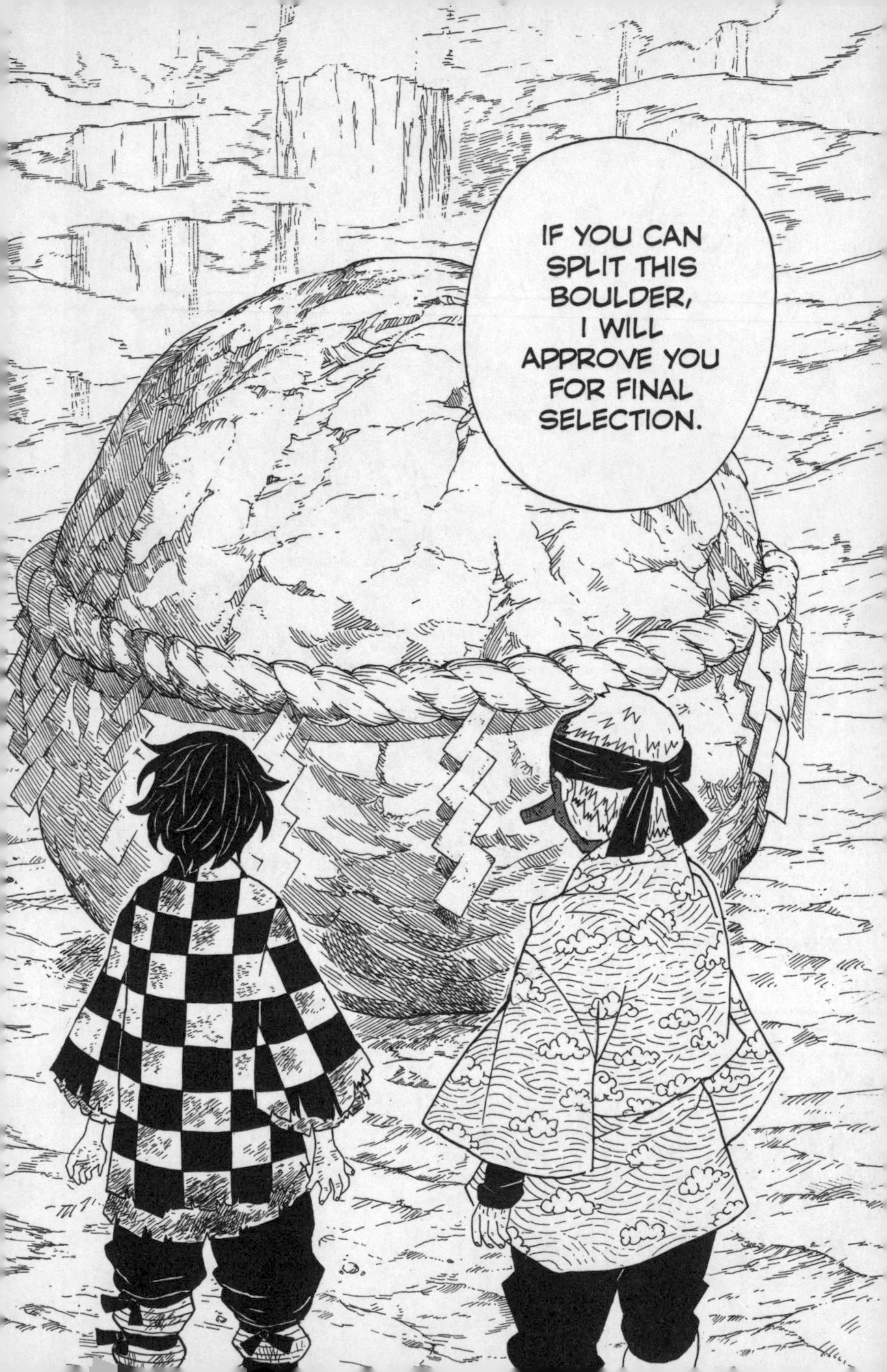
IF YOU CAN SPLIT THIS BOULDER, I WILL APPROVE YOU FOR FINAL SELECTION.

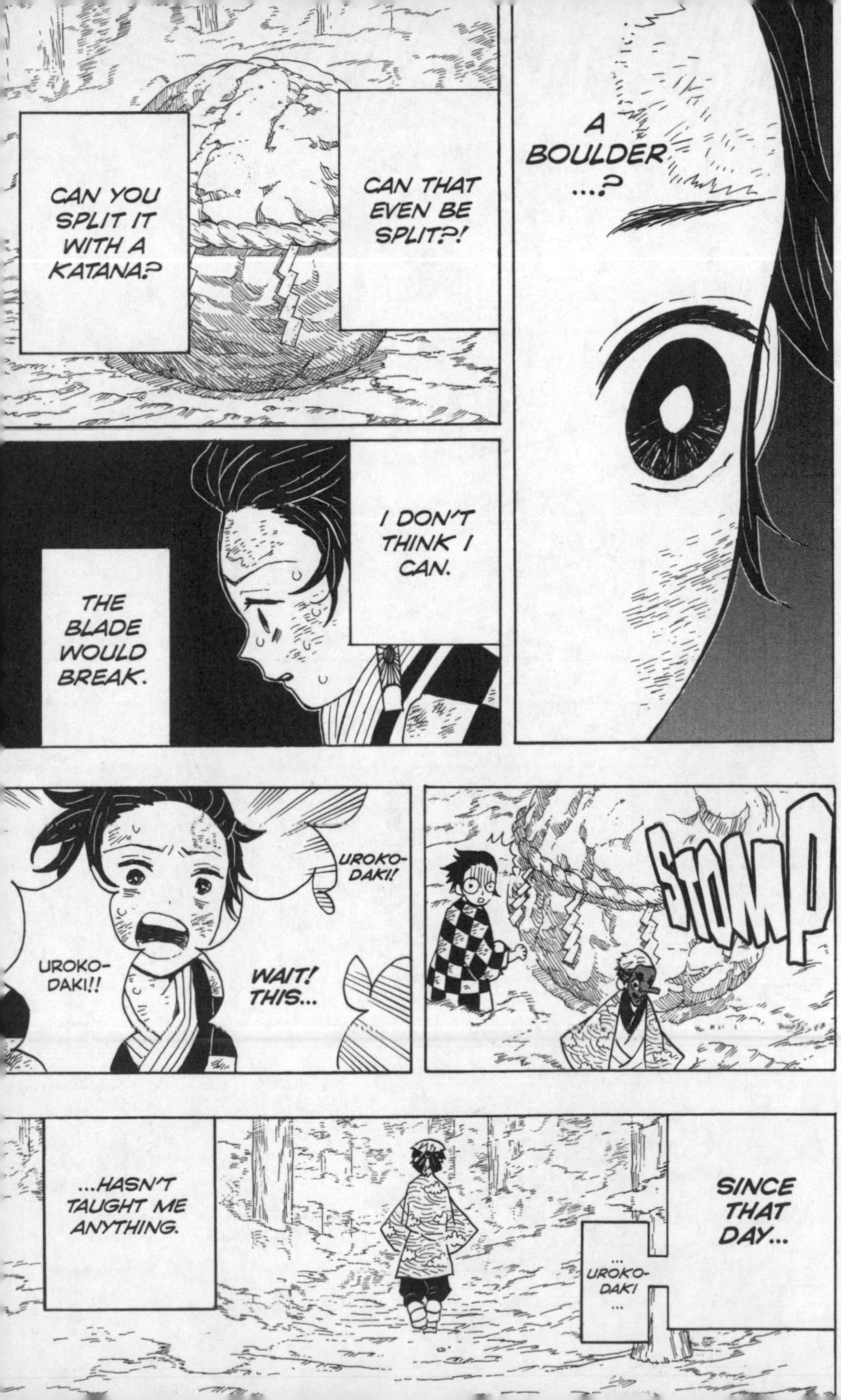
A BOULDER ...?
CAN THAT EVEN BE SPLIT?!
CAN YOU SPLIT IT WITH A KATANA?
I DON'T THINK I CAN.
THE BLADE WOULD BREAK.
STOMP
UROKO-DAKI!
WAIT! THIS...
UROKO-DAKI!!
SINCE THAT DAY...
...UROKO-DAKI...
...HASN'T TAUGHT ME ANYTHING.

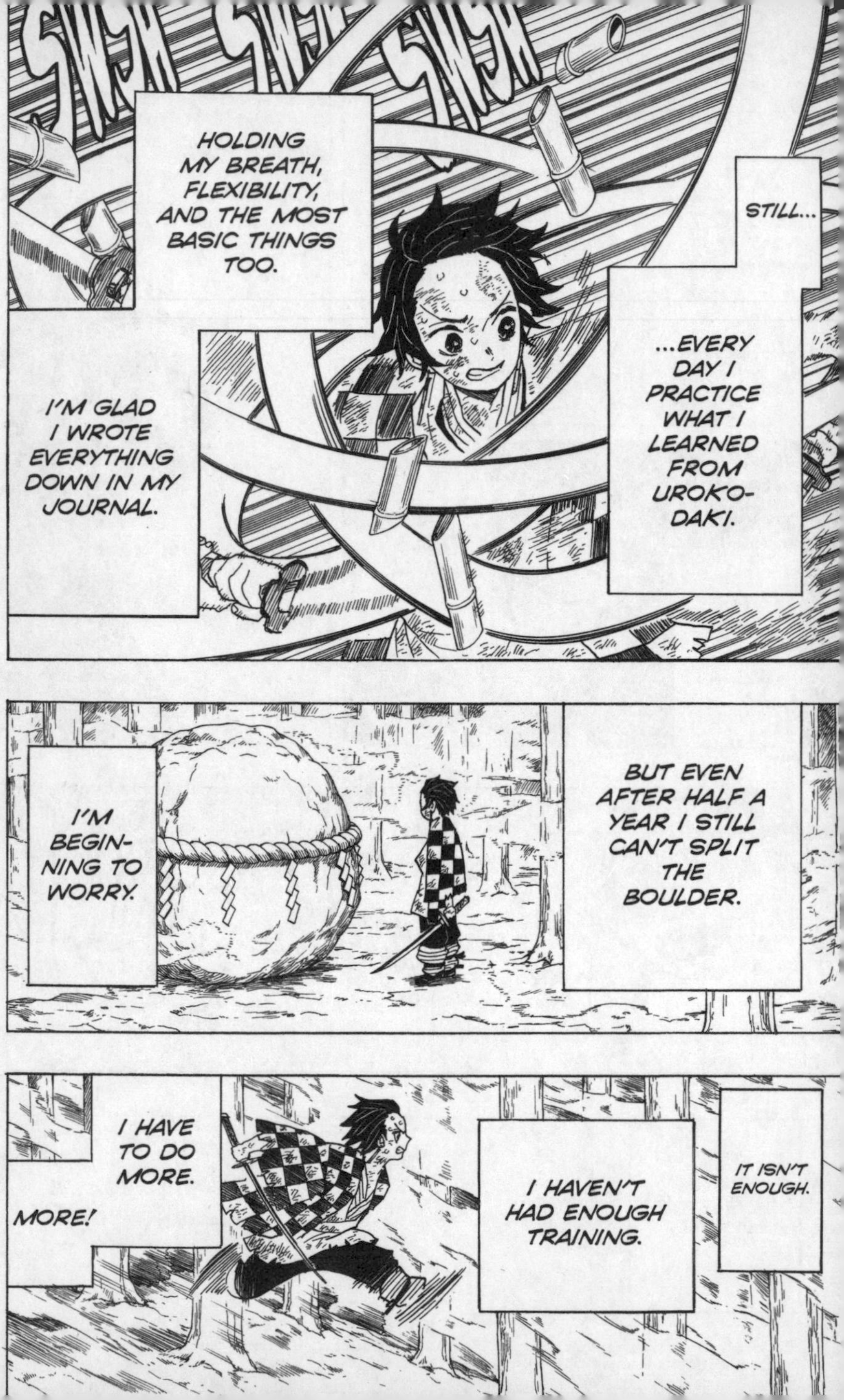
SWSH SWSH SWSH
STILL...
...EVERY DAY I PRACTICE WHAT I LEARNED FROM UROKO-DAKI.
HOLDING MY BREATH, FLEXIBILITY, AND THE MOST BASIC THINGS TOO.
I'M GLAD I WROTE EVERYTHING DOWN IN MY JOURNAL.
BUT EVEN AFTER HALF A YEAR I STILL CAN'T SPLIT THE BOULDER.
I'M BEGIN-NING TO WORRY.
IT ISN'T ENOUGH.
I HAVEN'T HAD ENOUGH TRAINING.
I HAVE TO DO MORE.
MORE!

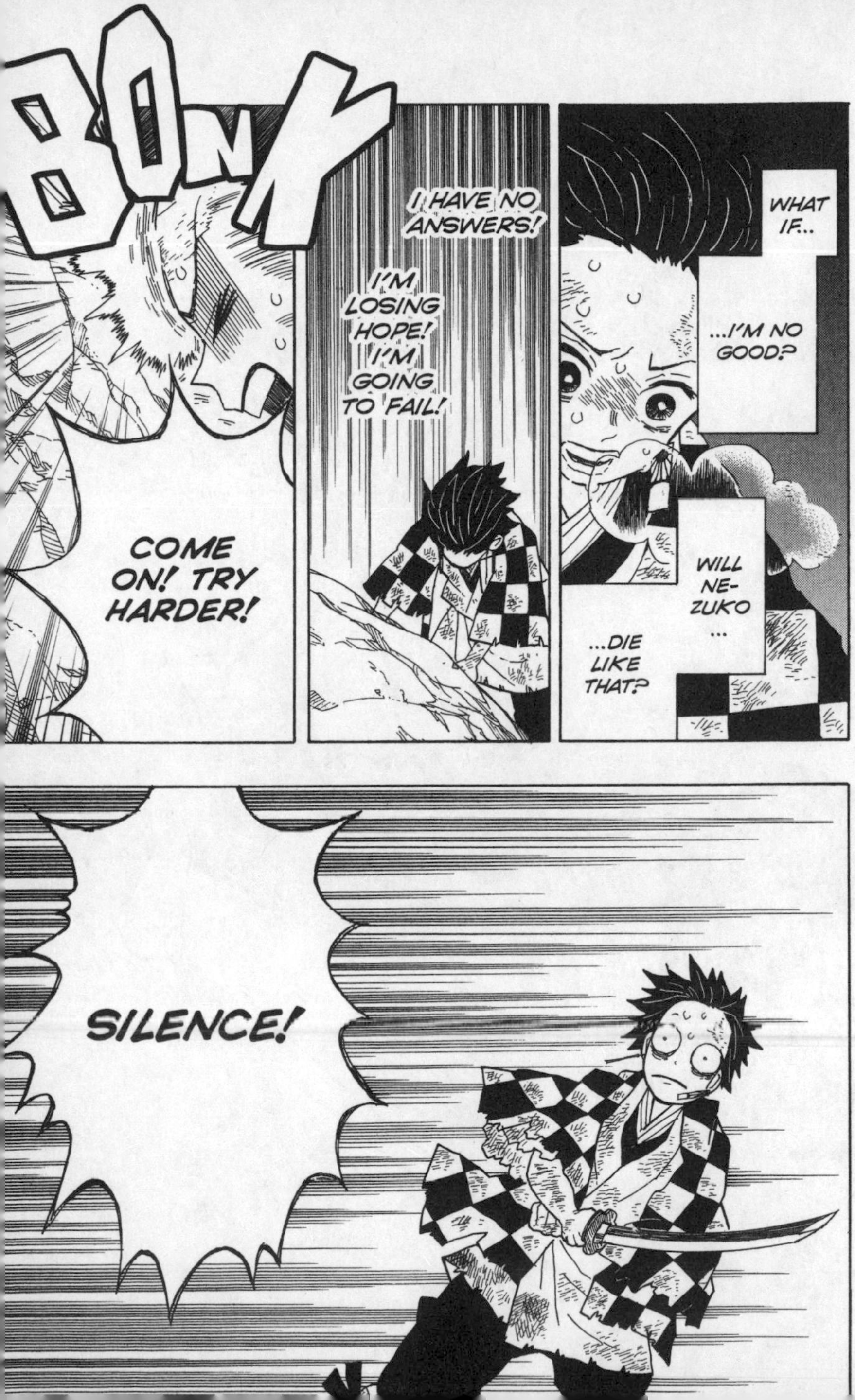
WHAT IF...
...I'M NO GOOD?
WILL NE-ZUKO...
...DIE LIKE THAT?
I HAVE NO ANSWERS!
I'M LOSING HOPE! I'M GOING TO FAIL!
BONK
COME ON! TRY HARDER!
SILENCE!

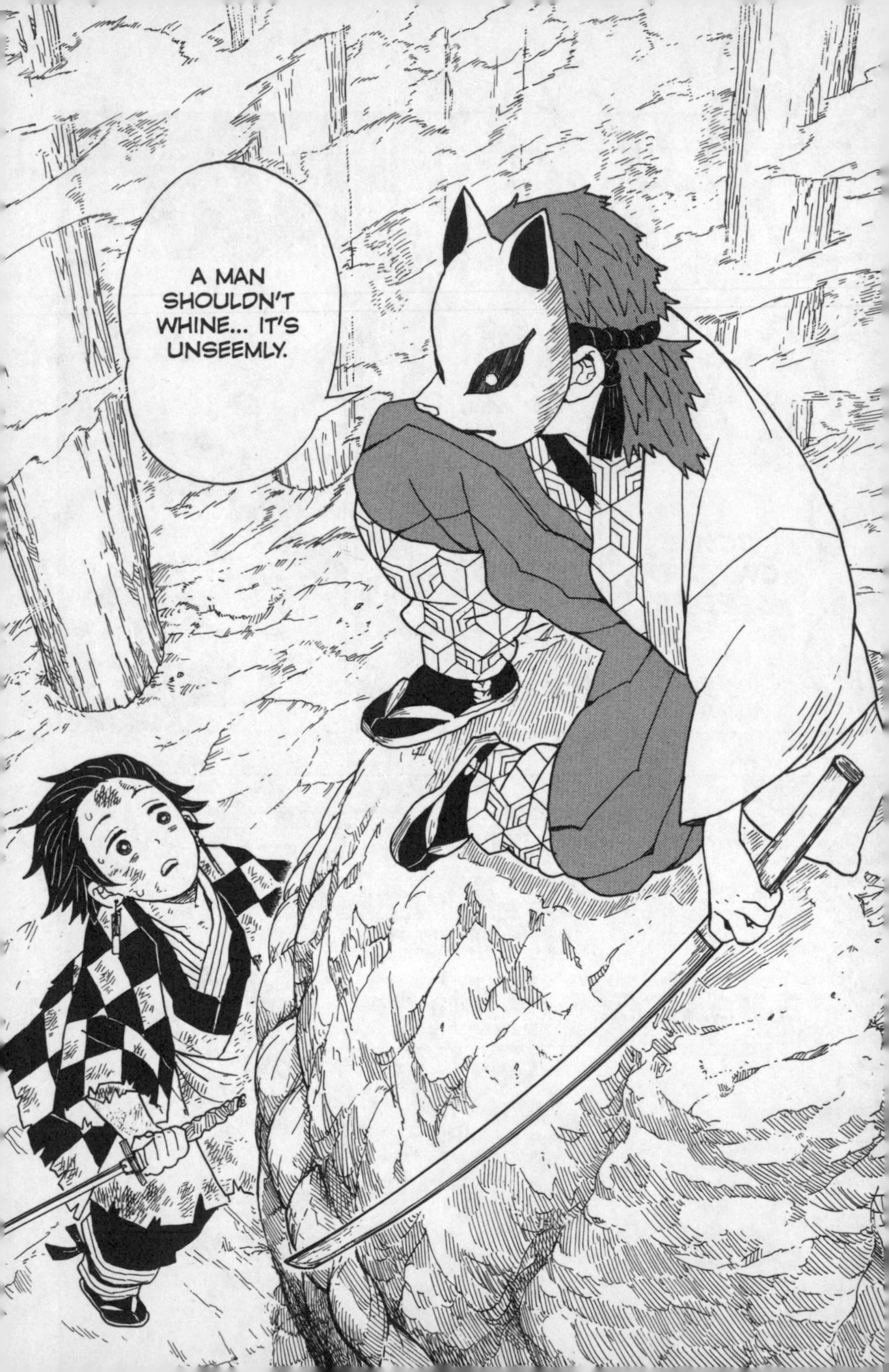
A MAN SHOULDN'T WHINE... IT'S UNSEEMLY.

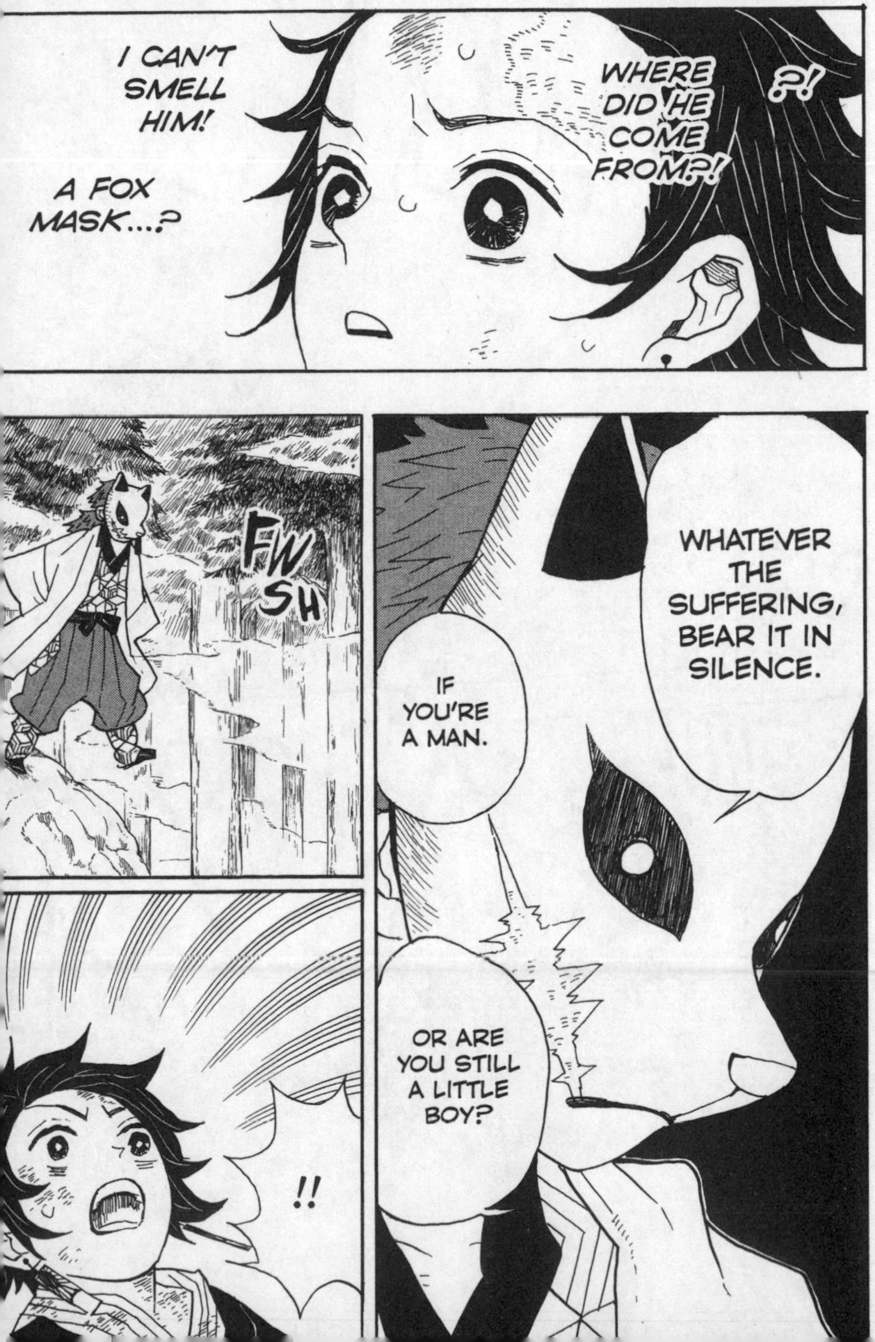
?!
WHERE DID HE COME FROM?!
I CAN'T SMELL HIM!
A FOX MASK...?
WHATEVER THE SUFFERING, BEAR IT IN SILENCE.
IF YOU'RE A MAN.
OR ARE YOU STILL A LITTLE BOY?
FWSH
!!

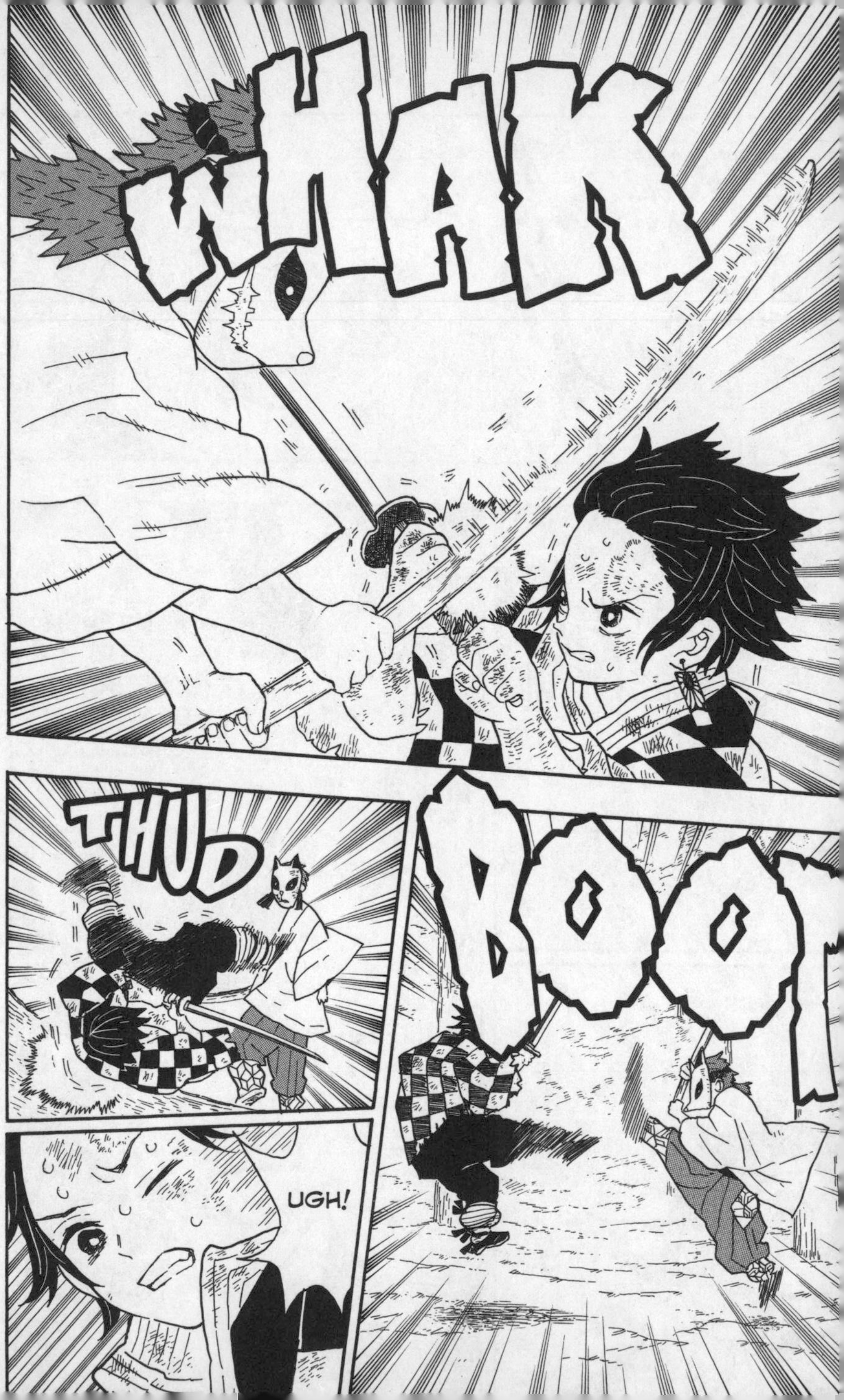
WHAK
BOO
THUD
UGH!

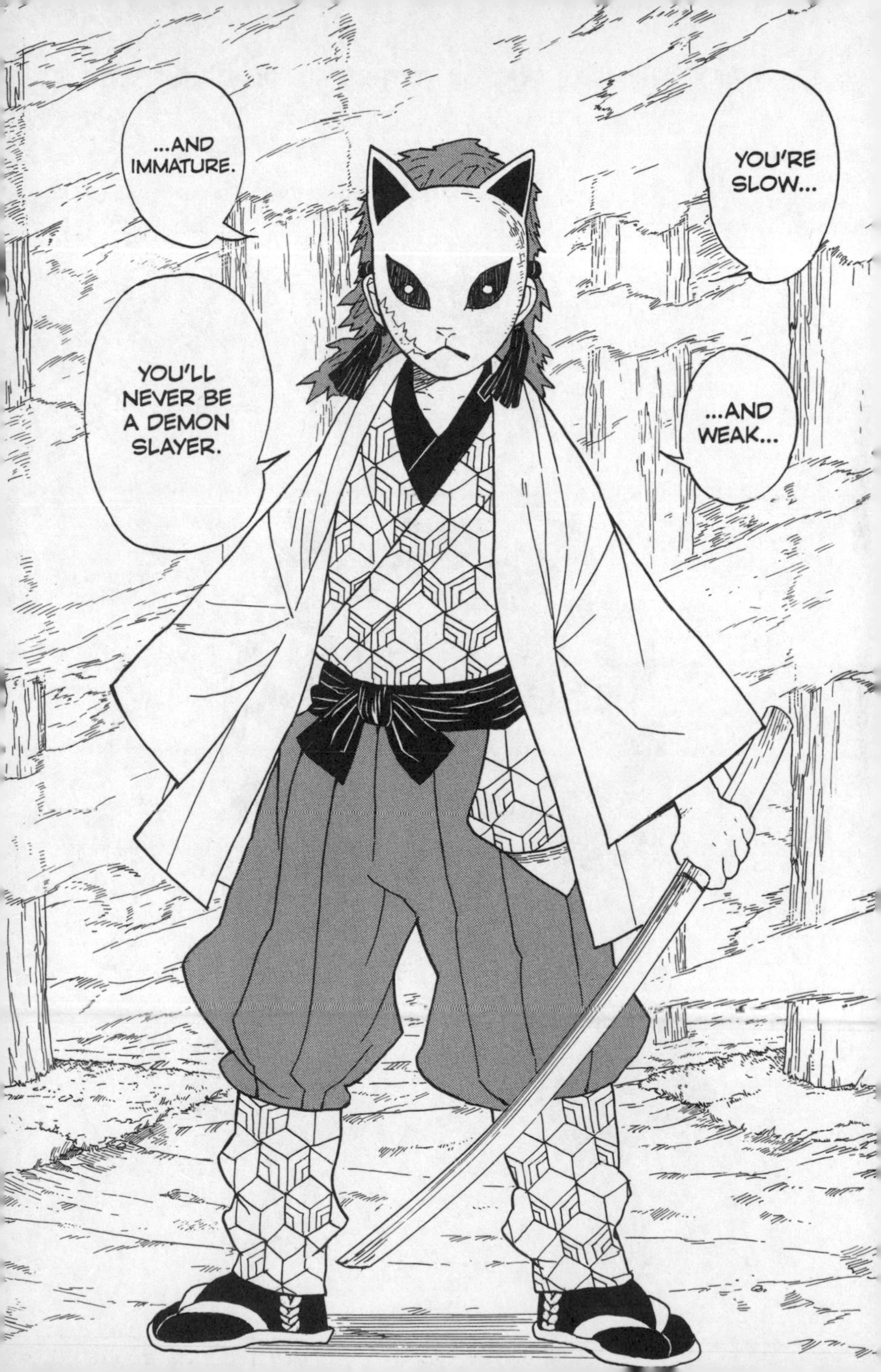
YOU'RE SLOW...
...AND WEAK...
...AND IMMATURE.
YOU'LL NEVER BE A DEMON SLAYER.

ADVERTISING ILLUSTRATION AT THE BEGINNING OF THE SERIES.

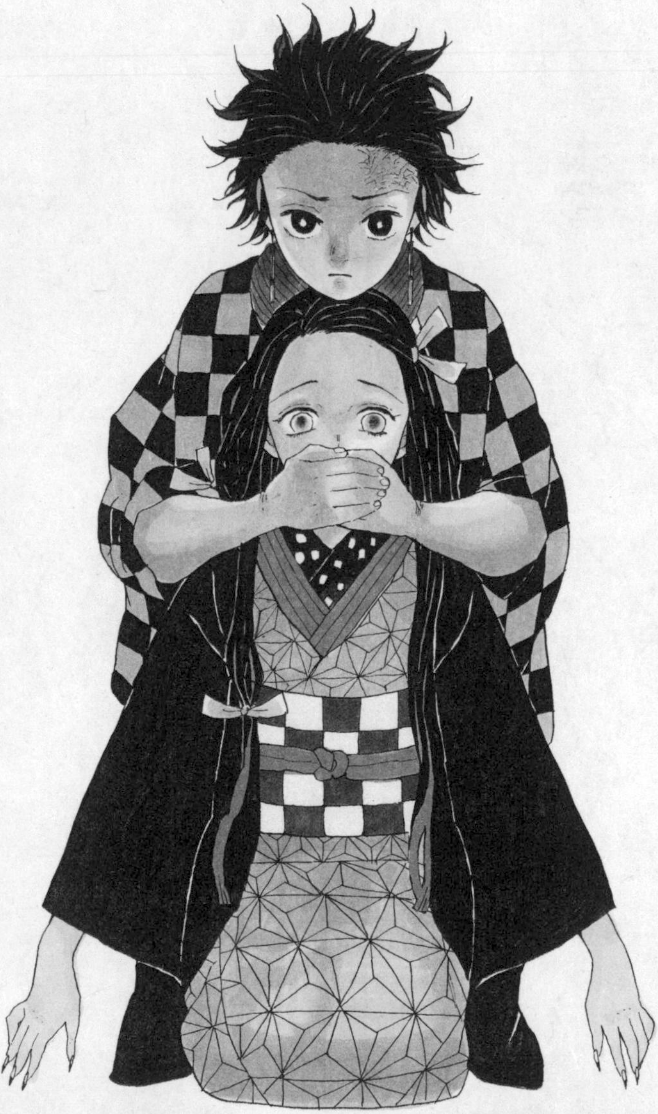

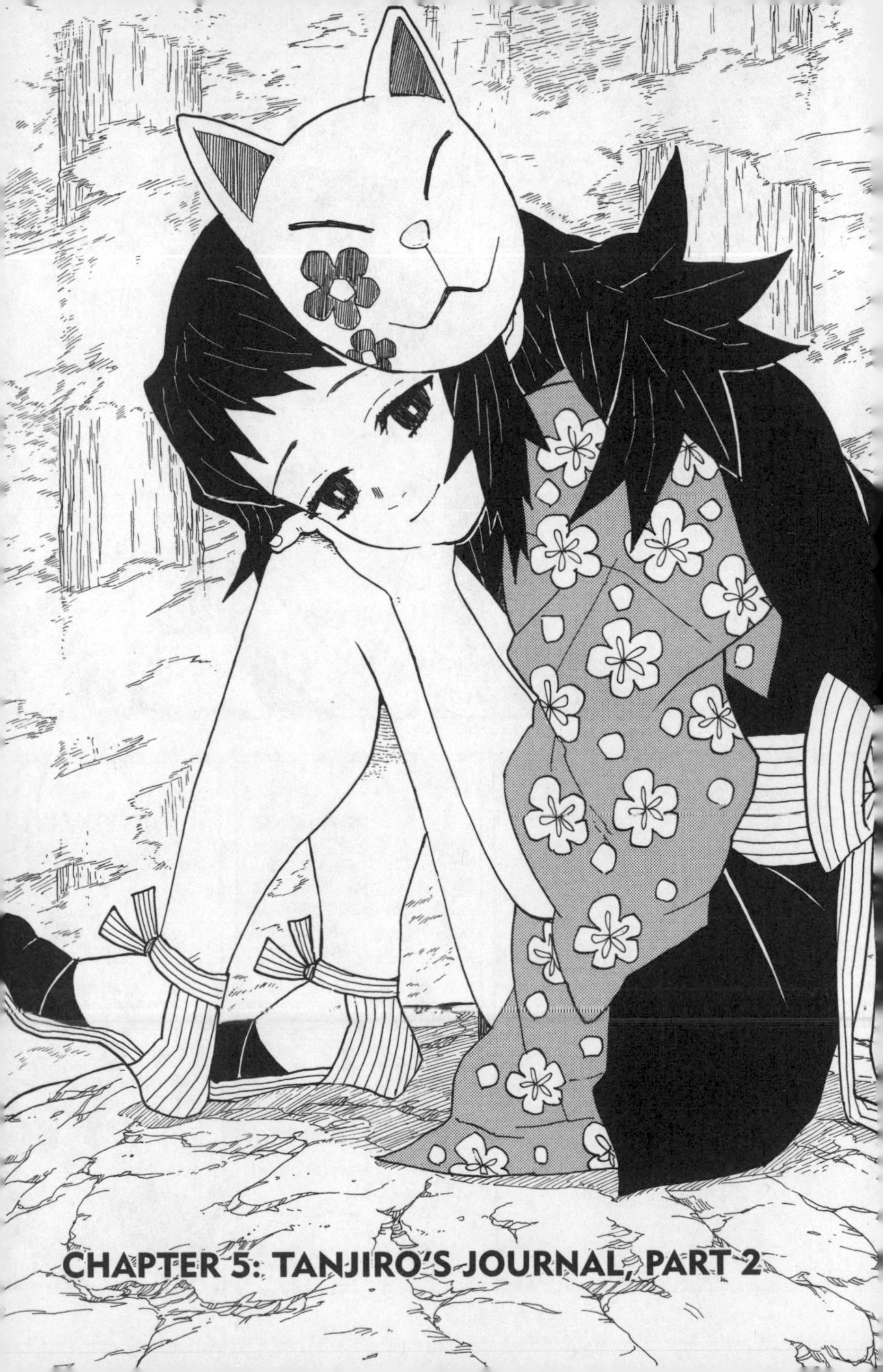

CHAPTER 5: TANJIRO'S JOURNAL, PART 2

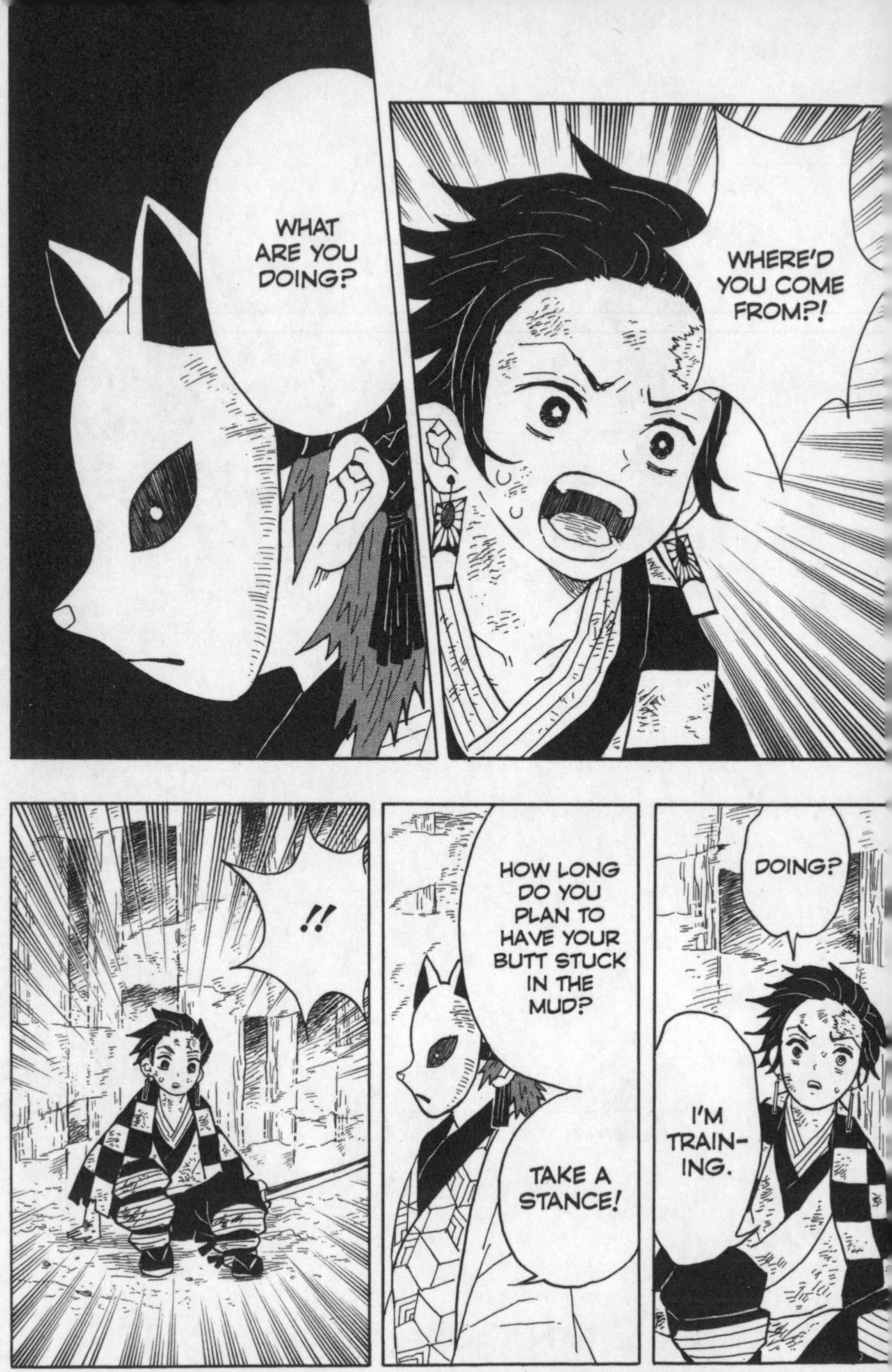
WHAT ARE YOU DOING?
WHERE'D YOU COME FROM?!
DOING?
I'M TRAINING.
HOW LONG DO YOU PLAN TO HAVE YOUR BUTT STUCK IN THE MUD?
TAKE A STANCE!
!!

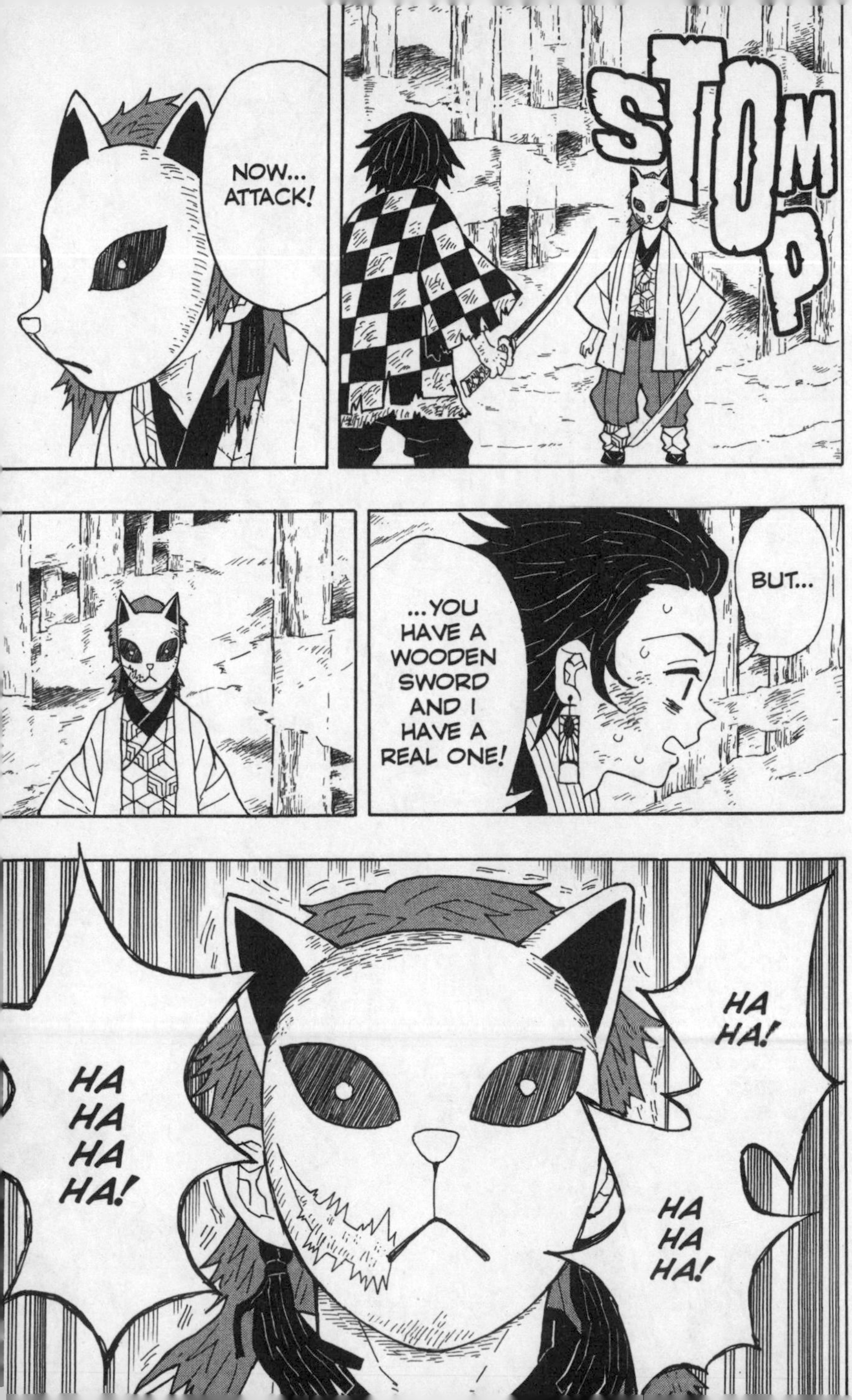
STOMP
NOW... ATTACK!
BUT...
...YOU HAVE A WOODEN SWORD AND I HAVE A REAL ONE!
HA HA!
HA HA HA!
HA HA HA HA!

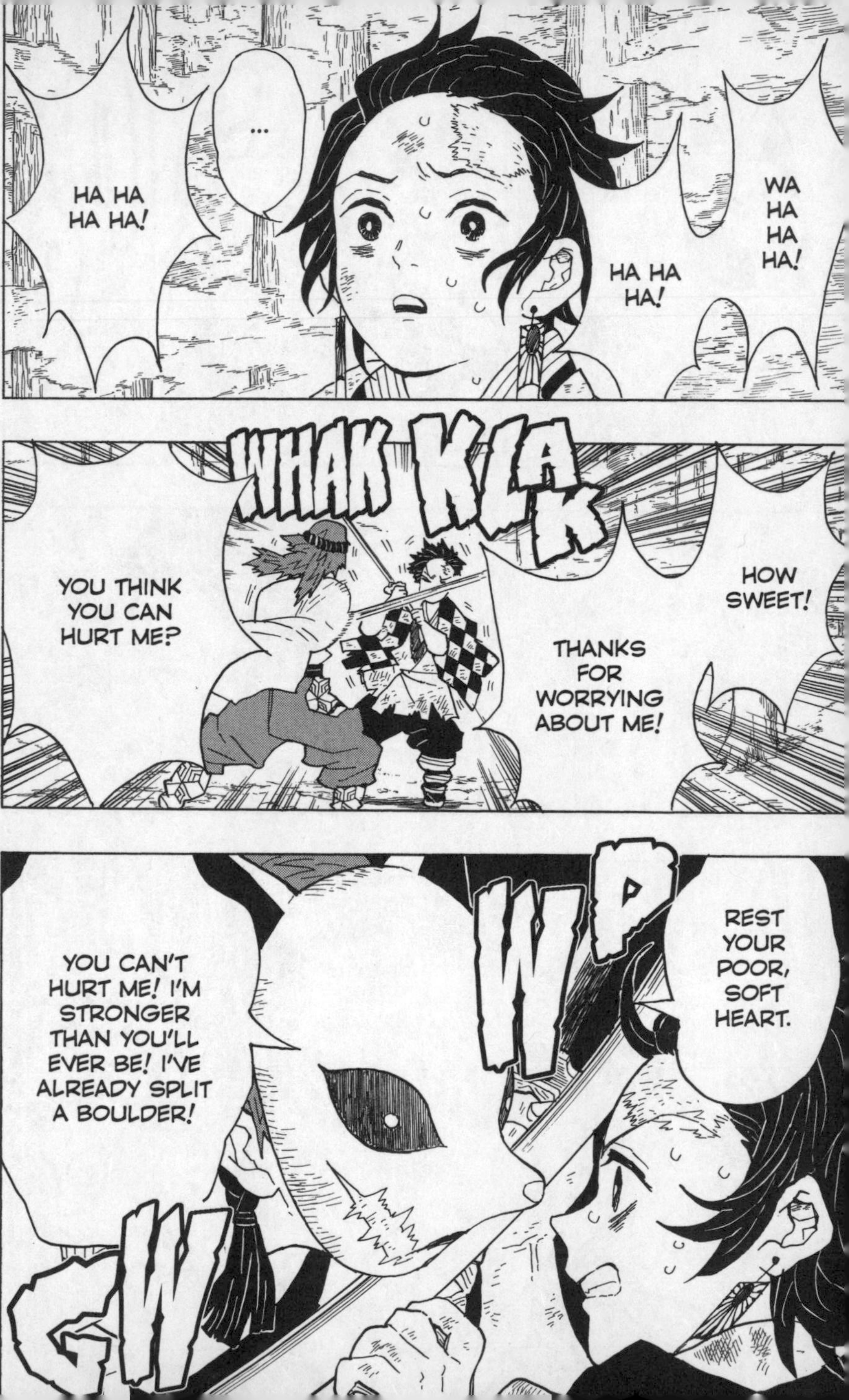
WA HA HA HA!
HA HA HA!
...
HA HA HA HA!
WHAK
KLAK
HOW SWEET!
THANKS FOR WORRYING ABOUT ME!
YOU THINK YOU CAN HURT ME?
REST YOUR POOR, SOFT HEART.
YOU CAN'T HURT ME! I'M STRONGER THAN YOU'LL EVER BE! I'VE ALREADY SPLIT A BOULDER!

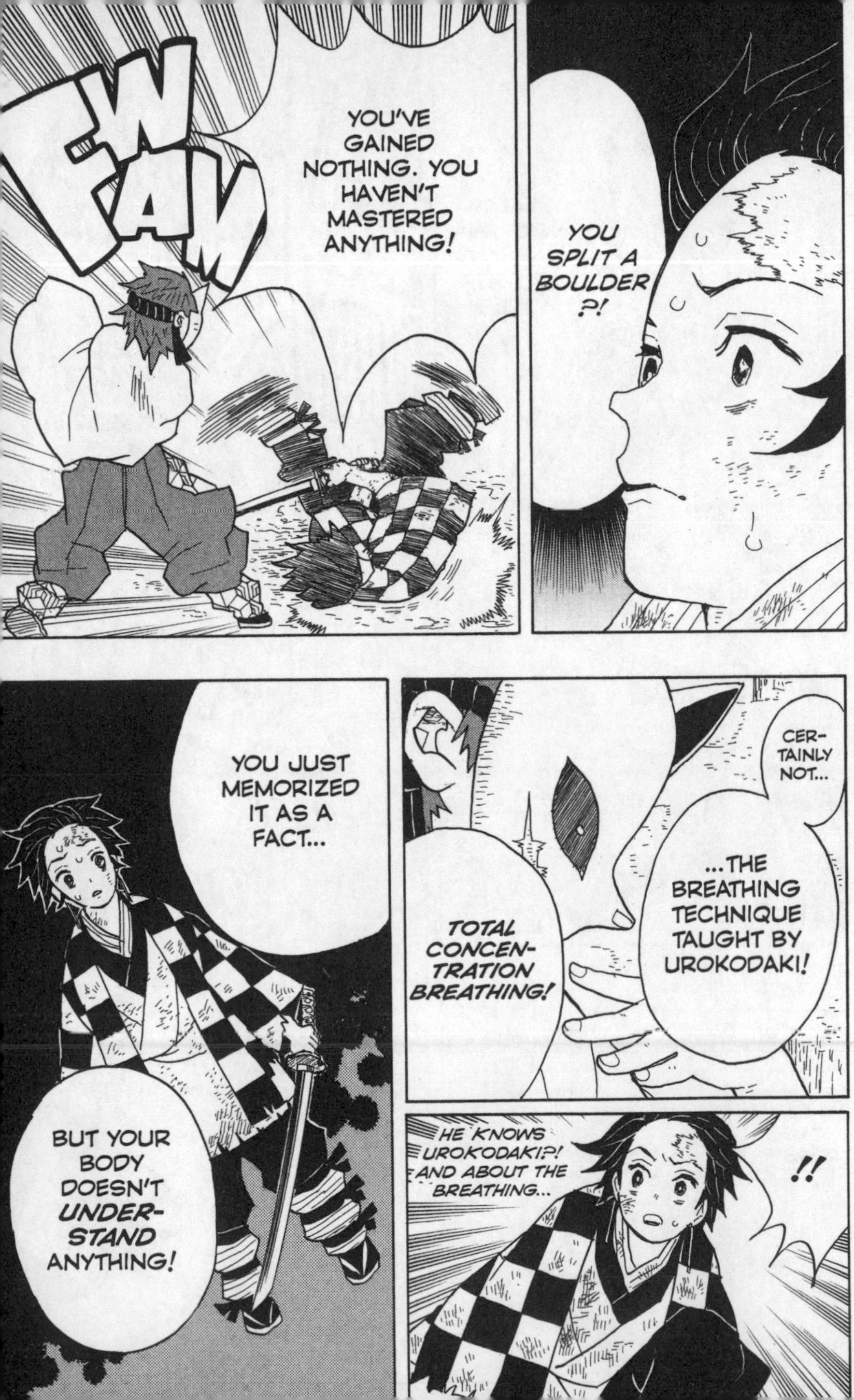
YOU SPLIT A BOULDER ?!
WHAM
YOU'VE GAINED NOTHING. YOU HAVEN'T MASTERED ANYTHING!
CER-TAINLY NOT...
...THE BREATHING TECHNIQUE TAUGHT BY UROKODAKI!
TOTAL CONCEN-TRATION BREATHING!
HE KNOWS UROKODAKI?! AND ABOUT THE BREATHING...
!!
YOU JUST MEMORIZED IT AS A FACT...
BUT YOUR BODY DOESN'T UNDER-STAND ANYTHING!

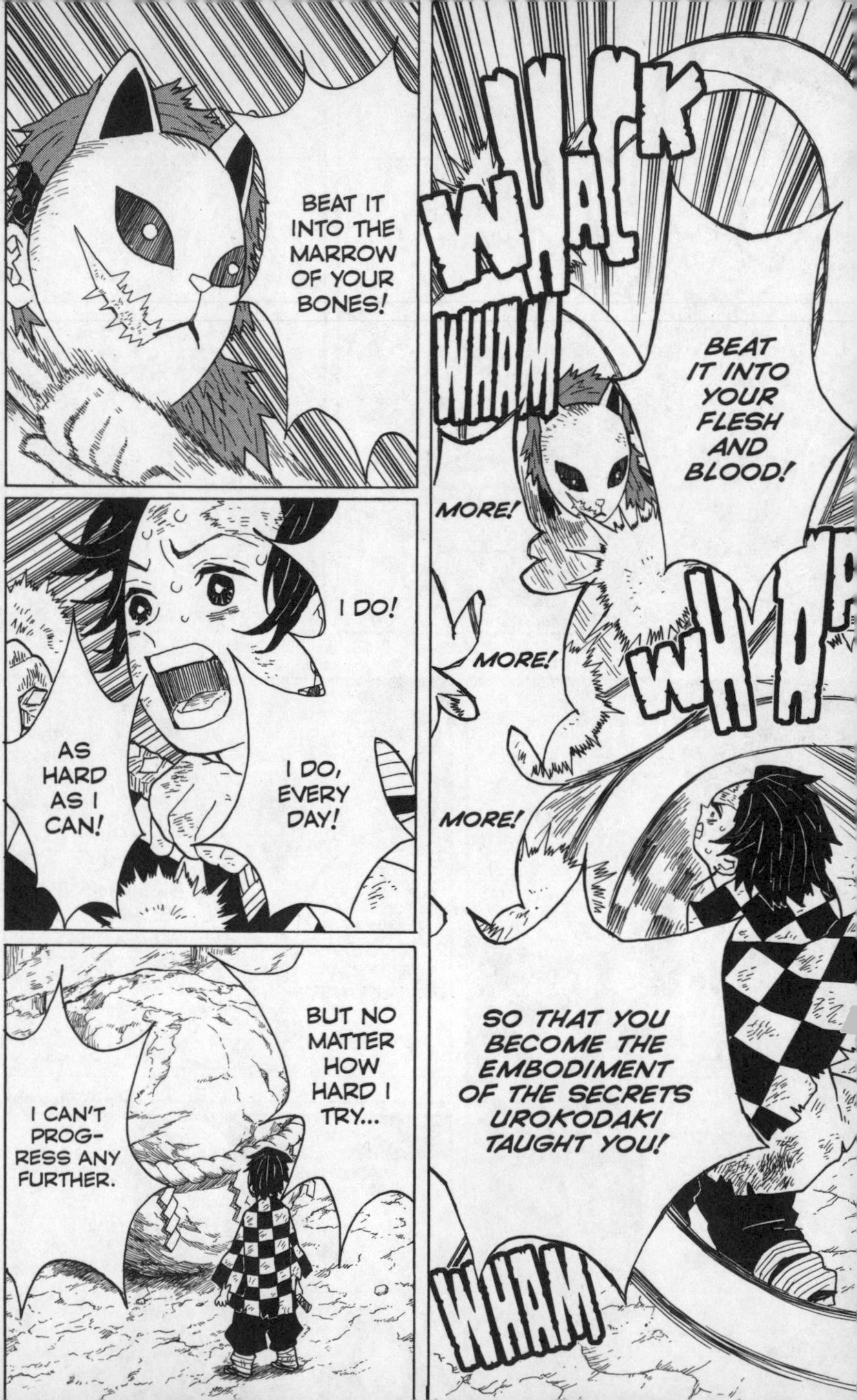
WHACK
WHAM
BEAT IT INTO YOUR FLESH AND BLOOD!
MORE!
MORE!
MORE!
SO THAT YOU BECOME THE EMBODIMENT OF THE SECRETS UROKODAKI TAUGHT YOU!
WHAM
BEAT IT INTO THE MARROW OF YOUR BONES!
I DO!
I DO, EVERY DAY!
AS HARD AS I CAN!
BUT NO MATTER HOW HARD I TRY...
I CAN'T PROG-RESS ANY FURTHER.

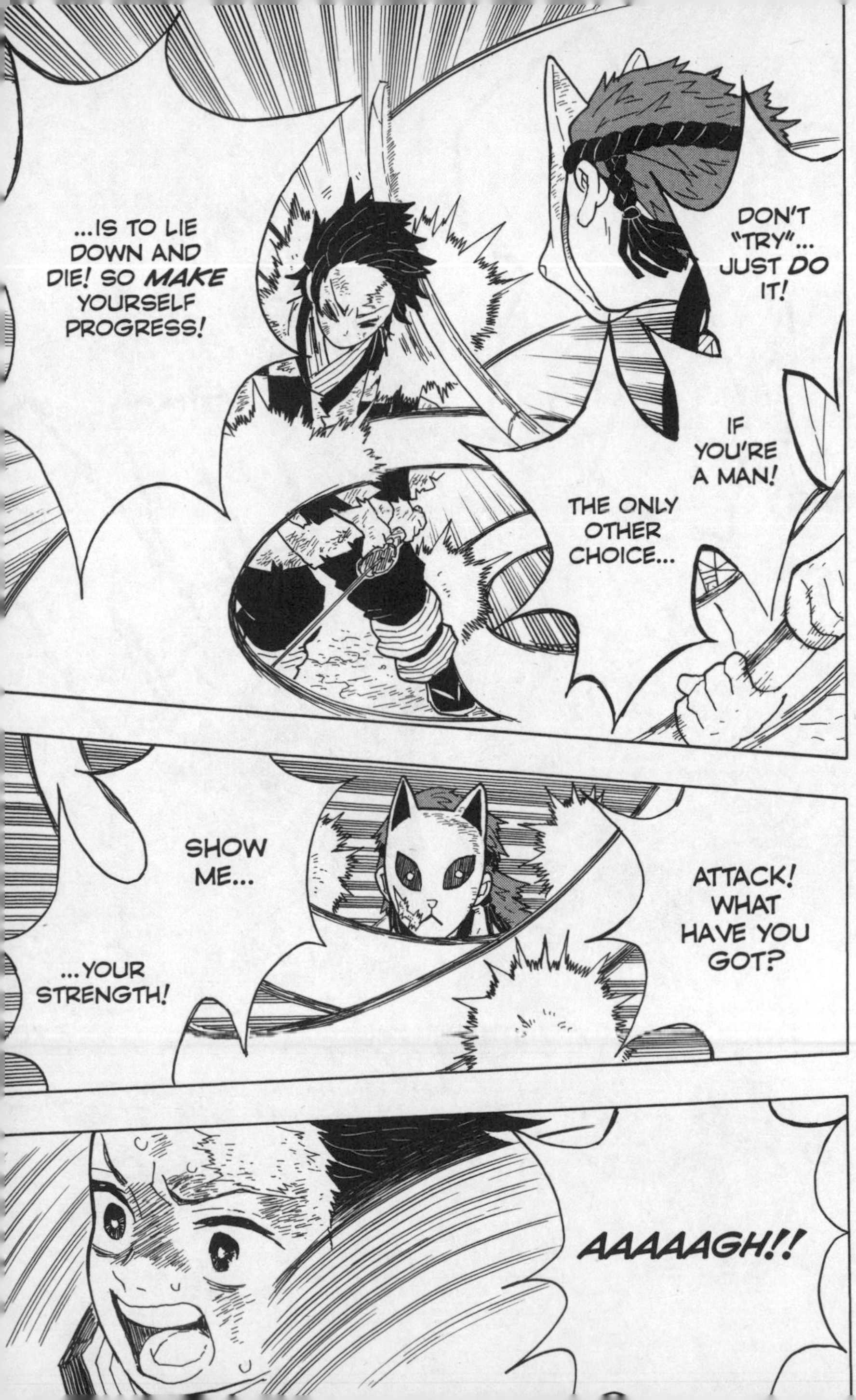
DON'T "TRY"... JUST *DO* IT!
IF YOU'RE A MAN!
THE ONLY OTHER CHOICE...
...IS TO LIE DOWN AND DIE! SO *MAKE* YOURSELF PROGRESS!
ATTACK! WHAT HAVE YOU GOT?
SHOW ME...
...YOUR STRENGTH!
AAAAAGH!!

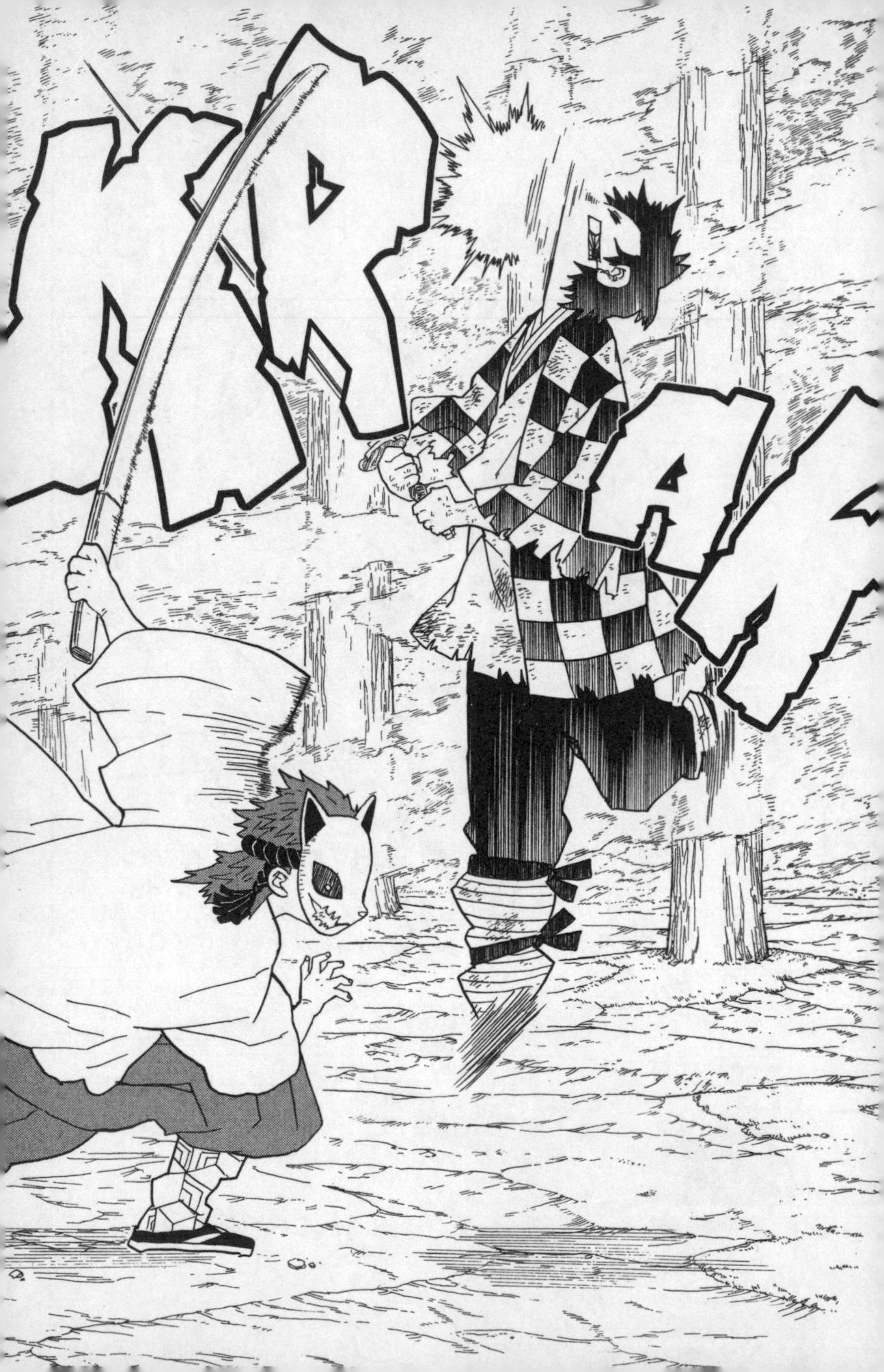
KRA

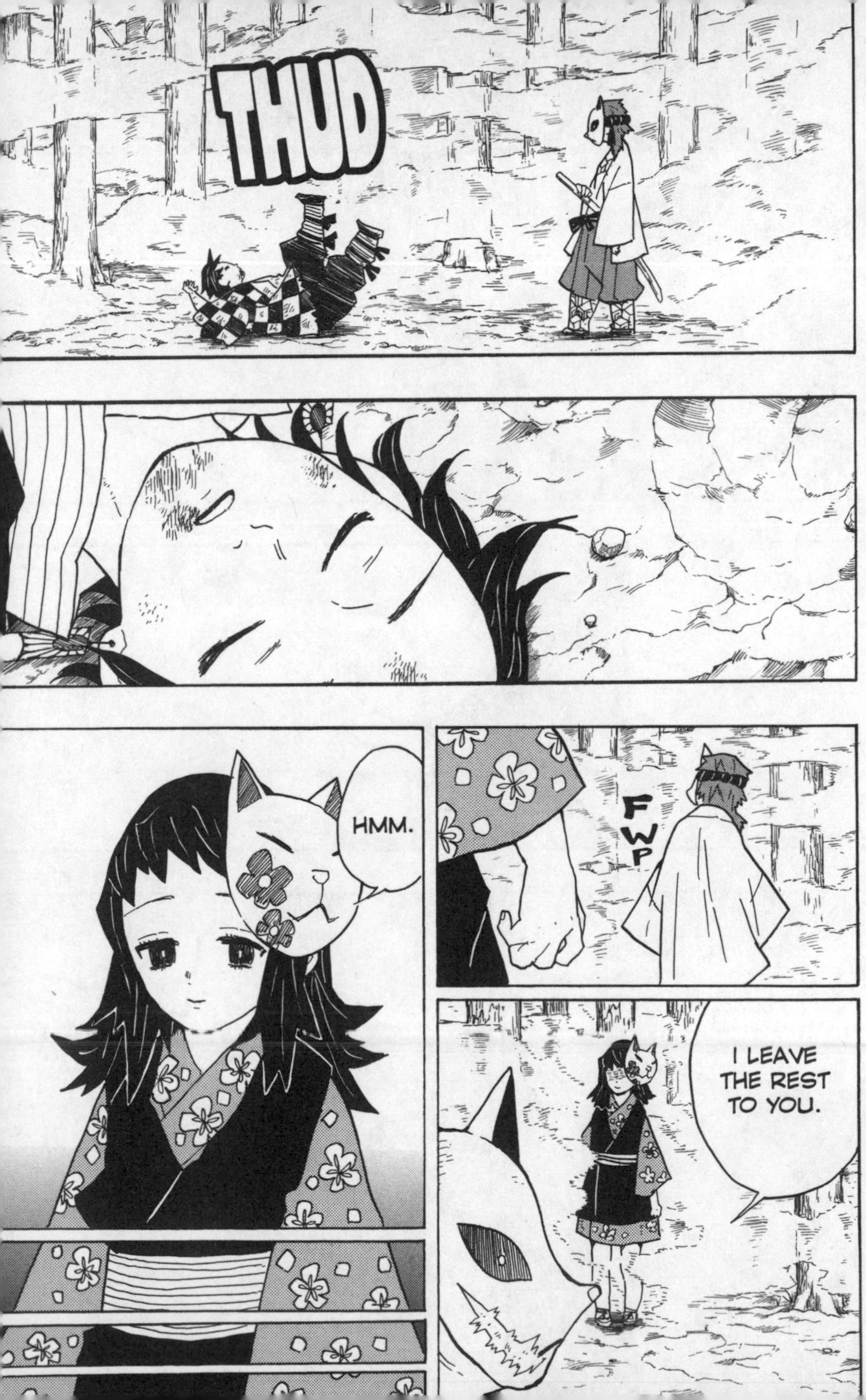
THUD
FWP
I LEAVE THE REST TO YOU.
HMM.

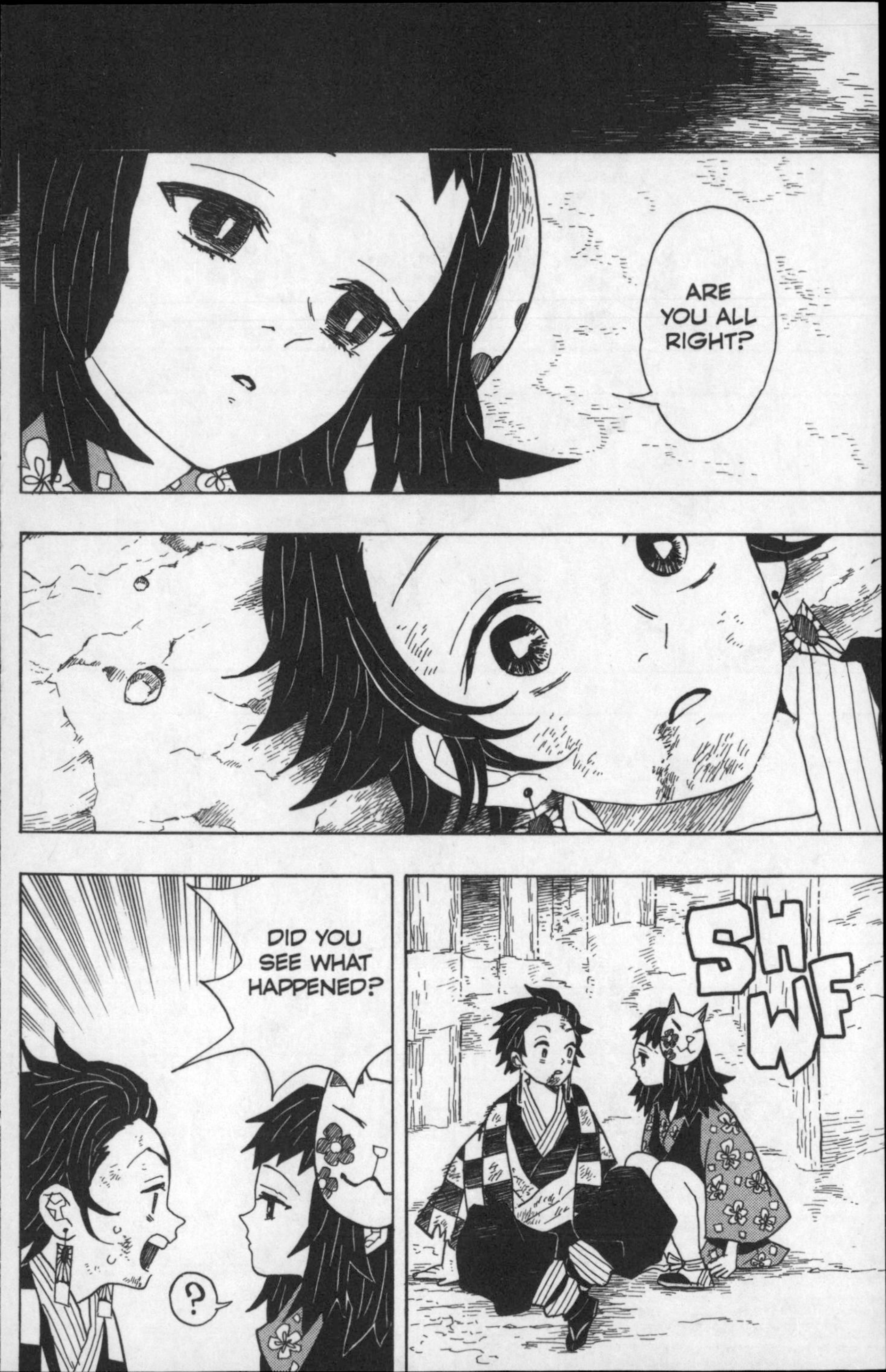
ARE YOU ALL RIGHT?
SHWF
DID YOU SEE WHAT HAPPENED?
?

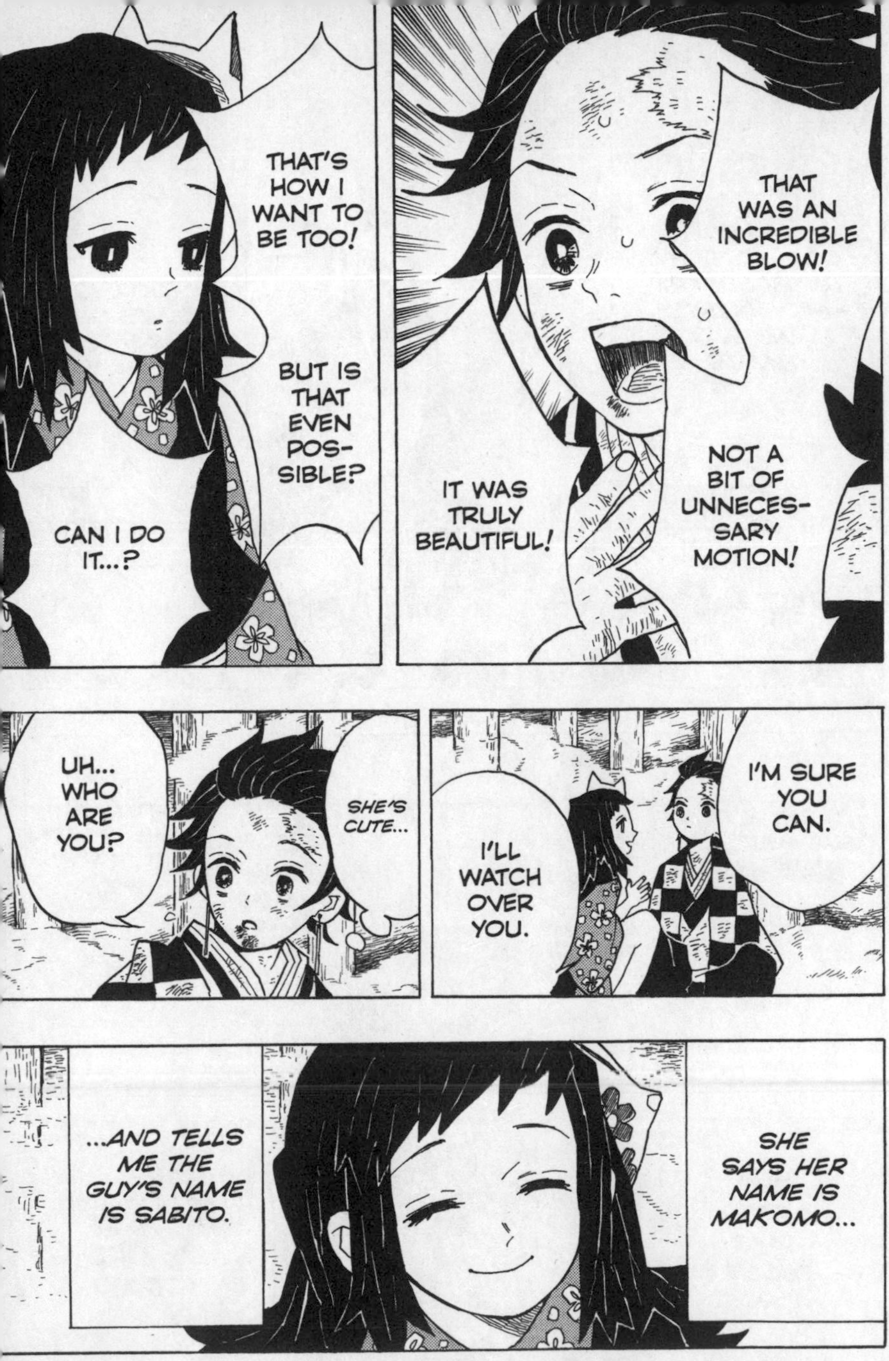
THAT WAS AN INCREDIBLE BLOW!
NOT A BIT OF UNNECESSARY MOTION!
IT WAS TRULY BEAUTIFUL!
THAT'S HOW I WANT TO BE TOO!
BUT IS THAT EVEN POSSIBLE?
CAN I DO IT...?
I'M SURE YOU CAN.
I'LL WATCH OVER YOU.
SHE'S CUTE...
UH... WHO ARE YOU?
SHE SAYS HER NAME IS MAKOMO...
...AND TELLS ME THE GUY'S NAME IS SABITO.

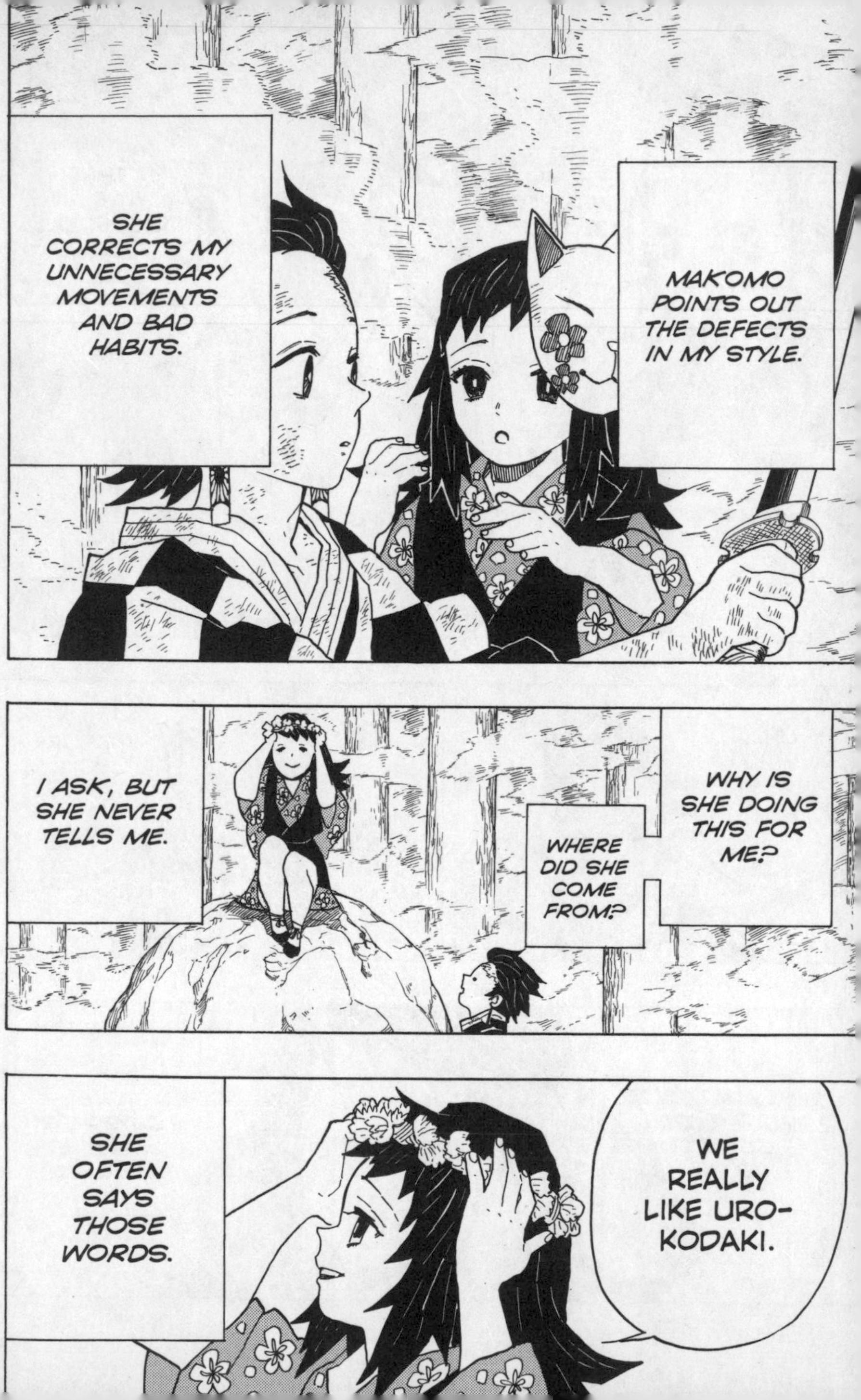
MAKOMO POINTS OUT THE DEFECTS IN MY STYLE.
SHE CORRECTS MY UNNECESSARY MOVEMENTS AND BAD HABITS.
WHY IS SHE DOING THIS FOR ME?
WHERE DID SHE COME FROM?
I ASK, BUT SHE NEVER TELLS ME.
WE REALLY LIKE URO-KODAKI.
SHE OFTEN SAYS THOSE WORDS.

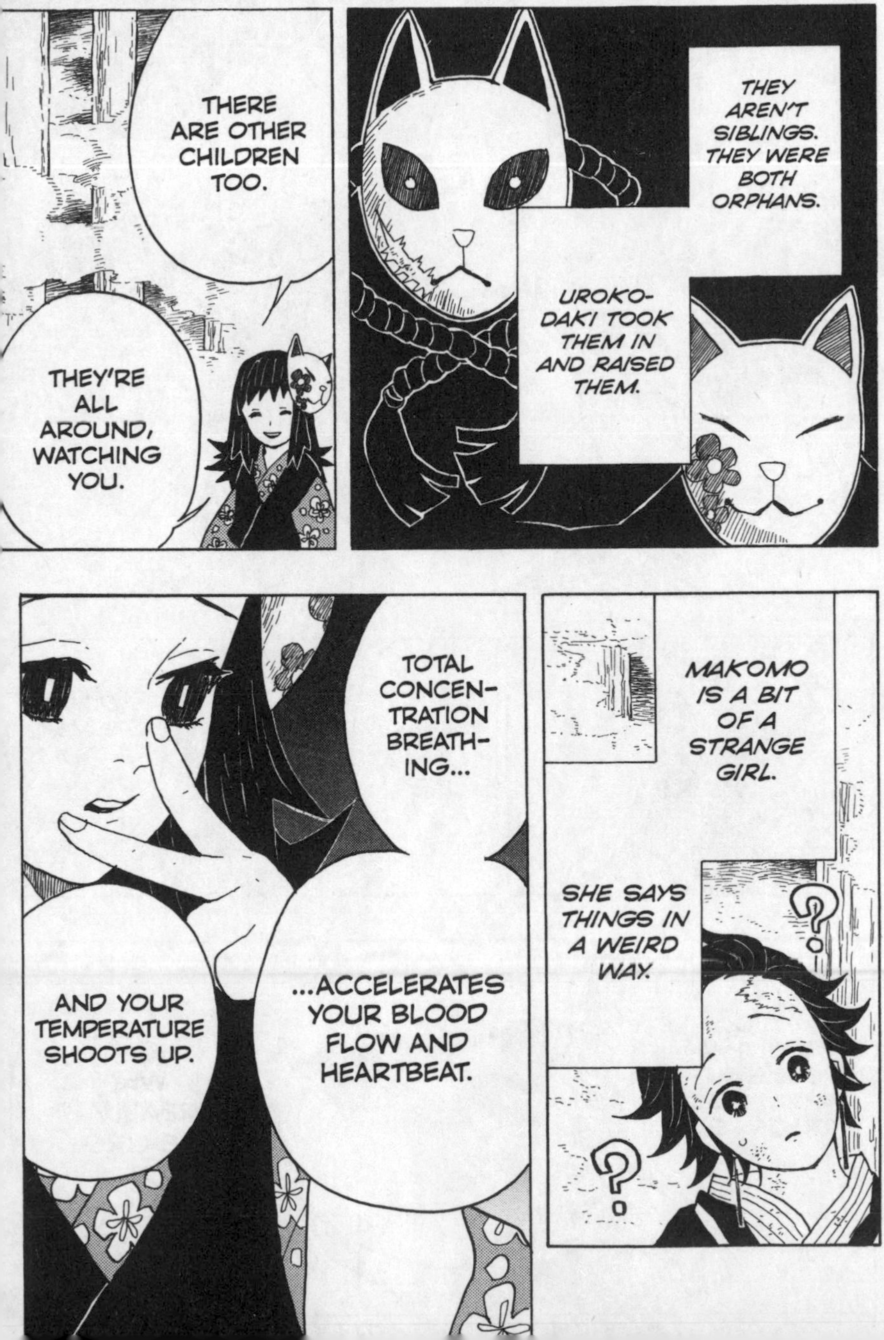
THEY AREN'T SIBLINGS. THEY WERE BOTH ORPHANS.
UROKODAKI TOOK THEM IN AND RAISED THEM.
THERE ARE OTHER CHILDREN TOO.
THEY'RE ALL AROUND, WATCHING YOU.
MAKOMO IS A BIT OF A STRANGE GIRL.
SHE SAYS THINGS IN A WEIRD WAY.
TOTAL CONCENTRATION BREATHING...
...ACCELERATES YOUR BLOOD FLOW AND HEARTBEAT.
AND YOUR TEMPERATURE SHOOTS UP.

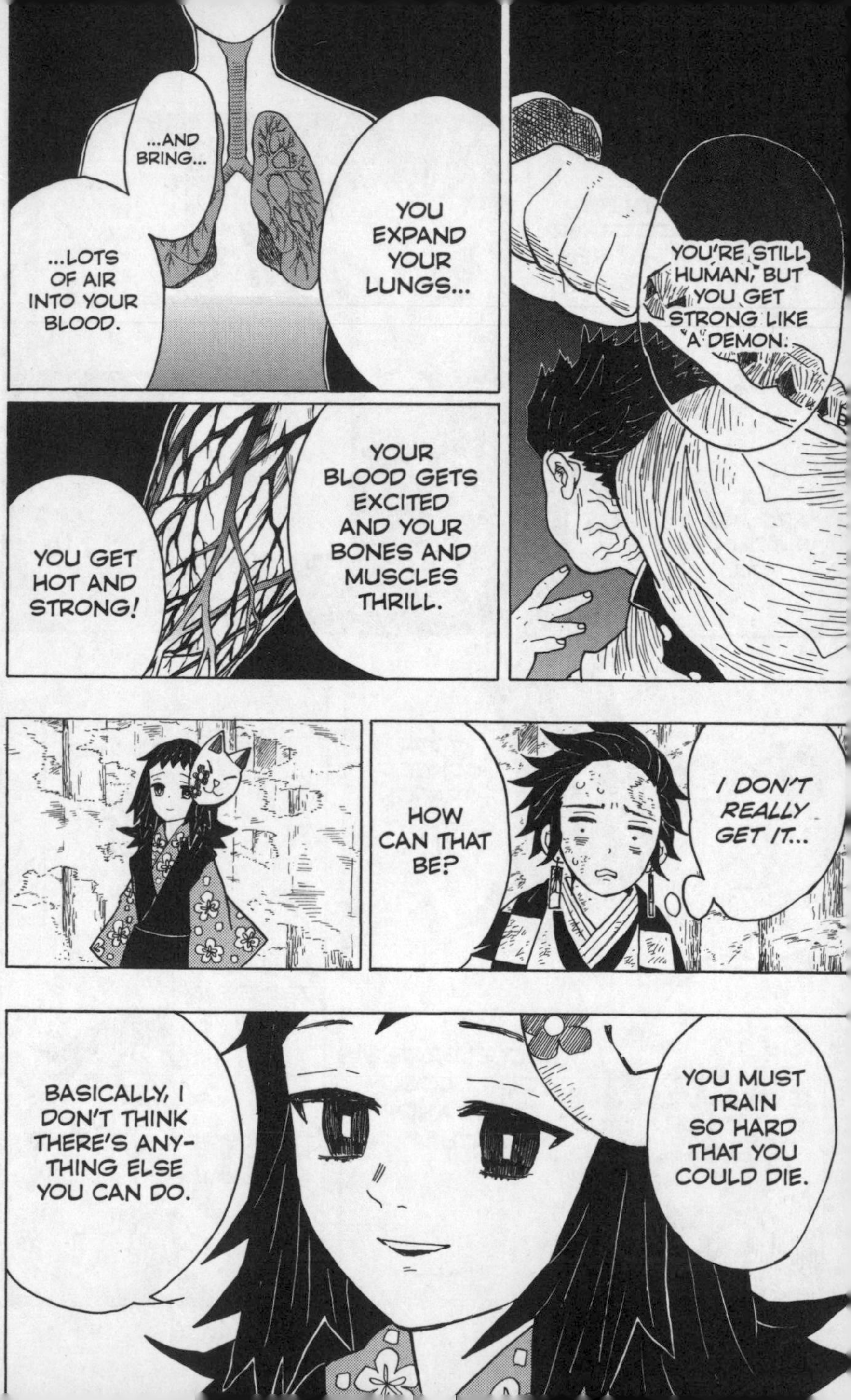
YOU EXPAND YOUR LUNGS...
...AND BRING...
...LOTS OF AIR INTO YOUR BLOOD.
YOUR BLOOD GETS EXCITED AND YOUR BONES AND MUSCLES THRILL.
YOU GET HOT AND STRONG!
YOU'RE STILL HUMAN, BUT YOU GET STRONG LIKE A DEMON.
I DON'T REALLY GET IT...
HOW CAN THAT BE?
YOU MUST TRAIN SO HARD THAT YOU COULD DIE.
BASICALLY, I DON'T THINK THERE'S ANY-THING ELSE YOU CAN DO.

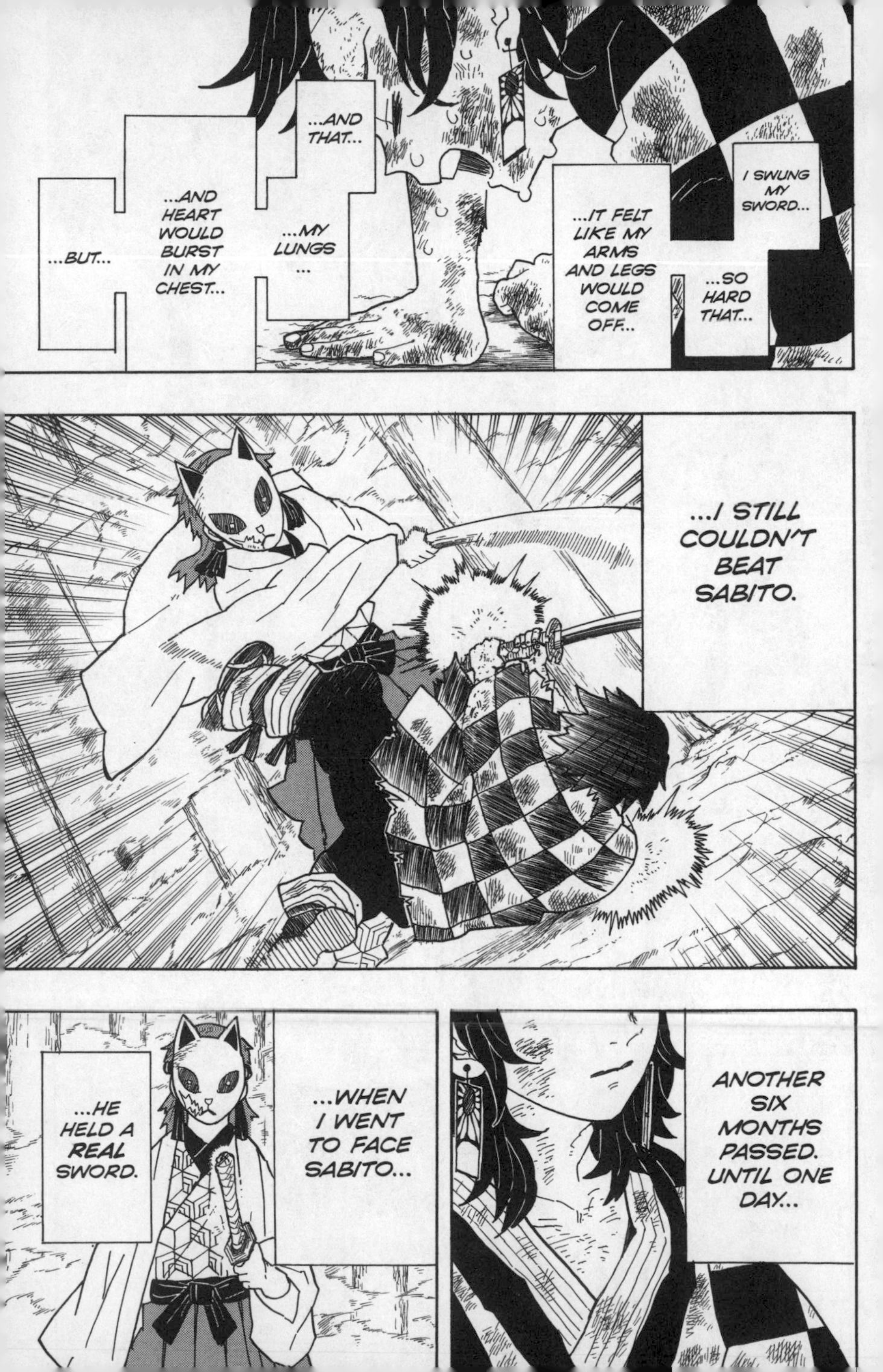
I SWUNG MY SWORD...
...SO HARD THAT...
...IT FELT LIKE MY ARMS AND LEGS WOULD COME OFF...
...AND THAT...
...MY LUNGS...
...AND HEART WOULD BURST IN MY CHEST...
...BUT...
...I STILL COULDN'T BEAT SABITO.
ANOTHER SIX MONTHS PASSED. UNTIL ONE DAY...
...WHEN I WENT TO FACE SABITO...
...HE HELD A REAL SWORD.

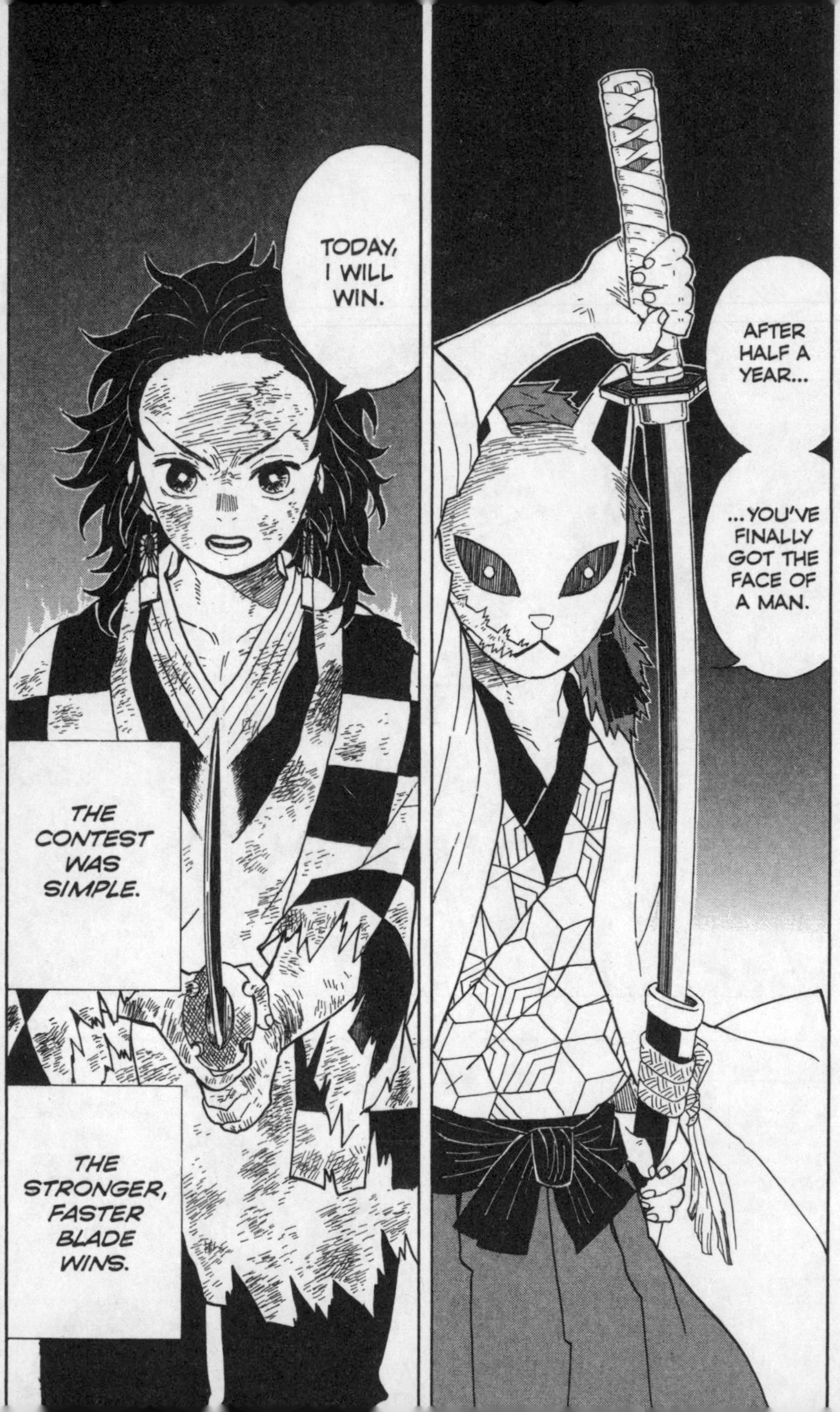
AFTER HALF A YEAR...
...YOU'VE FINALLY GOT THE FACE OF A MAN.
TODAY, I WILL WIN.
THE CONTEST WAS SIMPLE.
THE STRONGER, FASTER BLADE WINS.

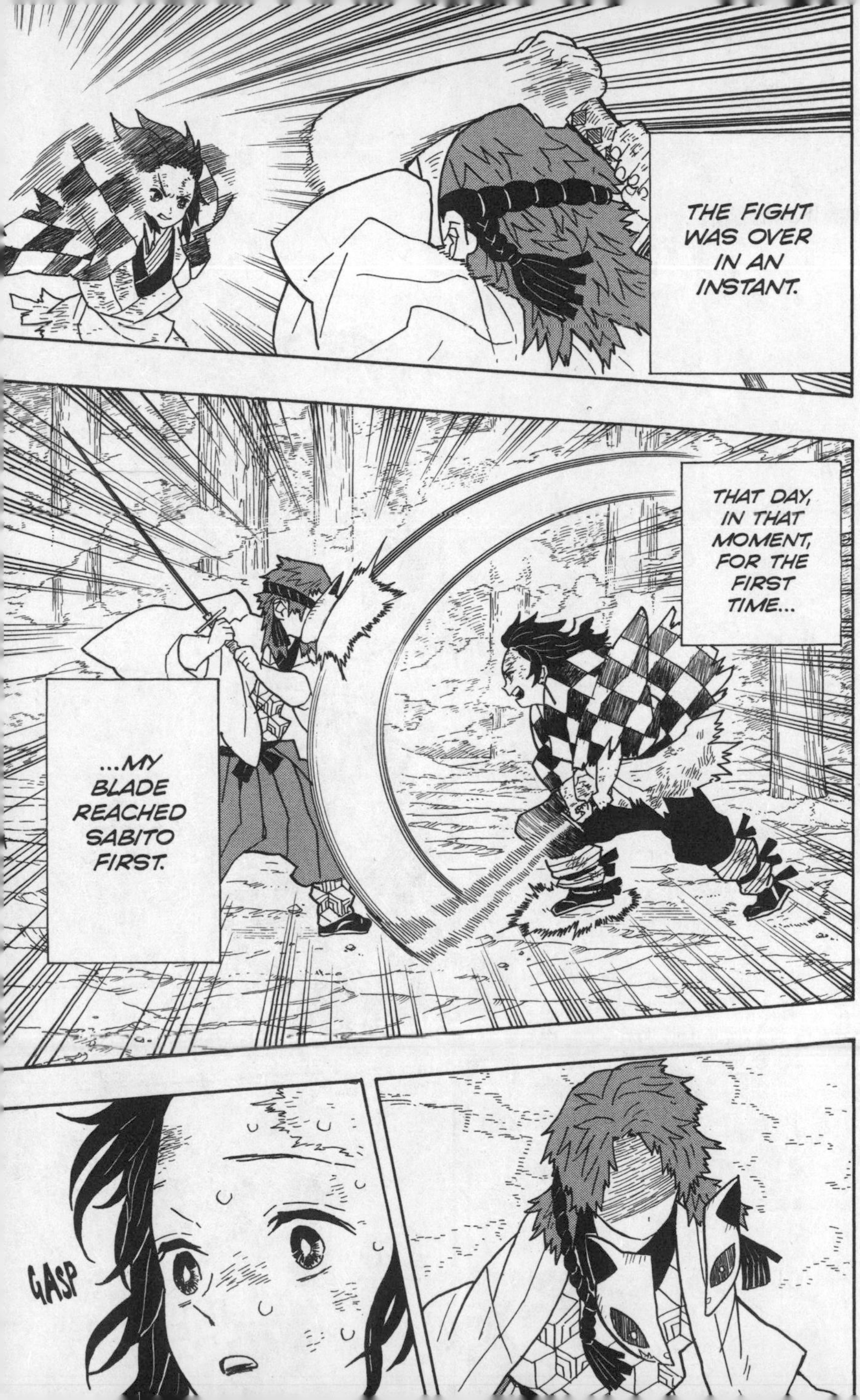
THE FIGHT WAS OVER IN AN INSTANT.
THAT DAY, IN THAT MOMENT, FOR THE FIRST TIME...
...MY BLADE REACHED SABITO FIRST.
GASP

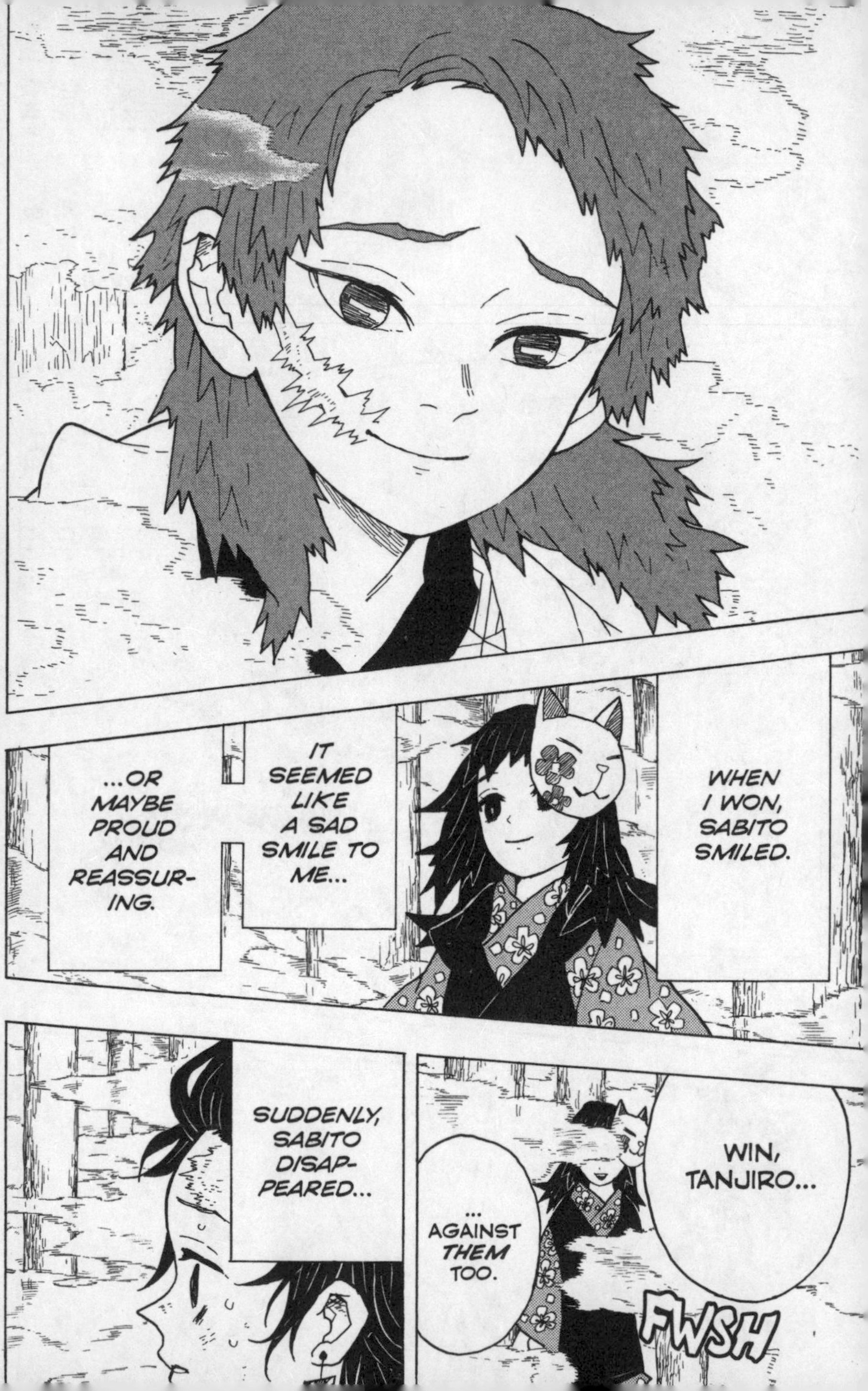
WHEN I WON, SABITO SMILED.
IT SEEMED LIKE A SAD SMILE TO ME...
...OR MAYBE PROUD AND REASSURING.
WIN, TANJIRO...
...AGAINST THEM TOO.
FWSH
SUDDENLY, SABITO DISAPPEARED...

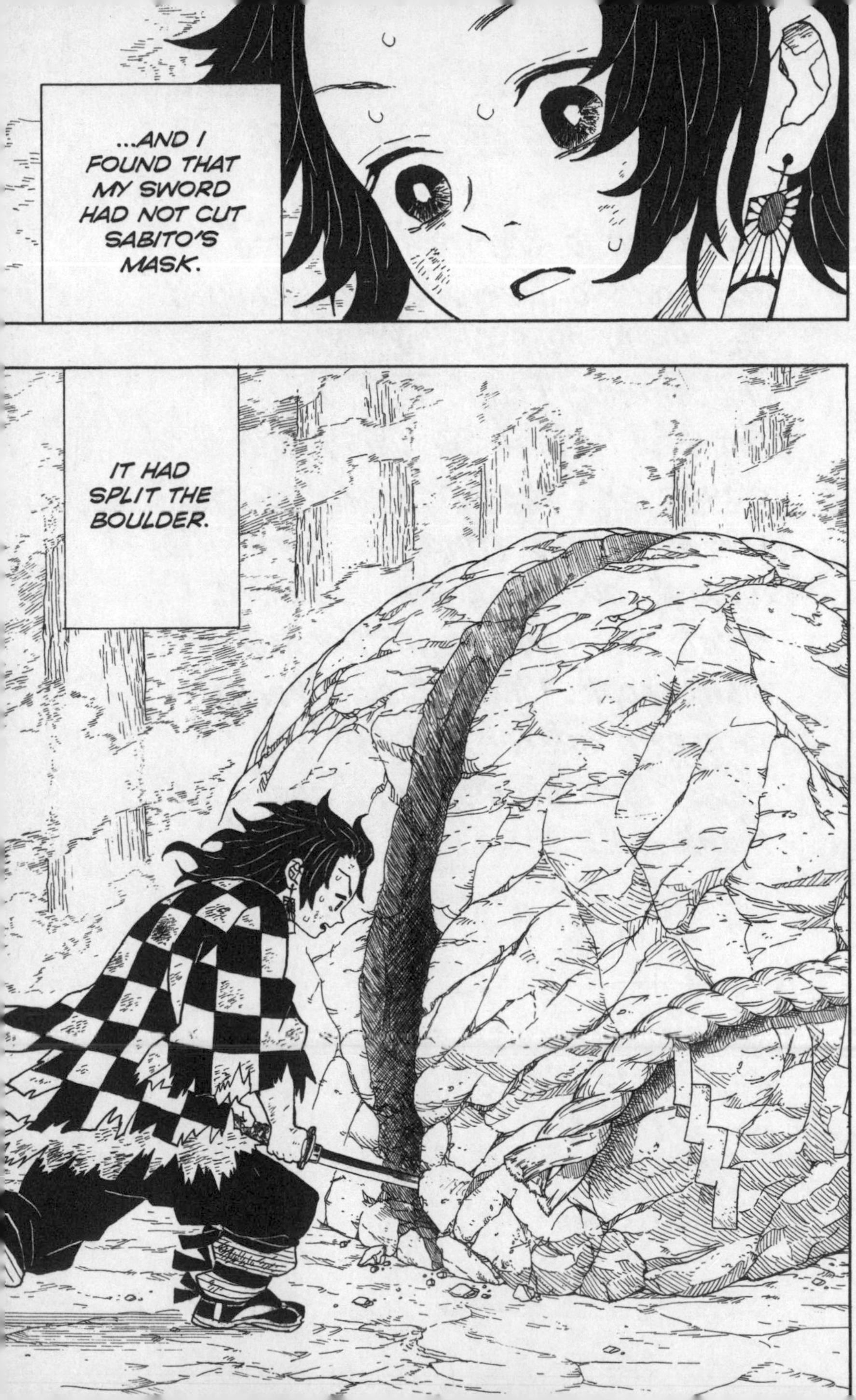
...AND I FOUND THAT MY SWORD HAD NOT CUT SABITO'S MASK.
IT HAD SPLIT THE BOULDER.

WORDS OF GRATITUDE

Thank you to everyone who read this work and to everyone who bought it. Thanks to your support, the series will continue. I can't tell you how thankful I am. Unlike water and food, manga isn't absolutely necessary for survival. Getting you to buy it is a tough job. Thank you very much. I create this manga with the help of many people. I'll work even harder to keep it interesting for you, so please keep reading. And again... thank you!!

I've gotten all your letters. Thank you. They make me so happy, but I can't reply, and that makes me very sorry. Forgive me, please. I'll keep doing my best!

Sorry...

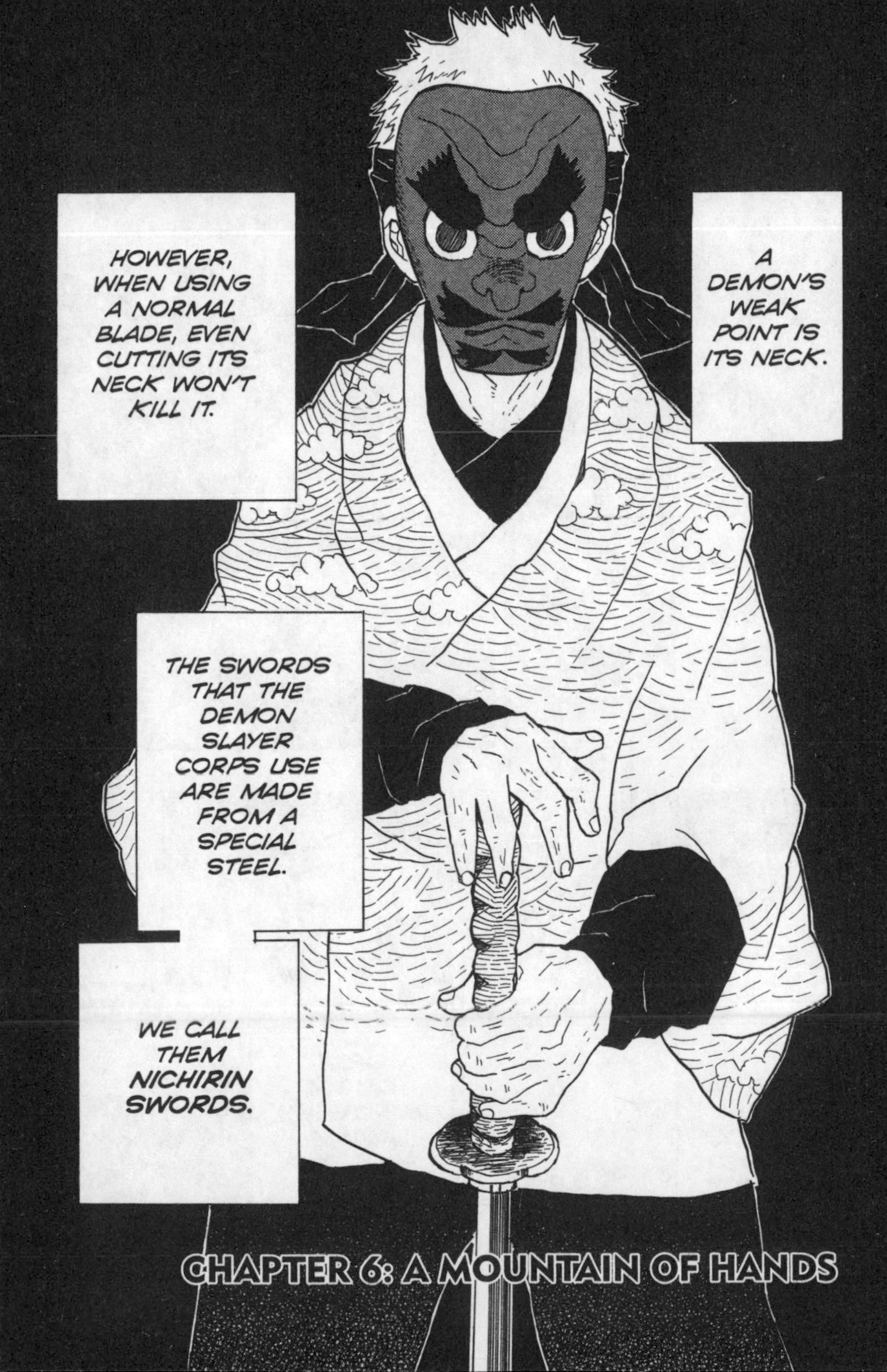
A DEMON'S WEAK POINT IS ITS NECK.
HOWEVER, WHEN USING A NORMAL BLADE, EVEN CUTTING ITS NECK WON'T KILL IT.
THE SWORDS THAT THE DEMON SLAYER CORPS USE ARE MADE FROM A SPECIAL STEEL.
WE CALL THEM NICHIRIN SWORDS.
CHAPTER 6: A MOUNTAIN OF HANDS

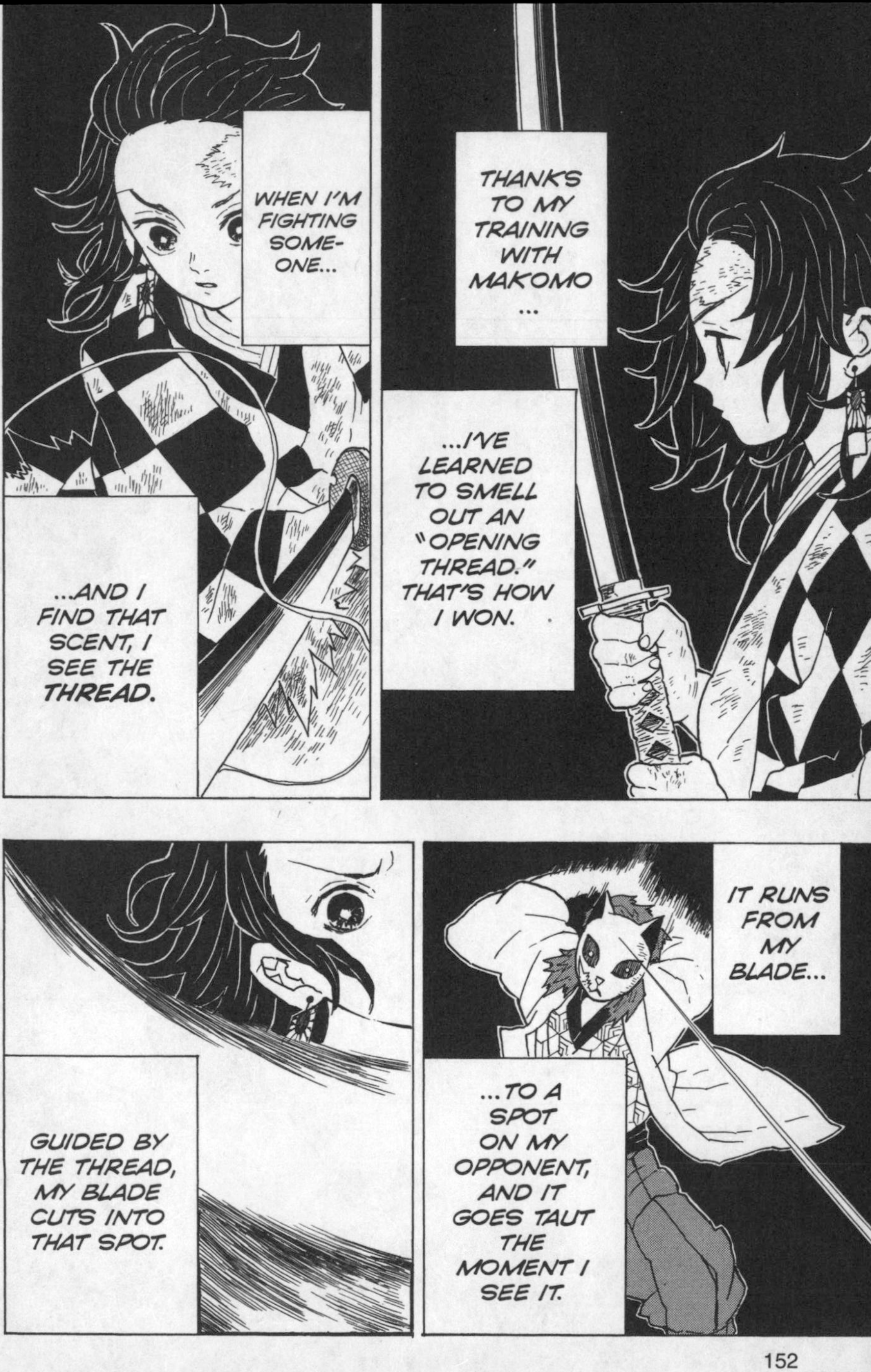
THANKS TO MY TRAINING WITH MAKOMO ...
...I'VE LEARNED TO SMELL OUT AN "OPENING THREAD." THAT'S HOW I WON.
WHEN I'M FIGHTING SOME-ONE...
...AND I FIND THAT SCENT, I SEE THE THREAD.
IT RUNS FROM MY BLADE...
...TO A SPOT ON MY OPPONENT, AND IT GOES TAUT THE MOMENT I SEE IT.
GUIDED BY THE THREAD, MY BLADE CUTS INTO THAT SPOT.

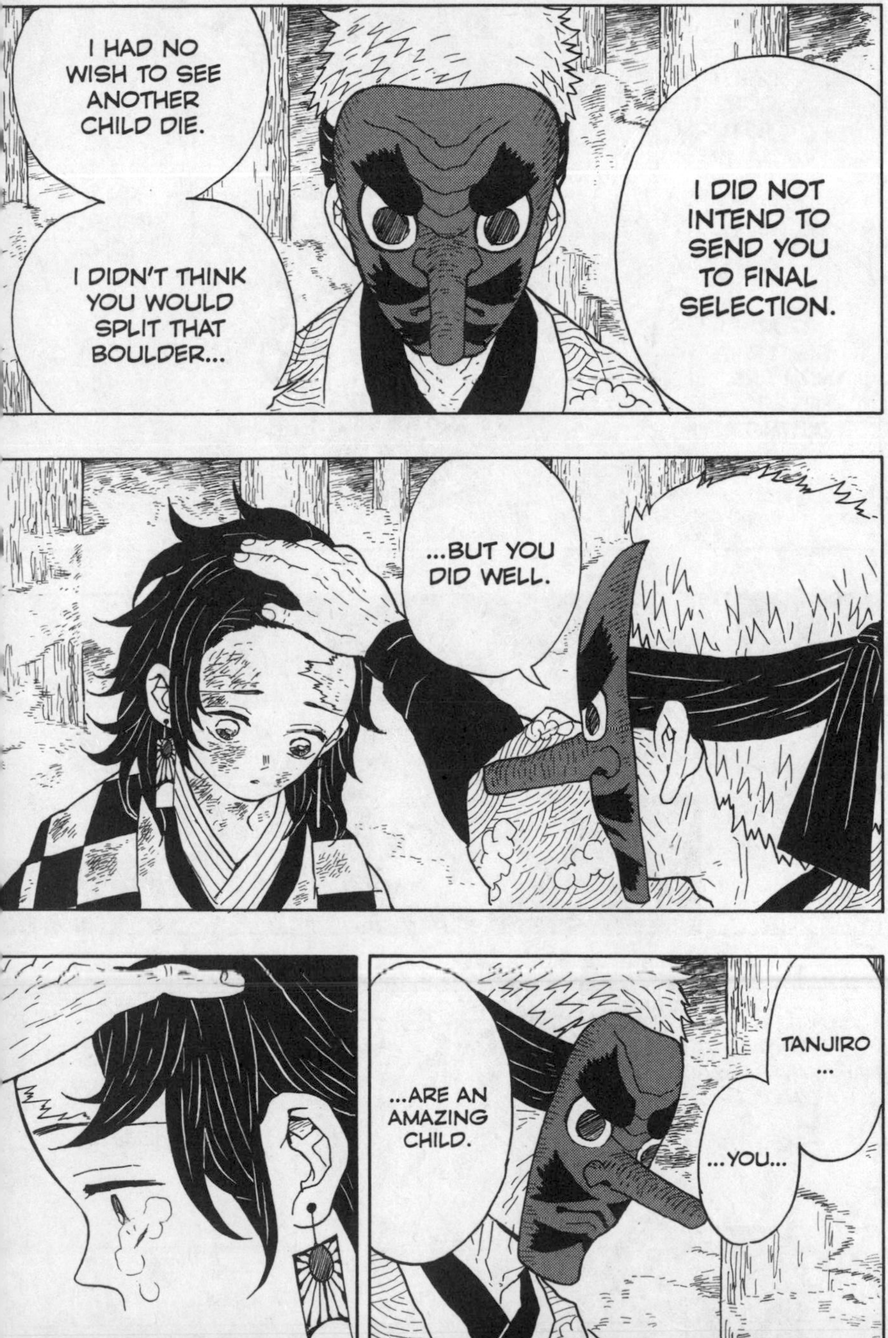
I DID NOT INTEND TO SEND YOU TO FINAL SELECTION.
I HAD NO WISH TO SEE ANOTHER CHILD DIE.
I DIDN'T THINK YOU WOULD SPLIT THAT BOULDER...
...BUT YOU DID WELL.
TANJIRO ...
...YOU...
...ARE AN AMAZING CHILD.

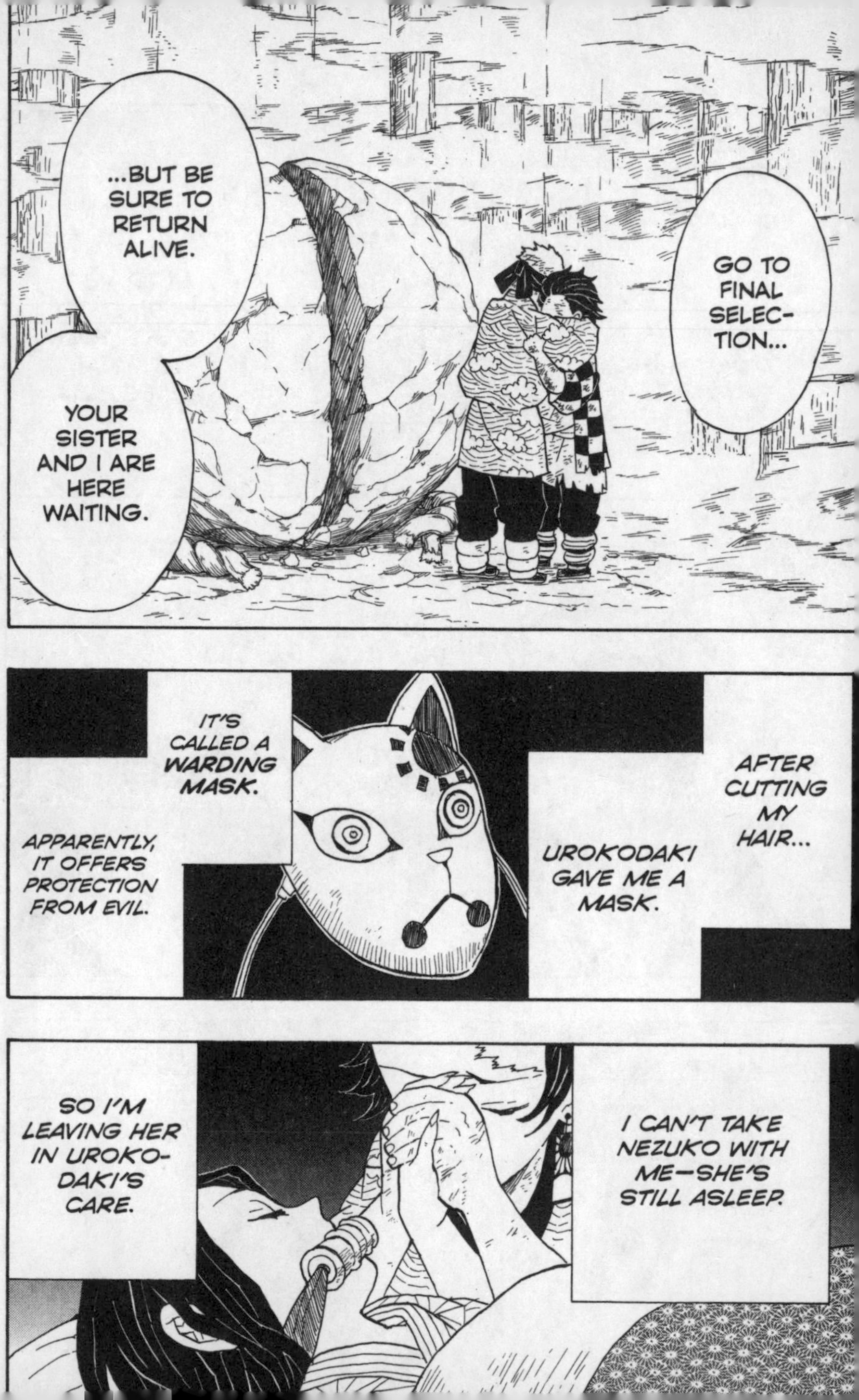
GO TO FINAL SELEC-TION...
...BUT BE SURE TO RETURN ALIVE.
YOUR SISTER AND I ARE HERE WAITING.
AFTER CUTTING MY HAIR...
UROKODAKI GAVE ME A MASK.
IT'S CALLED A WARDING MASK.
APPARENTLY, IT OFFERS PROTECTION FROM EVIL.
I CAN'T TAKE NEZUKO WITH ME—SHE'S STILL ASLEEP.
SO I'M LEAVING HER IN UROKO-DAKI'S CARE.

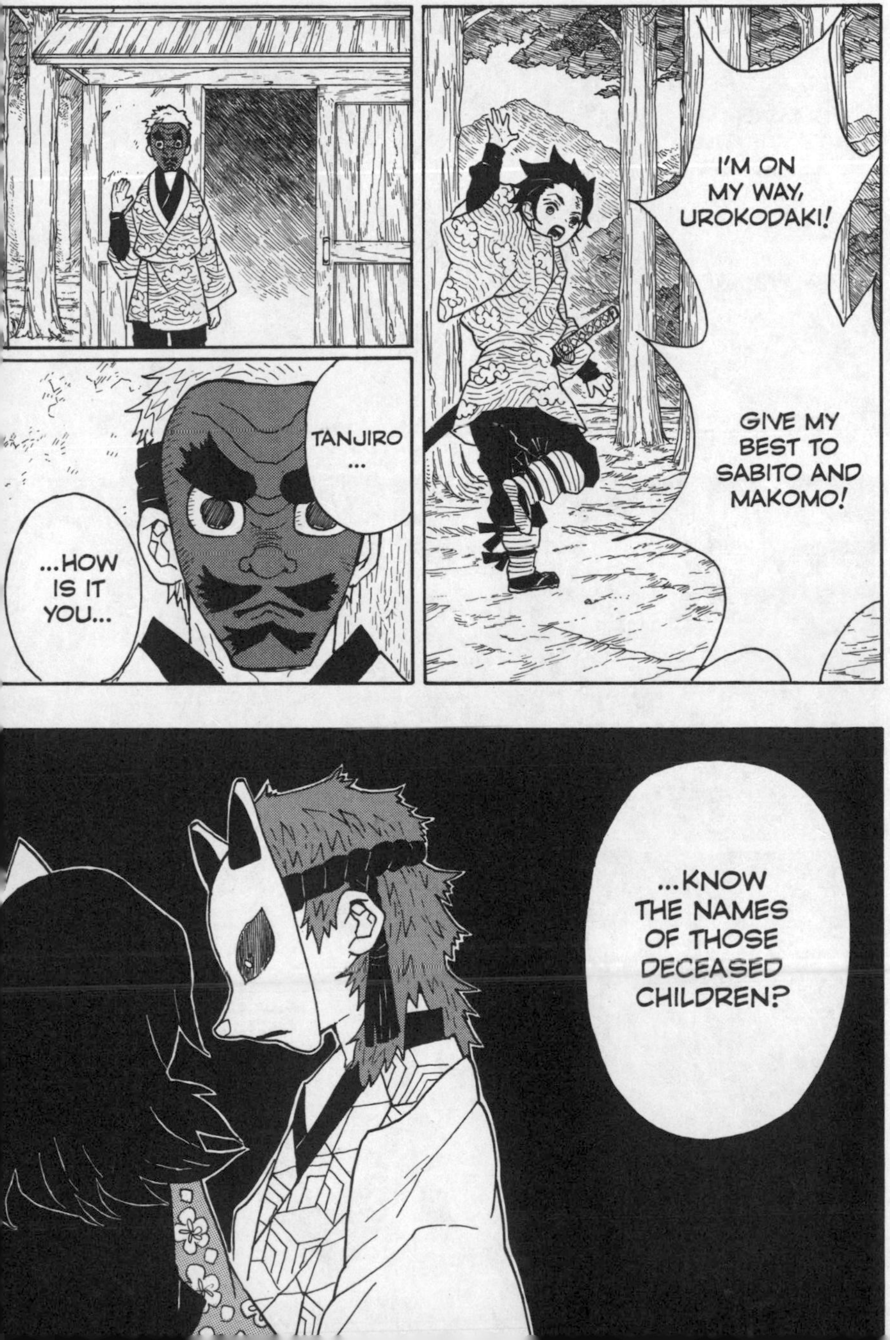
I'M ON MY WAY, UROKODAKI!
GIVE MY BEST TO SABITO AND MAKOMO!
TANJIRO ...
...HOW IS IT YOU...
...KNOW THE NAMES OF THOSE DECEASED CHILDREN?

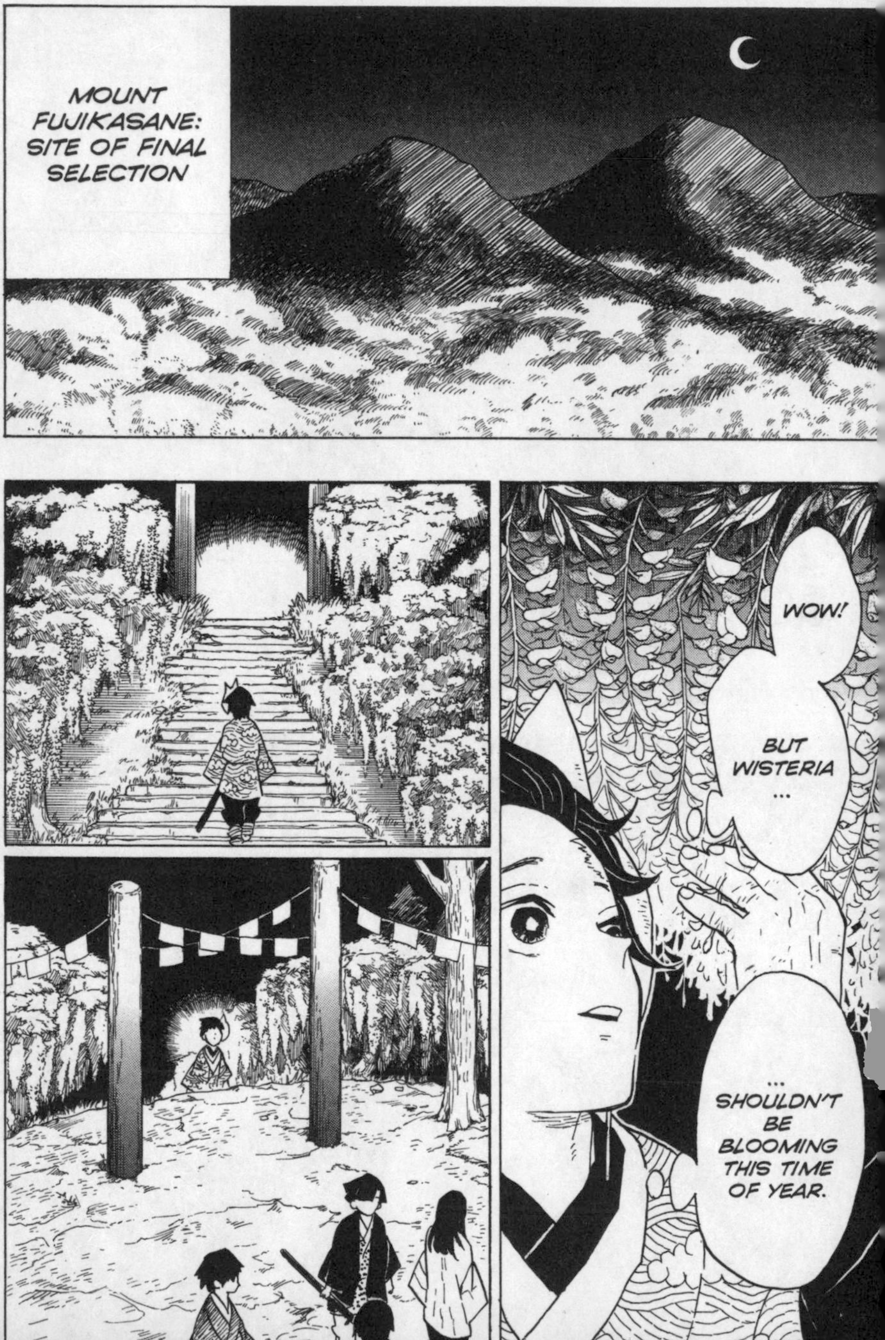
MOUNT FUJIKASANE: SITE OF FINAL SELECTION
WOW!
BUT WISTERIA ...
... SHOULDN'T BE BLOOMING THIS TIME OF YEAR.

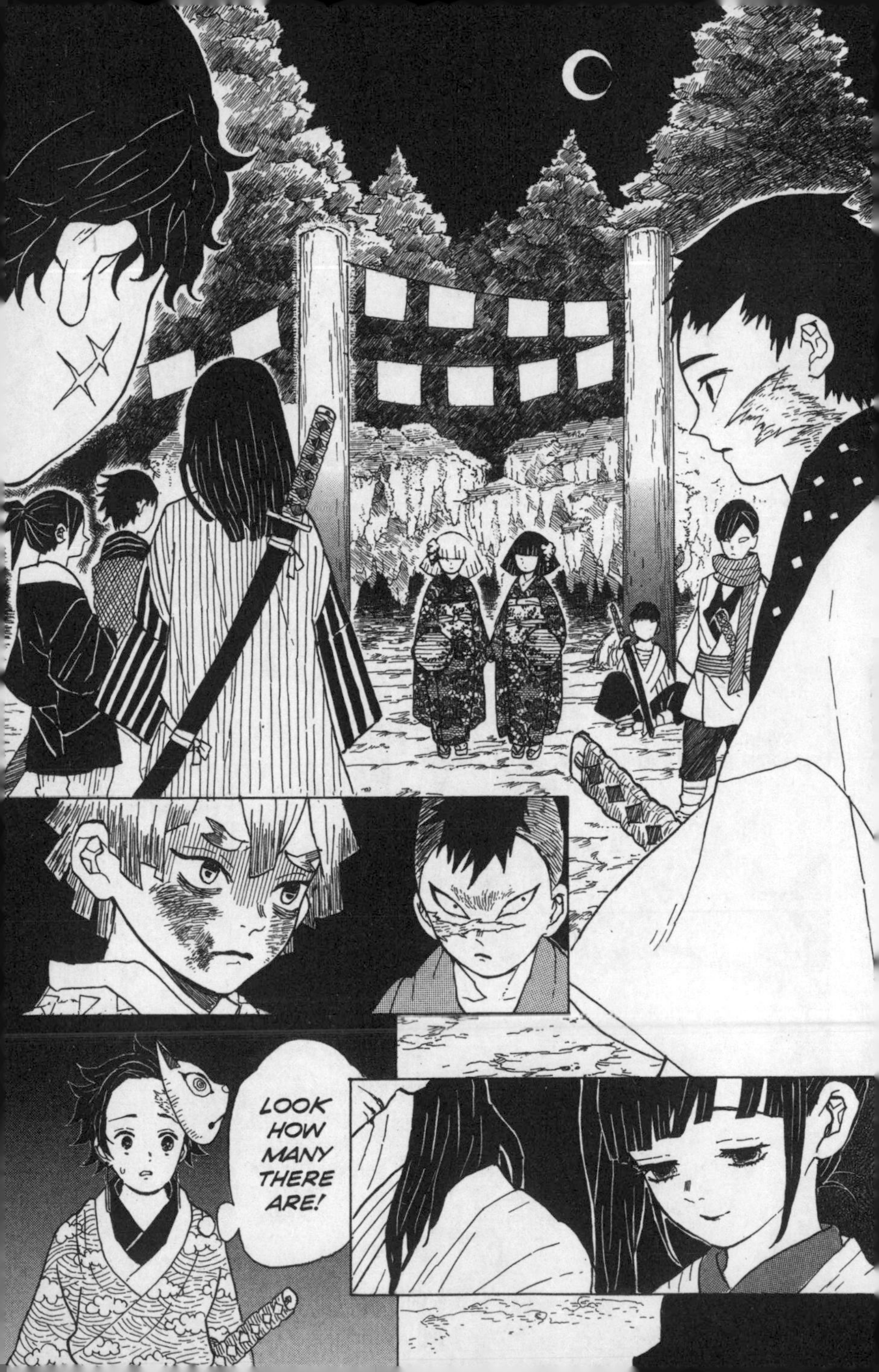
LOOK HOW MANY THERE ARE!

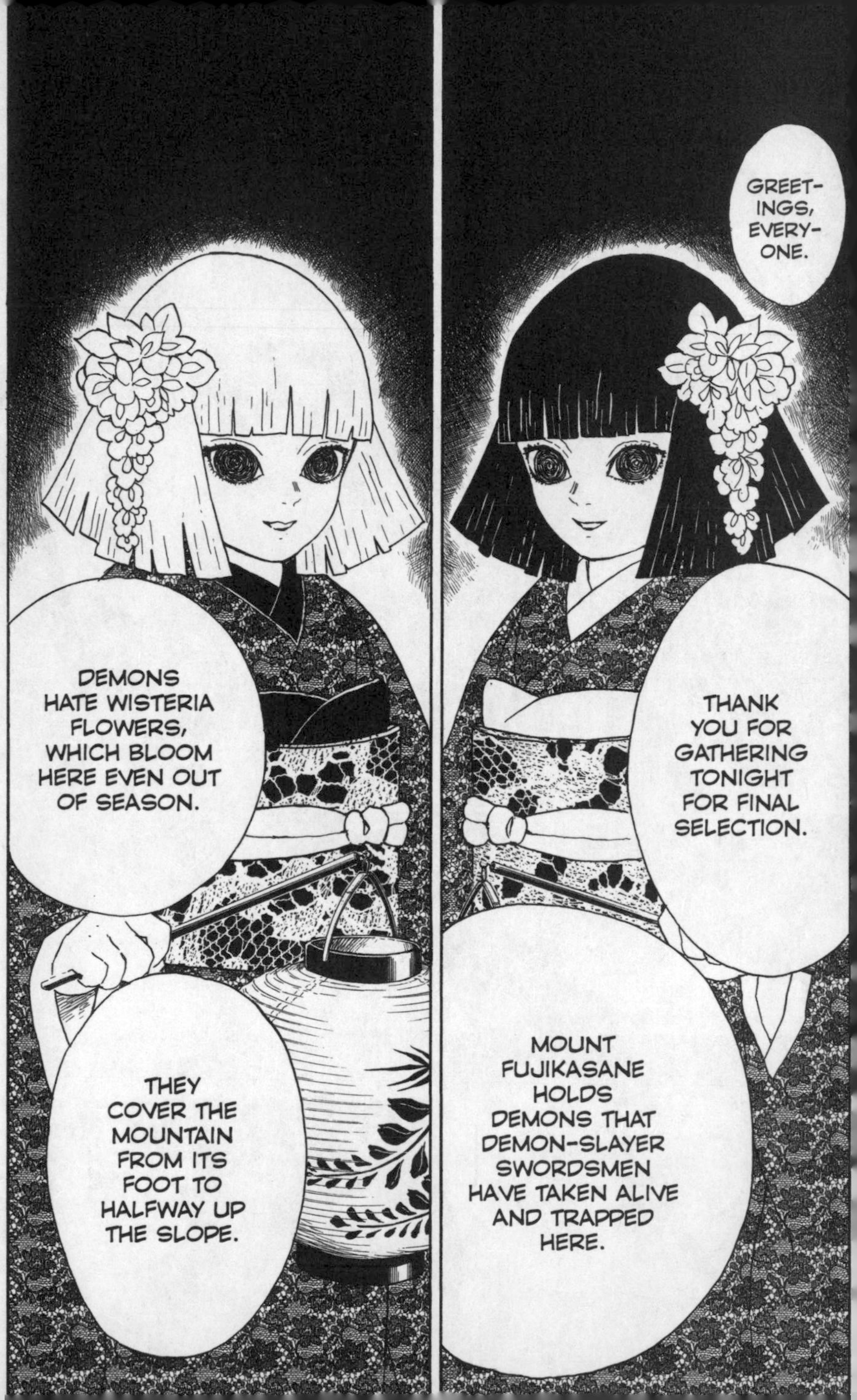
GREET-INGS, EVERY-ONE.
THANK YOU FOR GATHERING TONIGHT FOR FINAL SELECTION.
MOUNT FUJIKASANE HOLDS DEMONS THAT DEMON-SLAYER SWORDSMEN HAVE TAKEN ALIVE AND TRAPPED HERE.
DEMONS HATE WISTERIA FLOWERS, WHICH BLOOM HERE EVEN OUT OF SEASON.
THEY COVER THE MOUNTAIN FROM ITS FOOT TO HALFWAY UP THE SLOPE.

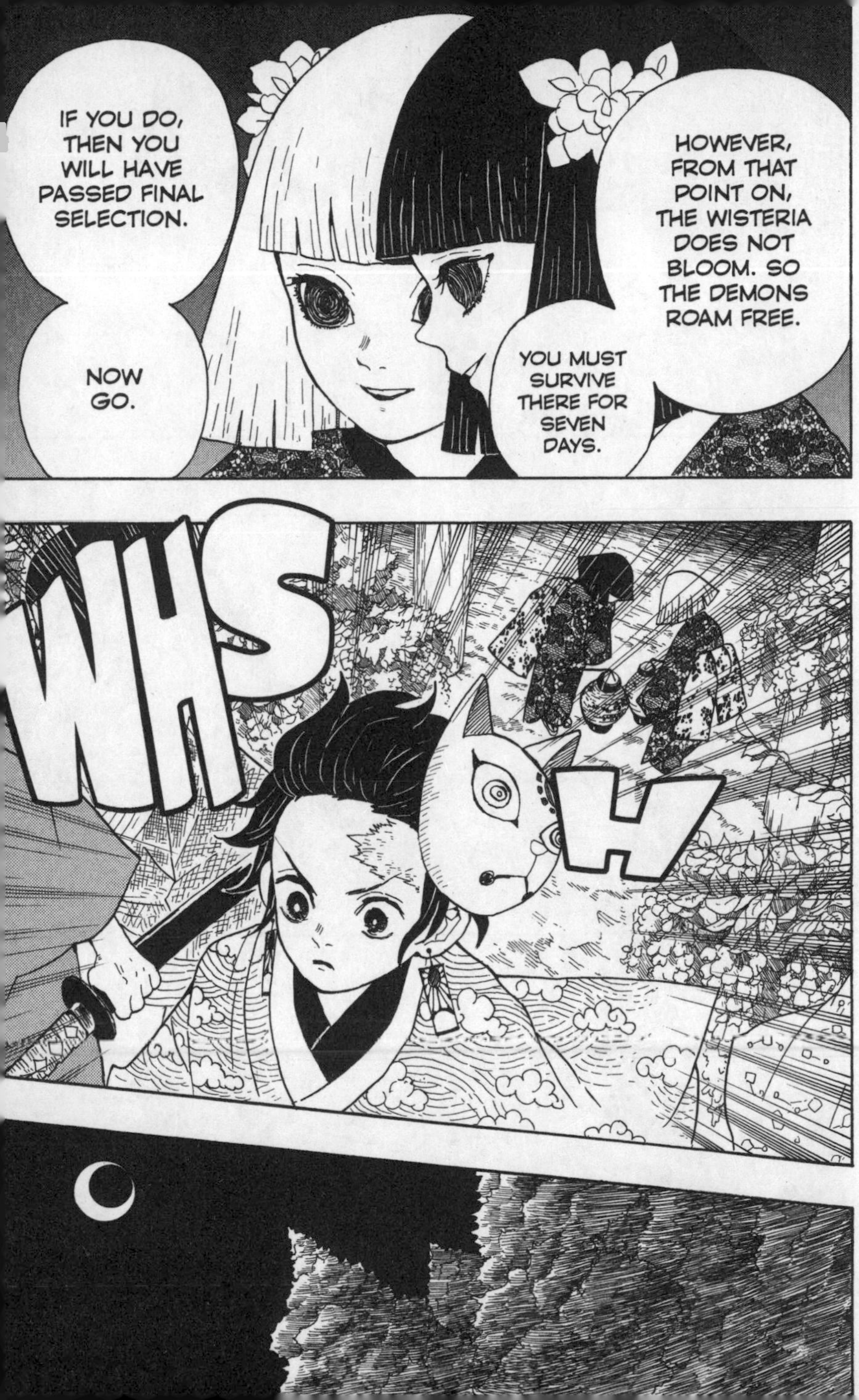
HOWEVER, FROM THAT POINT ON, THE WISTERIA DOES NOT BLOOM. SO THE DEMONS ROAM FREE.
YOU MUST SURVIVE THERE FOR SEVEN DAYS.
IF YOU DO, THEN YOU WILL HAVE PASSED FINAL SELECTION.
NOW GO.
WHS
H

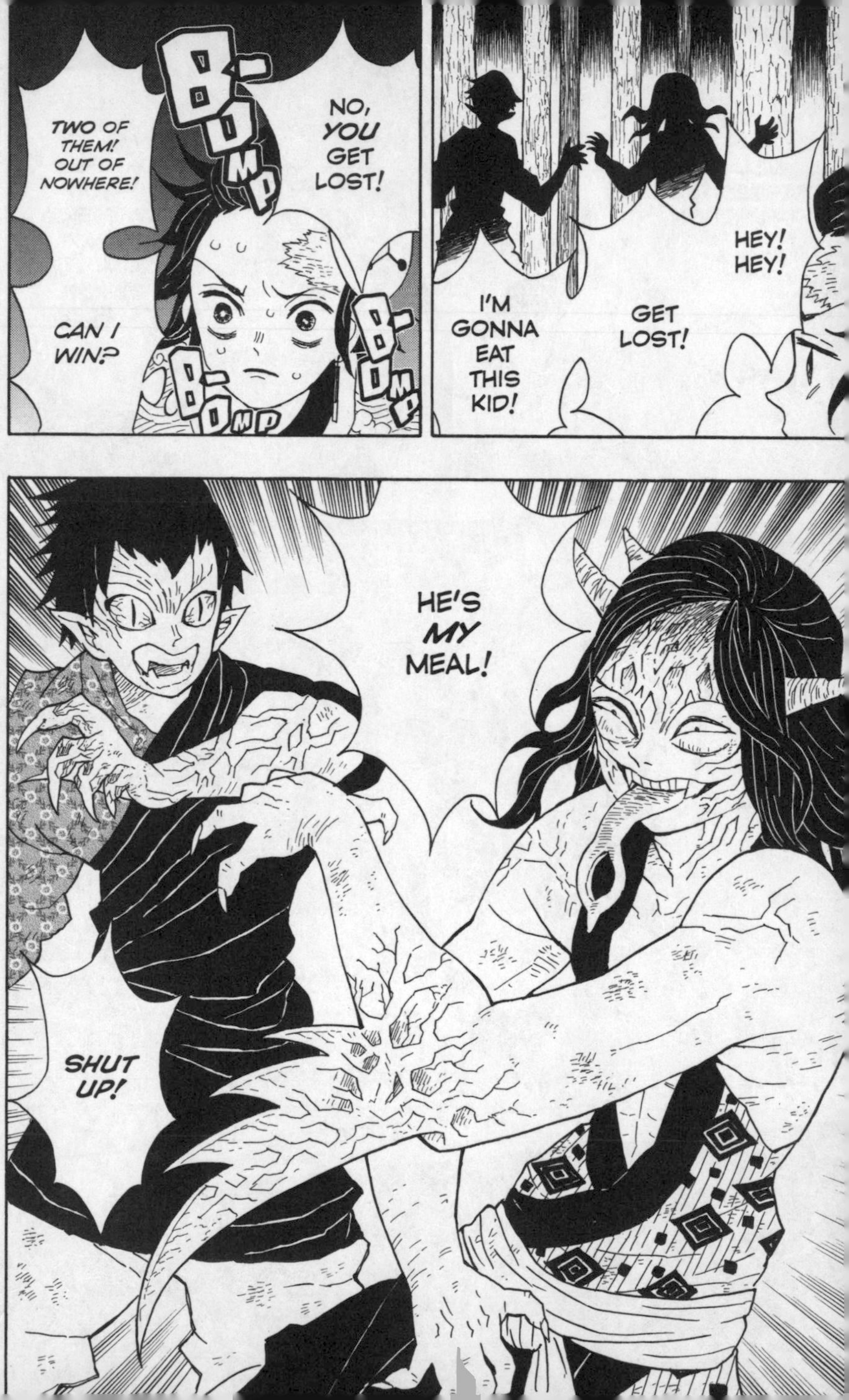
HEY! HEY!
GET LOST!
I'M GONNA EAT THIS KID!
NO, YOU GET LOST!
B-BUMP
TWO OF THEM! OUT OF NOWHERE!
B-BUMP
B-BUMP
CAN I WIN?
HE'S MY MEAL!
SHUT UP!

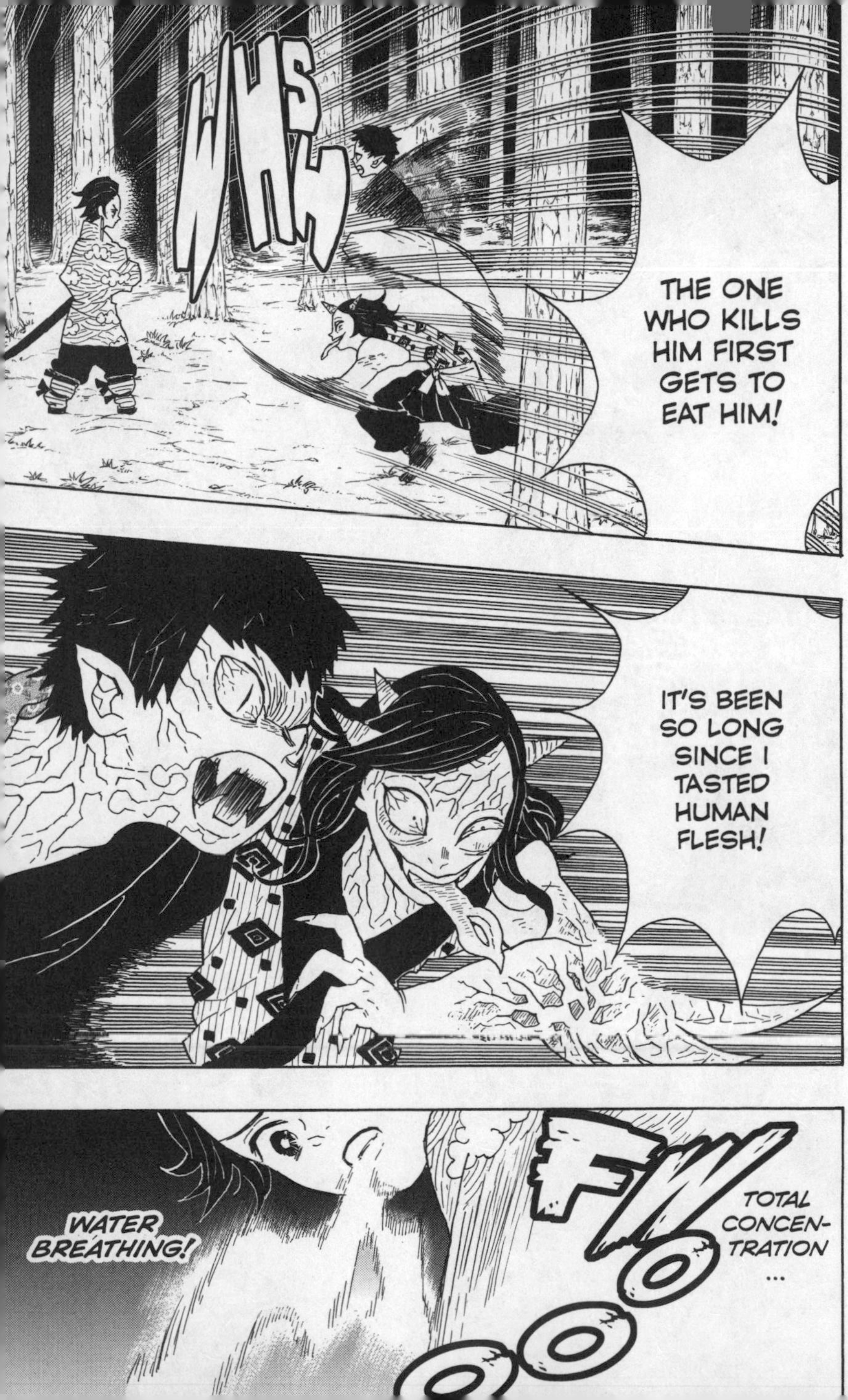
WHSH
THE ONE WHO KILLS HIM FIRST GETS TO EAT HIM!
IT'S BEEN SO LONG SINCE I TASTED HUMAN FLESH!
FWOOO
TOTAL CONCEN-TRATION ...
WATER BREATHING!

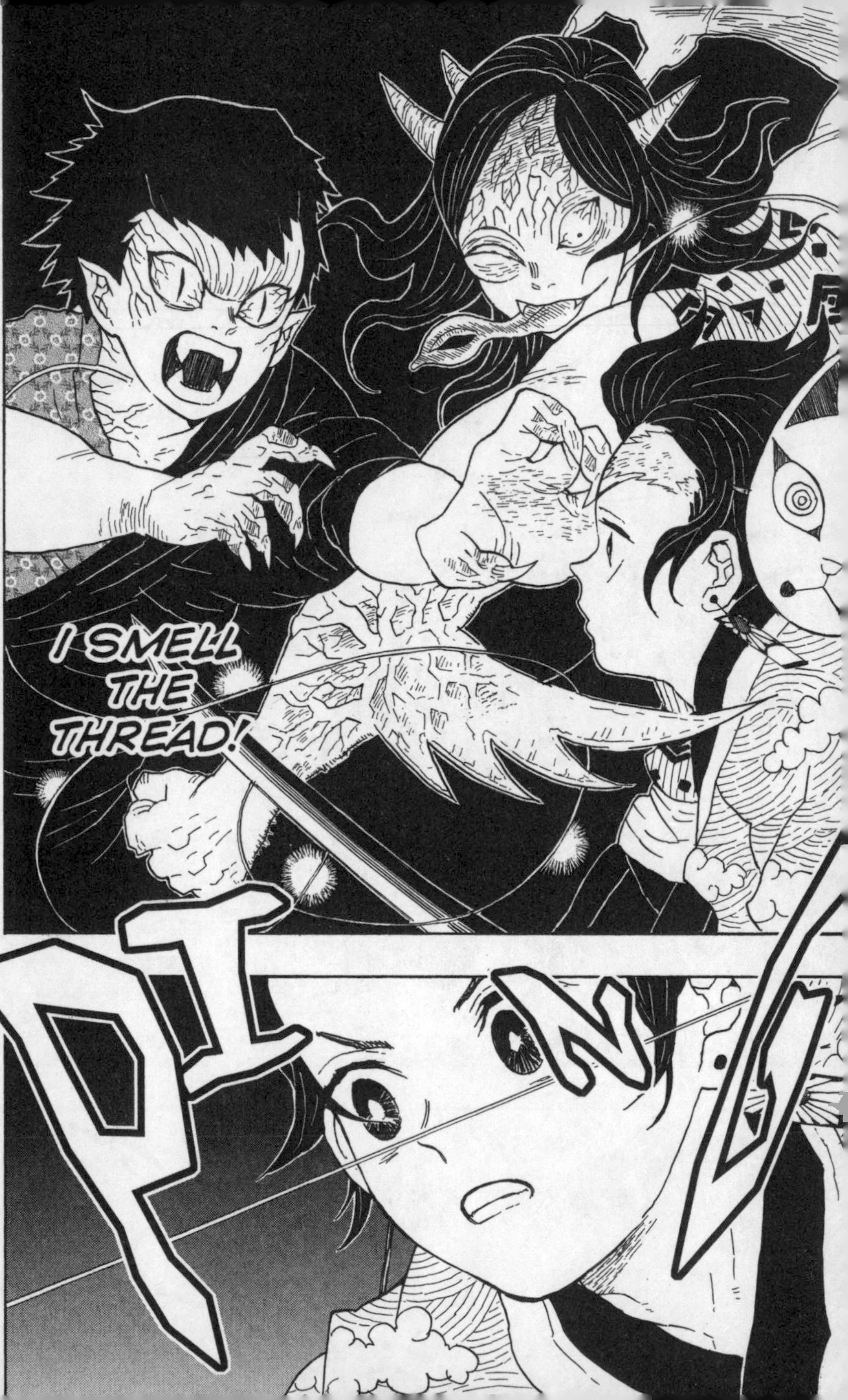
I SMELL THE THREAD!
DIN

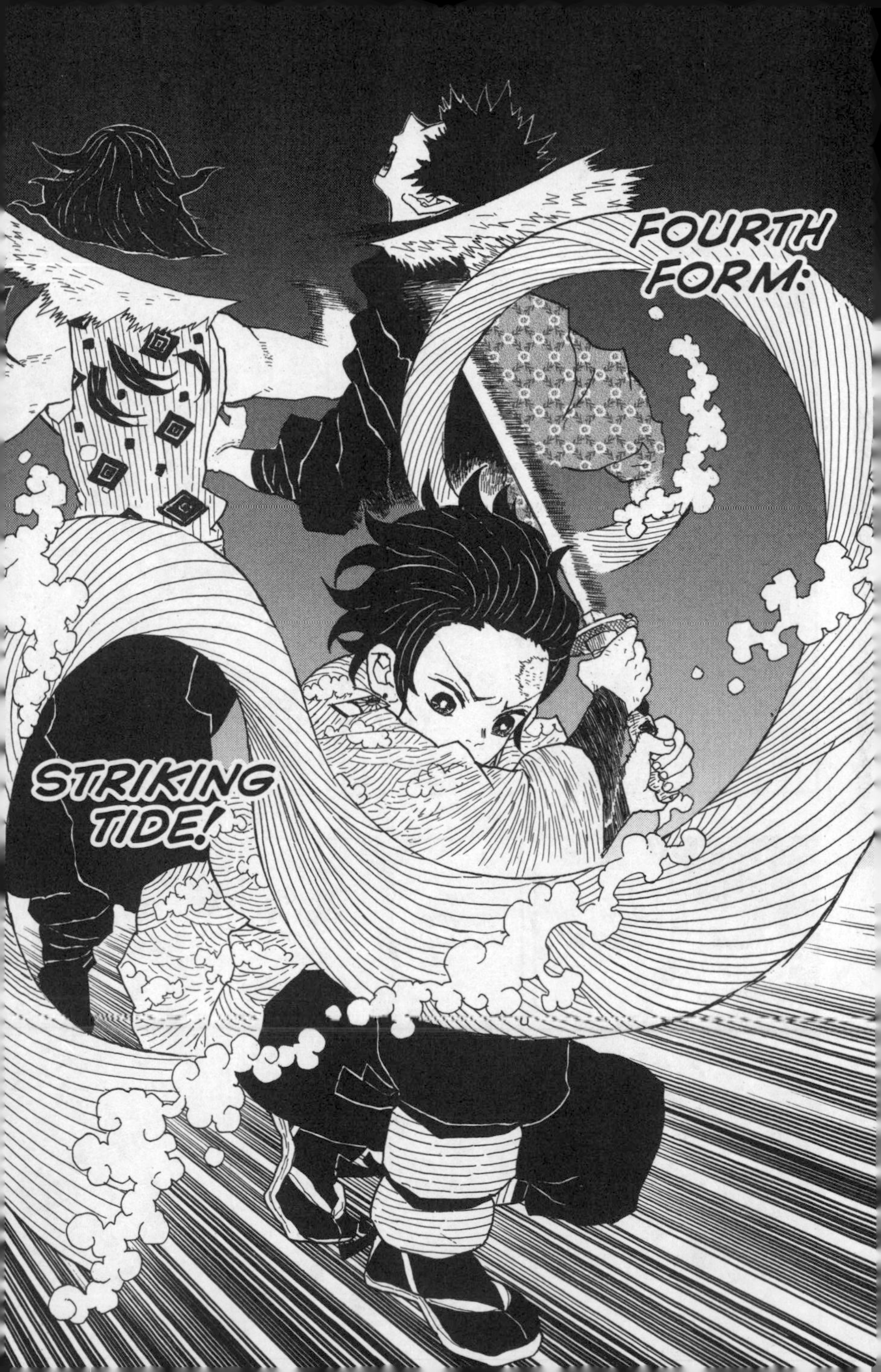
FOURTH FORM:
STRIKING TIDE!

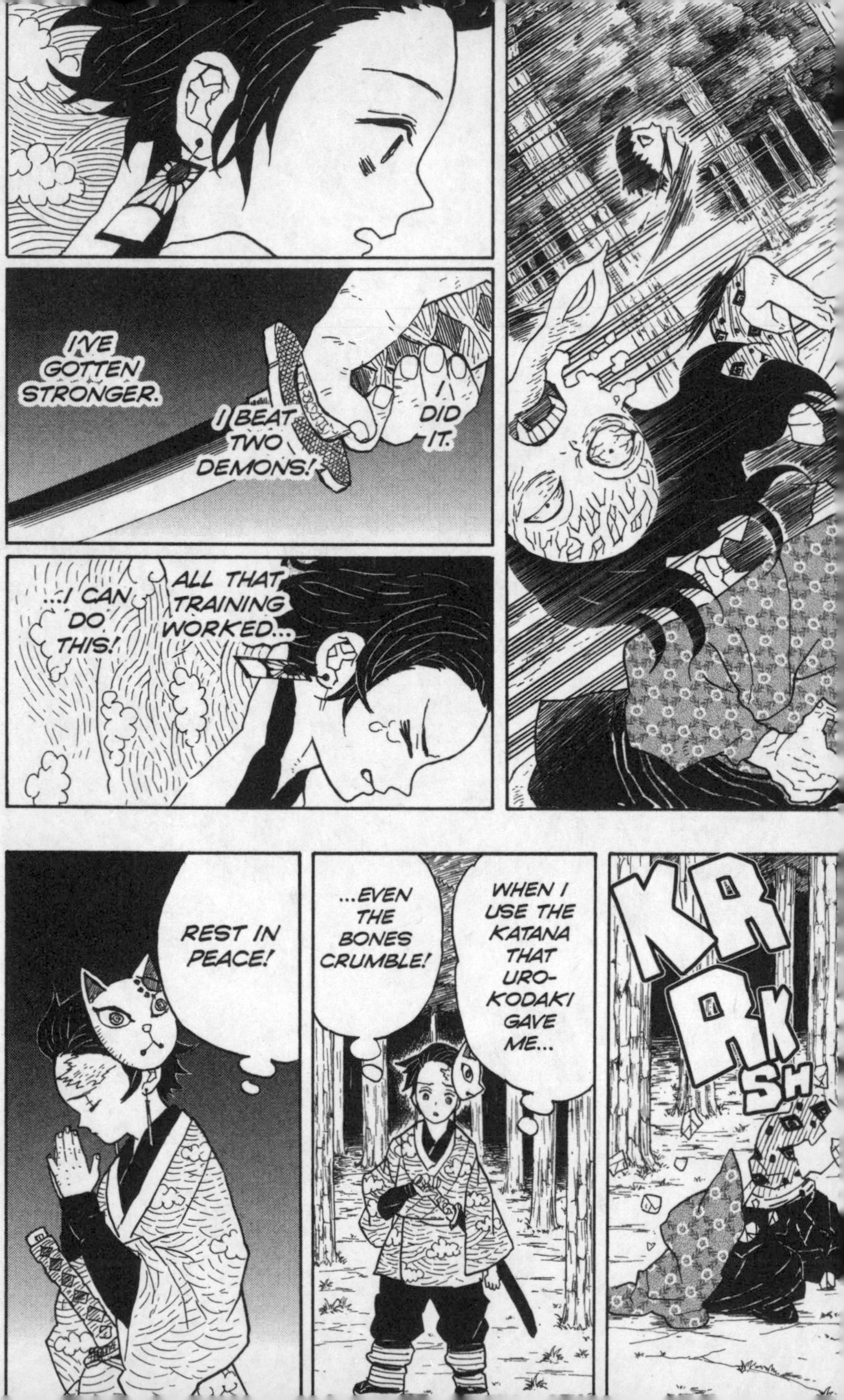
I DID IT.
I BEAT TWO DEMONS!
I'VE GOTTEN STRONGER.
ALL THAT TRAINING WORKED...
...I CAN DO THIS!
KRAKSH
WHEN I USE THE KATANA THAT URO-KODAKI GAVE ME...
...EVEN THE BONES CRUMBLE!
REST IN PEACE!

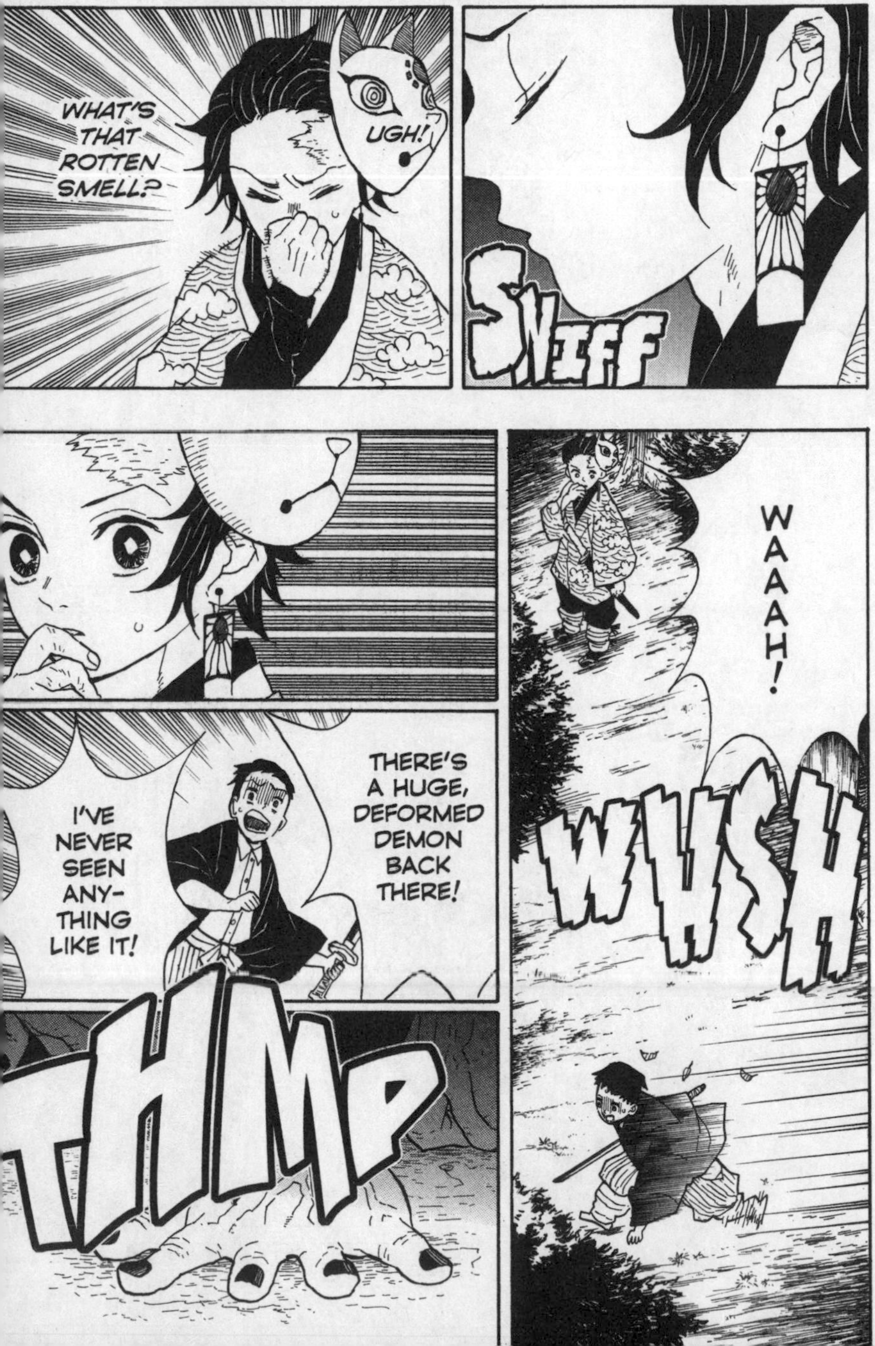
SNIFF
UGH!
WHAT'S THAT ROTTEN SMELL?
WAAAAH!
WHSH
THERE'S A HUGE, DEFORMED DEMON BACK THERE!
I'VE NEVER SEEN ANYTHING LIKE IT!
THMP

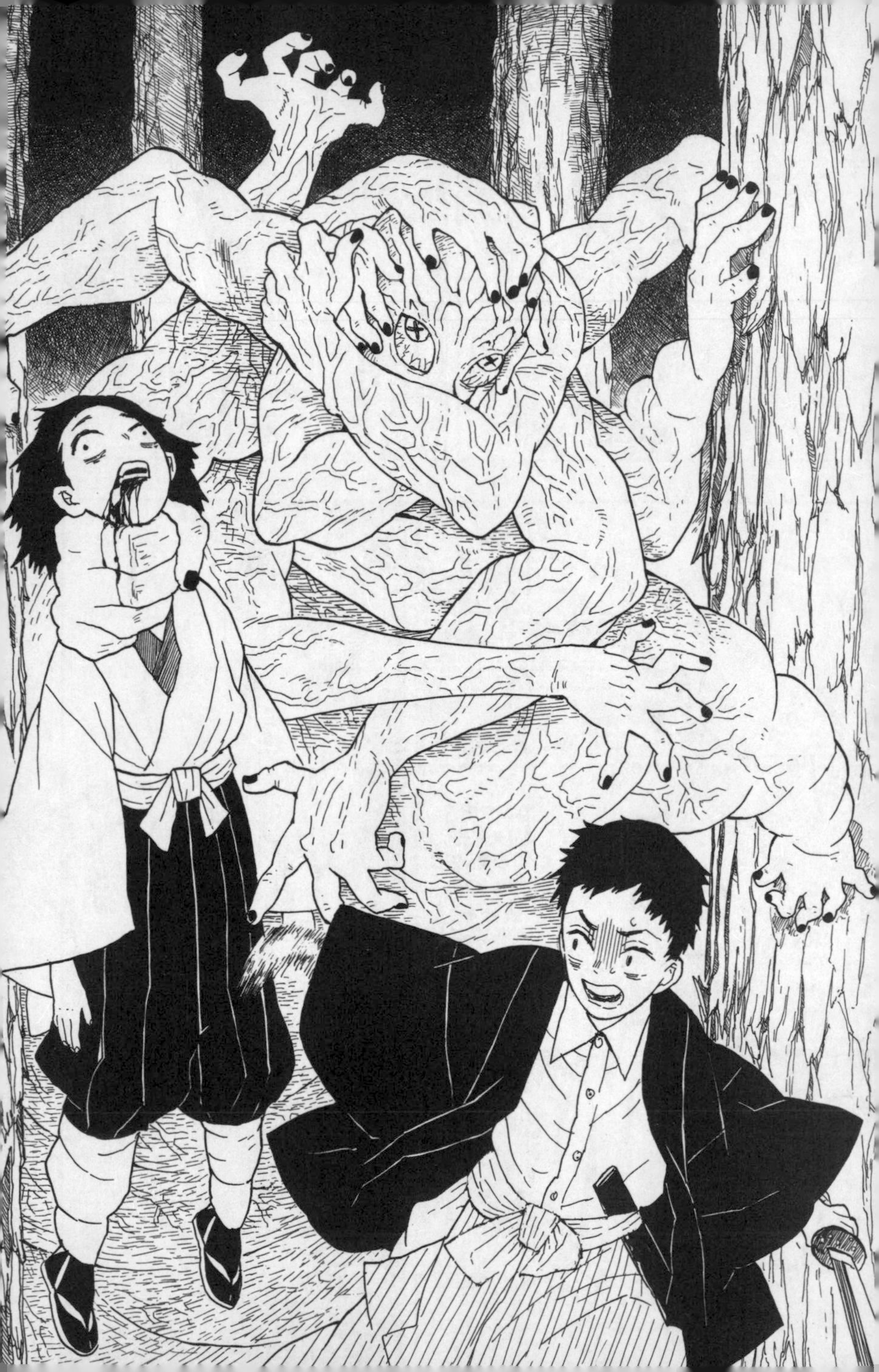

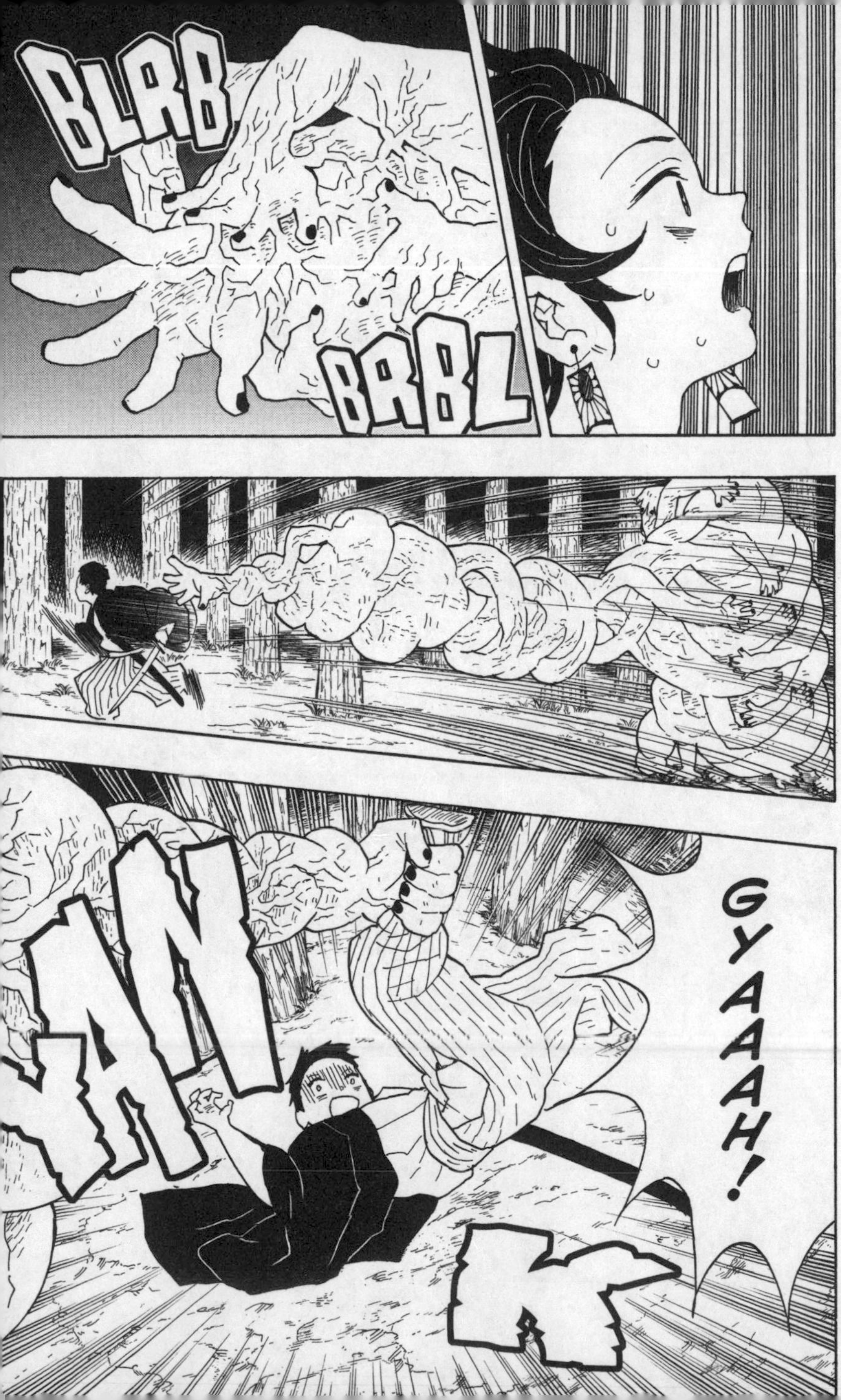
BLRB
BRBL
GYAAAAH!

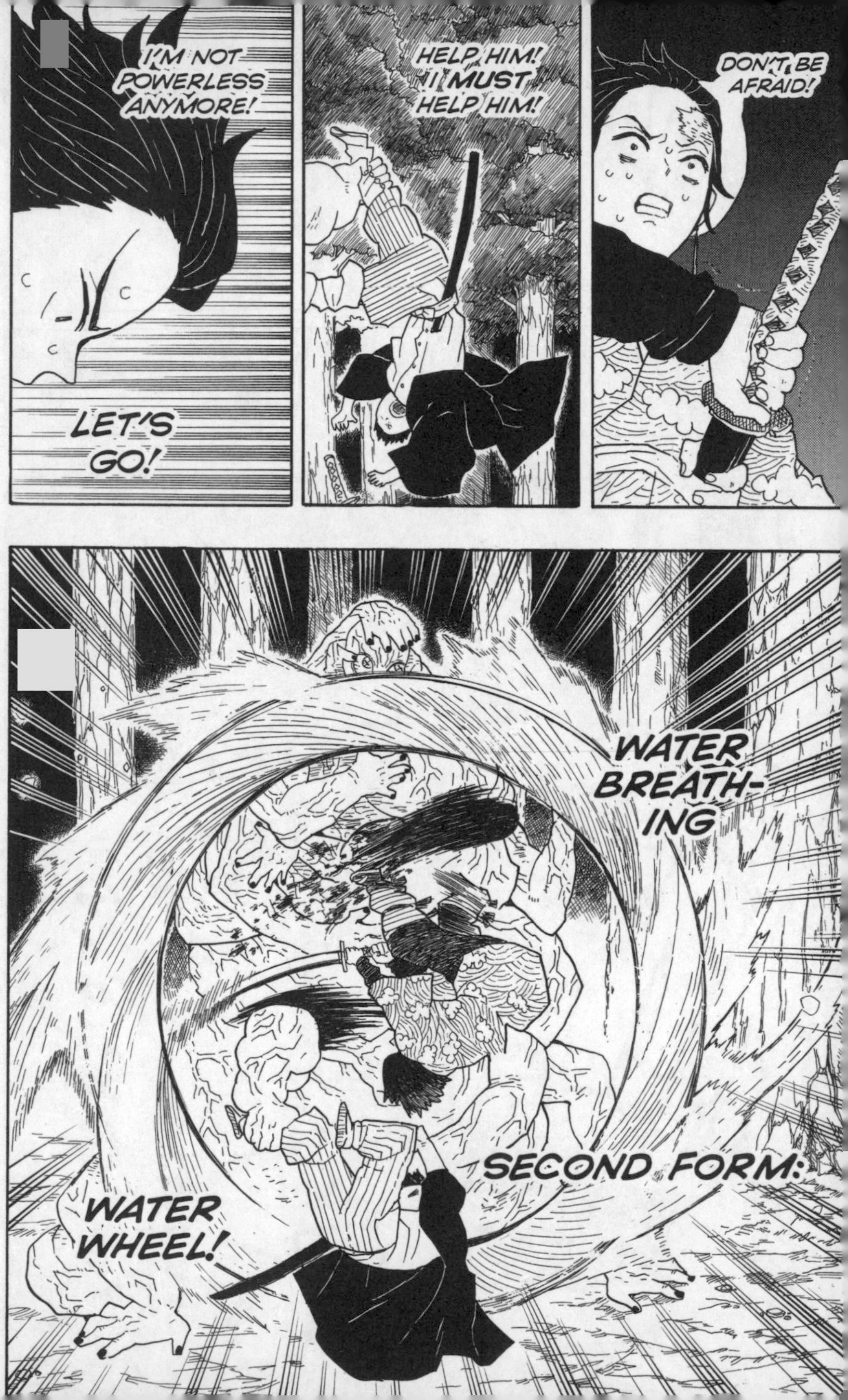
DON'T BE AFRAID!
HELP HIM! I MUST HELP HIM!
I'M NOT POWERLESS ANYMORE!
LET'S GO!
WATER BREATHING
SECOND FORM:
WATER WHEEL!

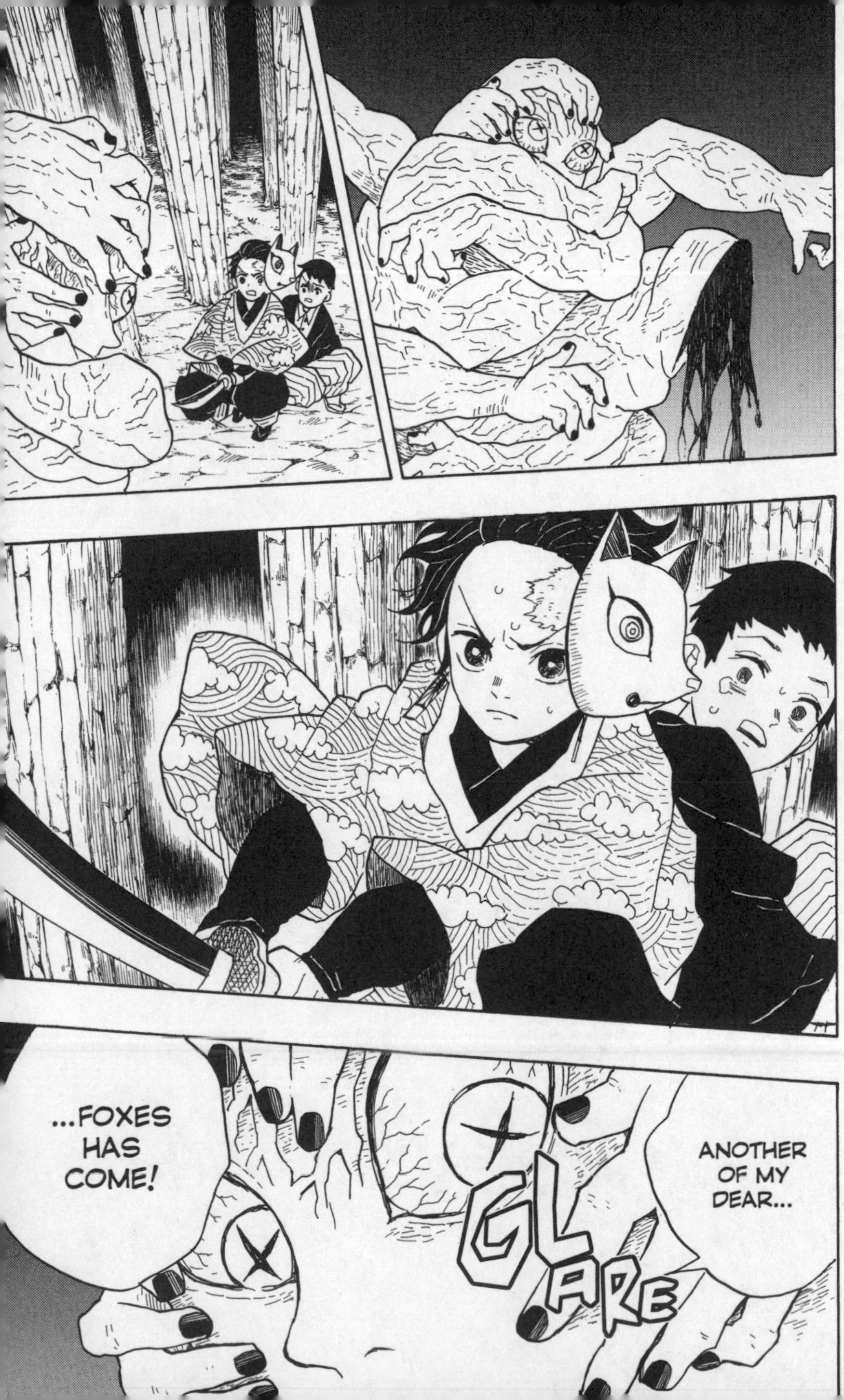
ANOTHER OF MY DEAR...
...FOXES HAS COME!
GLARE

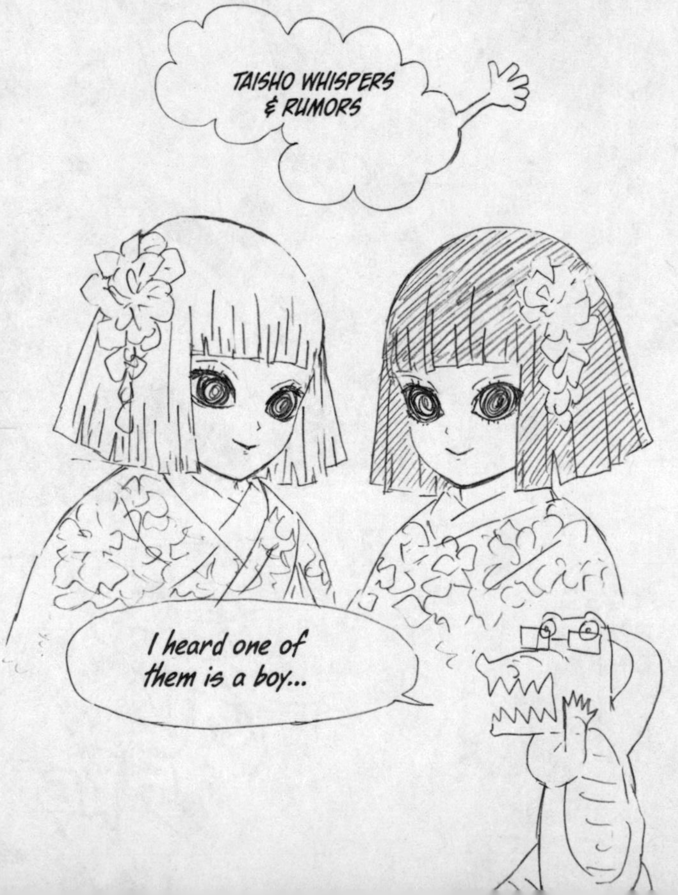
TAISHO WHISPERS & RUMORS
I heard one of them is a boy...

CHAPTER 7: SPIRITS OF THE DECEASED

DO YOU THINK...

...TANJIRO CAN REALLY DO IT?

SABITO ...?

AND YOU KNOW THAT...

...RIGHT?

...NO AMOUNT OF EFFORT IS TOO MUCH.

BUT...

I DON'T KNOW.

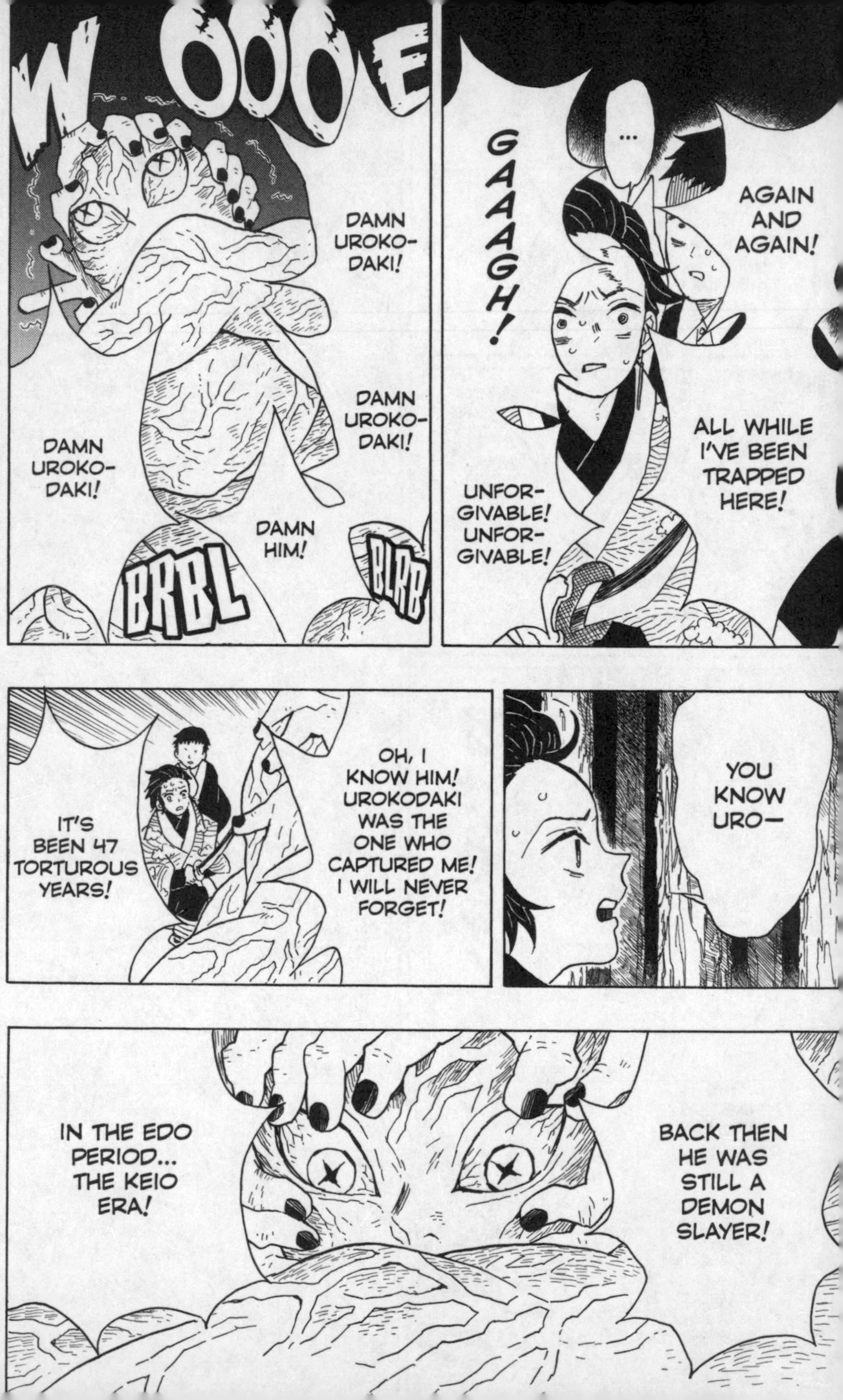
...
AGAIN AND AGAIN!
GAAAGH!
ALL WHILE I'VE BEEN TRAPPED HERE!
UNFORGIVABLE! UNFORGIVABLE!
WOOOE
DAMN UROKO-DAKI!
DAMN UROKO-DAKI!
DAMN UROKO-DAKI!
DAMN HIM!
BLRB
BRBL
YOU KNOW URO—
OH, I KNOW HIM! UROKODAKI WAS THE ONE WHO CAPTURED ME! I WILL NEVER FORGET!
IT'S BEEN 47 TORTUROUS YEARS!
IN THE EDO PERIOD... THE KEIO ERA!
BACK THEN HE WAS STILL A DEMON SLAYER!

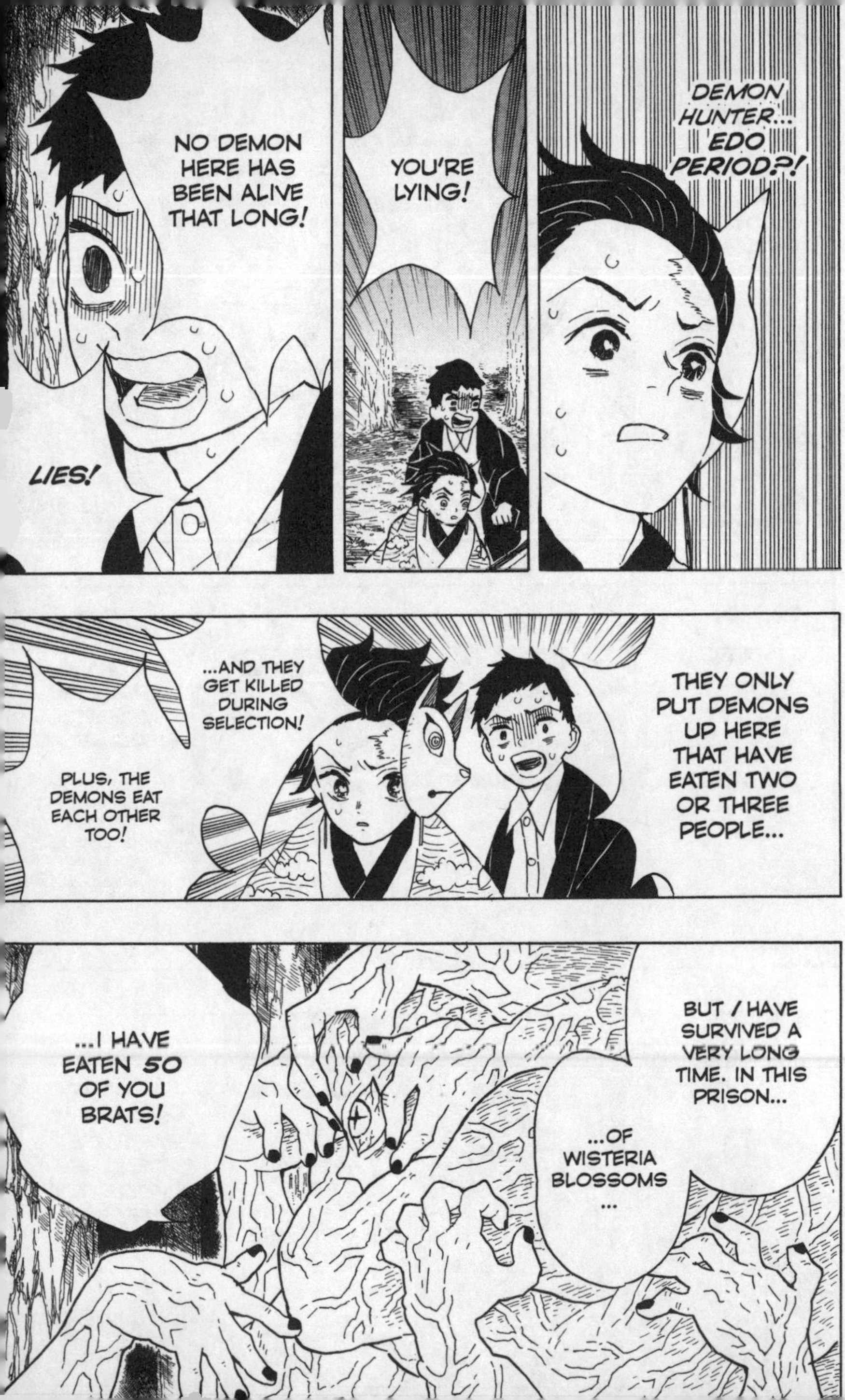
DEMON HUNTER... EDO PERIOD?!
YOU'RE LYING!
NO DEMON HERE HAS BEEN ALIVE THAT LONG!
LIES!
THEY ONLY PUT DEMONS UP HERE THAT HAVE EATEN TWO OR THREE PEOPLE...
...AND THEY GET KILLED DURING SELECTION!
PLUS, THE DEMONS EAT EACH OTHER TOO!
BUT I HAVE SURVIVED A VERY LONG TIME. IN THIS PRISON...
...OF WISTERIA BLOSSOMS ...
...I HAVE EATEN 50 OF YOU BRATS!

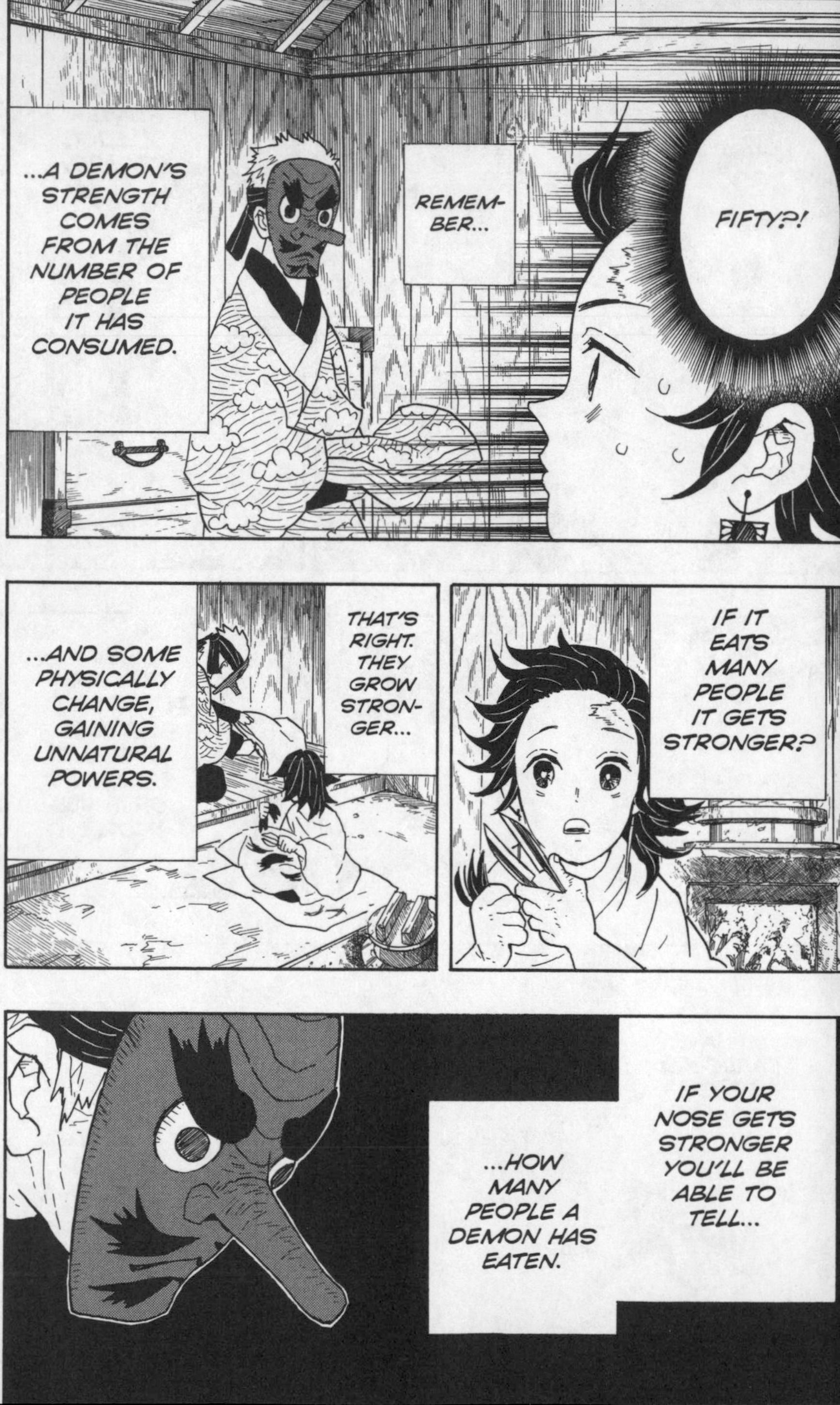
FIFTY?!
REMEMBER...
...A DEMON'S STRENGTH COMES FROM THE NUMBER OF PEOPLE IT HAS CONSUMED.
IF IT EATS MANY PEOPLE IT GETS STRONGER?
THAT'S RIGHT. THEY GROW STRONGER...
...AND SOME PHYSICALLY CHANGE, GAINING UNNATURAL POWERS.
IF YOUR NOSE GETS STRONGER YOU'LL BE ABLE TO TELL...
...HOW MANY PEOPLE A DEMON HAS EATEN.

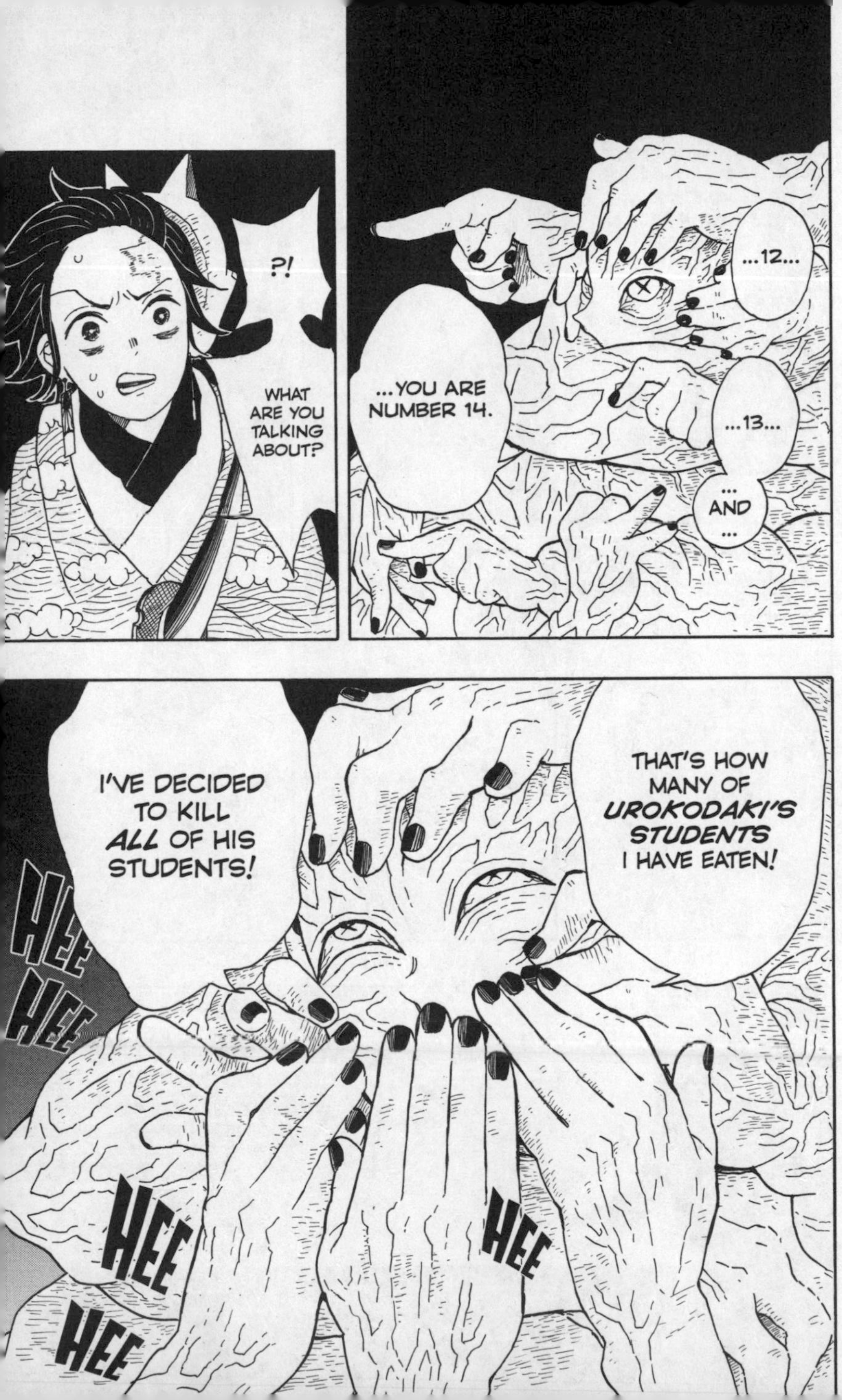
...12...
...13...
... AND ...
...YOU ARE NUMBER 14.
?!
WHAT ARE YOU TALKING ABOUT?
THAT'S HOW MANY OF *UROKODAKI'S STUDENTS* I HAVE EATEN!
I'VE DECIDED TO KILL *ALL* OF HIS STUDENTS!
HEE
HEE
HEE
HEE
HEE

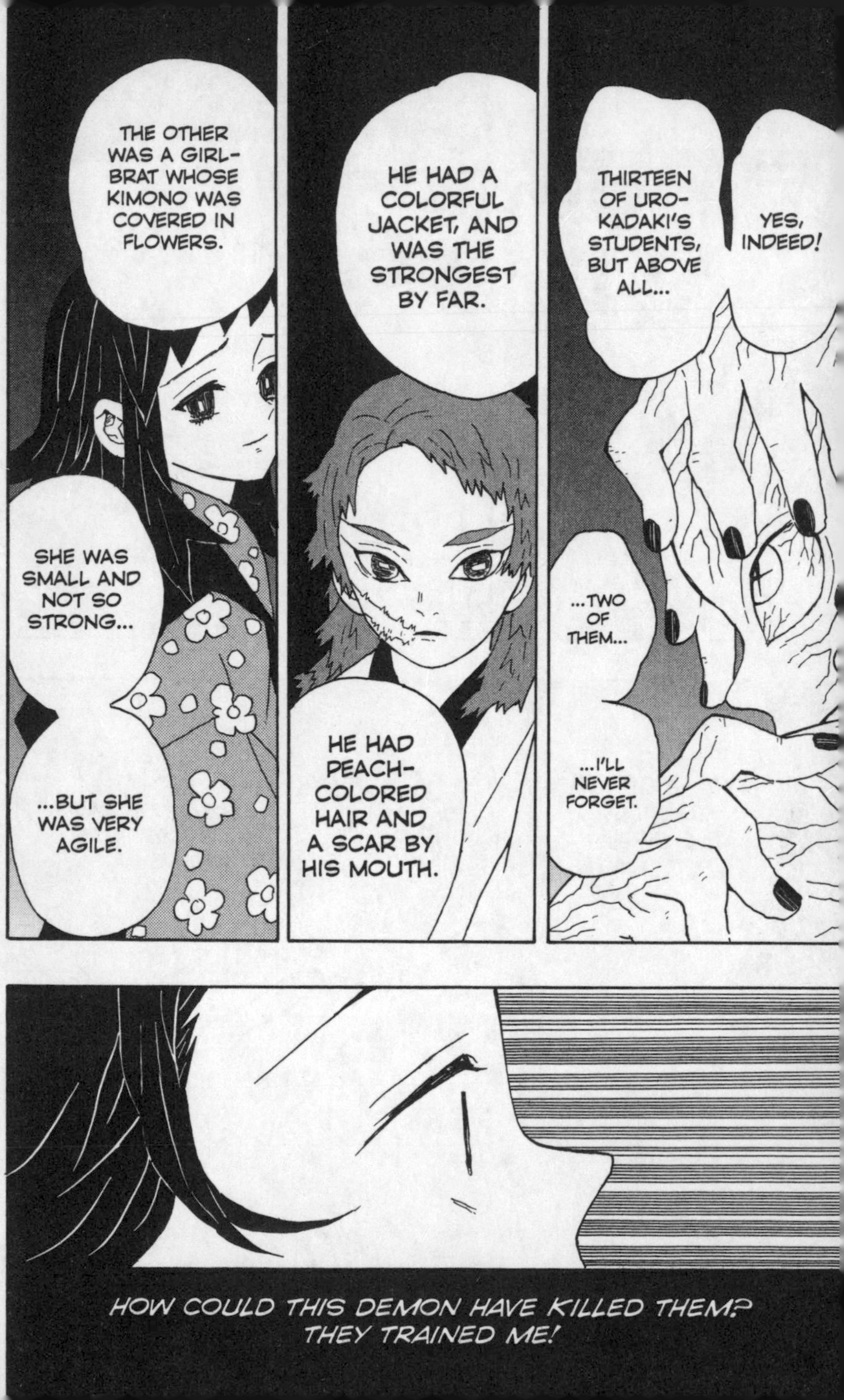
YES, INDEED!
THIRTEEN OF URO-KADAKI'S STUDENTS, BUT ABOVE ALL...
...TWO OF THEM...
...I'LL NEVER FORGET.
HE HAD A COLORFUL JACKET, AND WAS THE STRONGEST BY FAR.
HE HAD PEACH-COLORED HAIR AND A SCAR BY HIS MOUTH.
THE OTHER WAS A GIRL-BRAT WHOSE KIMONO WAS COVERED IN FLOWERS.
SHE WAS SMALL AND NOT SO STRONG...
...BUT SHE WAS VERY AGILE.
HOW COULD THIS DEMON HAVE KILLED THEM? THEY TRAINED ME!

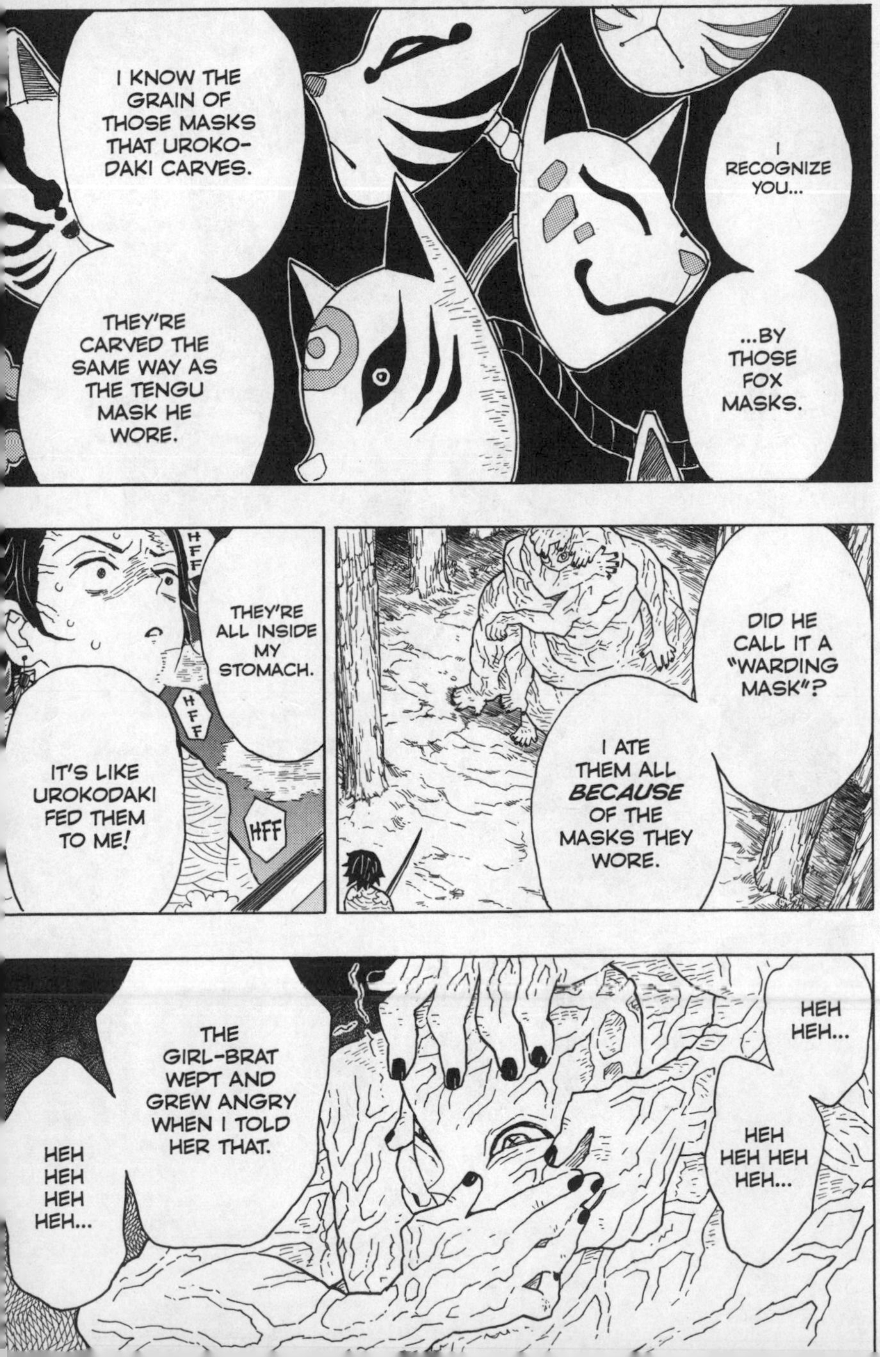
I RECOGNIZE YOU...
...BY THOSE FOX MASKS.
I KNOW THE GRAIN OF THOSE MASKS THAT UROKO-DAKI CARVES.
THEY'RE CARVED THE SAME WAY AS THE TENGU MASK HE WORE.
DID HE CALL IT A "WARDING MASK"?
I ATE THEM ALL *BECAUSE* OF THE MASKS THEY WORE.
HFF
THEY'RE ALL INSIDE MY STOMACH.
HFF
HFF
IT'S LIKE UROKODAKI FED THEM TO ME!
HEH HEH...
HEH HEH HEH HEH...
THE GIRL-BRAT WEPT AND GREW ANGRY WHEN I TOLD HER THAT.
HEH HEH HEH HEH...

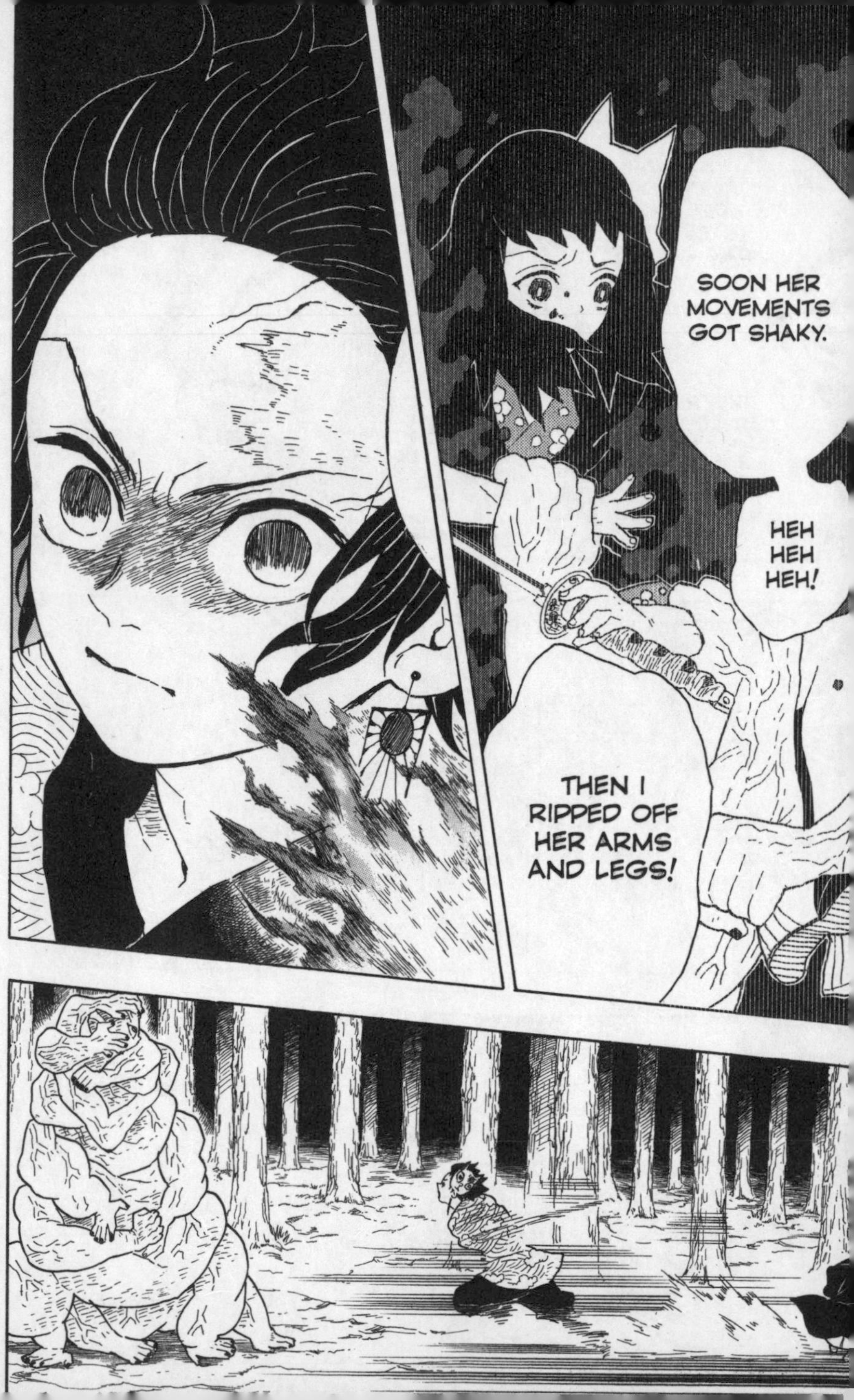
SOON HER MOVEMENTS GOT SHAKY.
HEH HEH HEH!
THEN I RIPPED OFF HER ARMS AND LEGS!

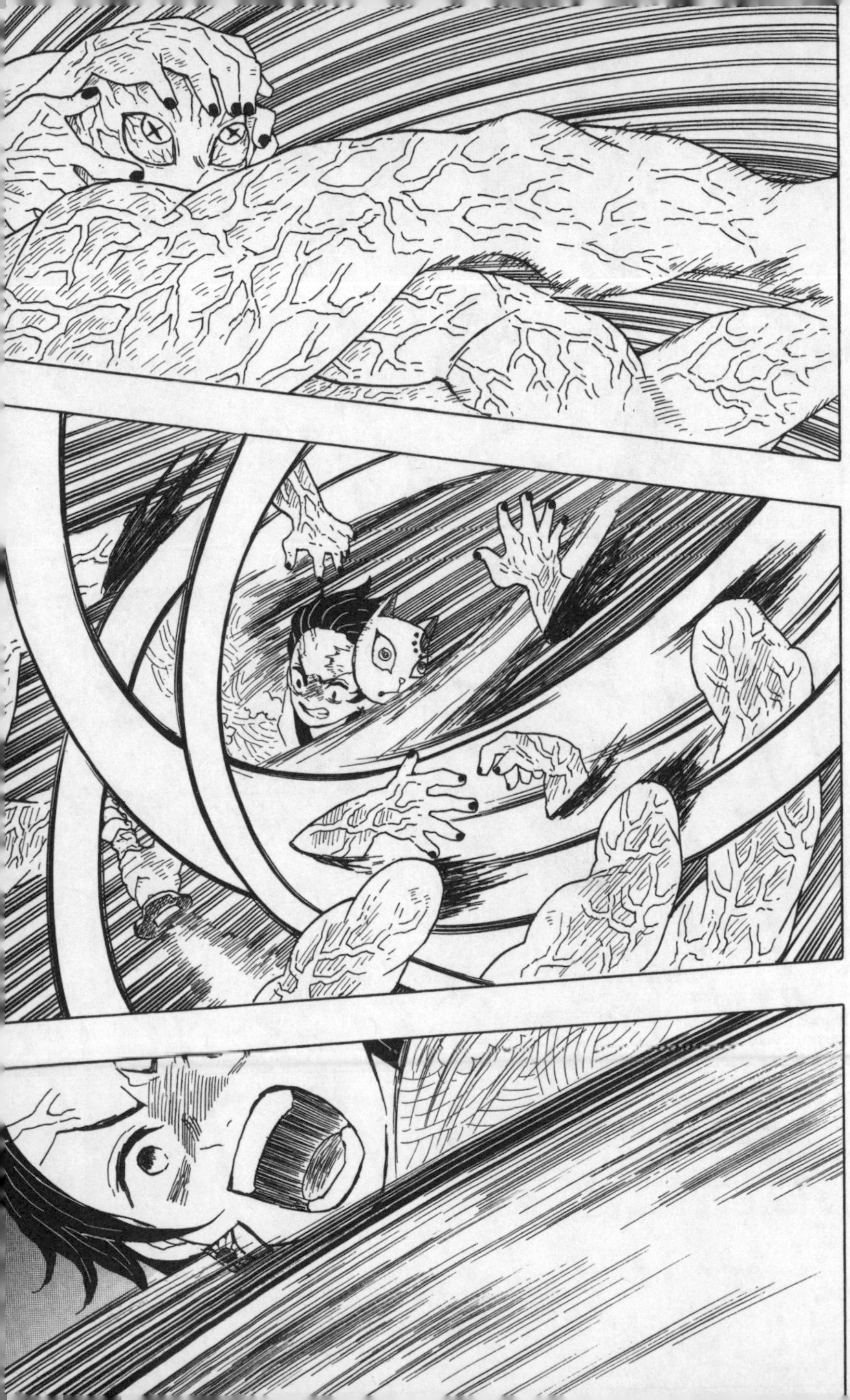

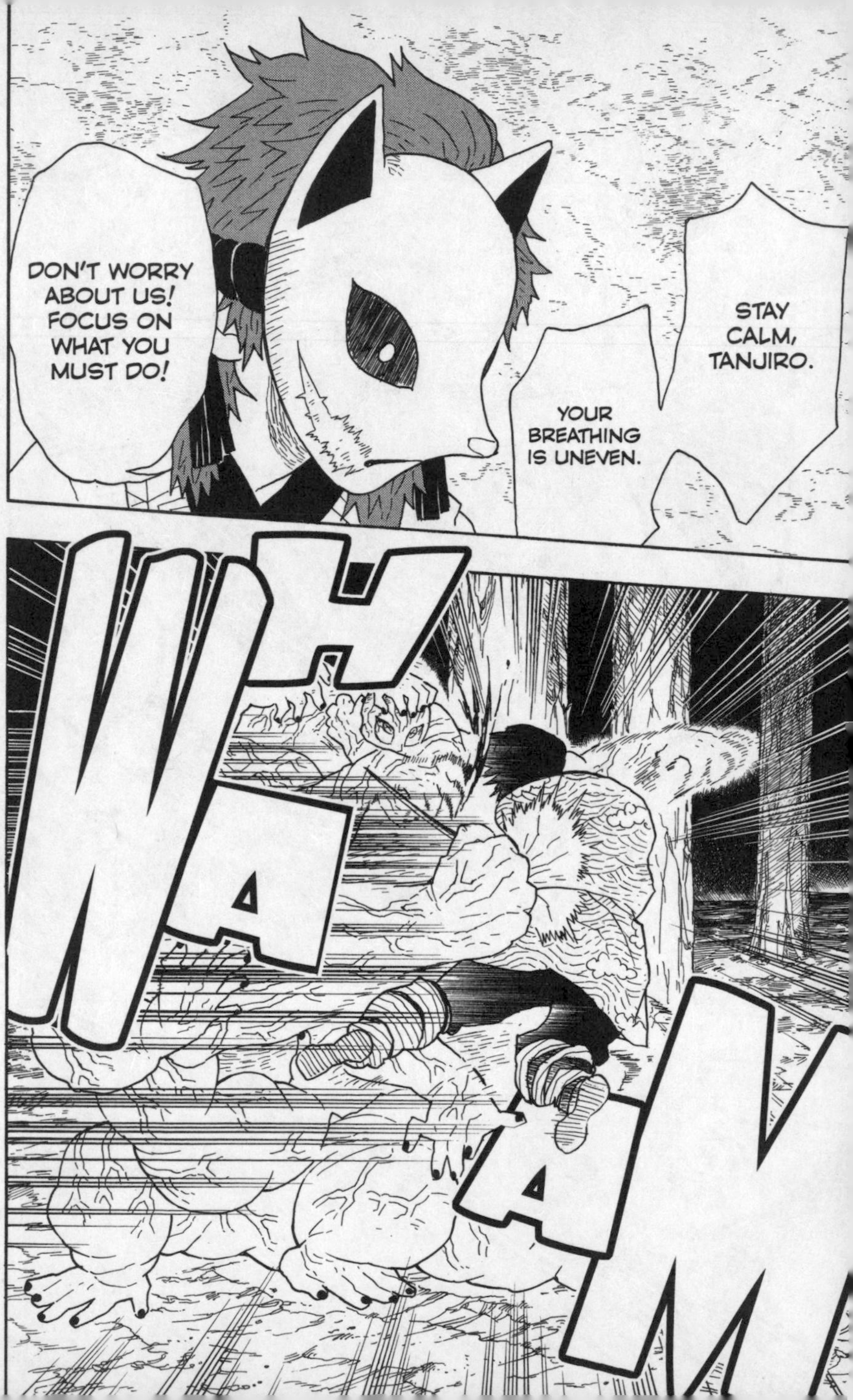
STAY CALM, TANJIRO.
YOUR BREATHING IS UNEVEN.
DON'T WORRY ABOUT US! FOCUS ON WHAT YOU MUST DO!
WHAAM

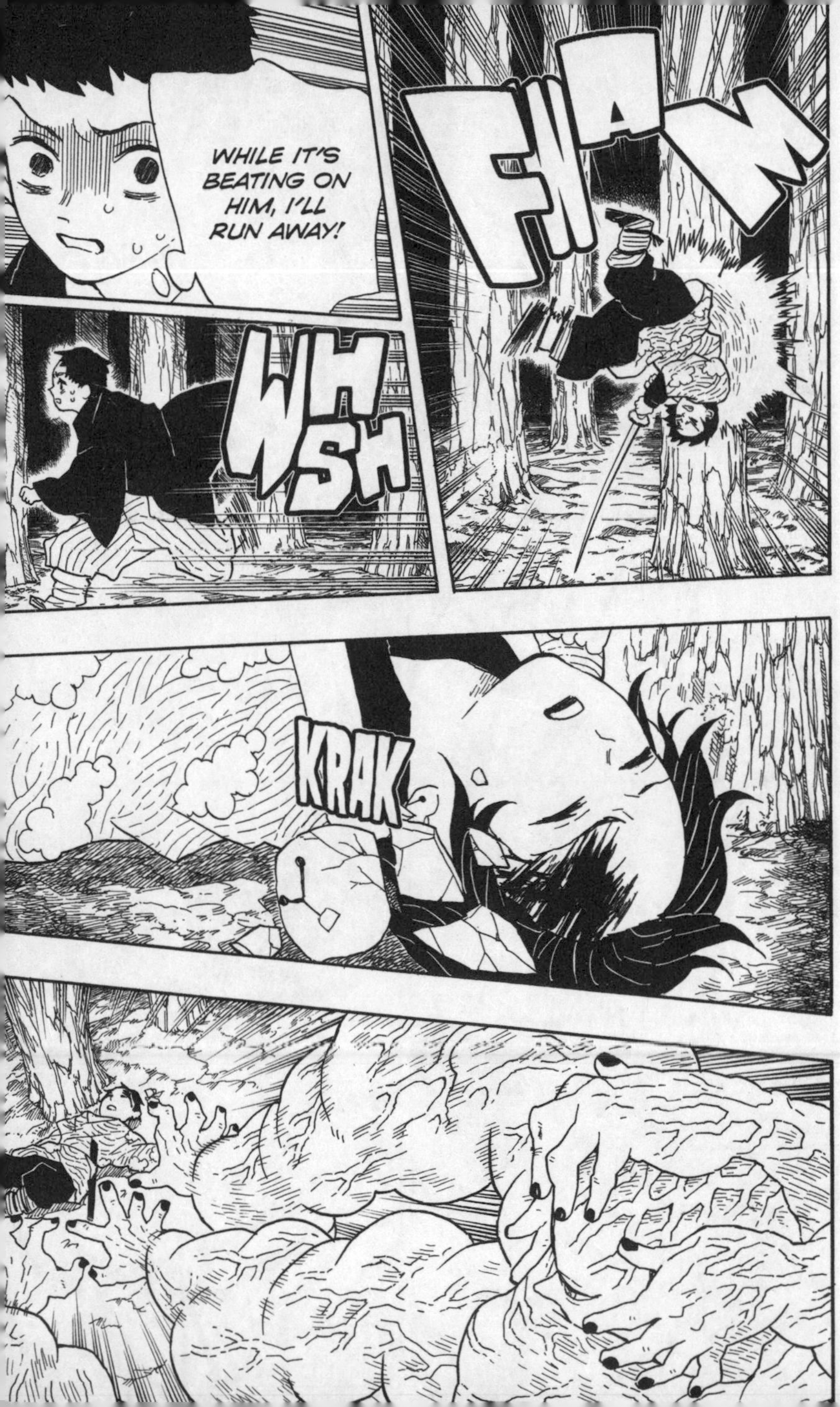
FWAM
WHILE IT'S BEATING ON HIM, I'LL RUN AWAY!
WHSH
KRAK

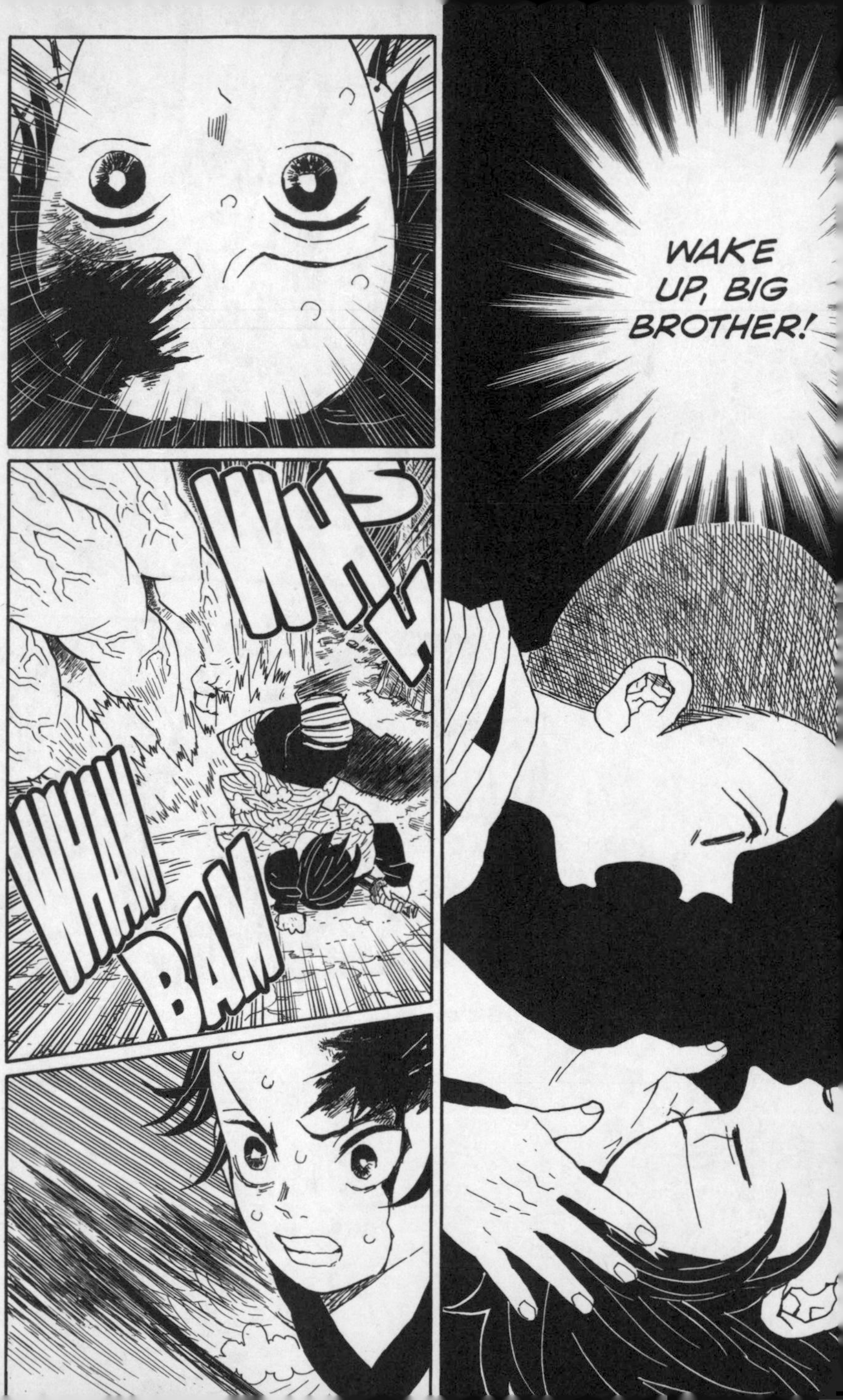
WAKE UP, BIG BROTHER!
WHSH
WHAM
BAM

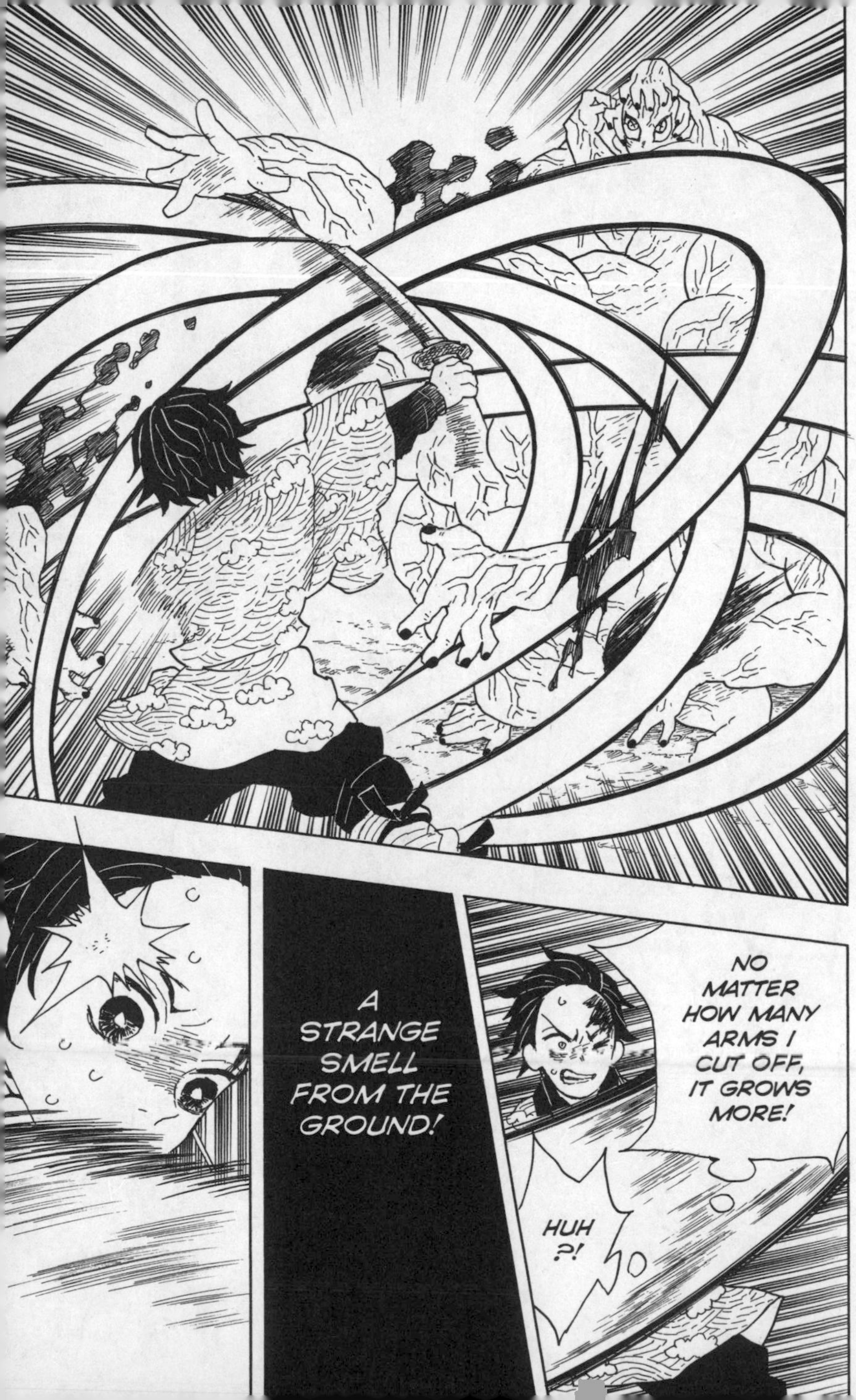
NO MATTER HOW MANY ARMS I CUT OFF, IT GROWS MORE!
HUH ?!
A STRANGE SMELL FROM THE GROUND!

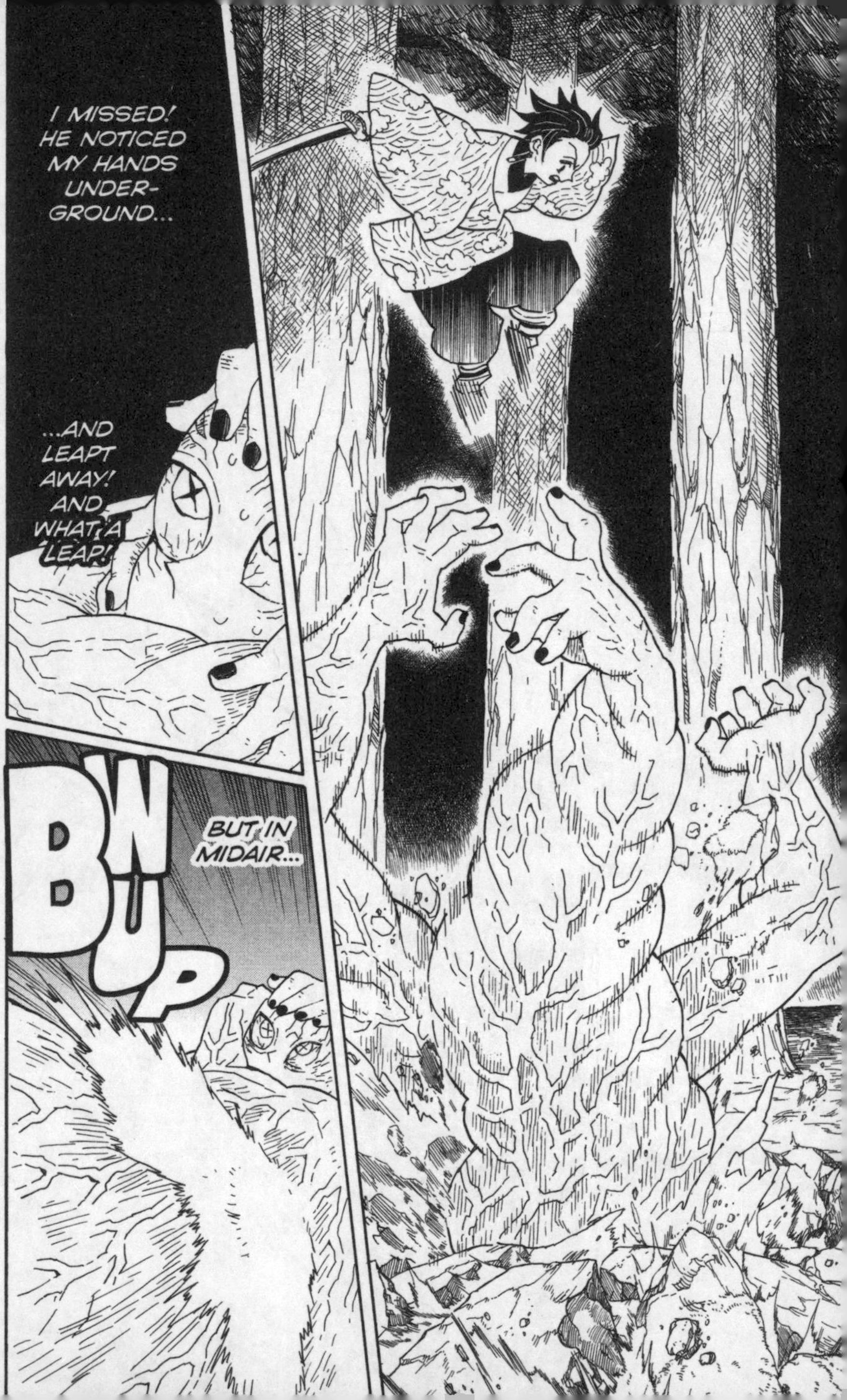
I MISSED! HE NOTICED MY HANDS UNDER-GROUND...
...AND LEAPT AWAY! AND WHAT A LEAP!
BWUP
BUT IN MIDAIR...

THE FOX-BRAT IS IN STRIKING RANGE!

I CAN'T GROW MORE IN TIME!

AND I'M OUT OF HANDS!

HE ESCAPED!

WATER BREATHING!

TOTAL CONCENTRATION.

EVEN THE PEACH-HAIR COULDN'T CUT IT!

BUT MY NECK IS HARD AND IMPERVIOUS!

SNIFF

...AND CRUSH IT, JUST LIKE I DID TO THE OTHER ONE!

WHEN HE FAILS TO CUT MY NECK, I'LL GRAB HIS HEAD...

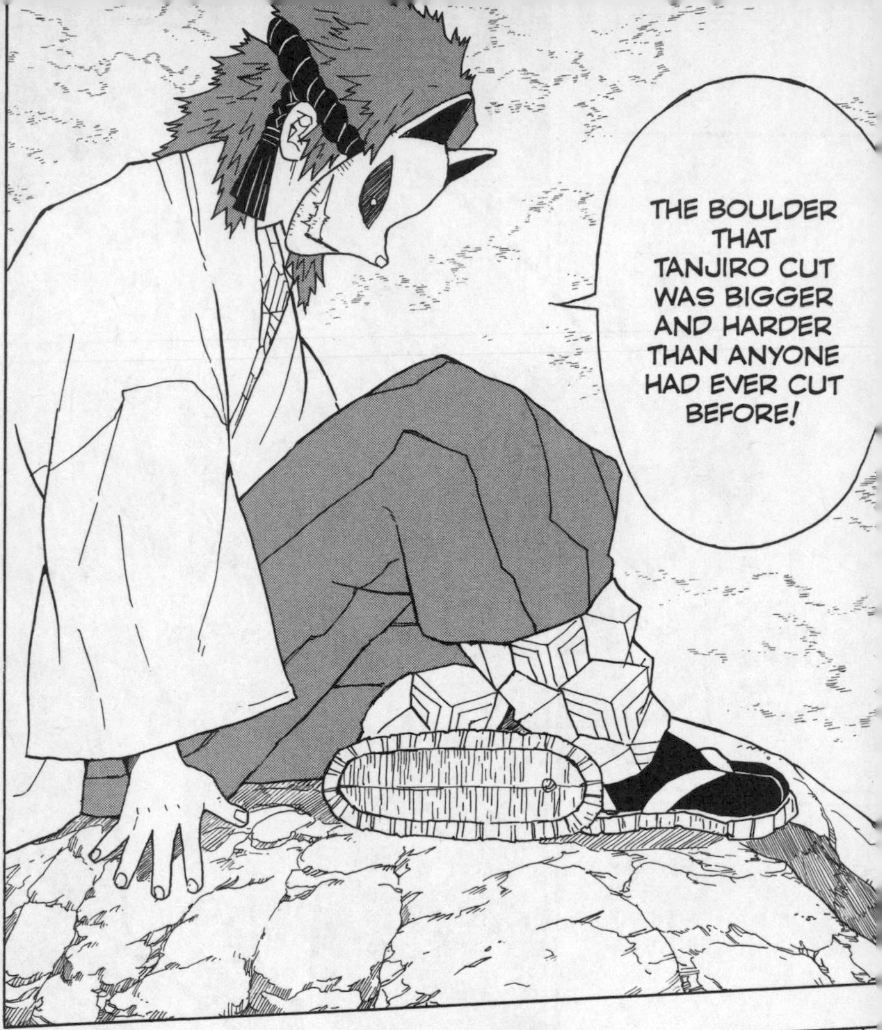
THE BOULDER THAT TANJIRO CUT WAS BIGGER AND HARDER THAN ANYONE HAD EVER CUT BEFORE!

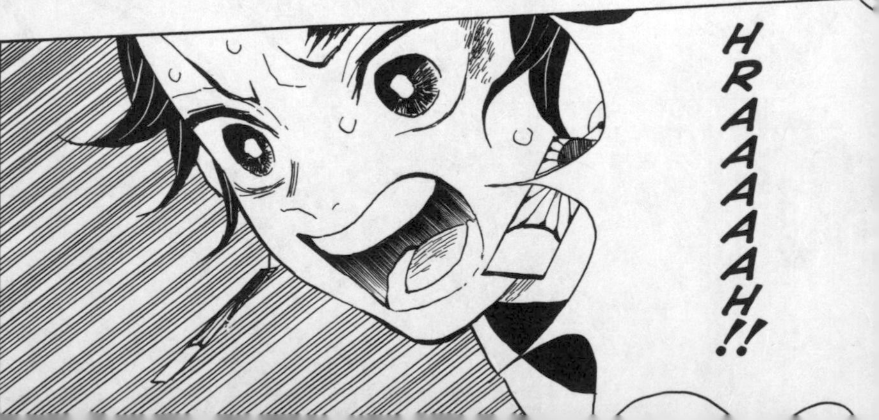
HRAAAAAAH!!

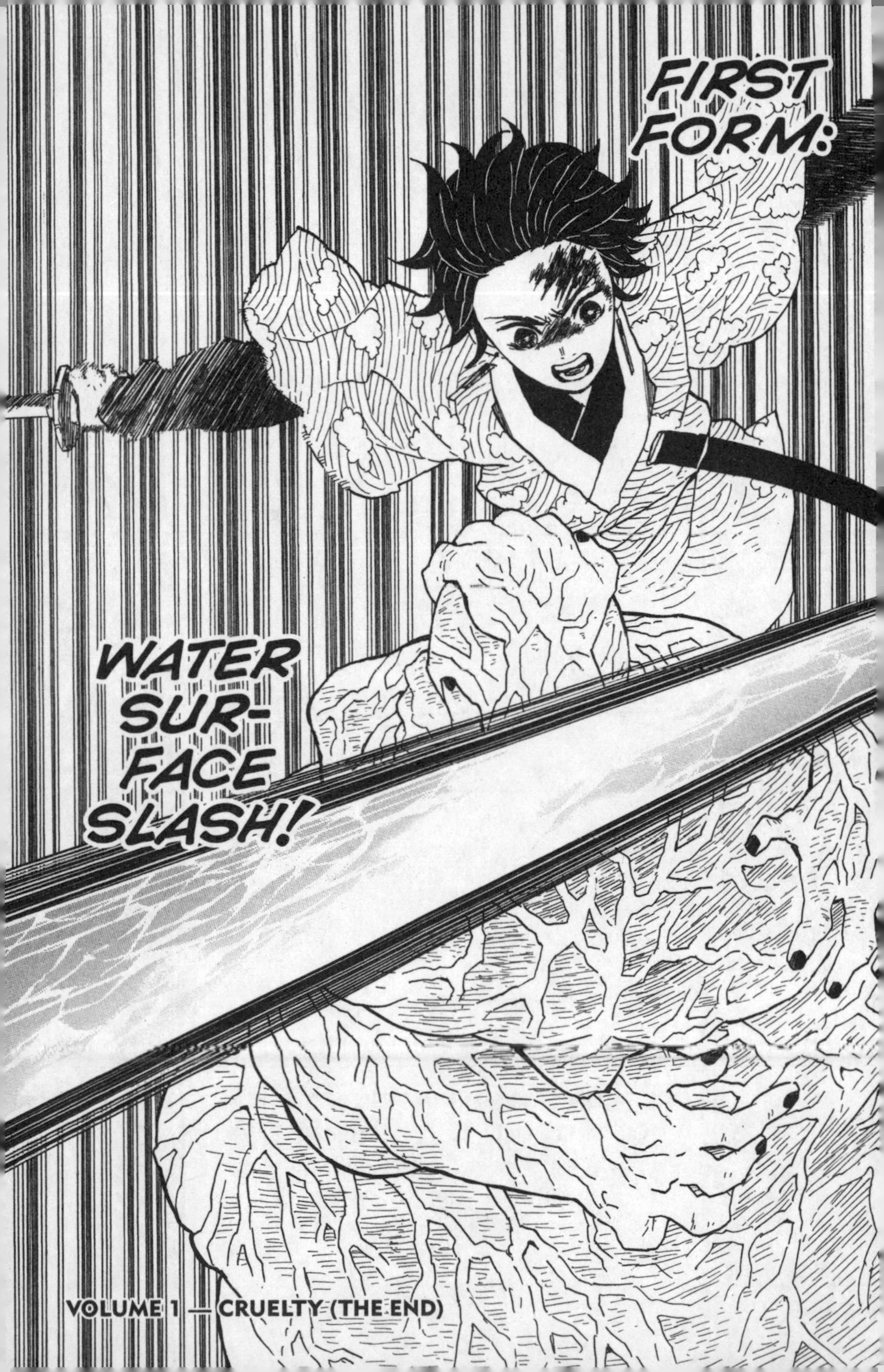
FIRST FORM:
WATER SUR-FACE SLASH!

VOLUME 1 — CRUELTY (THE END)

YOU'RE READING THE
WRONG WAY!

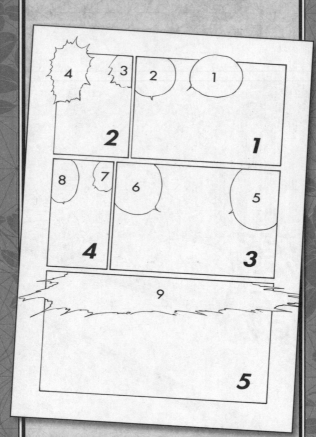

DEMON SLAYER: KIMETSU NO YAIBA
reads from right to left, starting in the
upper-right corner. Japanese is read from
right to left, meaning that action, sound
effects and word-balloon order are completely reversed from English order.